A CUP OF TREMBLING

DAVE HUNT

HARVEST HOUSE PUBLISHERS
Eugene, Oregon 97402

All Scripture quotations in this book are taken from the King James Version of the Bible.

Quotations from the Koran are taken from *The Glorious Koran: An Explanatory Translation* by Marmaduke Pickthall. Alfred A. Knopf, Everyman's Library, 1930, 1992.

The author's free monthly newsletter
may be received by request. Write to:

Dave Hunt
P.O. Box 7019
Bend, OR 97708

A CUP OF TREMBLING

Copyright © 1995 by Dave Hunt
Published by Harvest House Publishers
Eugene, Oregon 97402

Library of Congress Cataloging-in-Publication Data

Hunt, Dave.
     A cup of trembling / Dave Hunt.
        p.   cm.
     Includes bibliographical references.
     ISBN 1-56507-334-7
     1. Bible—Prophecies—Jerusalem. 2. Jerusalem—
Miscellanea. 3. Jerusalem in the Bible.   I. Title.
BS649.J38J86   1995
263'.042569442—dc20   95-14279
                                      CIP

Printed in the United States of America.

95 96 97 98 99 00 01 02 — 10 9 8 7 6 5 4 3 2 1

*In a plea for truth and freedom
and in protest against
the misinformation and propaganda
that enslave the mind and foment evil,
this book is dedicated to the peace of Jerusalem
and to the victims of terrorism and violence
by whomever initiated.*

Contents

*I [God] have chosen Jerusalem, that my name might
be there. . . . For now I have chosen and sanctified
this house [the Temple], that my name may be there
forever; and mine eyes and mine heart shall be there
perpetually. . . . In this house, and in Jerusalem,
which I have chosen . . . will I put my name forever.*

—2 Chronicles 6:6; 7:16; 33:7

*Great is the LORD, and greatly to be praised in the
city of our God. . . . Beautiful for situation, the joy of
the whole earth, is mount Zion . . . the city of the
great King. . . . God will establish it forever.*

—Psalm 48:1,2,8

*The LORD rebuke thee, O Satan; even the LORD that
hath chosen Jerusalem rebuke thee: Is not this a
brand plucked out of the fire?*

—Zechariah 3:2

*The LORD hath chosen Zion; he hath desired it for his
habitation.*

—Psalm 132:13

*If I forget thee, O Jerusalem, let my right hand forget
her cunning.*

—Psalm 137:5

1

Jerusalem, City of Our God

◆

There are cities in today's world which are renowned because of their strategic location, their great size, their climate and natural resources, or their industrial and manufacturing capability and capacity. Jerusalem has none of these advantages to commend it. Yet there is not a city on earth which is better known and more dearly loved by so many people of diverse nationalities and beliefs. And certainly there is no city which is of greater importance to world peace.

One hardly need argue that the peace of the world depends upon the peace of Jerusalem. That awesome fact is recognized by the United Nations today, for every effort is being made by its members to find some way of achieving a just and lasting peace between Arabs and Jews in Palestine—and significant progress has seemingly been made. As of this date, however, the question of *Jerusalem* still hangs in the balance and will be the deciding factor. Jerusalem is, in fact, unique among earth's cities both as to its history and its present and future impact upon the rest of the world.

Unique? Yes, unquestionably that timeworn city stands all by itself, in a category of its own. In contrast to any other place on earth, Jerusalem alone is singled out and its remarkable role in world destiny (quite evident today) is clearly expressed throughout the Bible in both its historical accounts and in its prophetic declarations. The biblical quotations at the beginning of this chapter are only a few among the 811 times Jerusalem is mentioned in Scripture.

A Preposterous Explanation?

These myriad references offer an apparently preposterous explanation for Jerusalem's astonishing position on today's world stage, a position which could never be true of any other city and which even most of Jerusalem's present inhabitants do not believe belongs to her. How could what ought to be just one more seemingly ordinary (if not even obscure) Middle East city reach such a position? If words have any meaning, the Bible's prophets declare unequivocally and with one resounding voice, century after century, that Jerusalem is "the City of our God," chosen by Him to play a special role in human destiny. We challenge the reader to find any other justification for Jerusalem's uniqueness.

Such an assertion is usually summarily rejected today, and for varied reasons. There are those who disclaim any belief in God and who deride the Bible as a collection of myths. How ironic that a high percentage of the inhabitants of what the Bible designates as "the City of our God" claim to be atheists! As such, however, they can neither deny Jerusalem's extraordinary role in world affairs nor can they offer a theory to explain it.

Other people, while claiming some religious interest and tolerance, are nevertheless wary of taking the Bible "too literally." And even the literalists sometimes disagree among themselves as to what the Bible's prophetic passages actually mean. To add to the confusion, increasing numbers of evangelicals are embracing Catholicism's long-held view that the church has replaced the Jews as God's people. The State of Israel is therefore seen by many as the illegitimate offspring of a misguided and obnoxiously zealous Zionism that got lucky at just the right time in history.

Most of today's Jews consider Israel's existence to be the result of fortuitous chance combined with blood, sweat, and tears rather than the fulfillment of prophecy (which scarcely anyone believes anymore). That could explain the strange statistic of more Jews moving out of Jerusalem than are moving in—a deficit of 6149 in 1993.[1] For the Arabs, of course, the suggestion that God promised Palestine to the Jews and is now fulfilling that promise is outrageous. For fundamentalist Muslims it is blasphemy. Though the words *Palestine* and *Canaan* do not even appear in the Koran, Islam teaches that this land belongs not to the Jews but to the Arabs. Therefore Israel's very existence and, above all, its control of Jerusalem are intolerable insults to Islam. Only by driving the Jews from Palestine can Arab honor be restored.

However, in spite of herculean Arab military efforts, employing overwhelming numerical superiority of manpower and machines and with the backing of the Soviet Union, tiny Israel has not only survived but has actually grown steadily stronger. The superiority of the Israeli fighting machine is a shocking but well-established fact that has made it necessary for the Arabs to come to the bargaining table at last. And no matter what objection the skeptics may make, the fact that (precisely as the Bible foretold) the peace of the entire world is tied to Jerusalem's future cannot be denied. Nor is there either a reasonable explanation or a logical refutation of this truly inconceivable state of affairs.

A Religious Rationale?

Some skeptics have proposed as a purely rational justification the irresistible spiritual appeal this "Holy City" holds for half of the world's population. It is held in reverence by about 1 billion Muslims, 1 billion Roman Catholics, 400 million Orthodox adherents, and 400 million Protestants. Yet that fact in itself only raises more questions and deepens the mystery of Jerusalem's astonishing character.

For example, Jerusalem is not mentioned even once in the Koran—a rather glaring omission if it is truly as sacred to Islam as today's Muslims believe. There was even an abortive attempt in the early days of Islam (for commercial reasons) to make it the center of Muslim worship, but that ploy was quickly rejected by the Muslim world. Historian Will Durant writes:

> In 684, when the rebel Abdullah ibn Zobei ᵕeld Mecca and received the revenues of its pilgrims, Abd-al-Malik, anxious to attract some of this sacred revenue, decreed that thereafter this rock [where Abraham had offered Isaac and the temple had stood in Jerusalem] should replace the Kaaba [in Mecca] as the object of pious pilgrimage. Over that historic stone his artisans [in 691] raised in Syrian-Byzantine style the famous "Dome of the Rock," which soon ranked as the third of the "four wonders of the Moslem world. . . ."
>
> Abd-al-Malik's plan to make this monument replace the Kaaba failed; had it succeeded, Jerusalem would have been the center of all the three faiths that competed for the soul of medieval man. But Jerusalem was not even the capital of the province of Palestine [under the Arabs]. . . .[2]

During the centuries when Jerusalem was under complete Arab control, no Arab ruler or Islamic leader ever made it the object of a religious pilgrimage—again a strange indifference toward a city which is now considered to be the third-holiest religious site in Islam after Mecca and Medina. We are confronted by an obvious question: How and why did the status of Jerusalem change so dramatically in modern times? The fact that the huge, flat stone within the Dome had been the site both of Abraham's offering of Isaac and of the Temple was not enough to stir the Muslim soul. It had to become the scene of a myth associated with Mohammed in order to arouse such sentiment.

A Muslim Inconsistency

The importance of Jerusalem popularly accepted by today's Muslims derives from the belief that within the Dome of the Rock lies the sacred site from which Mohammed allegedly ascended to heaven. That tradition, however, though now firmly established in the Muslim mind, is of very recent origin. It is, in fact, a fabrication invented by Yasser Arafat's uncle, Haj Amin el-Husseini, past Grand Mufti of Jerusalem. He promoted this myth in the 1920s and 1930s in order to arouse Arab sentiment against the growing Jewish presence in Jerusalem and to justify the location of the Dome of the Rock on the Temple site.

That such an idea was not the actual reason for the construction of this monument to Islam by Abd-al-Malik in 691 is evident from the fact that the one verse in the Koran (Surah 17:1) which, it is now claimed, alludes to this alleged event is not to be found among the verses from the Koran which are inscribed inside the Dome. The absence of that key Koranic passage speaks volumes. Obviously the interpretation now given to that verse was unknown in earlier times, and with good reason. The fact is that any normal reading of the verse, assigning normal meaning to the words, fails to suggest the tradition of Mohammed visiting that site and launching from there into heaven. The Koran doesn't say that at all, but its meager statement has been stretched into a now-accepted Islamic tradition. Here is the verse:

> Glorified be He who carried His servant by night from the Inviolable Place of Worship to the Far Distant Place [al-Aqsa] of Worship the neighbourhood whereof We have blessed, that We might show him of Our tokens! Lo! He, and only He, is the Hearer, the Seer.

The accompanying commentary states that the "Inviolable Place of Worship" is Mecca and that the "Far Distant Place of Worship" is Jerusalem. The first is, of course, true because Mecca had held that position from the beginning. The latter, however, has no substantiation because Jerusalem had never been the scene of Islamic worship to that time, nor would it be for centuries thereafter. As we have already noted, Jerusalem is not even mentioned by name in the Koran, either in this verse or anywhere else. So how could it be a place of worship for the Muslim who was never directed to it?

Quite obviously, the magnificent Dome of the Rock was erected on that particular spot not only in an attempt by Abd-al-Malik to gain potentially vast revenues from pilgrims, but also to prevent the Jews from ever rebuilding the Temple. No doubt it was thought that without that sacred structure the Jews would have no reason for regathering in Jerusalem. Thereby the stage was set more than a millennium ago for a future conflict which today threatens us all with a Third World War—a war over Jerusalem from which earth might very well never recover. We will have much more to say on that subject in subsequent chapters.

Internationalizing Jerusalem

That Jerusalem is unique is further attested to by the fact that most of the nations of today's world want it to be under international control. The Vatican even demanded the internationalization of Jerusalem during the U.N. debate in 1947 concerning the partitioning of Palestine. No such desire is expressed or makes sense for other cities, so why should it be imposed upon Jerusalem? It is unreasonable and unprecedented. Nevertheless, to this end the nations of the world have agreed among themselves that Jerusalem cannot be the capital of Israel, even though Israel so designated it and located its Knesset there in 1980. Did the outside world ever before dictate to a nation where it could or could not establish its capital? Then why to Israel? Surely secular governments don't believe what the Bible says about Jerusalem, so why do they consider this small, isolated Middle East city to be so special?

For a comparison, consider the case of East Germany. When that defeated country, in defiance of the Potsdam agreement, designated East Berlin as its capital, the nations of the world acquiesced immediately without a murmur of protest. Not so with Jerusalem. There is no international agreement giving other nations any control over Jerusalem. Yet it is treated as though it belongs not to Israel but to the rest of the world.

In fact, the world's major powers, in what is apparently an unwritten agreement among them, have determined that one day Jerusalem will be a world center for "peace" under international control. It is no coincidence that the Vatican has played a major role in that program and has recently worked its way into Israel's good graces in order to pursue this odd purpose. That Jerusalem holds the key to world peace is too obvious to argue. Yet the fact that Jerusalem, of all the world's cities, should play such a role makes no sense at all unless one accepts what the Bible says about it.

Like other nations, the United States, though it has been a supporter of Israel, has nevertheless placed its embassy not in Jerusalem but in Tel Aviv, contrary to Israel's wishes. Even the world's media go along with this open denial of Israel's right to direct its own affairs. For example, in high-handed fashion and in defiance of logic, the BBC and other European radio and television networks habitually refer to Tel Aviv as Israel's capital, an inexplicable twisting of the facts which persists like some giant conspiracy worldwide. On a recent German quiz show, to the question of the location of Israel's capital, Tel Aviv was judged the correct answer. How frustrating to Israel that the capital city it has chosen is not acknowledged as such by the rest of the world!

One can only ask again, "Why this unprecedented treatment of Jerusalem?" What makes it so special? Why does it hold such importance for all nations? The Bible alone offers a reasonable explanation. If the biblical answer to that question is rejected, then no other rationale can be found. Its religious significance, as we have seen, fails to fully explain Jerusalem's uniqueness, a uniqueness which holds an altogether irrational significance for the world's secular powers. Why should a world that doesn't believe the Bible's promises concerning Jerusalem nevertheless treat this city as though what the Bible said about it were true?

A Behind-the-Scenes Betrayal?

Surprisingly, Israel's leaders have been involved in considerable behind-the-scenes intrigue to bring about international control—negotiations which are tantamount to a betrayal of their country. According to the intelligence newsletter *Inside Israel*, Foreign Minister Shimon Peres sent a letter to Yasser Arafat in October 1993 "committing Israel to respect PLO governing institutions in Jerusalem." After Peres had denied that letter's existence, it was finally admitted that such a letter had been sent. That reluctant confession was followed by a most disturbing further revelation. Mark Halter, a close friend of Peres, "told the Israeli weekly *Shishi* that in May [1994] he delivered a letter from Peres to the Pope which outlined the Foreign Minister's plans for Jerusalem. According to Halter, 'Peres offered to hand over sovereignty of Jerusalem's Old City to the Vatican.' "

According to the secret (and to most Israelis, unthinkable) plan, the city would have both an Israeli and a Palestinian mayor, both of whom would be under the authority of the Vatican. The Vatican has made it clear that it considers the religious sites in Jerusalem too precious to be under the control of local authorities. It wants to shoulder that responsibility itself, and apparently Peres is willing to have it so. In apparent agreement with the Vatican, the "heads of the Christian community" in Jerusalem handed the Israeli government at the end of 1994 an unpublished document which also called for the internationalization of Jerusalem.[3] In an apparent attempt to assure all sides that he would deal with an even hand, Pope John Paul II declared in an exclusive interview for *Parade* magazine early in 1994:

> We trust that, with the approach of the year 2000, Jerusalem will become the city of peace for the entire world and that all the people will be able to meet there, in particular the believers in the religions that find their birthright in the faith of Abraham [obviously including the Muslims].[4]

Further confidential disclosures reveal that Jerusalem is to become the "second Vatican of the world," with all three major religions functioning there, as the Pope hinted, under the authority of Rome. A Palestinian state will emerge in confederation with Jordan, with its religious capital being Jerusalem but its administrative capital situated elsewhere, possibly Nablus. Israel's Foreign Ministry justifies this apparent betrayal by promising that Israel's new ties to the Catholic world will lead to trade, tourism, and prosperity and that Catholic governance of Jerusalem will provide a firm hand for quick settlement of future disputes between Jews and Arabs. An announcement coming out of Jordan in late 1994 seemed to confirm the above:

> Jordan last week renounced its religious links to Judea, Samaria, and Gaza, but retained its religious claims to Jerusalem. . . . Relations between Jordan and the Palestine National Authority (PA) grew strained after the July 25 signing of a Jordanian-Israeli declaration, in which Israel acknowledged a special Jordanian role in Jerusalem's Moslem sites. . . .
>
> In Jericho, the PA's Islamic affairs minister welcomed Jordan's decision to sever its religious ties with the territories.[5]

At the subsequent Washington Summit, Jordan's King Hussein, hoping to bolster his claim to Jordanian control over Jerusalem's holy sites, declared that "only God has the right to decide who will own the Temple Mount and Jerusalem." As one Jewish commentator noted, however, "He is, of course, correct. But the question then becomes, whose God? For . . . Hussein's Allah does not mention Jerusalem once in the Koran, while the Hebrew Bible and the New Testament together refer to the city over 800 times. The God of Israel has already exercised His right to decide. And He has given Jerusalem to the Jews as their inheritance in perpetuity . . . [a fact which] challenges the insidious 'interfaith' theology equating God with the Allah of Islam."[6]

The same writer, in reviewing a recent book by Eliyahu Tal titled *Whose Jerusalem?* accuses the "would-be redividers" of Jerusalem of being "intent on tearing the very heart out of the Jewish soul." His review presents the essence of a powerful book:

Tal tells it like it is. And for those who still choose historical legitimacy over the Islamic-inspired, oil-weighted claims of Iranian Shi'ites, Palestinian Arabs, Hashemites, Moroccans and Saudi Arabians, the data amassed in *Whose Jerusalem?* provide a solid platform from which to fend off the multiplying calls for the re-division of Jerusalem, or its otherwise demise as the exclusive capital of the Jewish state. . . .

Only the Jews have for centuries lived and died in the hope of being physically restored to this city. It is only when a Jewish king reigned here that the Shechina (glory of God) shone visibly in Jerusalem, and it is only to Jews that the city itself has thus been holy all these years.[7]

Arafat's Ominous Candor

Jerusalem seems to have a unique importance, too, in God's timetable of last days events. Jesus declared, "Jerusalem shall be trodden down of the Gentiles [non-Jewish nations] until the times of the Gentiles be fulfilled" (Luke 21:24). Could it be that the taking of Jerusalem by the Jews in 1967 marked the end of the Gentile era and brought Israel to center stage in God's program? If so, Jerusalem must remain in Jewish hands until Armageddon. This does not mean, however, that the battle for the control of Jerusalem is over. In fact, it will no doubt intensify as the time for the revelation of the Antichrist draws near.

That battle is certainly heating up already. Early in 1994, in a speech in a Johannesburg mosque, Yasser Arafat called for continuing *jihad* (holy war) by the Arabs to retake Jerusalem. When the contents of his speech, obviously intended for Arab ears only, became public knowledge, it created an understandable stir in Israeli quarters. Arafat tried to explain away his statement by saying that *jihad* also means a peaceful struggle.

There is, however, no such concept in the Koran; and "peaceful struggle" was certainly neither taught nor practiced by Mohammed. In fact, another remark in that speech by Arafat leaves no doubt as to Arafat's meaning: "This agreement [between the PLO and Israel], I am not considering it more than the agreement which had been signed between our Prophet Mohammed and Quraish." That reference was ominous.

The Quraish, Mohammed's own tribe, controlled Mecca but was not strong enough to withstand Mohammed's growing military power. Its people therefore signed a peace agreement with Mohammed, which, on a pretext, the Prophet broke two years later, killing the Quraish leaders and conquering Mecca. Thus Arafat was saying that the PLO's agreement with Israel is only a step in the avowed conquest of Israel and is as easily and with as good conscience broken, inasmuch as Mohammed himself set the example of such justifiable treachery. Israeli analyst Moshe Zak wrote:

> It was not lies or stupidity that characterized Arafat's Johannesburg remarks, but stupendous candor. His forthright, unambiguous remarks were reminiscent of *Mein Kampf*, in which the author [Hitler] was blunt about his plans, so much so that his adversaries didn't take him seriously. We all know now that by the time Hitler's Satanic program became a reality, it was too late to stop him.
>
> Arafat did *not* commit any slip of the tongue in Johannesburg: he used his call for a *jihad* and cited Mohammed's agreement with the Quraish tribe to test his thesis that Israel would swallow that, too.
>
> The PLO leader was sure that Israeli protests would strengthen his position among his own people—for he must never appear to be cooperating with Israel against Hamas and Islamic Jihad [two leading terrorist groups]. His rhetoric about a holy war to liberate Jerusalem was designed to remove all suspicion of such cooperation. . . .
>
> Whatever the interpretations of Arafat's statements, one thing is clear: the Palestinian masses understand his message about a holy war to liberate Jerusalem.[8]

Make no mistake: The world will have war or peace depending upon what happens in "the city of our God." In fact, we know what will happen there because the Bible has foretold it in great detail. We will refer to those prophecies in the following pages.

Like It or Not

Is it mere coincidence that Jerusalem, the present key to world peace, was originally called Salem, which means "peace"? It was ruled in those early days by one of the most enigmatic figures in history: Melchisedec, King of Salem. He suddenly appears out of nowhere on the pages of Scripture, then vanishes. This was pagan territory, yet Melchisedec was "*the* [not *a*] priest of the most high God" (Genesis 14:18; cf. Hebrews 7:1). Abraham, known as "the friend of God," looked up to Melchisedec as one greater than himself, honored him with a tithe, and accepted his blessing (Genesis 14:19,20; Hebrews 7:1,2).

Speaking to God, Solomon called Jerusalem "the city which thou hast chosen . . ." (1 Kings 8:44). Jerusalem, with its prophetic destiny about to reach full flower, presents a clear message to the world: Mankind is not the product of chance and blind evolutionary forces. Nothing in the universe, neither energy itself nor the myriad forms in which it is manifested, can be explained by chance. Quite clearly the laws of physics and chemistry did not initiate their orderly control over matter but were ordained by a law Giver; and just as obviously, the atom and living cell, with their incomprehensible organization and function, could only have been designed and brought into existence by an infinite Creator. In agreement with the universe surrounding it, Jerusalem declares to the world that mankind has a special place in God's creation and that a glorious destiny awaits those who will acknowledge and obey the God of Israel who chose Jerusalem as His city.

Whether one likes the implications or not, the fact remains that the rationally inexplicable role being played by Jerusalem was prophesied in the Bible thousands of years ago. And whether one likes the further implication or not, it remains also that these biblical prophecies offer the only rational explanation for Jerusalem's unique place on today's world scene.

The facts stand on their own and cannot be refuted even though many Israelis and Zionists reject their miraculous flavor. In subsequent chapters we will document these prophecies and their remarkable fulfillment.

Without the Bible one cannot possibly make any sense of human history. We are faced with only two choices: Either mankind is merely an accident which happened on one of billions of planets (and if here, perhaps on others scattered throughout the cosmos), or we were created by God for His own purposes. It is the God of the Bible who alone gives purpose and meaning to His creation, and He has decreed that Israel will play a key role in His plan.

Jerusalem! It is like no other city on earth. It stands at the center of history and at the very heart of God's purposes for this planet and all of its inhabitants. This is the "City of God," where God chose to place His name and for which He will have the last word. Like it or not, the whole world finds itself caught in the grip of that choice.

*The LORD had said unto Abram, Get thee out of thy
country . . . unto a land that I will show thee; and I
will make of thee a great nation, and I will bless
thee . . . and I will bless them that bless thee, and
curse him that curseth thee. . . .*

—Genesis 12:1-3

*In the same day the LORD made a covenant with
Abram, saying, Unto thy seed have I given this land,
from the river of Egypt unto . . . the river Euphrates. . . . To thee will I give it, and to thy seed forever.*

*And the LORD appeared unto him [Isaac], and
said . . . unto thee, and unto thy seed, I will give all
these countries, and I will perform the oath which I
swore unto Abraham thy father. . . .*

*And, behold, the LORD . . . said [unto Jacob], I am
the LORD God of Abraham thy father, and the God of
Isaac; the land whereon thou liest, to thee will I give
it, and to thy seed.*

—Genesis 15:18; 13:15; 26:2,3; 28:13

*I will bring you in unto the land, concerning which I
did swear to give it to Abraham, to Isaac, and to
Jacob; and I will give it you for an heritage; I am the
LORD.*

—Exodus 6:8

*Ye shall inherit their land, and I will give it unto you
to possess it, a land that floweth with milk and honey.*

—Leviticus 20:24

*Then will I cause you to dwell in this place, in the land
that I gave to your fathers, for ever and ever.*

—Jeremiah 7:7

2
Land of Promise

♦

From the foregoing verses it is quite clear that God gave Israel a *land* to possess *for ever and ever*. This was not the promise that the Jews would always have *some* land *somewhere* in the world but that they would possess a *specific* land as the heritage which God had promised to them. Such a promise was never made to any other nation or people. That fact alone makes both the Jewish people and the land of Israel absolutely unique. And until that fact is acknowledged both by Israel and all other nations this world will never know real peace.

As we shall see later, and as the prophets warned them, the Israelites were cast out of that land because of their disobedience to the God who had given it to them. As the centuries passed, the Jews now scattered around the world lost the conviction that the land of Israel belonged to them. At the same time, the persecution and slaughter which they experienced in their communities at the hands of the Gentiles around them made them long for a land of their own. They were a people without a country to call home; and the desire for a national Jewish homeland began to take root as anti-Semitism increased, particularly in Russia and Europe toward the end of the last century. That desire spawned the Zionist movement.

Zionism and the Promised Land

The first Zionist Congress was held at Basel, Switzerland, in 1897, inspired by the publication in 1896 of *The Jewish State* by Theodor Herzl. It must be understood that Herzl's motivation was not primarily inspired by faith in the God of Israel and His promises to Abraham, Isaac, and Jacob. He was not necessarily intent upon a return to the land that God had promised to His chosen people. It is questionable how many of the early Zionists actually believed that God existed and had made such a promise. Herzl's motivation was purely political and economic, aroused by the wave of anti-Semitism sweeping Europe in the wake of the controversy surrounding the Dreyfus Affair (the false accusation of treason and wrongful conviction of Alfred Dreyfus, a young Jewish captain in the French Army). It had become more obvious than ever that Jews needed a safe refuge somewhere in the world which only a Jewish State could offer.

Many if not most of the early Zionists didn't care what land they were given so long as it belonged to them alone. It didn't necessarily have to be the ancient land of Israel. Some were even willing to take a territory in Africa. Theodor Herzl himself negotiated for a tract of land in the British Mandate that was not in the Holy Land but adjacent to it. When he was offered instead a 6000-square-mile area in East Africa, the Zionist movement split between those willing to accept this offer and those who insisted that the Jewish State must be in Palestine. That bitter controversy still had not been settled when Herzl died on July 3, 1904. Nevertheless, in honor of the vital role that Herzl had played, his body was taken to Israel in 1949 for reburial there.

Thus the Zionist movement itself split over the two opposing positions which one may take regarding Jerusalem and Israel. As we noted in the first chapter, either the Bible is true and a specific land was given to the Jews by God to be theirs forever, or else there is no God and the idea that the land of Israel was promised to the Jews is a myth. If the former is true, then Israel dare not barter away any of its land for "peace."

A Radical (but Biblical) Proposal

Furthermore, if God exists and the Bible is true, then instead of attempting to take land from the Jews, their Arab neighbors should be returning to Jewish control the entire territory which God promised to them, and the United Nations ought to be conducting itself with that understanding. This is a radical departure from the viewpoint of either Israel, the Arabs, or the rest of the world. However, such a course of action follows logically from what the Bible declares repeatedly and in the plainest of language.

The return of all of the promised land to Israel's control would not, of course, involve the expulsion of its present inhabitants. It would, however, give the Israeli government *jurisdiction* of that territory. That such a change in management would benefit the entire Middle East can hardly be doubted. To recognize the truth of that assertion, one need only make a comparison of the prosperity of the land of Israel with the previous destitution of that land before Jewish control and with the present poverty of its Arab neighbors, as any visitor to that area of the world well knows. As only one example, consider the following comparison of a few current statistics:

> The population of Israel is about 5.4 million, its gross domestic product is $61.5 billion, and thus its per capita gross domestic product is about $11,600 per annum. Jordan, Israel's next door neighbor, has a comparable population of about 4.5 million people. Their per capita gross domestic product, however, is less than $1/10$ of Israel's, or about $1,100 per annum. Israel's 5.4 million people export about $15 billion in products each year compared with Jordan's $1.25 billion for its 4.5 million people.
>
> In fact, it is the Israeli economy that holds up that of the Palestinians in the Gaza Strip and the West Bank.[1]

On the other hand, if the latter is true (no God and no promised land for Israel), then the mere fact that the State of

Israel came into existence in the Middle East in 1948 and has survived to this date is the result of pure chance and has no other significance. In that case, without God as the Creator of mankind, there is no purpose or meaning to any human existence. The struggles of individuals and nations for survival, possessions, and security are simply the savage instincts of creatures to whom evolution has granted the capability of developing more sophisticated and cruel methods of selfish aggression. The history of mankind is thus a meaningless continuation at a more destructive level of the fight for survival which its animal forebears fought with fang and claw and the animal world continues to this day. Without an intelligent and purposeful Creator, peace is a fantasy, progress is insanity, history is going nowhere, and the entire universe is a macabre joke.

Ecumenical Destruction of Truth

Of course, opinions vary among Christians, Muslims, and Jews, and even among those who claim to believe in God and in the Bible but who nevertheless disagree on the subject of Israel. But there can be not the slightest doubt as to what the Bible teaches: Palestine and much more—even to the Euphrates River—is the "Promised Land" given by God to the Jews forever. Nor can any honest person deny the existence of this God or the validity of His promises to Israel. For as we shall see, the Hebrew prophets who claimed to be inspired by the Creator of the universe put down in writing hundreds of prophecies concerning Israel which have come true hundreds and even thousands of years after they were made. The fulfillments are so numerous and so precise that chance is ruled out by the mathematics of probability. Any sincere observer is left with only one choice: to accept God's existence and what He has decreed and to realize that only through Him will there be a just, a meaningful, and a lasting peace among all nations.

Such a viewpoint, however, is relegated to the realm of religious superstition in our day, and, except for a few Islamic regimes, the "separation of church and state" is the rule. As a consequence, God, even if He does exist, is not allowed to interfere in "real life." A major reason for that prevailing opinion is of course the fact that there are so many different concepts of God and so many different religions. Only when they all agree can church and state come together; and perhaps only then will there be peace. Such is the hope of ecumenism.

Unfortunately, the ecumenical movement aims at resolving differences in belief by abandoning them, to arrive at a lowest common denominator acceptable to all. Such a development would not be progress but folly, for it is in itself a denial of truth and a rejection of the importance of any belief about which there are differences of opinion. Ecumenical unity is thus achieved at the expense of conviction and reason and is therefore a retreat from, not a step toward, a meaningful agreement.

Another way truth is denied is by the rule of consensus in our day. Anything that is not palatable or positive is rejected simply on that basis. Truth is often uncomfortable and is thus unpopular. What the Bible teaches is certainly not always palatable, whether about Israel or about man's moral responsibility to God. What we have seen from the Bible regarding the "Promised Land" seems a preposterous proposition to the vast majority of mankind. No one can deny, however, that the Bible declares it over and over in unequivocal terms. We cannot simply ignore this fact. If God's promises to Abraham, Isaac, and Jacob regarding the *land* are not true, then the Bible is not true in anything else it says. One must either accept or reject the whole package.

Two Alternatives with Serious Consequences

Neither can one escape the logical and practical consequences for Israel, depending upon which viewpoint one embraces. I remember standing in a group that was being shown around a kibbutz in Galilee by one of its leaders. He made it a point to boast that his kibbutz was atheistic and that most of the 300 others in Israel were atheistic as well. In fact, most were founded on Marxist principles. I asked him a simple question: "If there is no God, then this land was not, as the Bible says it was, given by God to the Jews. If that is the case, how do your people have any better claim to this land than the Arabs?"

It was a question to which he had no answer. Logically, if this is not the land of promise given by God to the Jews, then their only claim is to that small part of the land which was partitioned to them by the United Nations in 1947. They are obligated to give back all other land which they have taken since that time, and that includes Jerusalem. Israel cannot claim the "Promised Land" if its people do not believe in the God who promised it. A 23-year-old athlete who recently immigrated from Antwerp to Israel complained, "If anything bothers me in Israel, it's the [lack of] relation to the Jewish heritage."[2]

If the Bible is merely the human record of the ancient Hebrews presenting their traditions, then the Hebrew Scriptures are no better than the traditions of any other group of people on earth. Certainly there is no basis for giving the Jews title today to a land just because they occupied it more than 2500 years ago. One might as well try to unscramble the present ownership of property in Europe by establishing who its "original" inhabitants were, attempting to find their descendants, and giving each plot back to them in spite of the claims of present occupants.

On the other hand, if God exists and has indeed given to the Jews the land of Israel as its boundaries are outlined in the Bible, then we must honor His decision. Tradition stems from the past without any justification or compulsion for honoring it in the present. Traditions vary among peoples, so who is to say which tradition is the best or explain why it should be kept, much less expect others of different traditions to honor those that conflict with their own? Honoring ancient traditions is not the route to peace.

If God exists, however, then the same One who named Israel as His chosen people is still God today. Therefore His promises remain in force and He has the power to fulfill them in the present. Those who deny His existence and reject His promises will find themselves fighting against God to their own sorrow and loss.

No Favoritism with God

The very fact that the Bible calls the Jews God's "chosen people" and that He gave them the Promised Land arouses immediate anger and resentment. "Why should God favor *them*!" is the common complaint. There is no reason, however, for resentment against God or the Jews, for the Bible makes it clear that He did not give the land of Canaan to Israel because of mere favoritism.

At the time He promised that land to Abraham and his seed, God declared that it could not be theirs until the wickedness of its present inhabitants had reached the point where God would be justified in dispossessing and even destroying them: "But in the fourth generation they shall come hither again, for the iniquity of the Amorites is not yet full" (Genesis 15:16). God again made this point very clear to Israel through Moses:

> Speak not thou in thine heart, after the LORD thy God hath cast them out [the Canaanites] from before thee, saying, For my righteousness the LORD hath brought me in to possess the land; but for the wickedness of these nations the LORD doth drive them out from before thee . . . and that he may perform the word which the LORD swore unto thy fathers, Abraham, Isaac, and Jacob (Deuteronomy 9:4,5).

The Bible states repeatedly and clearly that the title deed to the land of Israel was given by God to the seed of Abraham, Isaac and Jacob to replace nations which had been cast out of that land because of their wickedness—and that it was given to Israel forever. Whatever one's prejudices or beliefs, what the Bible says cannot be denied. The promise of the land was not given once or twice but dozens of times and is repeated in almost every Old Testament book. Therefore, although the Arabs may claim to be descended from Ishmael (which they cannot prove), that is not good enough. They are definitely not of the seed of Isaac and Jacob, to whom the land was given. The Arabs prove this by their hatred and persecution of the Jewish people to this day.

It was *God* who promised this land to these people. Therefore anyone who tries to prevent them from receiving full possession and enjoyment of their land is rebelling against *God* and comes under the curse which He established: "I will bless them that bless thee, and curse him that curseth thee..." (Genesis 12:3). If we believe the Bible at all, then we must admit that the "Promised Land" belongs to those to whom God promised it. That being the case, we must do all we can to enable them to possess that land. It is not a matter of *human* agreement or disagreement, but of agreement with God Himself.

This Is God's Land

Three things must be remembered about God's promise of the land to Israel: 1) The promise was not made to present-day Jews (who may seem unworthy by their behavior), but to Abraham, Isaac, and Jacob, and therefore it is unconditional as far as the right of their descendants to the land, a land which belongs to them exclusively; 2) continued possession of the land is conditioned upon obedience to God, and those who disobey, though genuine descendants of Jacob, will be cast out if they do not repent and return to God; and 3) the promise was not for some limited time that has now passed but was for ever and ever and thus holds true today. These three points are made repeatedly and in the clearest language throughout the Bible. The following are only a few among the many examples that could be given:

> And Moses besought the LORD his God, and said ... Remember Abraham, Isaac, and Israel, thy servants, to whom thou swarest by thine own self ... all this land that I have spoken of will I give unto your seed, and they shall inherit it forever (Exodus 32:11,13).

The land shall not be sold forever, for the land is mine . . . (Leviticus 25:23).

And the LORD hath sent unto you all his servants the prophets. . . . They said, Turn ye again now everyone from his evil way . . . and dwell in the land that the LORD hath given unto you and to your fathers for ever and ever (Jeremiah 25:4,5).

And they shall dwell in the land that I have given unto Jacob my servant, wherein your fathers have dwelt; and they shall dwell therein, even they, and their children, and their children's children forever . . . (Ezekiel 37:25).

The words of the prophets could not be plainer as they repeatedly renewed God's promise, a promise that gave the land to Israel in perpetuity. One's opinion on this important and controversial subject is not a matter of being "pro-Israel" or "pro-Arab" or "anti" either of these peoples, but of acknowledging God's will in the matter. The simple fact is that in trying to take back land from Israel, the Arab nations are opposing God and rejecting His clear promises in the Bible and are thereby robbing themselves of the blessing that God promised to those who would bless Israel. The same is true of the Palestinians in demanding autonomous control over parts of that land which was promised to Israel.

How then can the Muslims justify their violent opposition to Israel? After all, they claim to believe in the God of the Bible. We will deal more fully with that question later, but suffice it to say at this point that Mohammed embraced another god, who is not the God of the Bible. Allah is clearly not the God of Abraham, Isaac, and Jacob. The Arabs prove that they follow another god by cursing those whom God has blessed. Moreover, the Koran, after accepting the Bible in its early pages, contradicts itself by later contradicting the Bible in many ways. Islam, too, contradicts the Bible, for example, in its claim that the Promised Land had been given to the Arabs and not to the Jews.

The Roman Catholic Attitude

The Arabs are not the only ones who denounce Jewish possession of the Promised Land. Over the centuries the idea developed in Roman Catholicism that because they crucified Christ, the Jews were to be persecuted and even killed. Certainly they no longer had any claim to the Promised Land, which now belonged to the (Roman Catholic) Church. The Crusaders sought to recover that land in order to preserve its "holy sites" of Christian memory. In fact, the Roman Catholic Church considers itself to be the new Israel of God.

Consequently, the Vatican has not been favorable toward Israel. It took the Catholic Church nearly 47 years to acknowledge the legitimacy of the State of Israel—and then it did so only for selfish motives, as we shall see. *After* Saddam Hussein's rape of Kuwait, Jerusalem's Catholic patriarch, Michel Sabbah, commended Saddam for "truly carry[ing] in his heart the Palestinian cause." He refused to concede that Saddam was "more dangerous" than President Bush.

Iraq's ranking Catholic leader, Patriarch Raphael Bidawid, defended Saddam's invasion and annexation of Kuwait and even its missile attacks upon Israel's civilians. "This entire war has been planned by Israel," said Bidawid from Rome, where he was conferring with the Pope and other Vatican officials about Middle East "peace." His remarks, which sounded hauntingly like Hitler's, were never reproved by the Vatican. One can therefore only conclude that he was presenting the official view. The Roman Catholic Church continues to oppose Jewish control of Jerusalem.

Acceptance of what the Bible says about the "Promised Land" belonging to Israel is made even more difficult by the extent of that land as the Old Testament describes it. The present worldly consensus is that Israel already possesses too much land, yet she occupies only a very small fraction of the territory which the Bible says belongs to her. Thus it is out of the question, by human wisdom, to look to the Bible at all for a solution to the Middle East crisis.

The Promised Land's Surprising Size

The boundaries of the Promised Land are given to us in Genesis 15:18-21. It comprised all of Lebanon and much of Jordan, including its capital, Amman. The 2½ tribes of Reuben, Gad, and half of Manasseh had their possession on the east side of Jordan. The tribe of Dan possessed what is now the Golan Heights and additional territory of what is now Syria. In fact, most of today's Syria, including its capital, Damascus, and beyond to the Euphrates was within the boundaries of the land that God gave to the descendants of Abraham, Isaac, and Jacob:

> In the same day the LORD made a covenant with Abram [later God renamed him Abraham], saying, Unto thy seed have I given this land, from the river of Egypt unto the great river, the river Euphrates: [naming the peoples in possession at that time] the Kenites, and the Kenizzites, and the Kadmonites, and the Hittites, and the Perizzites, and the Rephaims, and the Amorites, and the Canaanites, and the Girgashites, and the Jebusites (Genesis 15:18-21).

Israel never possessed all of the territory that belonged to her. However, much of what is now Lebanon, Syria, and Jordan were under David's control and also that of his son Solomon during his own reign. For example, we are told that "David smote also [King] Hadadezer... as he went to recover his border at the river Euphrates" (2 Samuel 8:3). Since the Euphrates was one boundary of the Promised Land, apparently David had previously taken much of what is now Syria, up to the Euphrates, and King Hadadezer came to recover it. The account continues:

> And when the Syrians of Damascus came to succor Hadadezer king of Zobah, David slew of the Syrians twenty-two thousand men. Then David put garrisons in Syria of Damascus, and the Syrians became servants to David, and brought gifts....

> And David took the shields of gold that were on the
> servants of Hadadezer, and brought them to Jerusa-
> lem . . . which also king David did dedicate unto the
> LORD, with the silver and gold that he had dedicated of
> all nations which he subdued: of Syria, and of Moab, and
> of the children of Ammon, and of the Philistines, and of
> Amalek, and . . . he put garrisons in Edom . . . and all
> they of Edom became David's servants. And the LORD
> preserved David wherever he went. And David reigned
> over all Israel . . . (2 Samuel 8:5-15).

Skeptics have tried desperately to discredit the Bible, but
archaeologists have been quietly at work for the last 150 years,
and everything they uncover only proves the accuracy of Scripture. Jewish students today study their amazing history from
the Old Testament, while archaeologists use its accounts to
find the sites of ancient ruins and geologists follow its descriptions in locating water and oil and ancient mines and minerals.
There is every reason to accept the biblical account. What a
transformation would be made in the Middle East if the nations
of the world were to govern their affairs on that basis!

Awakening Jewish Consciousness

It is amazing to see that even after the Holocaust so many
Jews, instead of immigrating to the Promised Land, are
returning to the scene of the slaughter of their forebears in
Europe. *Time* magazine recently reported: "In Budapest,
Prague, Warsaw, Moscow, Bratislava, Berlin, in hundreds of
towns and villages from the Baltic to the Black Sea, Jewish
communities are re-emerging and coming together in a kind of
Continental minyan, the quorum required for the holding of
religious services. Synagogues and schools are rising again,
some on the foundations of Jewish institutions dating from the
Middle Ages. Jews are proudly calling themselves Jews once
more, reviving traditions and cultures long buried in the ashes
of Hitler's ovens. 'That now there is the possibility to be a Jew
is mystical,' says 18-year-old Igor Czernikow, one of the founders of a Jewish youth club in Wroclaw in Poland's Silesia. 'It's

a historic change, in the history of our nation and the history of the individual.' "³

There were nearly 2 million Jews left in Europe after the war. Most of them had no desire to resettle in Israel. Nor did the majority of them have much feeling for their Jewishness, which "seemed to consist of little more than distinctive surnames and distant memories. Yet since the Iron Curtain was lifted and communism banished from the Soviet bloc, the lost generations are being found. Renewed interest in Judaism is part of a broad search for spirituality that has sprung up in the desert created by the demise of a discredited ideology. 'People are coming out of the woodwork and announcing they are Jewish,' says David Lerner, a British educator who helped found a Sabbath school in Minsk. 'Six years ago Jews were still being beaten up in Minsk. Now there are three religious congregations, the Sabbath school, a youth movement and a voluntary welfare organization.'

"It is the young, especially, who are discovering their Jewishness. 'In the very place where the Nazis created Auschwitz, we have young Jews trying to reclaim their heritage,' said Rabbi Michael Schudrich of the American Lauder foundation as he opened the latest youth center last week in Cracow, Poland. 'Many did not even know five years ago that they were Jewish.' In Budapest the 118-year-old Rabbinical Seminary, the only one in Eastern Europe, is training a new generation of religious leaders for Hungary. . . .

"Now some of the younger Jews are drawing their elders back to the faith. . . . Jan Rott, 73, a Prague architect and writer, is astonished at the revival. 'For 50 years only a few circumcisions were done here,' he says. 'It was difficult to gather the 10 men required to hold Sabbath prayers.' Now Prague's Altneu Schul, the main synagogue, holds services daily, and three study groups meet weekly to explore Jewish religion and culture. . . . The need to reintroduce children to their culture is especially urgent in Russia, where 70 years of repression and assimilation obliterated Jewish consciousness. . . ."⁴

"Many of Russia's Jews are flocking to Berlin and Hamburg, where Jewish communities once were, in search of opportunity. . . . At the beginning of 1992 the official count for the Jewish community in Germany was about 34,000. Since then another 20,000 have arrived from the East, and more are expected at a rate of about 10,000 a year for the foreseeable future . . . and it is upsetting to those who believe that Jews who leave Russia should be going to Israel, even the U.S., but in no case to Germany. 'They are going from one hell to another,' says Dov Shilansky, a member of the Israeli parliament from the rightist Likud group. 'They are living next to people who killed their brethren.'"

But others disagree with that attitude. "'If all of us fled Germany,' says Shlomit Tulgan, a student in Berlin, 'then Hitler would have achieved his desire of making Germany free of Jews. We can't let that happen.' Serge Klarsfeld, the French Nazi hunter, believes the Jews belong in Eastern Europe despite the Holocaust. 'To live in Cracow, in Prague or in Budapest is not to live with assassins. It is to live with the memory of Jewish life that once flourished there.'"[5]

Tradition or the Bible?

Conspicuous by its absence in the growing and often heated discussion about where Jews ought to live is any reference to the fact that the Bible says they belong in the Promised Land that was given to them by God. It is astonishing that in all of the excitement of a revived awareness of Jewishness there is almost no recognition of what it means, according to the Bible, to be a Jew.

For the millions of Jews living in the world today their Jewishness finds its meaning in tradition but not in the Bible. Or if in the Bible to some extent, then that sacred Book is considered to be of no more authority than tradition. Jesus is viewed by most Jews today as a rebel from Judaism. Yet no one can argue with the truth of His indictment of the rabbis in his day, an indictment which applies equally in our time:

> Thus have ye made the commandment of God of none
> effect by your tradition. Ye hypocrites, well did Esaias

prophesy of you, saying, This people draweth nigh unto
me with their mouth, and honoreth me with their lips,
but their heart is far from me. But in vain they do worship
me, teaching for doctrines the commandments [tradi-
tions] of men (Matthew 15:6-9).

Rabbi Shlomo Riskin, who has a regular column in the
international edition of *The Jerusalem Post*, uses that medium
to call Jews back to their tradition and roots. He writes,
"Our ability to remain on Israeli soil—and not to be exiled—
depends upon our fealty to traditional Jewish teaching, the
continuity of our ethical, moral and ritual conduct which links
us to our glorious past." He argues further:

> Only those Jews who return to Israel because it was
> the land of their forebears, yearned for by their grand-
> parents, can re-endow the land of Israel with its original
> sanctity. And only those Jews who value their history,
> and whose ethical, moral and traditional mores are inex-
> tricably linked to the great chain of Jewish being, will be
> allowed to maintain this land and their rights to live in
> it.[6]

One wonders "who" or "what" is the power that decides
Jewish "moral and traditional mores" and removes from the
Promised Land those who don't measure up. Is it perhaps "the
great chain of Jewish being" which somehow has the mysterious power to determine what Jewishness means and to purge
from Israel those who fall short of its mystical standards?
While the rabbi also mentions God and "the Divine will," one
is not sure what he means. In any event, it is surely not the
personal God of Abraham or David who determines Israel's
destiny, but Jewish "tradition" itself.

Topol, in *Fiddler on the Roof*, seemed to agree that "tradition" had become everything. But tradition is really nothing if
it does not agree with God's immutable laws and purposes. In
fact, as Jesus said, such tradition contradicts and nullifies
God's purpose for Israel and for all mankind. How astonishing

that in spite of the Holocaust and in spite of God's judgment— and also in the face of God's undeniable and merciful fulfillment of His promises to Abraham, Isaac, and Jacob by bringing their descendants back into their land—the vast majority of Jews disbelieve those promises today.

Perhaps what the Bible says is too much for them to believe, for, as we have noted, the "Promised Land" given by God extends far beyond that small territory now known as Israel. Could that unbelief explain why Israel's leaders are bartering part of that too-small territory for the seductive promise of "peace" with their neighbors?

Early in February 1995, in a brief military ceremony, Israel turned back to Jordan 340 square kilometers of land. Radio Jordan announced triumphantly, "Jordan has achieved full sovereignty over lands that Israel had occupied."[7] By such deeds Israel is repudiating the very promises of God which are her only title to that land. Instead, she desperately needs to hold onto what little she has and to trust God to give her the rest.

With more Jews returning home from all over the world, especially from the former Soviet Union, even burial space is inadequate. "Experts estimate that within two years, three at most, there will be no burial room in cemeteries from Haifa to Jerusalem. The only solution is to bury people deep underground in layers, a proposal which is now under careful consideration."[8] Where then shall all of the Jews live who are yet to return to that land?

Islam or the Bible?

If it were only the Arabs as rational beings dealing with Israel, reason might prevail as to what would be best for that region of the world. There is, of course, the natural human pride which plagues not only Arabs but all mankind (Jews as well) and which stands in the way. The major roadblock, however, is Islam. That religion is the driving force behind much of the terrorism not only in that region but around the world today. And so much of the terrorism, no matter where it is found, has its roots in the Islamic determination to annihilate Israel. As one Middle East observer explains:

> Suddenly, in 1948, not so far from Mecca, the very heart of Islam, a Jewish state emerged with its own president, parliament, government, prime minister, and army; it had everything which distinguishes a genuine national community. A new nation had been born, and this was a clear demonstration of the fulfillment of what had been written by the prophets:
>
> > *I will bring back the captives of My people Israel; they shall build the waste cities and inhabit them. . . . I will plant them in their land, and no longer shall they be pulled up from the land I have given them, says the* LORD *your God* (Amos 9:14a,15).
>
> The rebirth of the Jewish state right in the midst of the Arab countries is a direct contradiction of Islamic teaching. Has not Allah finished with the Jewish people? And if Allah has predetermined all things, how is it possible that a Jewish state should have come into existence once again?
>
> For Muslims the worst humiliation is that this Jewish state has Jerusalem as its capital. On July 30, 1980, the Knesset (the Israeli parliament) passed a law declaring the City of Jerusalem to be "eternal and indivisible."
>
> Jerusalem . . . after Mecca and Medina, is the third-most-holy place in Islam. . . . And this same Jerusalem is now the capital of a Jewish state which, in Muslim eyes, should never have come into being![9]

Though we may sound repetitive, we cannot emphasize enough the fact that both the land and the people of Israel are unique. This is God's land, the place where He has chosen to place His name, the heritage He has given to His people. Its destiny is in His hands.

As for the Jebusites the inhabitants of Jerusalem, the children of Judah could not drive them out. . . .

—Joshua 15:63

And Joshua said unto the children of Israel, How long are ye slack to go to possess the land which the LORD God of your fathers hath given you?

—Joshua 18:3

And the children of Benjamin did not drive out the Jebusites that inhabited Jerusalem. . . .

—Judges 1:21

Nevertheless David took the [Jebusites'] stronghold of Zion; the same is the city of David.

—2 Samuel 5:7

I [God] will set up thy seed after thee . . . and I will establish the throne of his kingdom forever . . . thy throne shall be established forever.

—2 Samuel 7:12-16

Once have I sworn by my holiness . . . unto David. His seed shall endure forever, and his throne as the sun before me.

—Psalm 89:35,36

So David slept with his fathers, and was buried in the city of David.

—1 Kings 2:10

. . . that David my servant may have a light always before me in Jerusalem, the city which I have chosen me to put my name there.

—1 Kings 11:36

3

The City of David

◆

Freed at last from slavery in Egypt, the Israelites quickly became rebellious, ungrateful, and disobedient even on their way to the Promised Land. God's discipline was to keep them wandering for 40 years in the Sinai wilderness until all of that generation of rebels had died. The next generation was brought into the land, but they proved to be no better than their parents. Inside the land, with the fulfillment of God's promises only awaiting their cooperation and diligence, they failed to conquer and take possession of what God had so graciously given to them.

One such area was Jerusalem, which remained under Jebusite control. These resourceful idol worshipers were securely established in an impregnable fortress on the rocky summit of Mount Zion and could not be dislodged. The Israelites finally gave up trying. Here was the site that God had chosen for His Temple, but it remained in pagan hands in the very heart of the Promised Land.

David and the Messiah

When, however, David became king some 400 years later, he led his men in an attack against the Jebusites and conquered them. Now all of Jerusalem was under Jewish control at last. David made it the capital of Israel and called it "the city of David," a title given to Jerusalem more than forty times in the Bible. In fact, Jerusalem will forever be known both as "the city of God" and "the city of David." There David established his throne and ruled over Israel.

David's name will be perpetually attached to Jerusalem not only because he was its conqueror but because God promised to establish David's throne there in perpetuity: "I have chosen Jerusalem that my name might be there, and have chosen David to be over my people Israel. . . . And thine house and thy kingdom shall be established forever before thee; thy throne shall be established forever" (2 Chronicles 6:6; 2 Samuel 7:16).

Obviously such promises meant that the Messiah, whose reign was to be eternal, would be descended from David and would rule Israel and the world from David's throne in Jerusalem:

> I have made a covenant with my chosen, I have sworn unto David my servant, Thy seed [the Messiah] will I establish forever, and build up thy throne to all generations. . . .
>
> I have found David my servant; with my holy oil have I anointed him, with whom my hand shall be established; mine arm also shall strengthen him. . . .
>
> His seed [the Messiah] also will I make to endure forever, and his throne as the days of heaven. If his children forsake my law and walk not in my judgments, if they break my statutes and keep not my commandments, then will I visit their transgression with the rod, and their iniquity with stripes.
>
> Nevertheless my lovingkindness will I not utterly take from him, nor suffer my faithfulness to fail. My covenant will I not break, nor alter the thing that is gone out of my lips. Once have I sworn by my holiness that I will not lie unto David. His seed shall endure forever, and his throne as the sun before me (Psalm 89:3,4,20,21,29-36).

Repentance and Grace

David himself presents a remarkable picture of God's grace in action. Far from perfect, he sinned grievously in committing adultery with Bathsheba and having her husband, Uriah the Hittite (one of his mightiest warriors and most faithful servants), slain in battle to make it appear that he was just another casualty of war. In contrast to Saul, however, who had been king before him and only made excuses for his sins, David was a broken man when Nathan the prophet confronted him with the great sin he had committed, and David repented fully.

That God spared his life at that time was an act of grace. Nevertheless, David endured severe discipline from God in the retributive destruction of his own family. Psalm 51, which David wrote in bitter remorse at that time, has been an inspiration to many others who have likewise found themselves overtaken by a temptation to which they have yielded and have fallen into sin:

> Have mercy upon me, O God, according to thy lovingkindness; according unto the multitude of thy tender mercies blot out my transgressions.
>
> Wash me thoroughly from mine iniquity, and cleanse me from my sin. For I acknowledge my transgressions, and my sin is ever before me.
>
> Against thee, thee only, have I sinned, and done this evil in thy sight. . . . Purge me with hyssop, and I shall be clean; wash me, and I shall be whiter than snow. . . .
>
> Create in me a clean heart, O God, and renew a right spirit within me. Cast me not away from thy presence, and take not thy Holy Spirit from me. Restore unto me the joy of thy salvation. . . .
>
> The sacrifices of God are a broken spirit; a broken and a contrite heart, O God, thou wilt not despise.

Apart from that heinous lapse of obedience, David lived an exemplary life—so much so that God said of him, "I have found David the son of Jesse, a man after mine own heart, which shall fulfill all my will" (Acts 13:22). That relationship with God did not come in a moment but was developed over long years of faithful pursuit of God and His will. How tragic that today's Israeli leaders lack that same passion!

Revising Israel's History

It was because of his trust in God that David was able to conquer not only Jerusalem but the rest of the land which God had given to His chosen people, even to the River Euphrates. In contrast, today's Israel, though as yet possessing only a small fraction of the domain God promised her, is giving land back to its enemies in exchange for the promise of an insincere "peace." Israeli Foreign Minister Shimon Peres recently justified that less-than-Davidic policy by suggesting that David's military victories were not "acceptable to Judaism or to me."[1]

Peres was challenged by Knesset members on December 14, 1994, for his and Prime Minister Rabin's acceptance of the Nobel Peace Prize arm in arm with that longtime terrorist and murderer of Israelis, Yasser Arafat. What "peace" is that? Presenting an astonishing revisionist view of the Hebrew Scriptures, Peres defended current "peace policy" with the assertion that Judaism never supported military conquest or ruling over non-Jews.

Apparently, in Peres' revised Old Testament, the ancient Israelites fought no battles. Instead, the nations occupying the land of Canaan graciously handed it all over as a gift to Joshua and walked away in self-imposed exile! In fact, the Scriptures repeatedly declare what David often acknowledged: that every victory he won was only because of God's hand guiding and protecting him in the military conquest of the land and the Lord's enemies.

Unfortunately, political correctness and expediency now dictate Israeli policy. How tragic that today's leaders lack that same faith in God and that intimate relationship with Him that David enjoyed and which was the secret to his success!

Humility and Exaltation

One of David's outstanding qualities was a deep and sincere humility in recognition of the fact that he was totally dependent upon God. In spite of his great talents and unusual abilities, he was willing to do the most menial tasks assigned to him. It was this very humility that caused his father and brothers to overlook his incredible potential and actually to despise him.

God revealed to the prophet Samuel that the man He had chosen to replace the erring King Saul was one of Jesse's sons, whom he was to anoint with the special oil (reserved for prophets, priests, and kings) as king over Israel. Samuel, accordingly, came to Bethlehem and invited Jesse and his sons to a feast. Jesse introduced each of his sons to the prophet in turn. They were a handsome and virile group of men, each one seemingly fit to be king. Samuel was therefore confused when God told him that none of the men before him was the one He had chosen to rule Israel.

There was only one possibility: Jesse must have another son who was not present, even though Samuel had specifically told him to bring all of them. When Samuel asked if this might be the case, Jesse seemed embarrassed, as though he had either forgotten the youngest or had considered him unworthy to attend such an important affair:

> Samuel said unto Jesse, Are here all thy children? And he said, There remaineth yet the youngest, and, behold, he keepeth the sheep. And Samuel said unto Jesse, Send and fetch him, for we will not sit down till he come hither.
>
> And he sent and brought him in. . . . And the Lord said, Arise, anoint him, for this is he. Then Samuel took the horn of oil and anointed him in the midst of his brethren; and the Spirit of the LORD came upon David from that day forward (1 Samuel 16:11-13).

Why the Messiah Would Be Despised

David presents a remarkable picture of the Messiah, a picture which offers an insight into a Scripture that must have been difficult for Israel to comprehend: ". . . when we shall see him [the Messiah], there is no beauty that we should desire him. He is despised and rejected of men, a man of sorrows and acquainted with grief; and we hid as it were our faces from him; he was despised and we esteemed him not" (Isaiah 53:2,3). How could such a description fit the Messiah? Would *the Messiah* be physically repulsive? Surely not! Indeed, He would have to be the epitome of manhood, the perfect man, all that God intended man to be! Then why would Israel see no beauty in Him and even despise Him?

We find the insightful answer to this enigma in David. He was so humble that no one recognized his great qualities and abilities. Indeed, his very humility, so contrary to human nature, unconsciously condemned the pride of others and blinded them with their own resentment against him. David was the greatest harpist and songwriter in Israel, but no one knew it. He had been content to sing to God alone, with only that flock of sheep as witnesses. In response to the sincerity and humility of his heart, God gifted David with talents that made him the greatest psalmist of all time. And because of his willingness to faithfully care for that small flock of sheep in spite of abilities that fitted him for greater tasks, God promoted him to be the shepherd-king over Israel.

Would the Messiah be despised and rejected because He was inept and unattractive? Obviously not. David was despised and rejected, yet he was the handsomest and wisest and most capable warrior and administrator in Israel. After he was taken into the palace, his musical gifts greatly pleased the king. Yet when war broke out with the Philistines, David was sent back to tend the sheep (1 Samuel 17:1,15) because no one thought he would be of any use in a battle. Imagine treating Israel's mightiest warrior in that manner just when he was needed the most! Such blindness tells us much!

There was an adviser of the king, however, whose eyes were opened by God to see in David the real man whom no one else recognized. This unnamed servant is a picture of those whose hearts have been opened to see the Messiah as He truly is— "altogether lovely" (Song of Solomon 5:16)—though the rest of mankind finds Him unattractive. Here is how this man described David to the king:

> Then answered one of the servants and said, Behold, I
> have seen a son of Jesse the Bethlehemite that is cunning
> in playing [the harp] and a mighty, valiant man, and a
> man of war, and prudent in matters, and a comely [hand-
> some] person, and the LORD is with him (1 Samuel 16:18).

No higher praise could be given! Yet David was despised
even by his own family because of his self-effacing humility. In
David, its greatest king, Israel was given a picture to explain
why the Messiah would be so unattractive except to those few
who saw Him from God's perspective rather than from man's.
Indeed, the Messiah would be the perfect Man as God had
intended all men to be, without the ravages of sin in spirit,
soul, and body. His perfections, however, being those that
pleased God, would be despised by egocentric and sinful
people living in rebellion against God and intent upon becoming little gods themselves.

The Unrecognized Deliverer

His father, Jesse, sent David to bring some homemade cakes
to his older brothers, where Israel's army was in position
confronting the Philistines. Arriving on such a humble mission, David was astonished to see Israel's mightiest warriors
tremble with fright when the giant, Goliath, appeared to taunt
them. When he challenged anyone from Israel's army to fight
him, David could not understand why no one stepped forward
immediately.

Not himself part of the army, David was unfamiliar with the
situation. So he began to inquire of those about him in an
attempt to understand what was happening. When David's
brothers learned of his inquiries, they berated him mercilessly.
It was treatment he had received all his life. The blindness of
his brothers to his capabilities was astonishing and the injustice of the false motives they attributed to him must have been
exasperating, but David remained unruffled:

> Eliab his eldest brother['s] ... anger was kindled
> against David, and he said, Why camest thou down

> hither? And with whom hast thou left those few sheep in
> the wilderness? I know thy pride, and the naughtiness of
> thine heart; for thou art come down that thou mightest
> see the battle.
>
> And David said, What have I now done? Is there not a
> cause? And he turned from him . . . (1 Samuel 17:28-30).

Humility falsely accused of pride; honesty and sincerity
unjustly accused of selfish motives. How amazing! What an
illustration of the blindness of the human heart, and what
proof of David's purity before the God whom alone he served,
with no concern for what others might think of him. And what
a convicting example of complete faith in God David presented
to Israel's trembling army:

> David said to Saul, Let no man's heart fail because of
> him [Goliath]; thy servant will go and fight with this
> Philistine (1 Samuel 17:32).

David had absolutely no fear because he trusted in God.
This confidence in the face of impossible odds (which had
become part of David's everyday experience) was unknown to
Saul and his men. David's bravery seemed to them, who
remained blind to the real David, to be the foolhardy enthusiasm of youth. Thus when David offered to face Goliath and
defeat him, the king was certain that David would be an easy
prey for the giant. Once again we see how David's Messiah-like
humility made it impossible for the macho warriors to recognize that he was their champion:

> Saul said to David, Thou art not able to go against this
> Philistine to fight with him, for thou art but a youth, and
> he a man of war from his youth.
>
> And David said unto Saul, Thy servant kept his father's
> sheep, and there came a lion and a bear and took a lamb
> out of the flock; and I went out after him and smote him,
> and delivered it out of his mouth; and when he arose
> against me, I caught him [both the lion and bear] by his
> beard and smote him. . . . Thy servant slew both the lion
> and the bear. . . .

The LORD that delivered me out of the paw of the lion and out of the paw of the bear, he will deliver me out of the hand of this Philistine (1 Samuel 17:33-37).

A Stunning Victory Through Faith

Unable to persuade him not to confront the giant, Saul offered David the use of his armor. It was a well-intentioned but completely mistaken attempt to help. Remember, it was said of Saul that "from his shoulders and upward he was higher than any of the people" (1 Samuel 9:2). That was the situation before David was born. Obviously David was not the scrawny teenager often depicted in Sunday school materials. He must have been as tall and well-built as Saul or the king would not have put his armor upon him. David refused it, not because the armor didn't fit, but because he had another way of fighting the giant.

David had a simple weapon, the sling, with which he could hurl a stone with deadly velocity and hit the smallest target. No doubt he had practiced long hours each day during those lonely years of guarding the sheep. His trust, however, was not in his well-practiced accuracy, but in God alone, a trust which today's Israeli military unfortunately lacks:

> [David] took his [shepherd's] staff in his hand, and chose him five smooth stones [the giant had four brothers] out of the brook . . . and his sling was in his hand; and he drew near to the Philistine. . . .
>
> And the Philistine said unto David, Am I a dog, that thou comest to me with staves? And the Philistine cursed David by his gods. . . .
>
> Then said David to the Philistine [as he ran toward him], Thou comest to me with a sword and with a spear and with a shield, but I come to thee in the name of the LORD of hosts, the God of the armies of Israel, whom thou has defied.
>
> This day will the LORD deliver thee into mine hand . . . that all the earth may know that there is a God in Israel. And all this assembly [of Israel] shall know that

> the LORD saveth not with sword and spear; for the battle
> is the LORD's, and he will give you into our hands. . . .
>
> David hastened, and ran toward the army to meet the
> Philistine . . . and slung [a stone], and smote the Phi-
> listine . . . that the stone sank into his forehead; and he
> fell upon his face to the earth . . . but there was no sword
> in the hand of David.
>
> Therefore David ran, and stood upon the Philistine,
> and took his sword . . . and slew him, and cut off his head
> therewith. And when the Philistines saw their champion
> was dead, they fled (1 Samuel 17:40-51).

A single well-aimed shot from his sling and a stroke of the
giant's own sword in David's hands inspired Israel's army to a
great victory that catapulted David to honor. Saul wisely made
him commander of the army, but his jealousy of David soon
drove him to attempt his murder. The rest of this remarkable
story of the shepherd who became Israel's greatest king is
well-known and need not be repeated here.

David is, of course, remembered and greatly honored even
in Israel today. David's God, however—the God of Abraham,
Isaac, and Israel—is dishonored and even defied by His own
people. Instead of trusting in Him, Israel's modern military
leaders trust in themselves. That same mistake became Israel's
folly after the death of David and his son, King Solomon. Pride
and departure from God was ancient Israel's downfall. Jerusalem's rebellion brought God's just and long-deferred judgment
upon His chosen people.

A City Given to Destruction

Jerusalem, the City of God and the City of David, and the
Temple where God had revealed Himself in the Shekinah glory
that "filled the house of the LORD" (1 Kings 8:11), was given
over to destruction by invading armies. Instead of protecting
Jerusalem, God punished her for her sins by allowing her
enemies to do their worst. The history of Jerusalem became
the history of terror, of siege and famine, of repeated slaughter
and devastation. That history stands as eloquent witness to the

accuracy of the prophets who, in the name of the God of Abraham, Isaac, and Israel, warned the people of Israel to repent of their sin and told them of the judgment that would follow if they did not.

From the time of its destruction by Nebuchadnezzar as the instrument of God's retribution in 587 B.C., Jerusalem, the city of peace where God had placed His Name, has never again known lasting peace. Its history has been a never-ending litany of war, insurrection against its conquerors, desecration of the Temple, and the slaughter, enslavement, and dispersion of its people.

The walls of Jerusalem had been in ruins for more than 140 years when they were rebuilt under the leadership of Nehemiah about 445-440 B.C. Never again would the city regain its former glory, but it would be the continual target of invading armies, forever a ruin in the painful process of repair. In 320 B.C., when Ptolemy Soter attacked Jerusalem, the Jews refused to fight on the Sabbath. The city was taken and many of its people were led captive, some as far away as Africa, where they were sold as slaves.

Again in about 167 B.C. Antiochus Epiphanes desecrated the Temple and slaughtered Jerusalem's Jews by the thousands. He put the Holy City to the torch and beat down its walls. Once again many of those who were not slain were sold into slavery. Foreign peoples were brought in to resettle what was left on the site. A new fortress was built upon Mount Zion, and a garrison of troops was left there to rule the city in the name of Antiochus Epiphanes. At times, it seems, Antiochus thought of establishing and requiring the worship of himself as a god—even as the Antichrist, of whom Antiochus is a vivid picture, will eventually do (2 Thessalonians 2:4; Revelation 13:8,15).

Two years later Judas Maccabaeus led an army to a great victory over Antiochus. No foreign invaders conquered the city for the next hundred years. Yet during that time of "peace," internal strife among political and religious factions claimed at least another 50,000 dead, with multitudes more maimed and wounded. In 63 B.C., after a siege and much destruction, the city was captured once more, this time by Pompey. Six years later the city was conquered yet again, on this tragic occasion by a Roman army led by Herod the Great.

About 4 B.C. the Jews revolted against Herod the Great's successor, Archelaus, whose troops slew about 3000 insurgents. At the following feast of Pentecost there was another stubborn uprising and "great slaughter; the Temple cloisters were burned to the ground, the treasures of the sanctuary were plundered by the legions, and many Jews killed themselves in despair. . . . Varus, governor of Syria, entered Palestine with 20,000 men, razed hundreds of towns, crucified 2,000 rebels, and sold 30,000 Jews into slavery."[2]

The Final Diaspora

And so it has been down through the sad centuries for the City of Jerusalem. The City of Peace has known only repeated war. No wonder God has urged us, "Pray for the peace of Jerusalem" (Psalm 122:6). Having researched and written the entire history of civilization, Will Durant declared:

> No people in history has fought so tenaciously for liberty as the Jews, nor any people against such odds. From Judas Maccabee to Simeon Bar Cocheba, and even into our own time, the struggle of the Jews to regain their freedom has often decimated them, but has never broken their spirit or their hope.[3]

Jerusalem's last major destruction came in 70 A.D. at the hands of Titus and his Roman legions, who sacked the city and destroyed the Temple. Josephus accompanied Titus to the siege of Jerusalem and was a witness to its terrible devastation. From the Roman lines he pleaded with his countrymen to surrender, but they fought on to the last. Hundreds of thousands died in the siege. Of those who were captured alive, thousands were crucified—so many that Josephus reports, "Room was wanting for the crosses, and crosses were wanting for the bodies." Durant tells us that "in the later stages of the five-month siege the streets of the city were clogged with corpses . . . 116,000 bodies were thrown over the walls. . . .

"Having taken half the city, Titus offered what he thought were lenient terms to the rebels; they rejected them . . . the Romans set fire to the Temple, and the great edifice, much of it of wood, was rapidly consumed. . . . The victors gave no quarter, but slew all Jews upon whom they could lay their hands; 97,000 fugitives were caught and sold as slaves; many of them died as unwilling gladiators in the triumphal games. . . . Josephus numbered at 1,197,000 the Jews killed in this siege and its aftermath. . . . Judea was almost shorn of Jews, and those that remained lived on the edge of starvation. . . .[4]

"The flight or enslavement of a million Jews so accelerated their spread through the Mediterranean that their scholars came to date the *Diaspora* from the destruction of Herod's Temple. We have seen that the prophesied Dispersion had begun six centuries before in the Babylonian Captivity, and had been renewed in the settling of Alexandria. Since fertility was commanded and infanticide sternly forbidden by Jewish piety and law, the expansion of the Jews was due to biological as well as economic causes; Hebrews still played a very minor role in the commerce of the world."[5]

Prophecy Fulfilled

Israel was reaping what she had for centuries sowed. No one could doubt that the many solemn prophecies of God's judgment—of which the following are but a small sample—were being fulfilled:

> It shall come to pass, if thou wilt not hearken unto the voice of the LORD thy God, to observe to do all his comandments and his statutes which I command thee this day . . . the LORD shall send upon thee cursing, vexation, and rebuke . . . until thou be destroyed . . . because of the wickedness of thy doings whereby thou hast forsaken me. . . .
>
> The LORD shall cause thee to be smitten before thine enemies . . . and [thou] shalt be removed into all the kingdoms of the earth (Deuteronomy 28:15,20,25).

> And the LORD said unto Moses, Behold, thou shalt
> sleep with thy fathers; and this people will rise up and go
> whoring after the gods of the strangers . . . and will for-
> sake me and break my covenant which I have made with
> them.
>
> Then my anger shall be kindled against them in that
> day, and I will forsake them, and I will hide my face from
> them, and they shall be devoured, and many evils and
> troubles shall befall them, so that they will say in that
> day, Are not these evils come upon us because our God is
> not among us? (Deuteronomy 31:16,17).

Most striking is the frequent warning, to which we have
already referred, that the Jews would be removed into every
nation and every corner of the earth. Will Durant makes this
significant comment:

> Fifty years before the fall of Jerusalem, Strabo, with
> anti-Semitic exaggeration, reported that "it is hard to
> find a single place on the habitable earth that has not
> admitted this tribe of men, and is not possessed by it."
> Philo, twenty years before the Dispersion, described
> "the continents . . . full of Jewish settlements, and like-
> wise the . . . islands, and nearly all Babylonia."
>
> By A.D. 70 there were thousands of Jews in Seleucia
> on the Tigris, and in other Parthian cities; they were
> numerous in Arabia, and crossed thence into Ethiopia;
> they abounded in Syria and Phoenicia; they had large
> colonies in Tarsus, Antioch, Miletus, Ephesus, Sardis,
> Smyrna; they were only less numerous in Delos, Corinth,
> Athens, Philippi, Patra, Thessalonica.
>
> In the west there were Jewish communities in Car-
> thage, Syracuse, Puteoli, Capua, Pompeii, Rome, even
> in Horace's native Venusia. All in all we may reckon
> 7,000,000 Jews in the Empire—some seven percent of
> the population, twice their proportion in the United
> States of America today.[6]

Still, those Jews remaining in Jerusalem and its surround-
ings, blind to the reason for their troubles, continued their

efforts to shake off their oppressors. Instead of repentance and a return to God, there was more rebellion. "Under the leadership of Simeon Bar Cocheba, who claimed to be the Messiah, the Jews made their last effort in antiquity to recover their homeland and their freedom (132 A.D.). Rabbi Akiba ben Joseph, who all his life had preached peace, gave his blessing to the revolution by accepting Bar Cocheba as the promised Redeemer. For three years the rebels fought valiantly against the legions; finally they were beaten by lack of food and supplies.

"The Romans destroyed 985 towns in Palestine, and slew 580,000 men; a still larger number, we are told, perished through starvation, disease, and fire; nearly all Judea was laid waste. Bar Cocheba himself fell in defending Bethar. So many Jews were sold as slaves that their price fell to that of a horse. Thousands hid in underground channels rather than be captured; surrounded by the Romans, they died one by one of hunger, while the living ate the bodies of the dead."[7]

Thus ended the last organized attempt by the ever-more-widely-scattered Jews to regain their homeland until in 1897, more than 17 centuries later, the first Zionist Congress was held in Basel, Switzerland. However, when Israel would become a nation in her own land once again, it would not be through the efforts of the Zionists, but through a sovereign act of God.

After 2500 years of exile, and the continued slaughter of Jews and repeated destruction of Jerusalem, the City of David, a new phase in her history has obviously been reached. As we shall see, the prophets have not left us in ignorance concerning what is yet to come.

*The Lord shall inherit Judah his portion in the holy
land, and shall choose Jerusalem again.*

—Zechariah 2:12

*They shall come which were ready to perish in the
land of Assyria, and the outcasts in the land of
Egypt, and shall worship the LORD in the holy mount
at Jerusalem.*

—Isaiah 27:13

*He that putteth his trust in me shall possess the land,
and shall inherit my holy mountain.*

—Isaiah 57:13

*In mine holy mountain, in the mountain of the height
of Israel, saith the Lord God, there shall all the house
of Israel, all of them in the land, serve me; there will I
accept them.*

—Ezekiel 20:40

4

The Holy Land

◆

W hen God promised the land of Canaan to Abraham and
to his descendants after him it was not an arbitrary
decision but one determined in His justice. The inhabitants of
that land were so steeped in evil (idolatry, child sacrifice,
homosexuality, spiritism, and necromancy) that the day would
come when God's patience and mercy would be exhausted and
He would be forced to remove these people from the earth. At
that time He would use Israel as the instrument of His judgment. Only then would the land be given to the descendants of
Abraham, Isaac, and Jacob.

At the time He promised him the land, God told Abraham,
"The iniquity of the Amorites is not yet full" (Genesis 15:16).
Until the day came when these evil and idolatrous nations must
be destroyed, Abraham's descendants would be held as slaves
in a strange land for 400 years. After that, God would free
them and bring them into the Promised Land.

Israel's slavery in Egypt and eventual deliverance fulfilled
this prophecy and promise to Abraham. Only at that appointed
time were the patriarch's descendants at last given their land.
And Israel was to remember this fact; she was never to indulge
in the vain thought that God had favored her because she was
better than other nations:

The LORD did not set his love upon you nor choose you because ye were more in number than any people, for ye were the fewest of all people, but because the LORD loved you, and because he would keep the oath which he had sworn unto your fathers . . . (Deuteronomy 7:7,8).

Speak not thou in thine heart after the LORD thy God hath cast them [the Canaanites] out from before thee, saying, For my righteousness the LORD hath brought me in to possess this land. . . .

Not for thy righteousness, nor for the uprightness of thine heart, dost thou go to possess their land, but for the wickedness of these nations the LORD thy God doth drive them out from before thee, and that he may perform the word which the LORD swore unto thy fathers, Abraham, Isaac, and Jacob.

Understand therefore that the LORD thy God giveth thee not this good land to possess it for thy righteousness, for thou art a stiffnecked people. . . . From the day that thou didst depart out of the land of Egypt until ye came unto this place, ye have been rebellious against the LORD (Deuteronomy 9:4-7).

The Call to Holiness

What Moses passed on to the people of Israel from God was hardly a flattering speech calculated to build up their self-esteem. Instead, God in His wisdom and grace was telling the Israelites the truth about themselves. He was warning them even before He brought them into the land that if they continued in rebellion He would cast them out as He had done with the previous inhabitants. However, they would not be replaced by anyone else. The land would be left unattended and would revert to wilderness before He brought them back into it in the last days just before the Messiah's return to rule the world from Jerusalem.

In contrast to those nations which she dispossessed, Israel was to exemplify to the world the righteousness which God desired all nations and individuals to practice. The land that had been so wicked was to become the Holy Land by virtue of the holiness of the Israelites who came to possess it and the holiness of the God who had given it to them. "Be ye holy, for I am holy" was His oft-repeated charge to Israel (Leviticus 11:44,45; 19:2; 20:7; etc.):

> I have said unto you, Ye shall inherit their land, and I will give it unto you to possess it, a land that floweth with milk and honey; I am the LORD your God, which have separated you from other people. . . .
> And ye shall be holy unto me, for I the LORD am holy, and have severed you from other people that ye should be mine (Leviticus 20:24,26).

> For thou art an holy people unto the LORD thy God; the LORD thy God hath chosen thee to be a special people unto himself, above all people that are upon the face of the earth (Deuteronomy 7:6; cf. 14:2).

What a privilege—yes, and responsibility—God was giving to the children of Israel! We have cited only a very few of the many declarations in the Old Testament that God had chosen Israel to be His special people and that as such they were to live lives of holy obedience to Him. Whether they lived up to that high calling or not would determine whether they would prosper in the land or be cast out of it, as had been the fate of the nations inhabiting it before them.

Who Is a Real Jew?

The Bible makes it crystal clear that merely being a Jew by birth does not automatically entitle one to the Promised Land or to God's promised blessing. The land is only for those who have faith in God and who enjoy that same relationship with God which Abraham had. It is true that the land had been promised to Abraham's descendants. A mere physical relationship to Abraham, however, was not enough.

A real Jew must be a spiritual as well as a physical descendant of Abraham, a person whose life reflects the same faith in and obedience to God that had characterized the progenitor of his race. If the Jews were to continue in their land, they had to conduct themselves as the spiritual descendants of Abraham, truly loving and obeying God and trusting Him for guidance and protection. The following are only a very few of the many such reminders:

> It shall come to pass, if thou wilt not hearken unto the voice of the LORD thy God, to observe to do all his commandments and his statutes which I command thee this day, that all these curses shall come upon thee ... and ye shall be plucked from off the land whither thou goest to possess it (Deuteronomy 28:15,63; etc.).

> But take diligent heed to do the commandment and the law which Moses the servant of the LORD charged you, to love the LORD your God, and to walk in all his ways, and to keep his commandments, and to cleave unto him, and to serve him with all your heart and with all your soul (Joshua 22:5).

The land was to be holy because God called its new inhabitants, the Jews to whom He had given it, to set the example before the world of a holy people who lived pure lives in subjection to Him. Not only the priests were to be holy, but every citizen was to be as a priest before God: "Ye shall be unto me a kingdom of priests, and an holy nation . . ." (Exodus 19:6).

Failure and Tragedy

Tragically, Israel failed to obey God and to live up to the standard which He had set for her. Instead of exemplifying holiness, Israel became even more wicked than the people whom God had cast out in order to give her their land. It seems unbelievable, but it is sadly true, that in spite of the warnings of coming judgment from the prophets whom God sent, Israel increased in wickedness until she actually *exceeded* in infamy the pagan nations surrounding her! The following indictments of Israel by the prophets whom God sent to warn her are only a small sample of literally scores which we could cite:

> Manasseh made Judah and the inhabitants of Jerusalem to err, and to do worse than the heathen, whom the LORD had destroyed before the children of Israel (2 Chronicles 33:9).

> The LORD hath sent unto you all his servants the prophets . . . but ye have not hearkened. . . . They said, Turn ye again now every one from his evil way, and from the evil of your doing, and dwell in the land that the LORD hath given unto you and to your fathers for ever and ever; and go not after other gods to serve them, and to worship them. . . .
>
> Yet ye have not hearkened unto me, saith the LORD, that ye might provoke me to anger with the works of your hands to your own hurt (Jeremiah 25:4-7).

> Therefore thus saith the LORD: Behold, I will give this city into the hand of the Chaldeans, and . . . [they] shall come and set fire on this city, and burn it with the houses, upon whose roofs they have offered incense unto Baal, and poured out drink offerings unto other gods, to provoke me to anger.
>
> For the children of Israel and the children of Judah have only done evil before me from their youth . . . for this city hath been to me as a provocation of mine anger and of my fury from the day that they built it even unto this day . . . because of all the evil of the children of Israel and of the children of Judah . . . they have not hearkened to receive instruction, but they set their abominations in the house [Temple] which is called by my name to defile it, and they built the high places of Baal . . . (Jeremiah 32:28-35).

> Thus saith the Lord God: This is Jerusalem; I have set it in the midst of the nations and countries that are round about her. And she hath changed my judgments into wickedness more than the nations, and my statutes more

> than the countries that are round about her; for they have
> refused my judgments and my statutes, they have not
> walked in them (Ezekiel 5:5,6).

> Thus saith the Lord GOD unto Jerusalem. . . . As I
> live, saith the Lord GOD, Sodom thy sister hath not
> done, she nor her daughters, as thou hast done, thou and
> thy daughters. . . . Neither hath Samaria committed half
> of thy sins; but thou hast multiplied thine abominations
> more than they . . . [yet] I will remember my covenant
> with thee . . . and thou shalt know that I am the LORD
> (from Ezekiel 16).

One finds it difficult to imagine that the descendants of
Abraham, Isaac, and Jacob (Israel) would knowingly forfeit
the Promised Land by their rebellion. Having seen the miracle
of the Red Sea opening before them, the manna that came
every morning to feed them, and the water issuing from the
rock, having heard the voice of God speaking to them from
Mount Sinai and seen the guiding pillar of cloud by day and of
fire by night and having been brought into the land that God
had promised them, it seems unbelievable that they could then
rebel against God so flagrantly that they must be cast out of
that holy land! Yet that is exactly what happened.

God was extremely patient with His chosen people. He gave
them many warnings, yet they heeded not His prophets.
Finally, because of the great evil they continued to commit,
God allowed invading armies to destroy Jerusalem and the
Temple and to carry her people into captivity:

> The LORD said unto me, Proclaim all these words in
> the cities of Judah and in the streets of Jerusalem, say-
> ing . . . I earnestly protested unto your fathers in the day
> that I brought them up out of the land of Egypt, even unto
> this day, rising early and protesting, saying, Obey my
> voice.
> Yet they obeyed not, nor inclined their ear, but walked
> every one in the imagination of their evil heart; therefore
> I will bring upon them all the words of this covenant.

> . . . They are turned back to the iniquities of their fore-
> fathers, which refused to hear my words; and they went
> after other gods to serve them. . . . Therefore thus saith
> the LORD, Behold, I will bring evil upon them which they
> shall not be able to escape . . . (Jeremiah 11:6-8,10,11).

As the prophets foretold, the Jews were scattered to every corner of the earth, where they experienced the very persecution and death which the prophets had warned would overtake them. Knowing all of that history, it is even more astonishing that today, having been brought back into their land after 2500 years of homeless wandering, the Jews seem to have learned nothing from the past. Israel seems bent upon provoking God to pour out His wrath and judgment upon her yet again. How tragic!

Today's Repetition of Evil

It is ironic indeed that most of today's Israelis and Jews around the world have no concern for that holiness which God clearly said was their responsibility as caretakers of the Holy Land. Indeed, very few Jews either in Israel or anywhere else really believe that Israel is God's land, the place where He put His name forever and to which He brought His chosen people. Tragically, few believe in the God who has given them through their own history the full proof of His existence!

Instead of being an example of holiness, Israel falls prey to the same moral problems that plague the rest of the world. Israeli wife-beating, so common among Arabs because it is condoned in Islam, is on the rise, with increasing numbers of the battered women being killed. Yet the Israeli courts are criminally soft on their killers. Israeli psychologists are calling for "treatment" or "education" for the murderers, making it appear that murdering one's wife isn't really a crime but a "weakness" that can be blamed on one's childhood.[1]

Sins are rampant which were unknown in the days of Isaiah and Jeremiah. Drug addiction is increasing. There are now 200,000 Israeli drug users. Police Minister Moshe Shahal has said, "Every seven seconds a car is broken into . . . [usually]

the tape decks are stolen to be sold for money for drugs."[2] This is "the Holy Land"?

Television can be almost as addicting as drugs. It presents the most pervasive and persuasive influence in modern society and is corrupting youth as much in Israel as elsewhere. Even secularists are bemoaning the fact. As the result of a recent study he made in Israel, Dr. Raphael Schneller of Bar-Ilan's University commented:

> The growing addiction to television has serious implications on the youth's health, education, social development and culture. They are cut off from reality and don't know the real world. Everything is imaginary. . . . Normal terms of reference don't exist for them. They don't meet real-life characters and cannot hold a normal conversation. . . .[3]

Worst of all is the contempt for God and His law that is projected on TV. Its viewers are brainwashed into accepting the perverted lifestyles presented as "normal" for today. Certainly biblical morals, far from being favorably portrayed on TV, are despised and have long since been abandoned by society at large. A concerned Israeli teacher writes:

> Cohabitation prior to marriage, or in place of it, has become the norm. The divorce rate is on the rise. . . . Homosexuality is practiced more openly.
>
> British Chief Rabbi Jonathan Sacks has incisively charted this social transformation. Sin becomes immorality, immorality becomes deviance, deviance becomes choice, and all choice becomes legitimate.[4]

Leadership's Rejection of God

Sadly, government has taken the lead in legitimizing and promoting depravity not only in the United States but in Israel as well. In December 1994, for example, the Israeli Supreme Court handed down a decision granting legal status to homosexual or lesbian couples.[5] Imagine the highest court in the

Holy Land approving the sin for which God destroyed Sodom and Gomorrah!

Ariel Rosen-Zvi, dean of the Tel Aviv University law faculty, is concerned that "the constitution has become the arena of the struggle over the Jewishness of Israel" and is leading to "a growing polarization between religious and secular Jews. . . ."[6] Even from a purely logical and secular standpoint, the Court's decision is irresponsible and makes no sense, as a lecturer in Jerusalem's Center for Advanced Jewish Study for Women pointed out so clearly:

> The fundamental impulse of a healthy society is to perpetuate itself. In the case of the Jewish people, this has been a millennial obsession in the face of unabated oppression. The State of Israel is an expression of the collective will of the Jewish people to continue, even after the Holocaust. . . . When we choose a lifestyle that does not include bearing and raising Jewish children, we fail as citizens of the Jewish people. . . .
>
> By endorsing homosexual partnerships, the court has sent a message to all Jews, relieving them of the responsibility to consider the future of our people. . . . The star witness . . . the nuclear family, entered the court, weary from decline. It emerged ignored and dejected, to encounter a scene of jubilation.[7]

This is only one of many ways in which modern Israel continues on the downward path of her ancestors in violating divine law. God's judgment will fall, or He must apologize to those whom He has judged in the past for the same sins. We may be certain that modern Israel will yet taste God's wrath as did ancient Israel—and even worse—for the Hebrew prophets themselves have declared it. Jeremiah spoke of that coming judgment as "the time of Jacob's trouble" (Jeremiah 30:7).

The Israeli government and the military quite clearly have neither an understanding of their God-given role in the Holy Land nor a regard for God's command to be holy as He is holy. That fact is evident in many ways. As one example, consider the new code of ethics issued by the Israeli military early in

1995. Not surprisingly, the document, called "IDF Spirit— Values and Basic Rules," ignores the Ten Commandments that God gave to Israel through Moses and has little to do with morals. Its "11 core values" are: "operation persistence, responsibility, reliability, personal example, human life, purity of arms, professionalism, discipline, loyalty, representation and camaraderie."[8]

King David's Example

What a glaring contrast to the attitude of King David, the greatest warrior and military leader in Israel's history! One would think that today's military leaders would hold David in great admiration and pay close attention to what he said was the secret of his phenomenal success. On the contrary, they seem intent upon defying the very God whom David said was his sword and shield in battle.

David's Psalms are classic testimonies to his faith in God, a faith which today's secular Israeli government apparently thinks is obsolete or at least unnecessary. One of the best-known and most treasured gems of literature in the world is the 23rd Psalm. In that classic, King David declares that he is like a sheep and God is the Shepherd to whom he looks for his sustenance and protection each moment of each day. The Psalm ends with David's confident assurance of God's protection in this life and of eternal bliss in God's presence when his time on this earth has ended: "Surely goodness and mercy shall follow me all the days of my life, and I will dwell in the house of the Lord forever."

David's passion was to honor and obey the God of Israel, who had brought His people into the Holy Land and whom David knew intimately and loved with all his heart. That fact is apparent as one follows his steps and is confronted by the undeniable reality of God's guidance and protection throughout David's remarkable career. And what this extraordinary shepherd-boy-become-king writes is obviously not fantasy, not the wishful dreams of his own ambition, but truth and reality demonstrated in brilliant exploits and a triumphant life.

His devotion clearly springs from a heart that has been in continual and deeply personal communion with the God of the universe and as a result has come to a profound understanding of life's purpose:

O LORD our Lord, how excellent is thy name in all the earth! who hast set thy glory above the heavens. . . .

When I consider thy heavens, the work of thy fingers, the moon and the stars, which thou hast ordained, what is man, that thou art mindful of him? (Psalm 8:1,4).

The LORD is my light and my salvation; whom shall I fear? The LORD is the strength of my life; of whom shall I be afraid? . . . Wait on the LORD; be of good courage, and he shall strengthen thine heart . . . (Psalm 27:1,14).

Blessed is the man that maketh the LORD his trust. . . . Many, O LORD my God, are thy wonderful works which thou hast done, and thy thoughts which are to usward. . . . I delight to do thy will, O my God; yea, thy law is within my heart. . . . Let all those that seek thee rejoice and be glad in thee; let such as love thy salvation say continually, The LORD be magnified (Psalm 40:4,5,8,16).

I will praise thee, O LORD, with my whole heart; I will show forth all thy marvelous works. I will be glad and rejoice in thee; I will sing praise to thy name, O thou Most High (Psalm 9:1,2).

O God, thou art my God, early will I seek thee; my soul thirsteth for thee, my flesh longeth for thee, in a dry and thirsty land where no water is, to see thy power and thy glory. . . . Because thy lovingkindness is better than life, my lips shall praise thee. Thus will I bless thee while I live. . . .

I remember thee upon my bed, and meditate on thee in the night watches. Because thou hast been my help, therefore in the shadow of thy wings will I rejoice. My soul followeth hard after thee; thy right hand upholdeth me (Psalm 63:1-4,6-8).

What a contrast between King David and Israel's secular leadership today! And how thoroughly David proves the folly of the popular demand for "the separation of church and state." Instead of God being barred from public affairs, under David's leadership Israel looked to God for His wise counsel and safekeeping in every situation. The secret of David's extraordinary success lay in His faith in God, a faith which grew out of his love for His Creator and Redeemer and his continual communion with Him. David's Psalms have inspired millions with the desire to know, trust, and obey his God:

> One thing have I desired of the LORD, that will I seek after: that I may dwell in the house of the LORD all the days of my life, to behold the beauty of the LORD and to enquire in his temple (Psalm 27:4).

> Give unto the LORD, O ye mighty, give unto the LORD glory and strength. Give unto the LORD the glory due unto his name; worship the LORD in the beauty of holiness (Psalm 29:1,2).

> Rejoice in the LORD, O ye righteous, for praise is comely for the upright. Praise the LORD with harp; sing unto him with the psaltery and an instrument of ten strings. Sing unto him a new song; play skilfully with a loud noise. For the word of the LORD is right, and all his works are done in truth (Psalm 33:1-4).

King David's Rebuke

No one faced greater difficulties, overcame more insurmountable odds, or rose from a lowlier position to mount such a glorious throne than David. Nor did any king of Israel, before or after him, win greater military and political victories. Yet David takes none of the credit for any of this but gives it all to God. David's Psalms overflow with praise and thanksgiving to the One who guided his steps, protected him in danger, delivered him from his enemies, and made him by far the greatest warrior and military leader in Israel's history, and perhaps of any nation. Consider the following excerpts from Psalm 18 and take note that David gives God all the glory:

> I will love thee, O LORD my strength. The LORD is my rock and my fortress and my deliverer, my God, my strength, in whom I will trust; my buckler and the horn of my salvation and my high tower. I will call upon the LORD, who is worthy to be praised; so shall I be saved from mine enemies. . . .
>
> It is God that girdeth me with strength, and maketh my way perfect. He maketh my feet like hinds' feet. . . . He teacheth my hands to war, so that a bow of steel is broken by mine arms. . . .
>
> For thou hast girded me with strength unto the battle; thou hast subdued under me those that rose up against me. Thou hast also given me the necks of mine enemies. . . . Thou hast delivered me from the strivings of the people, and thou hast made me the head of the heathen. . . .
>
> It is God that avengeth me and subdueth the people under me. He delivereth me from mine enemies. . . . Therefore will I give thanks unto thee, O LORD, among the heathen, and sing praises unto thy name.
>
> Great deliverance giveth he to his king, and showeth mercy to his anointed, to David, and to his seed for evermore.

How appropriate would David's words be today as a rebuke to the secularists presently occupying that holy land and to those who imagine that Israeli ingenuity, industry, technology, and military might is sufficient! In addition to calling his people to praise the Lord, David had harsh words for atheists, of which today's Israel has an abundant supply:

> The fool hath said in his heart, There is no God. They are corrupt, they have done abominable works, there is none that doeth good.
>
> The LORD looked down from heaven upon the children of men, to see if there were any that did understand, and seek God.

They are all gone aside, they are all together become filthy; there is none that doeth good, no, not one (Psalm 14:1-3).

Blessed is the nation whose God is the LORD, and the people whom he hath chosen for his own inheritance. . . .
There is no king saved by the multitude of an host; a mighty man is not delivered by much strength. . . .
Behold, the eye of the LORD is upon them that fear him, upon them that hope in his mercy. . . .
Our soul waiteth for the LORD; he is our help and our shield (Psalm 33:12-20).

Rivals for the Holy Land

Though her people and leaders do not acknowledge God's purposes for Israel, millions of others consider her land to be holy, among them Catholics and Muslims. Yet one cannot escape the irony of Israel being called the "Holy Land" by Muslims and Catholics when one considers the viciousness with which both groups have sought to expel from this land the very people to whom God gave this land as a possession forever (Genesis 13:15; Exodus 32:13; Joshua 14:9; etc.).

The PLO's vow expressed in its charter—to exterminate the entire nation of Israel—has never been renounced and can never be so long as Islam continues to teach that "the Holy Land" was given by God not to the Jews but to the Arabs. Yasser Arafat's failure to renounce the terrorism that has escalated against Israel since its accord with the PLO[9] was excused by an assistant as due to the inability to express himself in English. He certainly hasn't expressed any regrets for terrorism in Arabic, in which he is fluent! "He's [Arafat] not a very good public speaker," said the PLO spokesman, "but in his heart and mind, he is absolutely set in this direction [of eventually denouncing terrorism?]."[10]

As for Roman Catholicism, it claims to be the new Israel and teaches that the Jews are no longer God's chosen people. Vatican II tries to hide that fact with double-talk, but its meaning is nevertheless quite clear:

He [God] therefore chose the Israelite race to be his own people and established a covenant with it. He gradually instructed this people . . . and made it holy unto himself. . . .

Christ instituted this new covenant . . . in his blood; he called a race made up of Jews and Gentiles . . . [to] be the new People of God.[11]

As Israel according to the flesh which wandered in the desert was already called the Church of Christ, so too, the new Israel [the Roman Catholic Church] which advances in this present era in search of a permanent city is called also the Church of Christ.[12]

This is the sole Church of Christ which in the Creed we profess to be one, holy, catholic and apostolic, which our Saviour, after his resurrection, entrusted to Peter's pastoral care. . . .[13]

Replacing Israel

So while the Roman Catholic Church acknowledges that the Jews were once God's people, this Church maintains that they no longer have that national role but must individually join "the *new* people of God," the Roman Catholic Church. The "church" which was once Israel exists no longer, and in its place there is now the "one, holy, catholic and apostolic" Church headquartered in Rome, a Church which all mankind, Jews and Gentiles, must join and to whose leadership they must submit if they are to be saved from God's wrath. So Israel, as the people of God, is finished. The Jews have no better claim to the land of Palestine than do the Arabs, and it is clear that the Vatican favors the latter.

One is reminded that the Catholic Crusaders fought to take back what they called "the Holy Land" not only from the Turks but from the Jews to whom God had given it. Upon reaching Jerusalem, the knights of the First Crusade herded the Jews into a synagogue and set it ablaze. Obviously the "holiness" that Catholics came to recognize regarding that land derived from its now belonging to the Church.

While evangelicals do not attribute holiness to inanimate objects such as land, Israel is holy to them because God declared it to be so. And this land is of deep interest to evangelicals because Christ once lived there and because Jerusalem is where He died for the sins of the world and the place to which He will return in power and glory. Evangelicals have never fought for this land, nor have any genuine Christians. Those who fought to take it from the Jews and were called "Christians" were, in fact, Roman Catholics. Documentation for that statement may be found in *A Woman Rides the Beast*, written by this author and published in 1994.

Consistently, for the past 1500 years the Catholic Church either banned (when it had the power to do so) or favored banning all Jews from Jerusalem as part of the punishment they deserved for "murdering Jesus Christ." In 1904 Pope Pius X told Theodor Hertzl, founder of the Zionist movement, "The Hebrews have never recognized Our Lord. Therefore, we cannot recognize the Hebrew People."[14] With a history of centuries of Jewish persecution on her hands, it is incomprehensible that Israel would now welcome the Vatican as a partner in its affairs and contemplate putting Jerusalem under its control!

Catholicism and Islam

The Muslims consider the land of Palestine "holy" because they believe it was given to the Arabs by Abraham. Thus any Arab who accepts the teachings of Islam must consider it his duty to drive the Jews from that "Holy Land" as the Catholic Crusaders once did. Such a passion is held by most of the Arab world today, though pursued in deed rather than only in word by a relative few. As though blind to the real facts, even the Israeli media speak of those few as Islamic "radicals" or "extremists," and that is the image evoked by the term "Islamic fundamentalist." Yet these terrorists are not truly religious fanatics at all, but are simply practicing fundamentally what the Koran teaches, as we shall see.

Consistent with her past, the Roman Catholic Church has sided with the Palestinians against the Jews from the beginning. Pope John Paul II began building a close relationship with Yasser Arafat when he was still regarded by most of the secular world as the terrorist he had thoroughly demonstrated himself to be. Vatican II even makes this surprising statement:

> But the plan of salvation also includes those who acknowledge the Creator, in the first place amongst whom are the Moslems: these profess to hold the faith of Abraham, and together with us they adore the one, merciful God, mankind's judge on the last day.[15]

Here we find a reflection of the anti-Semitism which has characterized Rome since the Middle Ages. How can the Catholic Church pretend that Muslims "hold the faith of Abraham"? That they do not do so is quite clear from their hatred of the Jews, the true children of Abraham through Isaac and Jacob. Nor do Muslims "adore the one, merciful God . . ." in whom Christians believe. The God of Israel, Jahweh, is most surely not the same being as Allah, or else the Muslims would love those to whom God gave the Promised Land rather than doing all they could to drive them from it.

The Roman Catholic Church believes in a triune God who is three Persons (Father, Son, and Holy Spirit) yet one God. In contrast, Allah, according to the Koran, is a single rather than a triune being, is not a father, has no son, and loves only the righteous, not sinners. The very fact that Islam rejects the trinitarian concept of Father, Son, and Holy Spirit is enough to prove that Allah is not the God of the Bible, as Roman Catholicism professes. Yet Vatican II goes on to say:

> Over the centuries many quarrels and dissensions have arisen between Christians and Muslims. The sacred Council now pleads with all to forget the past, and urges that a sincere effort be made to achieve mutual understanding; for the benefit of all men, let them together preserve and promote peace, liberty, social justice and moral values.[16]

What About Truth?

There can be no "mutual understanding" when the disagreeing parties do not even speak the same language. It is a fraud to pretend a meeting of the minds when each party to the "agree-ment" attaches a different meaning to the words used therein. How much more impossible to reach a "mutual understand-ing" about worshiping God and about His purposes for man-kind when the parties each believe in a different God! The Vatican has its own meaning and its own purpose, from which it has never wavered. Islam, too, has a similar agenda: to conquer the world for Allah and to do so by the sword if necessary. Can Israel be so deceived by fine words as to grant a sworn enemy a launching pad for terror and conquest within its own borders? Does truth no longer matter at all?

What folly for Israel to enter into an agreement with the Vatican and to trust the words it speaks today when they contradict 1500 years of history, a history which consistently proved that today's words mean just the opposite! Nor do we have to go very far back in history to see this phenomenon. As Rabbis Meir Zlotowitz and Nosson Scherman remind us in *Shoah*:

> Even when the [Roman Catholic] Church engaged in isolated rescue activities [during the Holocaust], the motives seem to have been to bring the rescued Jews into the bosom of Christianity [Catholicism]. Thousands of Jewish children were taken into monasteries, and after the war, many were not returned to their people and faith even after relatives pleaded for their release.[17]

Present actions also confirm the past. At a July 6, 1994, ceremony in Vienna, the Vatican presented Austrian President Kurt Waldheim with a papal knighthood for "safeguarding human rights" during his term as U.N. Secretary-General from 1972 to 1981. Yet Waldheim, a German military intel-ligence officer during World War II, has been implicated in war crimes against Jews. The *Washington Post* reported:

> The papal honoree is the same man who, according to an Austrian government report prepared by an indepen-dent panel of historians, knew about and did nothing to

stop atrocities against Jews. He is the same man Attorney General Edwin Meese blocked from entering the United States because of evidence he provided intelligence and other support that enabled others to kill, torture and deport people to slave labor camps.[18]

The Vatican recently made overtures to such terrorist-supporting regimes as Iran and Libya to gain their support against abortion at the Cairo Conference on population control, and has asked the U.N. to ease the embargo on Iraq. Her overtures to Israel are for equally selfish reasons: She wants to have a say in the "peace process" for the Middle East.

Facts no longer matter so long as smiles brighten the atmosphere. If the promises are pleasing, then don't ruin the partnership by suggesting that the words may not be sincere. Out of deep concern, Israeli Rabbi Neveh Tzuf writes:

> The recent image on TV of Achinoam Nini singing her "Ave Maria" on Shabbat in St. Peter's Square in Rome for an audience which included the pope and Mother Theresa, indicates the direction Israeli society is heading. . . .
>
> That Jews over the centuries have preferred to die at the stake rather than acknowledge any of the icons of Catholicism is, apparently, no more than a distant historical episode to Nini.
>
> Nini isn't alone in her indifference. Foreign Minister Shimon Peres's audacious disregard for history is almost breathtaking. Most recently, he appealed to German Chancellor Helmut Kohl . . . to send German troops to participate in a peacekeeping force on the Golan. Kohl, aware of the German-Israeli military face-off that could result, and not as sure as Peres that the world has forgotten the last such confrontation, turned him down flat. . . .
>
> Nini chose to ignore the martyrdom of thousands of Jews who were persecuted by the church that sponsored her performance. Peres, no less avid in his quest for expanded vistas, is happy to forget the murders of hundreds of Jewish civilians at the hands of his partners [the Vatican and PLO] in the peace process. After all, memory can limit options. And Freedom is all-important. . . .

Judaism and its obligations, Jewish history and religion, have come to be regarded as an albatross, as
something that must be shaken off, to allow Israelis a full
measure of freedom in their political and cultural lives.

But the natural outcome of that would be the disappearance of the Jewish state into the homogeneity of
Western materialism.[19]

The Modern Folly

Unfortunately, the "Jewish state," which should be an
example of holiness in the Holy Land, is already caught up in
"Western materialism" and worse. She is behaving consistently with her past. For the first 490 years of its existence, the
Jewish state, chosen to be "a holy nation," was so dishonoring
to God that He used Nebuchadnezzar to destroy it in 587 B.C.
Nor has Israel since then, as reconstruction was attempted
several times, been any nearer to what God originally intended
for it. Neither is the Jewish State today, as we have already
seen, even pretending to be an example of holiness to the
world.

Instead of looking to God, Israel is seeking "peace" in the
most naive of partnerships with its two most implacable enemies in history, the Vatican and Islam. Yet Israel remains blind
to the truth. Even Israeli rabbis see roses where Tzuf sees
thorns. Rabbi Jacobovits, the former Chief Rabbi of Britain
and the Commonwealth, enthuses:

> The prospects of eventual peace should prompt new
> visions of fulfilling the Jewish destiny and restoring the
> Jewish national purpose. So long as Israel had to devote
> its resources to fighting for physical survival, the spiri-
> tual test of seeking to become a light unto the nations
> could not begin.
>
> Hopefully, this is the time to nurture at least the
> yearning for a realization of this prophetic goal. Our
> religious leadership ought to inspire a renewed quest for
> spiritual and moral pioneering, fulfilling the promise to
> Abraham—"through you shall be blessed all the families
> of the earth."[20]

Spiritual and moral *pioneering?* What modern folly is this?
Morals are either absolute and unchangeable, established by
God, or they are nothing. God's standards of holiness have not
changed. Either God gave Israel the *holy* land or He didn't. If
He did, then only by returning to the holiness which He
demands can Israel find lasting peace. To suggest *pioneering*
new ethical and moral standards is to deny that there are any
standards at all. As for all nations being blessed through
Israel, that was quite clearly a promise to be fulfilled only
through the Messiah. Only that greatest Jew of all can bring
blessing to all the world.

It is evident to anyone willing to face the facts that, as the
result of escalating criticism and under the threat of boycott
and isolation, Israel will be forced to make increasing concessions—concessions that would not be necessary were she
living in holiness in that holy land and trusting God for His
protection.

What will happen to Israel, and when? We need not specu-
late about the future. The prophets whom God sent to Israel
more than 2000 years ago foretold it all.

*Now Sarai Abram's wife bore him no children; and
she had an handmaid, an Egyptian, whose name was
Hagar. And Sarai said unto Abram, Behold now, the
LORD hath restrained me from bearing; I pray thee,
go in unto my maid; it may be that I may obtain
children by her. And Abram hearkened to the voice of
Sarai.*

—Genesis 16:1,2

*Behold, thou [Hagar] art with child, and shalt bear
a son, and shalt call his name Ishmael. . . . And he
will be a wild man; his hand will be against every
man, and every man's hand against him. . . .*

*And Hagar bore Abram a son; and Abram called
his son's name, which Hagar bore, Ishmael.*

—Genesis 16:11,12,15

*And God said, Sarah thy wife shall bear thee a son
indeed; and thou shalt call his name Isaac; and I will
establish my covenant with him for an everlasting
covenant, and with his seed after him.*

—Genesis 17:19

*And Sarah saw the son of Hagar the Egyptian, which
she had born unto Abraham, mocking [Isaac].
Wherefore she said unto Abraham, Cast out this
bondwoman and her son; for the son of this bondwoman shall not be heir with my son, even with Isaac.*

—Genesis 21:9,10

5

Conflict and Bitterness

◆

The present bitter conflict between Arabs and Jews has its origin in the distant past. For more than a thousand years the Middle East has been a unique battleground between Jews, Christians, and Muslims. This seemingly unsolvable rivalry for the land of Israel continues to this day and threatens the peace of the entire world. If we are to understand this conflict and dare to hope for a solution, then we must probe its deep roots. Of course, a major part of the discord between Arabs and Jews that threatens to engulf us all in a Third World War involves a disputed inheritance. Both groups claim to be the descendants and heirs of Abraham and thus to be entitled to the land of Israel, which God promised to Abraham and his descendants as "an everlasting possession" (Genesis 17:8; 48:4; etc.).

The controversy, however, obviously involves something more than mere land. Israel is miniscule in comparison to the size of her neighbors, occupying about ⅙ of 1 percent of the land the Arabs possess. One Middle East specialist has stated:

> Neither can this strife be attributed to economic forces. . . . It is incredible that the nations round about Israel, with their vast territories, should want to take

over this little strip of land, which is like a postage stamp in comparison with the Arab countries.

Israel has no great rivers. Compared with the Nile, the Tigris, and the Euphrates, the Jordan is merely a stream. The conflict is not about water. Furthermore, Israel has no oil or gas, and no coal, diamonds, or gold. Clearly there can be no economic cause for the Middle Eastern problem. There must be a much deeper reason. . . .

[T]he conflict is one of *religion*. The battle is not between the might of Islam and the Jew, nor even between Islam and Zionism. Israel lies at the very heart of a violent confrontation between the spiritual powers of Islam and the Word of God (Daniel 10:13; Ephesians 6:12).

Islam is supremely confident. It teaches that it has the final revelation of the Word of God and that it represents the fulfillment of the work of God among the nations of the world. . . . Muhammad proclaims that Islam has replaced both Judaism and Christianity.[1]

In the early centuries of Islam its forces nearly took over Europe by the sword. It must be understood that such belligerence was not a mistaken zeal nor a holy resolve applicable only to the past, but is the very heart of Islam as Mohammed taught and practiced it and as it remains today. The conquest of the world is demanded by Islam as its unchangeable goal.

Islamic fundamentalists are playing out their special role in that conquest through terrorism. At the same time, the spread of Islam's mosques throughout the Western world accelerates even while Islam denies the same liberty for other religions in territories she controls. That intransigence is taking the world down the path toward the fulfillment of Islam's ultimate objective. It has been estimated that fully one-third of the world's population will have embraced this fastest-growing religion by the end of this century. Islam marches on!

A Contested Heritage: Ishmael or Isaac?

The Arabs lay claim to Palestine as the alleged descendants of Abraham through Ishmael, the illegitimate son born to him by Hagar, Sarah's maid. On logical grounds, it is inconceivable that an illegitimate child would take precedence over a true son. Furthermore, the Bible makes it very clear that Ishmael, the illegitimate son, was not the heir to the promise of the land of Canaan which Abraham received from God. That particular blessing belonged to Isaac, who is clearly designated in both the Torah and the New Testament—and the Koran, too—as the legitimate heir.

The Jews are without question the descendants of Abraham through his son, Isaac, by his wife, Sarah. That fact can be substantiated from both Old and New Testaments as well as from history. The claim of the Arabs, however, cannot be verified on either count. Of interest is the fact that the early part of the Koran honors the Torah as true (Surah 3:3,48, 65,93; 5:43ff.,66,68,61:6; etc.). The Koran itself testifies that the Jews, the descendants of Israel, and not the Arabs, are the legitimate heirs to the promised land. In "The Table Spread," for example, Mohammed writes:

> And (remember) when Moses said unto his people [the Israelites]: O my people! Remember Allah's favour unto you, how He placed among you Prophets, and He made you kings, and gave you that (which) He gave not to any (other) of (His) creatures.
>
> O my people! Go into the holy land which Allah hath ordained for you (Surah 5:20,21).

How then can the Arabs maintain their claim? After commending the Jewish Scriptures, the Koran proceeds to contradict them—and, of course, thereby to contradict itself. This was probably not deliberate on Mohammed's part but due to his ignorance of the Bible. Islamic scholars today, however, attempt to explain away this obvious inconsistency by claiming that after the Koran at first commended it, the Bible became perverted. That is why the Koran later supposedly corrects the errors which had crept into the Bible. This allegation is false, as we shall see. Nor can such passages in the Koran as that quoted above which agree with the Bible be explained away.

It is clear from many passages in the Bible that Ishmael was not Abraham's legitimate heir. Moreover, even if Ishmael were the son of promise, that would not help the Arab cause. Why? Because neither they nor anyone else can trace their ancestry back to Ishmael. The Arabs are actually descended from numerous nomadic tribes of uncertain origin. One researcher argues logically:

> If all the Arabs of the Middle East are the descendants of Abraham, whatever happened to all the Akkadians, Sumerians, Assyrians, Babylonians, Persians, Egyptians, Hittites, etc. that lived before, during, and after Abraham? What happened to all those millions of people who were not Abraham's descendants? Where did they go?[2]

There is no indication that Ishmael's descendants tried to keep themselves from intermarrying with the peoples around them, as we know that most of the Israelites did in obedience to God's specific command to them. There was no such command to Abraham's other descendants.

An Impossible Genealogy

No one disputes the fact that Ishmael was fathered by Abraham, but so were many other people whose descendants became many different nations. Ishmael and Isaac were not the only sons of Abraham, for after the death of Sarah he married Keturah, by whom he had six more sons (Genesis 25:1-4). Isaac also had two sons, Esau and Jacob. The former despised his inheritance and sold it to Jacob, who was later renamed Israel by God (Genesis 32:28). It was his descendants whom God brought into the land, which thus became known as the land of Israel.

There is no more justification to suggest that the land of Israel belongs to Abraham's numerous descendants by Keturah (which are unidentifiable today) than to say that land belongs to the descendants of Esau or Ishmael, which are also unidentifiable. Nor is the question of inheritance settled in the Bible by designating Isaac and his heirs alone. Let us clarify further.

The Bible states repeatedly and in the plainest language possible that it was to the descendants of Abraham, Isaac, *and Jacob* that the land of Israel was promised by God.[3] Indeed, the God of both Jews and Christians is repeatedly called, in both the Old and New Testaments, "the God of Abraham, Isaac, and Jacob."[4] He is *not once* called "the God of Ishmael" or "of Esau" or of any of the other sons of Abraham. Unfortunately, the descendants of Ishmael and all of the other sons of Abraham adopted a variety of pagan deities to worship and so fell into the very idolatry which God condemned.

There is thus an insurmountable problem preventing the Arabs from claiming the Promised Land: They cannot trace their ancestry back to Ishmael. Fortunately, Ishmael was not the true heir; for had he been, it would be impossible to determine to whom the "land of promise" belongs today. Consequently, God's promise that Abraham's seed would possess it "forever" could not be fulfilled and God would be proved to be a liar.

Ishmael's descendants unquestionably intermarried with the peoples around them and cannot now be identified. That fact alone is sufficient proof that Ishmael was not the true heir. God does not make promises and then fail to see them through to their fulfillment.

Already in the very next generation, because of intermarriage with those about them, Ishmael's descendants were described as 12 nations (Genesis 25:12-18). The fact that intermarriage also occurred between the descendants of Ishmael and Esau (Genesis 28:9), from whom there also came many nations, is clear. No doubt the descendants of Esau and Ishmael also intermarried with those of Abraham's other sons by Keturah. There would have been no reason for them not to have done so.

The Midianite nation was one result of Abraham's marriage to Keturah. These distant relatives became implacable enemies of Israel. Interestingly enough, they apparently became so mixed by marriage with the descendants of Ishmael that they were also called Ishmaelites (Judges 8:1,24). Such was the practice of intermarriage among related tribes that continued in the centuries that followed. Consequently, there is no certain people today who have retained the specific identity of being Abraham's descendants except the Jews. These alone can prove their descent from Abraham through Isaac, the son of promise, and his son Jacob, known as Israel.

Preservation of Jewish Identity

That the descendants of Isaac, the son of promise, through his son Jacob (Israel) retained their identity through the centuries in spite of being scattered all over the world is again additional proof that Isaac was, as the Bible repeatedly declares, the true heir to the land. The fulfillment of the many other prophecies concerning these people, the Jews, is additional, and in fact irrefutable, evidence that they are the heirs to whom the Promised Land belongs today. That retention of identity was as remarkable as it was essential for God's promise to be fulfilled. And to these identifiable heirs were given *all*:

> Abraham gave all that he had unto Isaac [not Ishmael].
> But unto the sons of the concubines [i.e., Hagar and
> Keturah] which Abraham had, Abraham gave gifts and
> sent them away from Isaac his son . . . (Genesis 25:5,6).

The Jews are undeniably the descendants of Israel. Furthermore, unlike the other descendants of Abraham through Ishmael, Esau, or the sons of Keturah, the Jews can trace in their Scriptures (the Old Testament) their history from Egypt, their deliverance therefrom, and their subsequent tortuous and lengthy journey to the land of Canaan that had been promised to Abraham. That history proves their right to the Promised Land of Palestine. The facts are indisputable. The Koran itself warns Muslims to obey the Torah and to bless the Jews:

> Again, We gave the Scripture unto Moses, complete
> for him who would do good, an explanation of all things,
> a guidance and a mercy. . . .

> And this is a blessed Scripture which We have re-
> vealed. So follow it and ward off (evil) that ye may find
> mercy (Surah 6:155,156).

Nor does the Koran offer the Arabs any help in this regard.
On the contrary, Islam's own Scriptures clearly designate the
children of Israel as the "people of the Book" whom Moses
originally led into the Promised Land and who therefore
have the preeminent claim to that land today (Surahs 2:63ff.;
5:19-24; 44:30ff.; etc.). Consider such passages as the following:

> Say: O People of the Book! Ye have naught (of guid-
> ance) till ye observe the Torah and the Gospel and that
> which was revealed unto you from your Lord. . . . We
> made a covenant of old with the Children of Israel . . .
> (Surah 5:68,70).

> And we brought the Children of Israel [not Ishmael!]
> across the [Red] sea, and Pharaoh with his hosts pursued
> them in rebellion . . . till, when the (fate of) drowning
> overtook him, he exclaimed: I believe that there is no
> God save Him in whom the Children of Israel believe. . . .
> And we verily did alot unto the children of Israel a
> fixed abode, and did provide them with good things . . .
> (Surah 10:90,94).

Bluster, anger, and terrorism cannot change the facts but
only further discredit those attempting intimidation with such
tactics. Those who oppose the right of the Jews to the Promised
Land are in fact not fighting only against Israel but against the
God of Israel, who will not be frustrated in His purposes. Even
the Koran says so.

The "Promised Land" in Arabia?

As we have already noted and shall see in more detail later,
the Koran, while it endorses the Bible in its early surahs, goes
on to contradict it, and thereby to contradict itself. The Torah is
very clear in stating that Abraham (when he was still known as

Abram) was called by God "from Ur of the Chaldees, to go into the land of Canaan" (Genesis 11:31), not into Arabia. It is equally clear that "into the land of Canaan they came . . . and the Canaanite was then in the land. And the LORD appeared unto Abram and said, Unto thy seed will I give this land; and there built he an altar unto the LORD . . ." (Genesis 12:5-7). The "land of Canaan" is not in Saudi Arabia but about a thousand miles to the north of Mecca; it included all of Palestine west of the Jordan River.

Furthermore, the biblical account relates that other than a brief excursion into Egypt during a lapse of faith (Genesis 12:10-20), Abraham remained in the land of Canaan, or Palestine, until his death. He returned from Egypt directly back to the area of the city of Sodom beside the Dead Sea and remained in the Promised Land thereafter (Genesis 13ff.). During this time God renewed His promise of that specific land to Abraham. God made it clear that the same land in which Abraham continued to graze his flocks was the land of promise: "I will give unto thee, and to thy seed after thee, the land wherein thou art a stranger, all the land of Canaan, for an everlasting possession; and I will be their God" (Genesis 17:8).

The Bible, in both Old and New Testaments, clearly and repeatedly declares that Abraham lived as a stranger in the Promised Land, which was the land of Canaan, or Palestine, *not* Arabia. Yet the Koran has Abraham and his descendants living in Arabia nearly a thousand miles to the south of Palestine, in Mecca! There is absolutely no biblical, historical, or archaeological support for such an idea. That allegation alone casts a cloud of doubt over the entire Koran, for if it is not accurate in this regard it could also contain other errors. In fact it does, as we shall see.

If Arabia, not Israel, is the Promised Land, why did Moses lead the Israelites to Palestine? And what is the quarrel over Israel today if it is not the Promised Land after all, but the area around Mecca? And if Palestine is the Promised Land, then why was Abraham living a thousand miles away in Mecca? Even to imagine that Abraham lived in Mecca is a denial of both history and the Bible and defies all reason. And if he did not live there, as all the evidence indicates, then the Koran proves itself once more to be false.

The Scriptures inform us, as we have seen above, that already in the days of Gideon there was no pure race descended from Ishmael, for Ishmaelites had intermarried at least with the Midianites and undoubtedly with others as well. Surely, then, there can be no pure descendants of Ishmael today, as the Arabs claim to be. As already noted, the Arabs are descended from a variety of nomadic peoples. As one encyclopedia on religion states:

> But the idea of the southern Arabs being of the posterity of Ishmael is entirely without foundation, and seems to have originated in the tradition invented by Arab vanity that they, as well as the Jews, are of the seed of Abraham—a vanity which, besides disfiguring and falsifying the whole history of the patriarch and his son Ishmael, has transferred the scene of it from Palestine to Mecca.[5]

The latter is an obvious and key point, and this is exactly what the false history in the Koran has done. It has Abraham living, as we have noted, nearly a thousand miles from the Promised Land where the Bible says he spent his days and years after leaving Ur of the Chaldees. Inasmuch as Mohammed's Quraish tribe evidently developed as a people in Arabia, the Koran attempts to locate Abraham there in order to establish a connection that didn't exist.

Proof from a Cave

The Cave of the Patriarchs in Hebron, known as the Cave of Machpelah, is one of the holiest sites for both Jews and Muslims. This is believed by both religions to be the place referred to in the Bible: "Isaac and Ishmael buried [Abraham] in the cave of Machpelah" (Genesis 25:9). Inasmuch as Arabs claim to be descended from Ishmael, it is understandable why the burial site of Abraham, Ishmael's father, would be revered by them.

Ishmael, however, was not buried in that same place, nor was he buried anywhere in the land of Israel. His burial site was somewhere in a region described as "from Havilah unto Shur, that is before Egypt, as thou goest toward Assyria" (Genesis 25:18). That fact again tells us that Ishmael was not considered to be among Abraham's true family members or he would have been buried with them.

Even the Arabs and Muslims admit that Abraham, Sarah, his wife, and his sons, Isaac and Jacob, were buried in Israel in the Cave of Machpelah, now recognized as one of Islam's holy sites. In fact, his sons took Jacob's body all the way from Egypt to bury it in the cave of Machpelah (Genesis 50:13,14). Why? Because that burial site had been purchased by Abraham in the Promised Land.

If Abraham had been living in Saudi Arabia, as the Koran says, then that must have been the Promised Land. Why then would Abraham have bought a burial site a thousand miles away in Canaan? And why would he make the impossibly long journey from Mecca to Israel to bury Sarah, then back again to Mecca? Why bother at all to bury her in faraway Palestine if Arabia was the Promised Land and Abraham lived in the heart of it, in Mecca? And why would Isaac make the incredible, nearly 2000-mile round-trip back across the desert to bury Abraham in Israel's cave of Machpelah . . . and Isaac himself be buried there, and so on, back and forth between Mecca and Israel? It neither makes sense nor does it fit the facts.

The Cave of Machpelah is also where Isaac's wife, Rebekah, was buried, as was Jacob's wife, Leah (Genesis 49:31), as well as Jacob himself. Since the Jews are descended not only from Abraham but also from Isaac and Jacob, they surely have a much stronger claim to this ancient burial site than do the Arabs or Muslims. Yet the latter, who cannot prove their descent from Ishmael, much less from Abraham, do not want to share it with the Jews who are truly descended from those buried therein. The Muslims have built a mosque on the site (as they have done on Temple Mount) to prevent both Christians and Jews from praying or worshiping there.

A Commonsense Distinction

That mosque was the tragic scene of a mass killing of 29 Muslim worshipers by a deranged Israeli settler, Baruch Goldstein, early in 1994. Riots by Arabs expressed their rage following the murders in the mosque. The passion for revenge among Arabs was so uncontrollable that the mosque was shut down for 8 ½ months before it was reopened—and then only under heavy armed guard. The slaughter at the mosque was a heinous crime and all Israel condemned it as such. It did not, however, warrant the resultant riots and violence initiated by Arabs nor the worldwide condemnation of Israel that followed. But what must the Arabs think when the Israeli government "did nothing to stop settler-supporters from building a shrine and publicly honoring Goldstein's memory" a year later?[6]

One must remember that the massacre at Machpelah was not the carefully planned act of an Israeli terrorist group. It was the work of one demented person and therefore must be distinguished from the continual terrorism plotted and carried out in cold blood year after year by Muslim organizations with apparent approval of most of the Arab population. Why haven't the Arabs or Palestinians *ever* rioted in protest of the carefully planned and repeatedly executed murders of Israeli citizens by Muslim terrorists? Why the difference? How amazing that armed attacks against Israeli civilians, in which many have been killed and maimed, are not condemned by Arab nations or peoples or even by the United Nations!

In fact, such attacks are generally commended as justified by the very presence of Jews in Israel. Let one mentally unbalanced Israeli run amok, however, and the world condemns Israel as though she planned the crime. Terrorist acts against both Palestinians and Israelis have increased greatly since the PLO took over the administration and policing of the West Bank, but the world has not condemned the PLO on that basis. There is an obvious and unjust double standard!

When the site of the Cave of the Patriarchs was reopened on November 7, 1994, there was bitter quarreling between Arabs and Jews, who hurled insults and threats at each other. Minwar

Ahmed Jabir expressed the sentiment of Muslims when he said:

> There will never be peace as long as Jews are allowed to pray here. Going inside with them in the mosque is like entering with a dog—it will desecrate the mosque. Our religion forbids us to pray while they are inside. We can allow Jews and Christians to come visit, but not to pray.[7]

What kind of "peaceful coexistence" is that? We have seen that the Israeli claim to the Cave of Machpelah is far more substantial than is that of the Arabs. Several of the most important ancestors of the Jews are buried there, but none of the Arabs' ancestors. Yet the Jews are not allowed to pray there? One can only conclude that Islam's purpose in building a mosque there betrays a similar purpose for the construction of the Dome of the Rock on Temple Mount.

A Blatant Error

To add to its errors, and to further contradict history and the Bible which it earlier endorsed, the Koran has Abraham and Ishmael rebuilding the Kaaba,[8] which was a temple housing numerous idols that were worshiped there. What an insult to Abraham, whose life proves that he would never have been guilty of building an idol temple or of worshiping therein!

The Bible makes it extremely clear that worship of idols is an abomination to the one true God whom Abraham worshiped. Will Durant's comments in his monumental *The Story of Civilization* are of interest:

> The desert Arab ... feared and worshiped incalcu lable deities in stars and moon ... confused by the swarm of spirits (jinn) about him. ... Now and then he offered human sacrifice; and ... worshiped sacred stones. The center of this stone worship was Mecca. This holy city ... [was] a convenient stopping point for the mile-long caravans ... that carried trade between southern Arabia

(and therefore India and Central Africa) and Egypt, Palestine, and Syria. The merchants who controlled this trade . . . managed the lucrative religious ritual that centered round the Kaaba and its sacred Black Stone.

In the belief of orthodox Moslems, the Kaaba was built or rebuilt ten times. The first was erected at the dawn of history by angels from heaven; the second by Adam; the third by his son Seth; the fourth by Abraham and his son Ishmael by Hagar . . . the ninth and tenth by Moslem leaders in 681 and 696; the tenth is substantially the Kaaba of today. . . .

In its southeast corner, five feet from the ground, just right for kissing, is embedded the Black Stone. . . . Many of its worshipers believe that this stone was sent down from heaven . . . [and] has been part of the Kaaba since Abraham. Moslem scholars interpret it as symbolizing that part of Abraham's progeny (Ishmael and his offspring) which, rejected by Israel, became, they think, the founders of the Quraish tribe. . . .

Within the Kaaba, in pre-Moslem days, were several idols. . . . One was called Allah, and was probably the tribal god of the Quraish . . . [who] as alleged descendants of Abraham and Ishmael, appointed the priests and guardians of the shrine, and managed its revenues.[9]

Mohammed's confusion is reflected in the fact that the Koran has Abraham practicing the very idolatry which the Bible condemns! Of course, such had been the religion of Mohammed's own people, the Quraish. For generations before Mohammed was born, his ancestors worshiped both Allah, the chief idol in the Kaaba, and this black stone as the god of the stones. It was said to have come down from heaven as a gift from the angel Gabriel to Abraham. The stone was worshiped by kissing it because it was believed to have the power to absorb sin when thus revered.

That Abraham would worship a stone or imagine that it could absorb sin is absolutely contrary to the Bible, to the God of the Bible, and to the means of cleansing from sin taught in Scripture from the days of Adam to Christ. Abraham very clearly knew that blood had to be shed for the cleansing of sin, a practice in which he engaged through the sacrifice of animals in obedience to God's specific instructions. He knew, too, that the blood of animals was only provisionary, and he looked forward to the Lamb of God whose death alone could atone for sin. Nevertheless, this blasphemous antibiblical element of calling Allah the true God and of kissing the black stone has been retained to this day in the religion founded by Mohammed.

Mohammed, the Jews, and Progressive Revelation

When he first began to practice the religion that became Islam, Mohammed treated the Jews well because they were, in his mind at that time, God's chosen people. And in response, the Jews in Medina, to which Mohammed had fled from Mecca, were in the beginning favorable toward the Prophet. He allowed them to continue to practice their own religion and to live in peace and enjoy equal rights with his followers. At this early stage, Mohammed looked with favor upon the Jewish Scriptures and even had his followers pray toward Jerusalem, though that city is not mentioned in the Koran.

It was not long, however, until the Jews began to feel uncomfortable concerning Mohammed's warlike tendencies. Nor could they take seriously his claim that he was the Messiah promised in their Scriptures because he didn't meet any of the necessary identifying qualifications. Most obvious of all, he was not descended from David. Smarting under their rejection, the Prophet turned viciously against the Jews.

Islam was still in the process of being developed. Part of that development was to define the official reaction toward those "infidels" who wouldn't accept the new religion. No sooner was a need expressed than it was met by new revelation. Much of the Koran came as progressive revelations from Allah to meet current problems as they arose in the Prophet's establishment of his power and authority. As would be expected, these utilitarian revelations only served to further discredit the Prophet in the eyes of skeptics such as the Jews.

For example, Mohammed fell madly in love with the beautiful young wife of his adopted son, Zaid. He therefore asked

Zaid to divorce her and give her to him as his wife. When Zaid and his bride refused, Mohammed just happened to receive a convenient new "revelation" that added to the ever-growing Koran. In it Allah coincidentally commanded Zaid to give his wife to the Prophet (Surah 33:35-39).

An equally opportune revelation came when his followers, during the period of the Prophet's residence in Medina, balked at attacking and robbing the caravans of their kinsmen from Mecca. Mohammed received this timely word from Allah which became a further part of the developing Koran:

> Jihad is ordained for you and you disliked it, and it may be that you dislike a thing which is good for you and that you like a thing which is bad for you. Allah knows but you do not know (Surah 2:216).

It was, therefore, not at all surprising that when the Jews rejected Allah as a pagan god salvaged from the Kaaba, Mohammed received a further apropos revelation from Allah. It accused the Jews of having corrupted the Scriptures, of having killed the prophets, and of having rejected their Messiah. At that time Mohammed abruptly changed the *qibla* (the point toward which Muslims must turn in prayer) from Jerusalem to Mecca and the Kaaba—a custom which had been part of the pagan worship of his ancestors for centuries.

A Ruthless Religion of Conquest

The Jews then accused Mohammed of returning to idolatry. So began the enmity between Muslims and Jews that continues to this day. For example, the Banu-Kuraiza Jews gave material aid to Mohammed's enemies, Abu Sufyan and the Quraish. In revenge, Mohammed forced them to surrender to his overwhelming army of 3000 warriors and gave them the choice of conversion to Islam or death. They chose the latter cruelty. Their 600 fighting men were slain and buried in the marketplace of Medina; their women and children were sold into slavery."[10] (Catholicism would also spread "Christianity" by the sword of Charlemagne and others, but it would not be the Christianity of Christ.)

When Mohammed's forces were strong enough, he marched to Mecca with 10,000 fighting men. Helpless before such overwhelming power, Mecca's leaders allowed him to enter the city peacefully. He destroyed the idols in and around the Kaaba but, perhaps in order not to leave the people with no ties to their old religion, left the Black Stone in its place and approved its worship, a practice followed by devout Muslims to this day.

At the same time, Mohammed proclaimed Mecca the Holy City of Islam and decreed that no unbeliever should ever be allowed to tread its sacred soil. It was only centuries later that Jerusalem's Temple Mount would also be declared an Islamic holy site. That was a decision which Mohammed never contemplated. It is clearly inconsistent with his rejection of the Jews and Jerusalem.

Unfortunately, that new post-Mohammed revelation has left the world with the impossible problem of Jerusalem. Here is a Holy City over which three religions, including Roman Catholicism, have fought through the ensuing centuries. Incredibly, in this day of science and skepticism when one would think that religion would no longer countenance, much less promote, such a superstitious, fanatical hold upon modern man, the quarrel over Jerusalem could now engulf the entire world in war.

A major part of the problem is the fact that from its very beginning Islam has been a religion of conquest. Mohammed himself led 27 invasions of neighboring towns, and during his lifetime his followers engaged in about 50 more. The conquered peoples were given the choice of conversion to Islam or death. At times a third alternative was granted: the payment of heavy tribute. Through these tactics, and from such a small beginning in Medina, Islam converted by conquest the vast regions which it now dominates and in which it forbids (often under penalty of death) conversion of a Muslim to another religion. And Islam claims Israel as its sole possession.

Islam's "Final Solution"

The United Nations is trying desperately to effect a peaceful solution to the enigma of Jerusalem. The Roman Catholic

Church has stepped in and Israel's leaders are apparently willing to turn Jerusalem over to the Vatican's administrative control and even to grant Jordan further power over Islamic religious sites there. Jerusalem is on the agenda, too, for further negotiations for an overall Middle East peace with the PLO. Even, however, if peace could be achieved for the city of Jerusalem, that would not be enough.

There remains one further fly in the ointment: Israel itself, which claims Jerusalem as its capital. That tiny country, in comparison to the Goliaths surrounding it, is like a mosquito on the back of an elephant. How then can it be so troublesome? Yet, after numerous attacks by the combined fighting forces of the surrounding Arab nations, and with the unlimited backing of the military might of what was once the Soviet Union, Israel remains the victor and stronger than ever.

To defeat this tiny David militarily from without is clearly a vain hope for the Arab Goliaths who have tried and failed repeatedly. She must be destroyed from within. An ideological battle is therefore underway, and at the heart of it is a "peace offensive." The Arab strategy is clear: Make overtures of peace, sign peace accords, and by whatever subterfuge that works gain a foothold within the borders of Israel from which to launch the final attack that will bring about her complete destruction.

Why must Israel be destroyed? Why not just leave her where she is and even force the despised Jews to remove themselves from the rest of the world and be confined there? Why not simply isolate her and reduce her to poverty by economic boycott? That would not be enough because it would leave the Jews in possession of part of the land which the Arabs claim as their right. The very existence of Israel stands as a rebuff to the declarations of the Prophet Mohammed, the Koran, and Islamic tradition which states that the land of Palestine belongs solely to the Arabs.

The Jewish State of Israel must be destroyed! Otherwise Islam has been proved a false religion. That is the issue. Clearly, and in spite of volumes of rhetoric and mountains of peace agreements, the Middle East conflict can be resolved in no other way than by the annihilation of Israel. To imagine otherwise or that the Arabs have any other intention is to be hopelessly deceived.

If ye transgress, I will scatter you abroad among the nations . . . unto the uttermost . . . yet will I gather them from thence and will bring them unto the place that I have chosen to set my name there.
—Nehemiah 1:8,9

[I] will cast off this city Jerusalem which I have chosen, and the house of which I said, My name shall be there.
—2 Kings 23:27

For, lo, I will command, and I will sift the house of Israel among all nations. . . .
—Amos 9:9

And the Lord shall scatter you among the nations . . . among all people, from the one end of the earth even unto the other. . . .
—Deuteronomy 4:27; 28:64

Fear not, for I am with thee; I will bring thy seed from the east and gather thee from the west; I will say to the north, Give [them] up, and to the south, Keep not back: bring my sons from far, and my daughters from the ends of the earth. . . .
—Isaiah 43:5,6

[T]hough I make a full end of all nations whither I have scattered thee; yet will I not make a full end of thee; but I will correct thee . . . and will not leave thee altogether unpunished.
—Jeremiah 30:11

Behold, I will bring them from the north country, and gather them from the coasts of the earth. . . .
Hear the word of the Lord, O ye nations . . . He that scattered Israel will gather him and keep him, as a shepherd doth his flock. . . .
—Jeremiah 31:8,10

6

Prophecy Becomes History

---------------- ◆ ----------------

One cannot begin to comprehend the enigma of seemingly insignificant Jerusalem's surprising importance in today's world except through a careful study both of its history and of the specific biblical prophecies which that history has fulfilled. Again its uniqueness becomes obvious. There are no prophecies in the Bible for cities such as Paris, Washington D.C., Moscow, London, or New York, cities so large and of such great political and commercial importance now and historically. In contrast, there are hundreds of prophecies about Jerusalem and the land and people of Israel.

These prophecies were pronounced thousands of years ago by men who claimed that God was speaking through them. Their fulfillment in detail centuries later provides irrefutable proof that God exists, that the Jews are His chosen people, and that He has indeed told us of the major events affecting Israel centuries—and in some cases thousands of years—before they happened. There is no other explanation.

It is extremely significant that the God of the Bible (in distinction from Allah) identifies Himself as the One who accurately foretells the future and makes certain that it unfolds as He said it would. In contrast to the Bible, which is about 30 percent prophecy (and most of it already fulfilled), there are no verifiable prophecies in the Koran, the Hindu Vedas, or the sacred scriptures of any major religion. The God of the Bible, however, points to prophecy as the irrefutable evidence of His existence and the authenticity of His Word.

God Proves His Existence by Prophecy

As we have pointed out in other writings, there are two major themes of prophecy in the Bible: Israel and the Messiah who comes to Israel and through Israel to the world. Every other topic of prophecy, whether it be the Antichrist, Christ's second coming, Armageddon, or whatever, finds its focus in relation to these two major themes. There is so much prophecy that has already been fulfilled in the minutest detail that we can have absolute confidence that those prophecies which still pertain to the future will in like manner be fulfilled as well.

"Ye are my witnesses," God says to Israel, "that ye may know and believe [in] me" (Isaiah 43:10). You are the irrefutable proof to yourselves and to the entire world that I am God and there is no other. Israel (the land and people) is the sign which God has given to the entire world for all generations.

God speaks of "Israel my glory" (not the Arabs, Germans, French, Americans, et al) (Isaiah 46:13) and refers to her alone as the one "in whom I will be glorified" (Isaiah 49:3). Speaking of the rescue of Israel at Armageddon, the subject of many Old Testament prophecies, God declares: "Thus will I magnify myself and sanctify myself; and I will be known in the eyes of many nations, and they shall know that I am the LORD" (Ezekiel 38:23).

God says that in contrast to the false gods of the world's many religions, He is the God of prophecy. He declares what will happen before it happens and watches over history to make certain that it does happen. The prophecies He has given concerning Israel and their fulfillment provide the irrefutable evidence for His existence and for the fact that He has a purpose for mankind (Isaiah 46:9,10). History is not merely happenstance; it is going somewhere. There is a plan, the plan of God. And prophecy reveals that plan in advance. At the heart of that plan the Bible places Israel as His great sign to the world and lets us know in advance the details of what her history will be.

Israel's Special Testimony

Though much that the prophets foretold concerning Israel is yet future, ten major prophecies involving specific and historically verifiable details have already been fulfilled precisely as foretold centuries beforehand. 1) As we have already seen, God promised a land of clearly defined boundaries (Genesis 15:18-21) to Abraham (Genesis 12:1-3; 13:15; 15:7; etc.). He renewed that promise to Abraham's son Isaac (Genesis 26:3-5), to his grandson Jacob (Genesis 28:13), and to their descendants after them forever (Leviticus 25:46; Joshua 14:9; etc.). 2) It is a historical fact that God brought these "chosen people" (Exodus 6:7,8; Deuteronomy 7:6; 14:2; etc.) into the "Promised Land," an amazing story of miracles in itself. 3) When the Jewish people entered the Promised Land, God warned them that if they practiced the idolatry and immorality of the land's previous inhabitants and for which He had destroyed them (Deuteronomy 9:4), He would cast them out as well (Deuteronomy 28:63; 1 Kings 9:7; 2 Chronicles 7:20; etc.). That all of this happened precisely as foretold is, again, an indisputable fact of history.

So far the story is hardly remarkable. Other peoples have believed that a certain geographic area was their "Promised Land" and after entering it have later been driven out by their enemies. The next seven prophecies, however, and their fulfillment, are absolutely unique to the Jews. The occurrence of these events precisely as prophesied could not possibly have happened by chance, and thus proves God's existence, that the Bible is God's Word, and that the Jews are God's special people. 4) God declared that His people would be scattered "among all people, from the one end of the earth even unto the other" (Deuteronomy 28:64; cf. 1 Kings 9:7; Nehemiah 1:8; Amos 9:9; Zechariah 7:14; etc.). And so it happened as to no other people in history. The "wandering Jew" is found literally everywhere.

The precision with which biblical prophecies fit the Jews alone becomes increasingly remarkable as fulfillment follows fulfillment, until the case for God's existence through His dealings with His chosen people can no longer be challenged. 5) God warned that wherever they wandered the Jews would be "an astonishment, a proverb, a byword . . . a curse and a reproach" (Deuteronomy 28:37; 2 Chronicles 7:20; Jeremiah 29:18; 44:8; etc.). Amazingly, this has been true of the Jews all down through history, as even the present generation knows full well. The maligning, the slurs and jokes, the naked hatred known as anti-Semitism, not only among Muslims but even among those who call themselves Christians, is a unique and persistent fact of history peculiar to the Jewish people. Even today, as we will document, in spite of the haunting memory of Hitler's Holocaust which once shocked and shamed the world, and in defiance of logic and conscience, anti-Semitism is still alive and is once again on the rise worldwide.

Furthermore, the prophets declared that these scattered peoples would not only be slandered, denigrated, and discriminated against, but 6) they would be persecuted and killed as no other peoples on the face of the earth had ever or would ever experience. History stands as eloquent witness to the fact that this is precisely what has happened to the Jews century after century wherever they were found. The historical record of no other ethnic or national group of people contains anything that even approaches the nightmare of terror, humiliation, and destruction which the Jews have endured down through history at the hands of the people among whom they have found themselves in their prophesied wanderings.

The Roman Catholic popes were the first to develop anti-Semitism to a science. Hitler, who remained a Catholic to the end, would claim that he was only following the example of both Catholics and Lutherans in finishing what the Church had begun.[1] Anti-Semitism was a part of Martin Luther's Catholicism, from which he was never freed. He advocated burning down the homes of Jews and giving them the choice between conversion and having their tongues torn out.[2] When

Rome's Jews were released from their papally imposed ghetto by the Italian army in 1870, their freedom at last ended about 1500 years of unimaginable humiliation and degradation at the hands of those who claimed to be Christians led by the Vicar of Christ.

Miraculous Preservation of the Jews

Even so, God declared that in spite of such persecution and the periodic wholesale slaughter of Jews, 7) He would not let His chosen people be destroyed but would preserve them as an identifiable ethnic, national group (Jeremiah 30:11; 31:35-37; etc.). The Jews had every reason to intermarry, to change their names and hide their despised identity by any possible means in order to escape persecution. Why preserve their bloodline when they had no land of their own, when most of them didn't take the Bible literally, and when racial identification imposed only the cruelest disadvantages?

To refrain from intermarrying made no sense. Absorption by those among whom they found themselves would have seemed inevitable, so that little trace of the Jews as a distinct people should have remained today, just as there is no trace of the descendants of Ishmael. After all, these despised exiles have been scattered to every corner of the world for the 2500 years since the destruction of Jerusalem by Nebuchadnezzar in 587 B.C. Could "tradition" be that strong without real faith in God? Or is this something God accomplished for His own purposes in spite of the Jews' lack of faith?

Against all odds and common sense, the Jews remain an identifiable people after all these centuries. That fact is an astonishing phenomenon without parallel in history and absolutely unique to this extraordinary "chosen" people. For most of the Jews living in Europe, Church law made it impossible to intermarry without converting to Roman Catholicism. Here again the Roman Catholic Church played an infamous role. For centuries it was a capital offense under the popes for a Jew to marry a Christian, preventing intermarriage even for those who desired it.

The Bible declares that God determined to keep His chosen people separated to Himself (Exodus 33:16; Leviticus 20:26; etc.) because 8) He would bring them back into their land in the last days (Jeremiah 30:10; 31:8-12; Ezekiel 36:24,35-38; etc.) prior to Messiah's second coming. That prophecy and promise, so long awaited, was fulfilled in the rebirth of Israel in her Promised Land in 1948, nearly 1900 years after the final Diaspora at the destruction of Jerusalem in 70 A.D. by the Roman armies of Titus. This restoration of a nation after 25 centuries is utterly astonishing, a phenomenon without parallel in the history of any other peoples and inexplicable by any natural means, much less by chance.

Even more remarkable, 9) God declared that in the last days before the Messiah's second coming, Jerusalem would become "a cup of trembling . . . a burdensome stone for all people" (Zechariah 12:2,3); and 10) that the Jews would be "like an hearth of fire among the wood . . . [to] devour all the people round about . . ." (Zechariah 12:6-8). We will deal with these last two prophecies in some detail in a later chapter.

An Incredibly Rebellious People

Almost as remarkable as the prophecies themselves and their fulfillment in detail has been Israel's resistance to God's pleas and warnings throughout history. Numerous prophecies foretold the multiple destructions of Jerusalem and the dispersion of the Jews to the four winds because of their persistent disobedience to God's laws. Generation after generation, God sent prophets to warn Israel of the coming judgment and to plead with His people to repent, but they would not. God has never dealt like this with any other city or people.

Unfortunately, Israel and the proud inhabitants of Jerusalem only hardened their hearts. Some of the most solemn warnings and saddest passages in Scripture relate to the judgment that God warned would befall Jerusalem and the people of Israel. Surely these offer valuable lessons for us today. Here are but a few examples:

> If ye turn away and forsake my statutes and my commandments . . . then will I pluck them [the Jews] up by

the roots out of my land which I have given them; and this house [Temple], which I have sanctified for my name, will I cast out of my sight, and will make it to be a proverb and a byword among all nations (2 Chronicles 7:19,20).

Because they have forsaken my law which I set before them, and have not obeyed my voice, neither walked therein, but have walked after the imagination of their own heart, and after Baalim [obscene idols] . . . I will scatter them also among the heathen . . . (Jeremiah 9:13-16).

Thus saith the Lord of hosts, the God of Israel: Ye have seen all the evil that I have brought upon Jerusalem, and upon all the cities of Judah; and behold this day they are a desolation . . . because of their wickedness which they have committed to provoke me to anger, in that they went to burn incense and to serve other gods. . . .

Howbeit I sent unto you all my servants the prophets, rising early and sending them, saying, Oh, do not this abominable thing that I hate. . . .

Then all the men which knew that their wives had burned incense unto other gods, and all the women that stood by . . . answered Jeremiah, saying . . . we will not hearken unto thee. But we will certainly [continue] . . . to burn incense unto the queen of heaven, and to pour out drink offerings unto her as we have done, we and our fathers, our kings, and our princes, in the cities of Judah and in the streets of Jerusalem; for then had we plenty of victuals, and were well, and saw no evil (Jeremiah 44:2-17).

Why 70 Years of Captivity in Babylon?

What an insult to God for His chosen people to credit idols with bringing the blessings He had showered upon them! Nor was rampant idolatry Israel's only sin. Greed and selfishness played their role as well in causing Israel to deliberately disobey specific commandments which God had given them at the time He brought them into the land of promise. These commandments involved their treatment of the land and one another. Here is what God had said:

> When ye come into the land which I give you, then shall the land keep a sabbath unto the Lord.
> Six years thou shalt sow thy field, and six years thou shalt prune thy vineyard, and gather in the fruit thereof; but in the seventh year shall be a sabbath of rest unto the land, a sabbath for the Lord; thou shalt neither sow thy field nor prune thy vineyard (Leviticus 25:2-4).

> At the end of every seven years thou shalt make a release. And this is the manner of the release: Every creditor that lendeth aught unto his neighbor shall release it; he shall not exact it of his neighbor or of his brother, because it is called the LORD's release. . . .
> And if thy brother, an Hebrew man or an Hebrew woman, be sold unto thee, and serve thee six years, then in the seventh year thou shalt let him go free from thee (Deuteronomy 15:1,2,12).

It is astonishing that Israel did not obey the above commandments even once! For 490 years these "chosen people," though they had been so blessed of God, selfishly refused to obey Him by observing the seven-year sabbath He had commanded. For that reason God sent Israel into captivity in Babylon for 70 years, leaving the soil untilled for the exact amount of sabbaths the land had missed. In judgment for having refused to forgive the debts owed to them by their fellows, God took all their possessions away from His people. And because they had refused for 490 years to let their fellow Hebrew slaves go free every seventh year, God allowed Babylon to enslave them for 70 years.

For nearly five centuries God had patiently pleaded through His prophets, urging His people to repent, but they had turned a deaf ear to His warnings: "The Lord hath sent unto you all his servants the prophets, rising early and sending them; but ye have not hearkened, nor inclined your ear to hear. . . . [Therefore] this whole land shall be a desolation . . . and these nations [the 12 tribes of Israel] shall serve the king of Babylon seventy years" (Jeremiah 25:4,11). Though God is patient and willing to forgive, willful disobedience and refusal to repent bring awful judgment at last.

The Prophesied "Last Days" Return

Judgment, however, was not all that the prophets foretold for these disobedient people. In spite of their rebellion against Him, God declared that in the "last days" just before Messiah's return, He would bring them back into their own land from wherever they had been scattered throughout the entire world. And He would do so not because of their repentance or goodness or any other merit, for they would remain in rebellion and unbelief to the very end. God would bring them back into the land solely to honor His promises to Abraham, Isaac, and Jacob:

> As I live, saith the Lord God, surely . . . [I] will gather you out of the countries wherein ye are scattered, with a mighty hand and with a stretched out arm, and with fury poured out. . . .
> And I will cause you to pass under the rod. . . . I will purge out from among you the rebels and them that transgress against me . . . and they shall not enter into the land of Israel; and ye shall know that I am the LORD (Ezekiel 20:33-38).

> And it shall come to pass in that day that the LORD shall set his hand again the second time to recover the remnant of his people . . . and shall assemble the outcasts of Israel, and gather together the dispersed of Judah from the four corners of the earth (Isaiah 11:11,12).

> But ye, O mountains of Israel, ye shall shoot forth your branches and yield your fruit to my people of Israel; for they are at hand to come. For behold . . . I will multiply men upon you, all the house of Israel . . . and the cities shall be inhabited. . . .
> Therefore say unto the house of Israel, Thus saith the Lord GOD: I do not this for your sakes, O house of Israel,

> but for mine holy name's sake, which ye have profaned
> among the heathen, whither ye went. . . . For I will . . .
> gather you out of all countries, and will bring you into
> your own land (Ezekiel 36:8-10,22,24).

Those promises and prophecies, of course, could not be fulfilled unless there remained a Jewish remnant that was ethnically and nationally identifiable and thus could be brought back into their land in the last days. That after 2500 years of dispersion to every corner of the world (since the destruction of Jerusalem and their Babylonian captivity) the Jews did remain an identifiable people is a remarkable occurrence without parallel in the history of any other people. And to be certain of that identification, Israel today has specific regulations for determining whether its citizens are really Jewish or not.

One of the most remarkable fulfillments of prophecy is the return to Israel of Jews from the former Soviet Union. That brutal regime had for years reduced emigrations to Israel to a mere trickle. However, since the breakup of the USSR into independent republics, immigrants have been arriving in Israel by the tens of thousands from the former Soviet Union. Who could deny that this amazing turnabout is a direct fulfillment of biblical prophecies? Consider these words, for example:

> I will say to the north, Give [them] up; and to the
> south, Keep not back: bring my sons from far, and my
> daughters from the ends of the earth (Isaiah 43:6).

> I will bring them from the north country, and gather
> them from the coasts of the earth (Jeremiah 31:8).

Our generation has had the privilege of witnessing this unfolding saga as Bible prophecies concerning Israel's rebirth as a nation continue to be fulfilled in our day. According to a recent report, "The Jewish population of the former Soviet union is dying. Out of a total Jewish population of 1.3 million, there are only 115,000 children. . . . Experts forecast that by the year 2000 only 500,000 Jews will remain in the CIS. . . . [S]ince the former USSR reopened its doors, some 800,000 Jews have left; 538,400 of them have come to Israel." Another 500,000 are expected to emigrate over the next five years, about 300,000 going to Israel and 200,000 elsewhere in the West.[3]

Breaking Free from Russia

As this book goes to press, "more than 100,000 Russian Jews have exit visas and would emigrate to Israel immediately if they had the means, according to On Wings of Eagles, a ministry of the International Fellowship of Christians and Jews. . . . The ministry is focusing on the Republic of Uzbekistan, where Muslim fundamentalism makes the situation dire for 12,000 Jews waiting to leave."[4]

Those rare creatures known as "refuseniks," who risked their freedom and their very lives in protest of the Soviet imprisonment of Jews, must be given much credit for the eventual reopening of the former Soviet Union to emigration. One of the best-known is Natan Sharansky. It is interesting that he in turn gives much of the credit for his survival and eventual freedom to an American Senator now deceased, Henry "Scoop" Jackson. At the height of the Cold War he coauthored the Jackson-Vanik Amendment, which made the granting of most-favored-nation status to the USSR conditional on the right of its citizens to emigrate.

Early in January 1995, former "refuseniks" held an international conference in Jerusalem on the twentieth anniversary of the Jackson-Vanik Amendment to honor the memory of the late Senator. In an interview at that event, Sharansky said:

> I first heard of the Jackson Amendment when I became active in the dissident movement in 1973. Only later did I learn that there was a person called Jackson.
> There are three landmarks in my life before leaving the Soviet Union: the Yom Kippur War, the Entebbe operation, and my arrest. But throughout, there was the Jackson Amendment. . . .

Suddenly we refuseniks realized we had a real ally. As Zionists we had a spiritual weapon: our Jewish heritage. But now we also had a historical and practical weapon: the Jackson Amendment.

The Soviet authorities immediately began blackmailing us. The KGB began detaining us, telling us it would become worse for us. . . . I sent hundreds of letters from refuseniks and dissidents, including [Andrei] Sakharov, to Jackson [by tourists], encouraging him to keep up his fight. . . . He was our symbol of hope. . . .

It [the Jackson amendment] was the turning point not only in the exodus of the Jews but in the ultimate victory of the West over the Soviet Union in the Cold War.[5]

How Few Believed!

The desire to return to Israel was not always as intense for Jews around the world as it was for Sharansky and his fellow Jews in the Soviet Union. During the many centuries of their dispersion from Israel, as the prophets had foretold, the Jewish consciousness had retained only a dim memory of the Promised Land. Only for a small minority of devout Jews did the psalmist's vow, "If I forget thee, O Jerusalem, let my right hand forget her cunning" (Psalm 137:5), remain a vital part of daily prayers.

Yes, some few individuals who could afford it made periodic visits to Jerusalem. On the part of most of those in the Diaspora, however, there was little real faith that God would bring His chosen people back to their land. In fact, very few had that desire. Why should they, so long as they were comfortable and prospering elsewhere?

In the distant past there had been occasional waves of Jewish refugees entering Palestine in their flight from persecution. One such influx occurred in 1492, when the Jews in Spain were faced with conversion to Roman Catholicism or expulsion. Other later immigrations of those fleeing persecution under the Russian Czars or from Poland brought a slowly growing Jewish presence in Safed, Jerusalem, Hebron, and Tiberias.

Yet in spite of Jewish attempts to gain the sympathy of leaders such as Kaiser Wilhelm II and Sultan Abdul-Hamid II, there was no recognition on the part of any political power that the Jews had any special claim to what had for centuries been their land, the Promised Land given by God to His chosen people.

Tragically, most Jews both in Israel and around the world today remain just as blind and deaf to God's Word as in the days of Jeremiah and the other ancient prophets who warned of impending judgment. As we have noted, 30 percent of today's Israelis claim to be atheists and very few of the remaining 70 percent really believe that God has brought them back into their land after 2500 years of dispersion all over the world. God declared that He would blind the understanding of His rebellious people and bring them back to their land in unbelief. How complete is the blindness that fails to realize that if God did not give them the land of Israel they have no better claim to it than the Arabs!

Even as recently as the early years of this century there seemed no hope for a recovery of the nation of Israel. The Zionist movement was making little headway and was scoffed at even by many Jews as an impossible dream. Rare was the Jew who actually believed the promises in the Torah, much less that God would ever literally fulfill them. Such was the hopeless climate when events began to unfold that would bring about the fulfillment of prophecy.

A Sudden Turn of Events

On January 22, 1917, President Woodrow Wilson laid down the conditions of peace which the United States would support. One requirement was the establishment of an international organization of the world's leading nations that would guarantee security for all independent states and the prevention of any future wars. The Zionists began to take fresh hope that a national homeland for Jews could be established and that it would come under such protection.

Then, seemingly out of the blue, came an unexpected and controversial statement by Arthur James Balfour, the British

Foreign Secretary. On November 2, 1917, he expressed Britain's approval of the establishment by undisclosed means of a Jewish homeland in Palestine. More a shrewd political maneuver than a reflection of conscience, the statement came at a crucial stage in World War I, before General Edmund Allenby's capture of Jerusalem. Britain was hoping to gain Jewish support for its war effort and to pacify Zionists. Known thereafter as The Balfour Declaration, it stated:

> His Majesty's Government view with favor the establishment in Palestine of a national home for the Jewish people and will use their best endeavors to facilitate the achievement of that object... it being clearly understood that nothing shall be done which may prejudice the civil and religious rights of existing non-Jewish communities in Palestine, or the rights and political status enjoyed by Jews in any other country.[6]

On April 25, 1920, the Supreme Council of Allied and Associated Powers gave the mandate for Palestine to the British in order for them to put into operation the provisions of the Balfour Declaration. Sir Herbert Samuel, a British Jew, was made governor of Palestine, and Jewish immigration was actively encouraged. In 1922 there were about 650,000 Arabs and 85,000 Jews living there. By 1935 the number of Jews had increased to about 250,000.

A majority of the Jewish immigrants were highly educated and skilled. That fact, together with the backing they received of Jewish financial support from around the world, gave the Jewish segment of the population in Palestine a considerable technological, financial, and commercial advantage over the Arabs. Unable to compete in many ways, the Arab population lost ground economically. Resentment against these immigrants exploded at last in a series of Arab riots against Jews during 1936-39. Finally, in May of 1939, Britain yielded to Arab pressure and issued its White Paper limiting Jewish immigration over the next five years to a total of 75,000, after which no more Jews would be admitted into Palestine.

The Zionists had understood the Balfour Declaration to guarantee the establishment of an independent Jewish state, but the White Paper denied that Britain had ever had such an intention. Instead, it promised the development of an Independent Palestine State that would be governed by both Jews and Arabs, closely tied to Great Britain and closed to further Jewish immigration. Neither the Jews nor the Arabs were happy with that proposal. The Jews felt betrayed: Britain had gone back on its earlier promise. The Arabs, of course, wanted control of Palestine to be in their hands alone.

Role of the Holocaust

Then came World War II with Hitler's slaughter of 6 million Jews. Amazingly, revealing to the world the horrible details of the Holocaust did not sufficiently arouse the world's conscience to end such crimes. The Holocaust continued with the postwar murders of many Jews when they tried to return to their prewar homes. In Kelsa, Poland, for example, 200 survivors of the original 25,000-member Jewish community were attacked—76 were killed—by townspeople who refused to give back homes the Jews had owned before being criminally hauled off to death camps.

What incredible evil resides in the human heart! Jewish survivors of Hitler's death machine were desperate to find a refuge where they would be safe from the satanic hatred that pursued their race. Wherever they turned in the world they found little genuine understanding or sympathy.

In April 1946, an Anglo-American Committee of Inquiry recommended admitting another 100,000 Jewish refugees from Europe to Palestine. Though this was a mere drop in the bucket compared with the desperate need, Britain refused to accept the recommendation and continued admitting Jewish refugees at the cruelly inadequate rate of only 1500 per month. Outraged by the heartless lack of real sympathy for their plight, desperate Jews began organized attempts to smuggle refugees into Palestine.

Britain retaliated by blockading the coast of Israel and confining in concentration camps on Cyprus those attempting to enter. These detainees soon numbered more than 55,000. Nevertheless, by 1947 the infiltration into Palestine of Holocaust survivors by presumably illegal but humanitarian means had brought the Jewish population to about 600,000.

At last Britain realized that the controversy was beyond her ability to resolve or control. The administration of this hotly contested land had become a burden which the British no longer cared to shoulder alone. Consequently, in February 1947 the British government asked for help and advice from the United Nations. That request was followed by Britain's unexpected announcement that it would terminate its mandate on May 15, 1948, and withdraw its troops from Palestine. The stage was being set at last for the fulfillment of one of the most remarkable prophecies in Scripture.

Volumes have been written in an attempt to explain how a loving God could have allowed the Holocaust. We will make no such attempt. One thing is certain, however: Without that slaughter, the State of Israel would not exist today. That was the catalyst which moved complacent Jews to desperation and momentarily aroused the conscience of the world. The Holocaust and the spectacle of its homeless survivors awakened sufficient public shame and sympathy for the world powers to take the necessary and long-delayed action to provide a national Jewish homeland. That action could not have taken place at any other time in history either before or since.

In April 1947, Britain, in order to relinquish its mandate with some sense of responsibility, asked the United Nations to convene a special session to determine a course of action. Moved by the plight of hundreds of thousands of Jewish Holocaust survivors who had nowhere to resettle, the U.N. held extensive hearings on the problem. Six months later, on November 29, 1947, by a vote of 33 to 13 with 10 abstentions, the United Nations General Assembly approved a plan to partition Palestine west of the Jordan River. About 18 percent was to be reserved for a Jewish homeland and the other 82 percent for Palestinian Arabs, with Jerusalem to remain under international administration. The Zionists were ecstatic.

Background to a Miracle

The Palestinians, however, were unwilling to allow the Jews to have any part of the Promised Land. We have explained why. As a good Muslim, Egypt's King Farouk declared: "I cannot and will not tolerate a Zionist state in the Middle East!"

Violent strikes, demonstrations, and riots against the Jews in the Arab nations and the Arab League threatened to undo any move toward partition. What the Arabs did not take into consideration, however, and very few Jews even believed, was that the time had finally come for the fulfillment of specific prophecies concerning the rebirth of Israel. Nothing could prevent that glorious event from taking place.

It had been hoped that Britain would oversee with its troops a smooth transition into partition, but the United Nations Commission for Palestine reported Britain's failure to fulfill these expectations and warned that the stage was being set for war. In fact, Haj Amin el-Husseini, the ex-mufti of Jerusalem who had supported the Nazi Holocaust, the Arab Higher Committee, and the Arab League called for a war to exterminate the Jews and warned that U.N. personnel would enter Palestine at their own risk.

In a sudden and unprovoked onslaught, the regular armies of Syria, Lebanon, Egypt, Iraq, and Transjordan (later known as Jordan) plus volunteer forces from Saudi Arabia, converged upon Palestine. Thus began the relentless and vicious attack against Jewish settlements and transport with little or no interference from the British military. On March 9, 1948, Haganah, the Jewish underground defense force, called for mobilization of all able-bodied Jews between the ages of 17 and 45. The 100,000 British troops, police, and civilian personnel in Palestine were evacuated. On May 13, Britain's blockade was officially lifted, allowing arms and those detained in camps on Cyprus to enter.

On May 14, 1948, in Tel Aviv, David Ben-Gurion, as its first Prime Minister, proclaimed the birth of the sovereign State of Israel. To any intelligent observer it was obvious that the

Arabs would make short work of the undermanned and under-equipped Jews. If Israel were to survive it would take a miracle to save her.

That she did more than survive is history. That Israel's problems, however, have only increased with each war she has won and the more territory she has gained is also history and a harsh reality today. So many prophecies fulfilled, yet so many troubles still! Could one reason be that in the proclamation of Israel's rebirth no mention was made of the God who gave her that land and whose prophets had foretold that great event?

Thus saith the Lord GOD: Behold I, even I, will both search my sheep and seek them out. . . .

And I will bring them out from the people, and gather them from the countries, and will bring them to their own land, and feed them upon the mountains of Israel. . . .

And they shall no more be a prey to the heathen . . . but they shall dwell safely, and none shall make them afraid. . . .

Thus shall they know that I the LORD their God am with them, and that they, even the house of Israel, are my people, saith the Lord GOD.

—Ezekiel 34:11,13,28,30

And I will multiply men upon you, all the house of Israel . . . and the cities shall be inhabited, and the wastes shall be builded . . . and I will . . . do better unto you than at your beginnings; and ye shall know that I am the LORD.

—Ezekiel 36:10,11

And I will bring again the captivity of my people of Israel, and they shall build the waste cities and inhabit them. . . . And I will plant them upon their land, and they shall no more be pulled up out of their land which I have given them, saith the LORD thy God.

—Amos 9:14,15

7

The Struggle to Survive

◆

The record stands unassailable. We have documented the precise fulfillment of numerous specific prophecies concerning the people and land of Israel. These prophecies could not have been fulfilled by chance. No one can deny the existence of the God of Abraham, Isaac, and Jacob or that the Jews are His chosen people. True, the world does not yet acknowledge the facts, and, tragically, neither does the vast majority of Jews, either inside or outside Israel. That lack of faith in God and His Word is the heart of the problem.

The Scriptures make it clear that the rebirth of Israel occurred in God's time and for His ultimate purposes. His promises to Abraham, Isaac, and Jacob are being slowly but surely fulfilled. Then why is the process accompanied by so much pain and the cost of so many lives? Simply because Israel has not yet repented and turned to God with her whole heart. Indeed, she has left Him out of her plans. God will use Israel to punish the nations that have mistreated her, but He will also use the nations to chastise Israel until she at last cries out to Him:

> I am with thee, saith the LORD, to save thee; though I
> make a full end of all nations whither I have scattered

> thee, yet will I not make a full end of thee, but I will
> correct thee in measure, and will not leave thee alto-
> gether unpunished (Jeremiah 30:11).

Israel's return to her land was effected by God, but because of her unbelief it was destined to be an agonizing process. In response to the founding of the Jewish State of Israel, the Arab Higher Committee and the Arab League renewed their shrill cry for a war of extermination against the Jews. Military operations were accelerated, the food supply of the 90,000 Jews living in the Jerusalem area was cut off, and Jerusalem was completely isolated from the other Jewish settlements. The Haganah, Israel's underground military, fought valiantly against overwhelming odds to keep contact with Jerusalem's Jews and to supply their needs.

A Terrifying Mentality

One tries to avoid the unbelievable and repugnant fact that the Arab mentality in the very shadow of the Holocaust was a reflection of the Nazi mind and was inspired by the same evil source. Yet such was the case, and to a large extent it remains the same today. At the beginning of World War II, Yasser Arafat's uncle, Haj Amin el-Husseini, was the Grand Mufti of Jerusalem. A great admirer of Hitler, Haj Amin openly and unashamedly declared that the Arabs supported the Axis Powers in the war because they promised a "final solution to the Jewish problem." S.S. leader Heinrich Himmler explained that "solution": "The Jewish race is in the process of being exterminated . . . that is our program . . . a splendid page in our history."

Himmler cabled his friend Haj Amin the welcome news: "The National Socialist Party has inscribed on its flag 'the extermination of world Jewry.' Our party sympathizes with the fight of the Arabs . . . against the foreign Jew." Haj Amin made his way to Germany. On Radio Berlin, March 1, 1944, he issued the following call:

> Arabs, rise as one man and fight for your sacred
> rights. Kill the Jews wherever you find them. This

pleases God [Allah] and religion [and] saves your honor.
God is with you.

Only in the context of such cries from Islamic leaders supported by the Koran and Mohammed's example can one begin
to comprehend the religious zeal with which the Arabs attacked the Jews in 1947-48. And how confusing to realize that
Muslims were willing to die in the holy cause of driving Jews
from the very land which the Koran declares God has given
them!

With memories of the Holocaust still fresh, the world stood
by as the Arab media continued to spew forth Hitler-like
hatred, and Arab armies attacked the Jewish settlers re-
lentlessly. In those days, before the current dishonest peace
offensive, there was no attempt to hide the Arabs' unalterable
goal of the extermination of all Palestinian Jews. It was the
Holocaust all over again and still the world hid its eyes. Today
the general perception in the West is that the Jews themselves
were to blame.

There was something more than hypocrisy, something
treacherously evil, about the Soviet Union's role. It had momentarily stepped out of character to cast the deciding United
Nations vote for the humanitarian partition of Palestine to
provide a homeland for Holocaust survivors. And yet, almost
in its next move, the USSR was backing the Arabs with
military means to exterminate the inhabitants of the very land
which the United Nations had given them. It continued openly
in that posture until its dissolution under Gorbachev, as do its
surviving independent republics today.

Refugees and Responsibility

Beyond the heavy casualties on both sides, one of the great
tragedies of the 1948 war of independence was the displacement of about 800,000 Palestinian Arabs, most of whom never
returned to their homes. Some of them happened to live within
that part of Palestine granted by the partition to Israel, while
others fled from the additional area that Israel captured in the

process of defending itself from the threatened extermination. The displacement of these unfortunate refugees has been blamed on both sides in the conflict. One author writes:

> Israel has maintained over the years that the exodus [of Palestinians] happened because Arab leaders, both inside and outside Palestine, ordered the masses to leave in order to clear the way for the invading armies. The Arabs contend that the flight resulted from a carefully orchestrated Jewish military campaign of expulsion that depopulated 250 villages and several major towns. A classified report prepared by the Israeli Defense Forces in 1948 and kept unpublished until 1986 supports, at least in part, the Arab Position. It says upward of 70 percent of the Palestinians fled because of Jewish military action or because of related psychological factors. . . .
>
> The truth probably lies midway between the two sides' claims and the exodus was the result of both Jewish militancy and Arab deceitfulness.[1]

Common sense would acknowledge that the Jews, on the verge of annihilation and in a desperate fight for their own survival, would have little time to think of protecting the rights of Palestinian Arabs. Furthermore, it would be very difficult and dangerous to attempt to acknowledge friends among those who spoke Arabic and dressed and looked exactly like the enemy who had sworn their extermination. While it could hardly be said that every Jewish defender always acted with the utmost fairness and concern for nonbelligerent Arabs, one's sympathies must lean toward the attacked rather than toward their attackers.

Looking back in 1988, *Time* magazine pointed out the obvious: "Had Egypt, Syria and the other Arab nations accepted Israel's right to exist in 1947, the Palestinians could have been living for the past 40 years in a state of their own."[2] After all, the Jews were content with the U.N. partition of the land. It was not they who attacked the Arabs in the first place, but the Arabs who attacked them.

Moreover, many Jews tried to persuade their fleeing Arab neighbors to remain. At least that was the on-the-scene opinion of the British chief of police in Haifa, A.J. Bridmead. In April 1948 he reported: "Every effort is being made by the Jews to persuade the Arab population to remain." Likewise, a foreign visitor observed, "In Tiberias I saw a placard affixed to a sealed Arab mosque that read:

> We did not dispossess them... [and] the day will come when the Arabs will return to their homes and property in this town. In the meantime let no citizen touch their property. Signed, *Jewish Town Council of Tiberias*

Consistent with the above eyewitness accounts, the reputable and presumably unbiased *London Economist* reported: "The Israeli authorities urged all Arabs to remain... [but] the announcement [was] made over the air by the Arab Higher Executive urging all Arabs to leave... [because] upon the final withdrawal of the British the combined armies of the Arab states would invade Palestine and drive the Jews into the sea."[3]

Again in apparent corroboration, and this time from an Arab source, the Jordan daily *Al Difaa* complained: "The Arab governments told us, 'Get out so that we can get in.' So we got out, but they did not get in."[4]

Israel's Expanding Borders

By God's grace, the outnumbered and outgunned Israelis were victorious overall in 1948. Separate armistice agreements were negotiated with each defeated Arab belligerent between February and July 1949. As she has always been, Israel was willing in exchange for acknowledgment of its right to exist to give back some of the land she had been forced to take in self-defense. Final boundaries were to be settled in the peace treaties growing out of the armistice agreements. However, those promised treaties never materialized, as the Arab nations refused to acknowledge Israel's right to exist—even that she did exist—and spurned the opportunity to negotiate such agreements. It took the Arabs 45 years to admit at last that negotiation was their only hope.

In the process of defending its very existence against the extermination intended by its Muslim neighbors, tiny Israel had expanded its borders to more easily defended positions. She now held most of Palestine, leaving the Arabs with the land east from Jerusalem to the Jordan River, known as the West Bank, and the Gaza Strip along the Mediterranean. The West Bank came under Jordanian control and Gaza under Egyptian. In those days no one, including the Palestinians themselves, had ever thought of an autonomous *Palestinian* state.

The 1947 partition had allotted to Israel such a narrow strip of land along the sea that it was indefensible. No one, therefore, could blame the Jews for holding onto at least some of the key positions they won as they pushed their would-be annihilators back in a victory that had seemed impossible. The boundaries of tiny Israel had to be enlarged if she was to survive the inevitable coming assaults from an enemy that daily swore its hatred and unashamedly broadcast its continued determination to destroy her. And today, 47 years later, the passion to destroy Israel still obsesses her Arab neighbors who are true to Islam, even though they are now talking "peace" in a new strategy of destruction.

As *Time* pointed out, had the new State of Israel been left in peace she would never have enlarged her borders. The extension of Israel's boundaries has *only* taken place as a result of wars she has been forced to fight against those who are bent upon her annihilation. What other nation would not do the same if surrounded by enemies who outnumbered it by 50 to 1 and continued to call for *Jihad* (Islamic holy war) against her?

The Palestinian Issue

Israel's problems, however, increased with each victory and each new piece of land she annexed. The Arab inhabitants of these territories presented an unsolvable problem for Israel.

As a result of their plight, the Arabs began to take on the image of oppressed underdogs in the eyes of the world. Israel came under increasing international criticism for her treatment of these unruly subjects.

Arabs living in those territories complain that they are not given Israeli citizenship and therefore lack basic rights. Israel responds that she would like to see them become citizens, but only if they swear allegiance to the State of Israel. Would the United States or any other nation grant citizenship to those who refuse to pledge their allegiance to her and who are determined to destroy her when the opportunity arises?

In justification of their hatred, the Palestinians see the Israelis as their conquerors and oppressors, so why should they not be determined to throw off the Israeli yoke? It is a stalemate with neither side willing to budge. Thus, paradoxically, each "victory" only increased the likelihood of Israel's ultimate defeat at the vengeful hands of those it had conquered. Yehoshafat Harkabi, former chief of Israeli military intelligence, has expressed the dilemma well:

> Our choice is not between good and bad. That is easy. Our choice is between bad and worse. Israel cannot defend itself if half its population is the enemy. The Arabs understand that if there is no settlement, then there will be hell, for them and for us. . . .
>
> We must learn to think internationally, to distinguish between grand design and policy. The Arabs' grand design may still be to destroy Israel, but their policy is different. We must deal not with the Arabs' vicious dreams, but with their policies. . . . We need a Zionism of quality, not of acreage.[5]

Following their repeated defeats, the Arab nations surrounding Israel steadfastly refused to admit that it even existed. For the past 47 years, the mere mention of Israel in an Arab country brought icy stares, stern rebuke, or worse. No one with an Israeli entrance stamp in his or her passport could enter an Arab country. For that reason, Israel issued its visas on a separate paper so that no Israeli stamp had to be put in one's passport. According to *The Jerusalem Report*, Israel was still not included on maps of the region distributed by an official Egyptian agency at the recent Casablanca economic summit.[6]

What a tragedy for both sides. What could be done to reach an amicable settlement? And with whom was Israel to negotiate? Jordan and Egypt had no more right to administer these territories than had Israel; and the Palestinians had never been united in a state of their own or even dreamed of such a possibility, so they had no elected representatives. That left the Palestinian Liberation Organization (PLO) as the only viable option, an option which Israel refused to accept for many years.

In fact, the PLO was not founded by a vote of the Palestinians it claims to represent but was created by Egypt's President Nasser, who appointed its first head. The Israelis were reluctant to deal with it for that reason as well as due to the fact that it was a terrorist organization whose very charter called for the extermination of Israel. Yet today these parties are shaking hands, smiling, posing together for pictures, and signing mutual agreements—and have even received the Nobel Peace Prize together!

The PLO's current leader, Yasser Arafat, was long ago "voted" president of the future Palestinian state to take effect whenever it could be formed. However, he was not voted to that position by the Palestinians over whom he would preside, but by the PLO Central Committee. How could Israel be certain that the Palestinians themselves really wanted the PLO to represent them? Nevertheless, Israel eventually realized that if a solution were to be reached, the Palestinians must have a voice in their own affairs, and the PLO seemed the only such voice available.

Placing the Blame

In all of the accusations against Israel for the territory she captured in defensive war, the big land grab by Jordan is never mentioned. In fact, Jordan annexed the large amount of remaining land that had been assigned by the U.N. to Palestinian

Arabs and which Israel had not captured, including that portion on the West side of the Jordan River known ever since as the West Bank. Furthermore, instead of integrating the displaced Palestinians into their society, Jordan and the other Arab nations have kept them in the squalor of refugee camps to this day. Thereby they have hypocritically managed to keep the focus of the world upon the "Palestinian refugee" problem even while bemoaning it.

The world media gives its sympathy to every demonstration made by Palestinians against what they consider to be the Israeli "occupiers" of their land. Some of these protests, such as the *intifadeh* (uprising), have been extremely violent and have cost many lives. No matter with what restraint Israel reacts, she is accused of oppression and murder. No sympathy is ever expressed for the Israelis killed in these incidents. Sympathy is reserved exclusively for the Arabs, even though they may have been killed or captured in the very act of trying to gun down or blow up Israelis. In fact, more Palestinians (who were perceived as not opposing Israel strongly enough) than Israelis have been killed by Palestinian terrorists.

We are not suggesting that Israel has no selfish interests or that she always acts with prudence and fairness. Even America's Jews have often raised their voices against Israel's treatment of Arabs who are protesting, sometimes violently, their lack of basic civil and political rights in the occupied territories. The American Jewish Congress called the beatings of Arab protesters "appalling and repugnant." The following cable was sent by Rabbi Alexander Schindler, president of the Union of American Hebrew Congregations, to Israeli President Chaim Herzog:

> The indiscriminate beating of Arabs, enunciated and implemented as Israel's new policy to quell the riots of Judea, Samaria and Gaza, is an offense to the Jewish spirit. It violates every principle of human decency. And it betrays the Zionist dream.[7]

Nevertheless, Israel's record has been far better than that of her Arab neighbors in dealing with protesting Palestinians. In only one uprising against Jordan in 1970, far more Palestinians were killed by the Jordanian army and police than have been killed by Israel in its entire history of trying to protect itself from terrorist attacks. The media, however, consistently presents a one-sided and anti-Israel picture. After all, Israel has been the conqueror for more than 40 years in a series of full-scale wars initiated by her Arab neighbors.

The Six-Day War

In 1967 Israel was once again forced to fight overwhelming odds for its very survival. In the process, for essential tactical reasons it took the West Bank, the Sinai, the Golan Heights, and Gaza. In fairness it must be acknowledged that, as always, Israel offered to give the land back—if the Arabs would recognize her right to exist. Indeed, David Ben-Gurion, in retirement, urged Israel to give back "all the captured territories very quickly" and warned that "holding on to them would distort, and might ultimately destroy, the Jewish state."[8]

Israel offered peace treaties to Egypt and Syria based upon international boundaries (already guaranteed by the United States and other Western powers) and the initiation of dialogue with Jordan to explore the possibility of trading land for peace. The Arab League, meeting in Khartoum, responded "with four implacable negatives: no peace, no bargaining, no recognition [of Israel] and no negotiation." Abba Eban's reaction was his famous quip, "Our Arab neighbors never lost a chance of missing an opportunity."[9] He suggested that had they taken the offer they would have been surprised by Israeli generosity.

It would be many years later, in 1979, when Egyptian President Anwar Sadat and Israeli Prime Minister Menachem Begin, with the encouragement of President Jimmy Carter, would sign a formal peace treaty at Camp David. In exchange for Egypt's recognition of her right to exist (the first by an Arab nation), Israel returned to Egypt all of the Sinai, which she had captured in 1967. For going against the teaching of Islam by that recognition of Israel, Sadat paid with his life at the hands of Islamic fundamentalists, who assassinated him as he reviewed a parade of troops.

Rewriting History

In one of the most blatant examples of rewritten history, a current textbook used widely in U.S. colleges, *Politics in the Middle East*, makes the outrageous claim that today's Palestinian Arabs "have much more of the ancient Hebrews' 'blood' than do present-day Jews." It even accuses the Israeli leaders of having rejected numerous overtures of peace by the Arab states, and accuses the Jewish settlers of having launched in 1948 an unprovoked surprise war of conquest against their Arab neighbors. The truth is exactly the opposite.

Politics in the Middle East makes only one brief mention of the fact that in ancient times the ancestors of the Jews who now live in Israel occupied the same country. (In fact, they possessed a far larger territory than Israel occupies today.) Continuing its deceit, the book rewrites Israel's other wars as well:

> Egyptian-Syrian rivalry and attempts by each to out-bid the other's radicalism, although neither had the intention of waging war, paved the way for the Israeli attack of June 1967.

I was in Egypt, Lebanon, and Syria just prior to the Six-Day War of 1967. To suggest that these Arab nations had no intention of waging war against Israel is to promote the most monstrous of lies. In fact, the Arab leaders made it crystal clear that they were at last going to fulfill their aim of annihilating Israel. The openly repeated threat of extermination neither caused embarrassment on the part of the Arabs nor brought rebuff from the rest of the world. Seemingly, the Israelis had it coming to them for having defended themselves so well in previous wars.

Setting the Record Straight

We were in Egypt in May 1967, when President Nasser returned from Moscow, where, with much fanfare and pretentious rhetoric on the part of the Soviets about their promotion of peace in the Middle East, he had been awarded the Soviet Peace Prize. As Nasser stepped off his plane in Cairo he was besieged by reporters asking what was going to happen to Israel. His blunt reply was that she would be driven into the Mediterranean.

In discussions with both civilians and military personnel, as we drove through Egypt at that time, we kept hearing a phrase that at first mystified us: "the 19-year war." What could it mean? What war had lasted for 19 years? It was only through judicious probing that we at last understood that in the minds of the Arab nations the war they had initiated by their attack upon the new State of Israel in 1948 had never ended. What Israel had thought were periods of peace between wars had been, for the Arabs, one continuous preparation to finish what they had attempted but failed to accomplish in 1948. And having spent the 19 years from 1948 to 1967 in that preparation, they were now confident that, with the military supplies and expertise of the Soviets (paid for with the money supplied by the oil-rich Arab states), Egypt, Jordan, and Syria were at last fully prepared to smash the Israeli military machine. Once again, however, it proved to be a vain ambition.

I sat with excited Arabs in the lounge of an Egyptian freighter on our way from Alexandria, Egypt, to Beirut, Lebanon, watching television. Again and again we were treated to scenes of Nasser reviewing his troops and tanks and air force and boasting of the imminent slaughter of Israeli forces. That the Arabs were soon going to attack was made clear. Nor was there the slightest suggestion of any danger that Israel might, as it actually turned out, make a preemptive strike first. The impression was given that the Israelis were cowering in fear, knowing that they would be overwhelmed by superior force. The day before the war broke out, *Newsweek* magazine expressed what the Israelis knew:

> Nasser has plunged too far into this affair to retreat now without suffering a grave loss of face among his fellow Arabs.[10]

Newsweek's subsequent article analyzing the astounding Israeli victory in what came to be known as the Six-Day War was titled "Terrible Swift Sword." The Israelis so overwhelmed the Arab forces that they could have taken over Damascus, Beirut, and Cairo had they not been restrained by the United States for fear of threatened Soviet intervention.

Today's university students hadn't yet been born when these events took place, so they missed the advantage of following the news as it developed. Even had they been alive and not actually present in the Middle East at the time, they probably would have gotten a distorted picture from the media. That is certainly the case today. Thus they are easily deceived by the falsehoods in their textbooks, by accompanying biased lectures, and the slanted reports we receive in the daily news.

Politics has the audacity to declare that "the October 1973 War was initiated by Egypt and Syria for the limited purpose of altering the context for diplomacy aimed at regaining the Sinai and Golan heights and possibly the West Bank and Gaza." Here is another piece of propaganda so bold that it is embarrassing to read. In fact, thousands of tanks pouring over the Golan and across the Sinai into Israel caught the Israeli military asleep in a lightning attack that was intended to overrun the entire country before resistance could be organized—and very nearly did. It was, again, the grace of God that kept Israel alive in spite of her continued denial that she needs such grace.

What About Today's Prospects for Peace?

When the Gulf War ended in early 1991, this author wrote the following in our monthly newsletter: "The war in the Gulf has ended much as expected. Thankfully, the end came swiftly to limit the loss of life on both sides. The Gulf region and the entire Arab world will never again be the same. The painful process ahead will bring new stability and hopes of peace—giant steps toward the New World Order. Pressure will increase upon Israel to give the Palestinians independence, forging a new Middle East 'peace' that will ultimately be guaranteed by Antichrist, whom Israel will embrace as her Messiah."

The "peace" which is now being negotiated in the Middle East is discussed prophetically in the Bible in both Old and New Testaments. Both agree that it will eventually be administered by the Antichrist. The prophet Daniel declared that "by peace" the Antichrist would "destroy many" (Daniel 8:25). Paul warned that when the world would say, "Peace and safety, then sudden destruction" would follow, "and they shall not escape" (1 Thessalonians 5:3).

Obviously, then, the time will come when the world will imagine that it has achieved "peace and safety," but this condition will not last. In fact, it will prove to be a giant step toward the Battle of Armageddon and horrible destruction both for Israel and the rest of the world. So says the Bible; and in view of the precise fulfillment of biblical prophecy which we have already documented, the world would do well to heed this warning.

From the evidence we have already given, one needs very little common sense to realize the truth of the above. That is evident from the fact that Islam requires Israel's destruction The current pledges of peace on the part of her Arab neighbors must also be understood in the context of the example which the Prophet Mohammed himself set for his followers: pledging "peace" only to turn upon and destroy those who laid down their arms in reliance upon his promises. Any means is moral so long as it furthers Islam's ultimate worldwide triumph.

That such a double cross awaits Israel at the right time has been made clear by the Arabs themselves. For example, the Palestine National Council's "Phased Plan" involves four stages: 1) The rejection of Israel's right to exist; 2) the establishment of an aggressive Palestinian state on any territory it can acquire [within Israel]; 3) the use of this territory to continue the war against Israel for the "liberation" of more of Palestine; and 4) the employment of confrontation states to assist in the final destruction of Israel.

Arafat has in the past repeatedly declared: "The goal of our struggle is the end of Israel and there can be no compromise." While his new strategy is to negotiate with Israel for "peace," he has never renounced such past declarations demanding her destruction. Yet Israel was condemned for years for its unwillingness to negotiate with the PLO for the establishment of a Palestinian state. To do so is insanity; yet Israel has no other choice.

The extermination of Israel is still the cry from radios and loudspeakers blaring forth in the streets of Arab countries. It is still taught in Islam's mosques around the world. The satanic spirit that inspired Hitler's Holocaust continues to call for "peace"—and demands the same price. Make no mistake: Yasser Arafat continues to see the extermination of the Jews as the sacred Islamic duty of the PLO even after the signing of the peace accord.

The "Occupied Territories"

The struggle for Israel's survival has turned from outright war to a battle of words, legal complexities, and internationally supervised negotiations for pieces of land where people live and die. The competition for land has actually heated up with the peace process. At one time Israel resisted the phrase "occupied territories." According to the promises God made to Abraham, Isaac, and Jacob, it is the Arabs who are occupying Jewish land, not the other way around. Now, however, it is commonly accepted terminology to speak of parts of Israel as "occupied territories," meaning that the Jews have occupied land that belongs to the Palestinians and is in the process of being returned to their control.

That change in attitude is even affecting Israeli settlements which once seemed unquestionably legitimate. One example is the Etzion Bloc, which includes Efrat, once seen as part of Greater Jerusalem. One disillusioned resident of Efrat expressed the frustration now felt by many of his neighbors:

> Since our decision to buy a home in Efrat, and in the less than four months we have lived there, I have only rarely encountered the negative reaction experienced by residents of many Jewish communities in Judea and Samaria. "You're not really settlers," I've been assured

more than once. "After all, everyone knows the history of the Etzion Bloc." . . .

Last week . . . stark headlines . . . told me that many of my assumptions were, in fact, illusions. [Experience since] has enhanced my growing feeling of betrayal by a government to which promises, and even court decisions, are meaningless. I feel taken advantage of by those who wish to make political statements at the expense of human beings.

While the struggle for the Land of Israel should not be just a struggle for homes and gardens and "quality of life," we do fear that, at best, Efrat's growth will stop forever, and that our home will remain at the very northern edge of the town. At worst, as I heard one resident say, "Camelot may soon come to an end." I hope he was exaggerating.

Even if the suggested compromise is implemented, the cabinet decision has blown the cover off a government which has lost all sense of proportion. It has lost the ability to establish or hold onto red lines, and is ready to abandon even the most legitimate and unassailable claims which we, as Jews, can make in the Land of Israel.

If we have no right to a barren hillside in the Etzion Bloc, then we have no claim to any other place between the river and the sea.[11]

The dispute over who really has a right to specific parts of the land of Israel continues to foul the machinery of the peace process. Israeli plans to expand the West Bank settlement of Efrat were halted by demonstrations by residents of the nearby Palestinian town of Al Khader, which blocked construction. Israeli settlers threatened their own demonstrations if construction were not resumed.

"To placate the settlers, Israel said building would be allowed on a different hill, closer to the settlement and farther from the Arab town. But this attempt at compromise satisfied almost no one. . . . Settlers accused Rabin of surrendering to Palestinian threats . . . [while] Palestinian Authority officials said one hilltop was the same as another. At either site, they

THE STRUGGLE TO SURVIVE ♦ 133

said, settlement building is unacceptable and a threat to peace talks."[12]

The Influence of Islam

The "peace process" is also made more difficult by the undeniable dog-in-the-manger attitude exhibited by the Arab world against Israel because of the latter's obvious superiority not only militarily but also agriculturally and industrially. The Israelis have taken a barren land of rocks and dry earth and swamp that had for centuries produced very little for its Arab occupants, and they have turned it back into the land that God gave to the descendants of Abraham, Isaac, and Jacob at the beginning: "a land that floweth with milk and honey" (Leviticus 20:24). And with the fruitfulness of the land have sprung up modern towns. The Arabs have resented Israel's success and have tried to destroy the fruit of Jewish labors and thus the very land which they hope to recover.

The Israelis have planted millions of trees, and the new forests have improved Israel's climate by attracting more rain. The Arab occupants of the land benefit as much as the Jews. Yet the Arabs periodically try to burn down these beneficial and beautiful woodlands. A letter received from a Jewish friend in Jerusalem just today reports sadly:

> We were out planting thousands of trees in Efrat last week—only to hear that the Arabs pulled them all up the next day.

Again we see the influence of Islam. One is reminded of the ancient war cry of the Prophet Mohammed: "Death means paradise, victory means pillage—and defeat means only the chance to try again." Behind the expediency of negotiating for a "peaceful settlement" remains the religious zeal that caused Algerian Prime Minister Houari Boumedienne to declare defiantly, immediately after Israel's resounding victory in 1967:

> The Arabs have lost the first battle. But we have not lost the war. We shall never accept the occupation of [Arab] lands by the Zionists!

The struggle for survival has reached an impasse because of the intransigence and conflicting interests of both sides. It will seemingly be resolved, but not as the Bible states nor even as the Koran agrees (where it does agree). Eventually, however, God will have His way and the prophecies concerning Israel will be fully realized. That cannot happen, however, without His will being effected, not merely concerning the land but in the hearts of those people, both Jews and Arabs, who occupy it. Sadly, that will not come about without further pain and destruction for both sides.

Yitzhak Rabin, a Major General and Israeli Chief of Staff at the time of Israel's smashing 1967 victory, boasted, "All this has been done by the Israel defense forces alone, with what we have, without anything or anybody else."[13] How different was King David's attitude, who won even greater victories and gave God all the credit! And how much suffering yet lies ahead of modern Israel until she learns to put her trust in the same One and realizes how desperately she needs David's God!

Say unto the children of Israel, I am the LORD, *and . . . I will take you to me for a people . . . and ye shall know that I am the* LORD *your God. . . .*

—Exodus 6:6,7

Thou art an holy people unto the LORD *thy God, and the* LORD *hath chosen thee to be a peculiar people unto himself, above all the nations that are upon the earth.*

—Deuteronomy 14:2

Ye shall be holy unto me, for I the LORD *am holy, and have severed you from other people that ye should be mine.*

—Leviticus 20:26

O ye seed of Abraham . . . ye children of Jacob his chosen . . . He is the LORD *our God. . . .*

—Psalm 105:6,7

The LORD *hath chosen Jacob unto himself, and Israel for his peculiar treasure.*

—Psalm 135:4

Thou, Israel, art my servant, Jacob whom I have chosen, the seed of Abraham my friend.

—Isaiah 41:8

Now hear, O Jacob my servant, and Israel, whom I have chosen . . . I, the LORD, *which call thee by thy name, am the God of Israel. For Jacob my servant's sake, and Israel mine elect . . . I am the* LORD . . . *there is no God beside me. . . .*

—Isaiah 44:1; 45:3-5

8

A *Chosen* People?

◆ ─────────────────

What the Bible clearly states about the Jewish people and the land of Israel can admittedly be very disturbing for Arabs and especially for Palestinians. However, the verses quoted on the facing page (representative of scores of others that could be cited) leave no question as to their meaning. The name *Israel*, referring either to the people or the land, is found more than 2500 times in the Bible, and reference to *the Jews*, or similar appelations, more than a thousand times. Obviously, this is a major topic of Scripture.

The Old Testament prophets declare with one voice that the Jews are a chosen people and that God has a special destiny for them and for the land which He has given them. The New Testament, too, makes the same divine declaration. In his second sermon, a few days after Pentecost, Peter referred to the Jews as "the children of the prophets and of the covenant which God made with our Father . . . Abraham" (Acts 3:25). Paul spoke of the "Israelites," his "kinsmen according to the flesh," as those "to whom pertaineth the adoption, and the glory, and the covenants, and the giving of the law, and the service of God, and the promises" (Romans 9:3,4).

Everything depends upon one's attitude toward Scripture. That the Bible is the infallible Word of God can be proved beyond the shadow of a doubt. Whether one believes the Bible is true or false determines the way one lives one's life, one's relationships with others, and one's hope for the hereafter. And in particular, whether one is a Jew or Gentile, Israeli or Palestinian, one's view of the Bible determines one's view of the land of Israel and the Jewish people, whether at home there or scattered around the world.

Human Tragedy

The need for an objective viewpoint such as the Bible provides is seen in the deep and fragmented feelings concerning Jerusalem which motivate Jews on one side and Arabs and Palestinians on the other. We are confronted with a Middle East crisis which threatens to engulf the entire world in the most devastating war in all of human history. Misinformation abounds, and to a large extent it determines the deep-rooted prejudices that inflame with anger and hatred those on both sides.

There are Palestinians and Arabs by the thousands who have been convinced of the astonishing lie (taught since infancy) that it was the Jews' naked aggression, not the attack upon the Jews by five Arab nations, which initiated the War of Independence in 1948. For most Palestinians and Arabs today, terrorists (who kill both Israelis and their own people who cooperate with the Israelis) are not terrorists at all but heroic patriots acting in self-defense. Even many of the younger generation of Israelis have now embraced that same revision of history through their enthusiasm for the "peace movement."

As an example, consider a book by a Jewish author, Penny Rosenwasser, *Voices from a 'Promised Land.'* In its pages one reads with deep sympathy the heartbreaking testimonies of Palestinians: of the hopelessness and despair of thousands of dispossessed people trapped without jobs in the occupied territories; of the filth, excruciating poverty, and crowded conditions in camps such as Jabalia in the Gaza Strip; of sudden midnight house searches by brutal Israeli soldiers without search warrants; of beatings, imprisonments, killings, deportations, and homes blown up.

By the time one is halfway through *Voices*, however, one is overtaken by an uneasy sense of being told only one side of a tragic story—and perhaps not even being told that side accurately. Totally absent is any hint that the Israelis might have at least some justification for their actions. Nor is there any suggestion that the PLO and many other terrorist organizations have ever done any wrong whatsoever.

Is There Another Side?

Remember, the PLO, Hamas, Islamic Jihad, and other similar organizations exist only to destroy Israel. They have waged a relentless war of terror against her civilians, killing women and children with abandon, yet one would never perceive that fact from reading *Voices*. There is no admission at all of any terrorist activity against Israel or of the multiplied deaths of Israelis that have resulted. Alya Shawa, for example, Gaza Strip hotel owner and a leader among the women's peace movement in the Gaza area, testifies in apparent sincerity:

> I'd just like the outside world to see that we are not terrorists, and to see who the real terrorists are [the Israeli soldiers], who have been for three years now killing the boys and beating kids and women. They are the terrorists. We are not.[1]

Over and over, the one-sided accusations are repeated in *Voices*. Typical is the following from a Palestinian woman who recounted in Arabic at a "Women Go for Peace" Conference in Jerusalem "how her husband had been deported just before their baby was born, [that] Israeli authorities are denying her an exit visa to visit him . . . a common harassment tactic used by the Israeli government to split up Palestinian families."[2] Absent is any documentation or explanation of *why* the Israelis may have found it necessary to deport her husband or any evidence to show that they acted unjustly. It is simply implied that whatever the Israeli government and soldiers do is wrong because they are evil Zionists who stole the Palestinians' land. The oppressed Palestinians are completely innocent victims who have never done anything to merit the Israeli reaction.

Consider the testimony of Rehab Essawi, who came to California as part of the Palestinian delegation to a "Beyond War" Conference. She is a Professor of Education at Hebron University in the West Bank. Her story of oppression and injustice evokes great sympathy for those who have suffered so much. Yet again it is so one-sided that it creates doubts concerning its reliability:

> [M]y father became very active in the revolution in 1936. Toward the end he was a political refugee in Iraq, and he was sentenced to death [in absentia] by the British three times. In 1970 I had a brother who was arrested and he spent twelve years in jail. I have another brother who was murdered in 1982 during the Lebanon invasion, and during the intifada other brothers have been arrested, as well as nephews. And I have been arrested three times.[3]

It is clearly implied that neither she nor her family nor any other Palestinians have ever done anything to merit arrest or punishment of any kind. The British were totally unjustified in sentencing her father to death. Three times they did it without any cause! This was not the Israelis, remember, but the British—who themselves favored the Arabs. Could it really be such a clear-cut injustice every time she or any member of her family (or any other Palestinian) is arrested? That is the obvious implication! The brother who spent 12 years in jail was apparently imprisoned for no reason at all. And so it must have been with the other brothers and nephews who were arrested during *intifada*. After dozens of stories like that, one begins to wonder.

By the time a reader has reached the last page, *Voices* (which at first aroused righteous anger against Israel for its treatment of Palestinians and deep sympathy for those oppressed peoples), begins to have the opposite effect. Surely something is missing in the tales the book tells. One's empathy is gradually turned toward the Israelis. No situation can be all white on one side and all black on the other. The thoughtful reader concludes that he is not being told the whole truth. And that fact causes distrust of those testifying, and, finally, sympathy for those whom they blame and accuse.

A Warped Point of View

Even Saddam Hussein is above reproach in *Voices*. What redeeming quality can be found in this mass murderer except that he has sworn to destroy Israel? That fact is apparently enough to outweigh his multiple crimes against humanity. In spite of his rape of Kuwait and his slaughter of thousands of his own people as well as Kuwaitis, Saddam is a shining hero because he threatens Israel with extermination and promises to turn all of its land back to the Palestinians.

Those interviewed in *Voices* express great resentment against the United States for having intervened in the Gulf War, even though that intervention prevented the slaughter of many more thousands of Arabs. They seem to think that the Gulf War interfered with peace. Saddam brought "peace" to the region? How the invasion of Kuwait (which would have continued right on into Saudi Arabia and other Gulf states without American intervention) can be interpreted as "peace" is not explained.

Zakaria Khoury, Palestinian guide for the U.S. Women's Peace Brigade 1990 tour, expresses shock that Palestinians were deported from Kuwait and Saudi Arabia during the war, even though their leader, Yasser Arafat, had expressed his solid support for Saddam. Khoury finds it incomprehensible that such action would be taken "against our people as a punishment for the position taken by the PLO regarding the Gulf crisis. . . ."[4]

Apparently there is nothing wrong with Saddam's brutal aggression against Iraq's neighbors or with launching Scud missiles into Israel or with his oft-repeated threats to destroy Israel. These obvious evils are the very factors, amazingly, which cause Saddam to be so admired by the Palestinian people and are the reason that the PLO was so enthusiastic in its praise of this Arab Hitler. The Palestinians supported Saddam in his vicious campaign against Kuwait and Saudi Arabia.

Yet they complained when those countries declared Palestinian workers to be security risks and sent them back to the West Bank or the Gaza Strip.

What about Israel? For decades she has had within her borders thousands of Arabs who have sworn to exterminate her and who carry on a terrorist campaign of mayhem and murder to accomplish that end. No worse security risks could be imagined. Yet when Israel finds it necessary for security reasons to deport a small percentage of the Palestinians (those who are actively working toward her destruction), instead of all Palestinians as Kuwait and Saudi Arabia did, there is an outcry from around the world, including even from Kuwait and the Saudis.

One despairs of ever reaching an equitable solution between Arabs and Israelis in the face of such deep-rooted prejudices and warped points of view. What is needed is a higher authority which both sides respect and are willing to obey. One might respond that the Catholics in Southern Ireland and the Protestants in the North both claim to believe in the same God and Jesus Christ, yet they have not been able to live at peace. The same could be said of the Serbian Orthodox and Croatian Catholics, who are killing one another in Yugoslavia. There is a difference, however, which it is vital to recognize: The Bible says nothing about Bosnia or Ireland, but it has much to say about the land of Israel.

God Has Spoken

It is obedience to God's Word which alone enables us to set aside all prejudices, whether between French and Germans, between Yankees and Southerners, between Americans and Mexicans, between parents and children, or between Arabs and Jews. We cannot allow ourselves to be influenced by the seemingly justifiable animosity on the part of both the Israelis and the Palestinians for the wrongs which they perceive they have suffered at each other's hands. The only hope for understanding, forgiveness, and peace is for all mankind to submit themselves to God. And God has something very definite to say not only about heaven and hell but about the land of Israel as well.

We have cited some of the prophecies about Israel, the fulfillment of which, centuries and even thousands of years later, proves beyond the shadow of a doubt that the God of the Bible, Creator of the universe, exists. He has demonstrated that fact by telling what would befall these unique people, the Jews, centuries before it happened. The fact that what God inspired His prophets to declare in advance concerning Israel occurred precisely as foretold cannot be explained as a mere series of coincidences. These fulfillments could not have happened by chance. The probability of that happening is a mathematical impossibility. No honest person can dispute the facts or reject the conclusion to which they point so clearly.

One dare not allow one's feelings, or preferences, or hopes, or dreams to determine one's opinion concerning Israel, the Arabs, and the Promised Land. It is not a matter of being pro-Arab or pro-Israeli, but of submitting to God's Word and will. What the Bible declares could not be clearer: that the Jews are God's "chosen people" and that the land of Israel was given by God to them more than 4000 years ago to be theirs *forever.* The very uniqueness of these people, which we have already documented, holds true even today and can be explained rationally on no other basis than what the Bible says.

The very importance of Jerusalem and the fact that it holds the key to world peace declares again that God has His hand upon both the Jews and their land. These are the people whom God scattered all over the world because of their gross disobedience and idolatry. And now, 2500 years after the Babylonian captivity, He has gathered them back into their land as He promised through his prophets He would do in the "last days." God has done this miracle in the sight of the whole world at this particular time in history to fulfill His Word and to demonstrate that He is God and that these are His people. Tragically, in spite of such overwhelming evidence, the vast majority of Jews remain in unbelief concerning His promises and warnings.

One may attempt to deny the truth of what the Bible says because of an unwillingness to believe in God and miracles, and in the vain hope of escaping accountability to Him. The fact that the Bible names the Jews as God's chosen people, however, and that its prophecies concerning them have come to pass, cannot be denied.

A Miracle in the Face of Unbelief

The miracle of modern Israel becomes even more amazing when one considers that the majority of Jewish people around the world do not believe in a literal interpretation of the Bible. Their sense of tradition may be strong, but there is no accompanying faith in God or His Word. This inexplicable state of affairs exists in spite of all that God has done to prove Himself to them.

Thus the modern nation of Israel has been created in spite of the Jews, not primarily because of them. It took the Holocaust to drive them from Europe and to awaken a passionate desire for a land of their own. Today their willingness to give up parts of Israel, the land God promised them, in exchange for a tenuous peace with those who have sworn their destruction, is sufficient proof that they do not consider the land of Israel to be their divine heritage, as it is described in the Bible.

When one considers the trend among Jews around the world to intermarry with non-Jews and thus to lose their God-given identity, it is apparent that the State of Israel was founded just in time. The rate of absorption into non-Jewish identities is accelerating as the Holocaust fades into the distant past and the Zionist dream becomes ever less real. Consider, for example, what has been happening in the former Soviet Union. In 1988, "73.2% of Jewish men were married out of the faith and 62.8% of Jewish women had intermarried . . . and the rate of mixed marriage is rising sharply and the birthrate dropping." Over the next five years in the former Soviet Union, because of "assimilation and negative population growth, about 500,000 are expected to be lost to Judaism."[5]

Furthermore, there are strong voices in Israeli society today arguing against any further gathering of Jews back to Israel

from around the world. The vision of a special land and a
special destiny is clearly being lost. The practical arguments
for this point of view, and the rejection of the Diaspora and
return to Israel as having any "religious" connotations, were
presented persuasively in a recent *Jerusalem Post* editorial
titled "The post-Zionist era is here":

> The vision of the Ingathering of the Exiles has sustained the
> nation through the ages, and aliya provided the sinews that
> enabled modern Israel to survive.
>
> But there are reasons to question whether it is truly Israel's
> ongoing mission to gather in the exiles, and the Diaspora's
> destiny to be gathered.
>
> Apart from its cardinal role as a haven for Jews in distress,
> Israel has promoted aliya in order to strengthen itself vis-a-vis
> the Arabs. The lengths to which it has gone to ensure that
> emigrants from the former Soviet Union come to Israel rather
> than the US reflect the healthy survival instinct of an embattled
> nation. But if national interest is the criterion, then aliya must
> be examined in that light, and not as a quasi-religious injunc-
> tion.
>
> In 1948, immigrants were rushed straight from ships to the
> battlefield at Latrun, where many met their deaths. But Israel
> no longer needs aliya to beef up its army, which already has
> difficulty coping with increasingly large numbers of recruits
> each year.
>
> Immigration boosts the economy, but its impact on popula-
> tion density has yet to be addressed. In the area north of
> Beersheba, where 93 percent of the population lives, density is
> already greater than in any other developed country, including
> Japan.
>
> The country is becoming so rapidly urbanized that some
> planners envision Israel approaching the Singapore-like para-
> maters of a city-state in 25 years. Is it in the national interest to
> speed up this process by beating the bushes around the world
> for immigrants? . . .
>
> The right of any Jew to settle here on his own must remain
> inviolate and so, too, Israel's role as a haven for Jews in
> distress. But promoting immigration is another matter. . . .
>
> Ought we not perhaps officially declare a Zionist victory
> after a century-long struggle, and begin thinking about the

post-Zionist era? These are questions that deserve public debate. So does the law of return, which gives automatic right of immigration to anyone with at least one Jewish grandparent. . . .

Israelis relate to the Diaspora as a spiritual limbo . . . where exiles weep for Zion beside the waters of Babylon. In fact . . . traditions cultivated in the Diaspora over the course of more than 2,500 years are an immense treasure, the likes of which no other nation can boast . . . [and maintaining] the Diaspora is clearly in Israel's national interest. . . .

The connection between Israel and the Diaspora is the major Jewish theme of our time. But the politically correct notion that Israel is where all Jews should aspire to come has outlived its usefulness.[6]

Another Compelling Argument

There are other reasons which Jews themselves find for rejecting belief in God and for denying their "chosen people" status or seeing any religious meaning in their return to their land. The most compelling is the Holocaust. Elie Wiesel tells how he came to reject the God of Israel. On the feast of Rosh Hashanah, 10,000 Jewish prisoners attended the solemn service inside the extermination camp of Buna. "Thousands of voices repeated the benediction, thousands of men prostrated themselves like trees before a tempest. 'Blessed be the Name of the Eternal!' Why, but why should I bless Him?" thought Wiesel:

Because He had had thousands of children burned in His pits? Because He kept six crematories working night and day, on Sundays and feast days? Because in His great might He had created Auschwitz, Birkenau, Buna, and so many factories of death? How could I say to Him: "Blessed art Thou, Eternal, Master of the Universe, Who chose us from among the races to be tortured day and night, to see our fathers, our mothers, our brothers, end in the crematory? Praised be Thy Holy Name, Thou Who hast chosen us to be butchered on Thine altar"? . . . In every fiber I rebelled.[7]

Even the horror and tragedy of the Holocaust, however, worse than any evil that has ever befallen any other people on earth, cannot change the prophecies that have existed in black and white in the Bible for thousands of years or the fact that they, against all mathematical odds, have been fulfilled to the very letter. The Holocaust may cause the Jews to question whether God is loving or merciful, but it cannot raise any legitimate uncertainty as to His existence and identity. That question has been laid to rest by the prophecies concerning the "people of the Book."

Even the Holocaust was foretold by the prophets—not in detail but surely in principle. Moreover, in the Holocaust itself and its repulsive violation of everything decent and humane, we have further proof of all that we have been trying to say about the uniqueness of the Jews and their Promised Land.

In thee shall all families of the earth be blessed.

—The promise to Abraham in Genesis 12:3

In thee and in thy seed shall all the families of the earth be blessed.

—The promise to Jacob in Genesis 28:14

Thou shalt become an astonishment, a proverb, and byword among all nations whither the Lord shall lead thee.

—Deuteronomy 28:37

I will . . . deliver them to be removed to all the kingdoms of the earth, to be a curse and an astonishment and an hissing and a reproach among all the nations whither I have driven them. . . .

In that ye provoke me unto wrath . . . burning incense unto other gods . . . that ye might be a curse and a reproach among all the nations of the earth.

—Jeremiah 29:18; 44:8

Their number, dress, diet, circumcision, poverty, ambition, prosperity, exclusiveness, intelligence, aversion to images, and observation of an inconvenient Sabbath aroused an anti-Semitism that ranged from jokes in the theater and slurs in Juvenal and Tacitus to murders in the street and wholesale pogroms.

—Will Durant, *The History of Civilization*[1]

9

The Mystery of Anti-Semitism

◆

It is indisputable that the hatred and persecution which is universally known as anti-Semitism goes far beyond the brutalization and mistreatment (in its intensity, duration, and universality) experienced by any other race or ethnic group. Once again, we find further evidence that the Jews are absolutely unique. And here too the obvious question arises as to why this should be.

Why should the Jews, in contradistinction to all other people, be pursued with such relentless hatred wherever they go in search of a secure home? There is something truly mysterious about this heinous phenomenon! Yet it cannot be without an explanation.

Are the Jewish people, after all, the most obnoxious, wicked, hateful people on the face of the earth? Have the Jews, in every generation and in every place, brought anti-Semitism upon themselves? Do they, to the last member of that race, really deserve such treatment? Some Jew-haters might say so, but this is surely not the consensus of rational people worldwide.

Then what is the explanation for this universal evil known as anti-Semitism? Why should the Jews, of all earth's races and throughout all earth's ages, be such objects of derision and contempt and outright hatred, even to their attempted annihilation as an ethnic group of people? And what must it be like to be born to such a fate!

The Maddening Injustice

There are many ethnic and even religious groups which are far larger than the 14 million Jews worldwide, and some of them are quite aggressive and open about their determination to take over the world. The total number of Jews on this planet is so small that it is ludicrous to accuse them of an "international Zionist conspiracy" to conquer the world. Yet that accusation has been thrown at them for centuries. Why should this be? The members of that hated and persecuted and slaughtered minority must have asked themselves that question a million times. Why are the Jews the perpetual focus of such an obviously false accusation?

Yes, the Jewish Scriptures, with which most Jews have only a passing acquaintance, declare that one day the Jewish Messiah will rule the world from Jerusalem. But there is no threat to the world in these prophecies. On the contrary, they offer the only hope for a lasting peace. The Hebrew prophets speak of no crusade by the Jews to take over the world. There is no suggestion of Jewish armies ravaging the earth and subjecting nations by force of arms. Rather, the Messiah comes to reign over the small land of Israel, and all nations are drawn to worship Him in Jerusalem because He is perfectly holy and righteous and because the God of the universe has given Him this position and power.

On the other hand, the Muslims, who have made themselves the chief enemies of God's people, openly speak of exterminating the Jews in Israel and of bringing the entire world into submission to Allah—and through violence, if need be. Yet Muslims, strangely enough, are never accused of wanting to take over the world. Even their threats to exterminate Israel are somehow justified or explained away. Arabs outnumber the tiny international Jewish community by nearly 100 to 1, yet the world sees the Jews as the threat to world peace. The Jews have threatened no one; they desire only to be left alone to live in peace, whereas the Arabs and especially the Muslims threaten and attack Jews continually. Why is this gross injustice promoted and accepted by the world?

What Jew today can answer that question either to his own satisfaction or on behalf of his children, who will share the same fate as they grow up? It is a destiny which parents wish they could spare their children, but which would require repudiating their Jewishness. Under increasing pressure, that repudiation is exactly what growing numbers of Jews are doing these days.

A Compelling Identity

While many thousands of Jews with no concern for their children's Jewish heritage are marrying non-Jews, something inexplicable continues to cause millions of others to cling to that universally despised heritage with a fierce pride. Is it, perhaps, respect for tradition? Can a sense of tradition be so strong as to overcome fear of persecution and even martyrdom? The reason is certainly not faith in the God of Abraham, since so few Jews profess that faith.

Why have the vast majority of Jews clung to their Jewishness even though it meant persecution and even death? Here we face still another mystery. The only answer seems to be that the God of Abraham, Isaac, and Israel said He would preserve these special people as an identifiable ethnic group so that, in the last days, He could bring them back into their land.

The pressure of persecution and false accusations can work both ways. While it causes some Jews to attempt to change their identity, it causes many others to acknowledge their identity with a certain sense of resignation. Given enough of the treatment which Jews have so long endured, self-loathing may even set in. How can so many people be wrong? Rozsa Berend, director of Budapest's Anne Frank High School, explains: "If they spit at you long enough, you feel like you must really be guilty of something. Most of the Jews of my generation went through that psychological misery."

Those who attempt to deny their Jewishness are often burdened with a sense of guilt for that betrayal. A member of today's Hungarian National Assembly, Matyas Eorsi, remembers how his father, to help his children escape future harassment, changed his name from the overtly Jewish *Schleiffer* to the indeterminate *Eorsi*. Years later, when his father was in the late stages of Alzheimer's disease, his son one day found him weeping and overheard his father's first coherent words in months: "I am Jewish!" How amazing that this was the one fact which his ravaged mind still held with conviction![2]

A Brief Look at Ancient History

Anti-Semitism is, of course, nothing new. It can be traced back to the earliest ages of antiquity. The Jews have been the object of persecution and of attempted extermination at least since the destruction of Jerusalem by Nebuchadnezzar scattered them far and wide 2500 years ago. What happened under Antiochus Epiphanes 400 years later is only one example of what the Jews have suffered repeatedly. Josephus informs us:

> Now Antiochus was not satisfied either with his unexpected taking of the city [Jerusalem, c. 167 B.C.], or with his pillage, or with the great slaughter he had made there; but being overcome with his violent passions, and remembering what he had suffered during the siege, he compelled the Jews to dissolve the laws of their country, and to keep their infants uncircumcised, and to sacrifice swine's flesh upon the altar; against which they all opposed themselves, and the most approved among them were put to death.[3]

The more familiar one becomes with history, the more one is driven back to that inexplicable fact: There is no ordinary explanation for the appalling fate the Jews have endured for thousands of years. And that this fate has been meted out consistently around the world and at so many times in history at the hands of such a wide variety of oppressors only adds to both the tragedy and the mystery. Will Durant provides his insight concerning Antiochus, which reveals a hatred of Jew-ishness that would do credit to any Hitler, yet it was held more than 2100 years earlier:

> Antiochus . . . marched up to Jerusalem, slaughtered Jews of either sex by the thousands, desecrated and looted the Temple, appropriated for the royal coffers its golden altar, its vessels, and its treasuries . . . and gave orders for the com-pulsory Hellenization of all Jews. He commanded that the Temple be rededicated as a shrine to Zeus, that a Greek altar be built over the old one, and that the usual sacrifices be replaced with a sacrifice of swine. He forbade the keeping of the Sabbath or the Jewish festivals, and made circumcision a capi-tal crime. Throughout Judea the old religion and its rites were interdicted, and the Greek ritual was made compulsory on pain of death. Every Jew who refused to eat pork, or who was found possessing the Book of the Law, was to be jailed or killed, and the Book wherever found was to be burned.
>
> The agents of Antiochus, having put an end to all visible expression of Judaism in Jerusalem, passed like a searching fire into the towns and villages. Everywhere they gave the people the choice between death and participation in Hellenic worship, which included the eating of sacrificial swine. All synagogues and Jewish schools were closed. Those who re-fused to work on the Sabbath were outlawed as rebels. On the day of the Bacchanalia the Jews were compelled to deck them-selves with ivy like the Greeks, to take part in the processions, and to sing wild songs in honor of Dionysus. Many Jews conformed to the demands, waiting for the storm to pass. Many others fled into caves or mountain retreats, lived on clandestine gleanings from the fields, and resolutely carried on the ordinances of Jewish life. . . . Women who had circumcised their newborn sons were cast with their infants over the city walls to death.
>
> The Greeks were surprised to find the strength of the old faith; not for centuries had they seen such loyalty to an idea. The stories of martyrdom went from mouth to mouth, filled books like the First and Second Maccabees. . . . Judaism, which had been near assimilation, became intensified in re-ligious and national consciousness, and withdrew into a pro-tective isolation.[4]

Triumph of Valor

One marvels that Judaism could survive at all, yet it did and against all odds. In spite of the diabolical persecution—or perhaps because of it—the Jews, with little real faith in the validity of their Scriptures, clung to at least the outer forms of their religion. And they did so even though that religion no longer seemed to offer the salvation from their enemies for which their ancestors had so long prayed.

In spite of persecution and lack of faith on the part of the majority, there have been times of great revival of Judaism throughout history. One of the most amazing came under the spectacular leadership of Judas Maccabee, a priest and warrior "whose courage equaled his piety; before every battle he prayed like a saint, but in the hour of battle 'he was like a lion in his rage.' "[5] Will Durant continues:

> The little army "lived in the mountains after the manner of beasts, feeding on herbs." Every now and then it descended upon a neighboring village, killed backsliders, pulled down pagan altars, and "what children soever they found uncircumcised, those they circumcised valiantly."
>
> These things being reported to Antiochus [Epiphanes], he sent an army of Syrian Greeks to destroy the Maccabean force. Judas met them in the pass of Emmaus; and though the Greeks were trained mercenaries fully armed, and Judas' band was poorly armed and clad, the Jews won a complete victory (c. 166 B.C.).
>
> Antiochus sent a larger force, whose general was so confident that he brought slave merchants with him to buy the Jews whom he expected to capture, and posted in the towns the prices that he would ask. Judas defeated these troops at Mizpah, and so decisively that Jerusalem fell into his hands without resistance. He removed all pagan altars and ornaments from the Temple, cleansed and rededicated it, and restored the ancient service amid the acclaim of the returning orthodox Jews (c. 164 B.C.) [an occasion ever since celebrated as Hanukkah]. . . .

Intoxicated with power, the Maccabeans now took
their turn at persecution, pursuing the Hellenizing faction vengefully, not only in Jerusalem but in cities that
bordered the frontier.[6]

With his troops overwhelmingly outnumbered, Judas was
eventually (c. 161 B.C.) slain in battle. His brother Jonathan
succeeded him, but he too was slain in war 18 years later. The
only surviving brother, Simon, carried on the leadership and,
with the support of an alliance with Rome, won Judean independence. "By popular decree Simon was appointed both high
priest and general; and as these offices were made hereditary
in his family, he became the founder of the Hasmonean dy-
nasty. The first year of his reign was counted as the beginning
of a new era, and an issue of coinage proclaimed the heroic
rebirth of the Jewish state."[7]

The Final Diaspora

After the destruction of Jerusalem and the Temple in 70 A.D.
by the armies of Titus, "even the poorest Jew had now to pay to
a pagan temple at Rome the half shekel that pious Hebrews had
formerly paid each year for the upkeep of the Temple at
Jeruslaem. The high-priesthood and the Sanhedrin were abol-
ished. Judaism took the form that it has kept till our own time:
a religion without a central shrine, without a dominant priesthood, without a sacrificial service. The Sadducees disappeared, while the Pharisees and the rabbis became the leaders
of a homeless people that had nothing left but its synagogues
and its hope."[8]

As further testimony to the persistence of anti-Semitism
and the miracle of surviving Judaism, let us follow history for
a few more years. In 130 A.D. the Roman Emperor Hadrian
declared his intention to erect a shrine to Jupiter on the site
where the Temple had previously stood. The next year,
he "issued a decree forbidding circumcision and public instruction in the Jewish Law. . . . Resolved to destroy the
recuperative virility of Judaism, Hadrian forbade . . . the

observance of the Sabbath or any Jewish holyday, and the public performance of any Hebrew ritual. A new and heavier poll tax was placed upon all Jews. They were allowed in Jerusalem only on one fixed day each year, when they might come and weep before the ruins of their Temple. The pagan city of Aelia Capitolina rose on the site of Jerusalem, with shrines to Jupiter and Venus, and with palaestras, theaters, and baths. The council at Jamnia was dissolved and outlawed; a minor and powerless Council was permitted at Lydda, but public instruction in the Law was prohibited on pain of death. Several rabbis were executed for disobeying this injunction. . . .

"No other people has ever known so long an exile, or so hard a fate. Shut out of their Holy City, the Jews were compelled to surrender it first to paganism, then to Christianity. Scattered into every province and beyond, condemned to poverty and humiliation, unbefriended even by philosophers and saints, they retired from public affairs into private study and worship, passionately preserving the words of their scholars, and preparing to write them down at last in the Talmuds of Babylonia and Palestine. Judaism hid in fear and obscurity while its offspring, Christianity, went out to conquer the world."[9]

A Tragic Misunderstanding

From earliest childhood Jews are taught the role of Christians in their persecution and pogroms. Yet the vast majority of Jews don't really know what being a Christian means. That confusion has caused the Jews to blame Christ and Christianity for anti-Semitism when, in fact, no true Christian would ever harbor such feelings toward God's chosen people. Here we have a tragic misunderstanding that persists to this day.

Out of ignorance, Jews equate Christianity with Roman Catholicism, unaware that the Roman Catholic Church, though it claims to be Christian, has killed far more Christians than it has Jews. For example, in one campaign the army of Pope Innocent III, in what he called the "crowning achievement of his papacy," killed 60,000 Albigensian Christians when it wiped out the entire town of Beziers, France. Over the next century the Albigensians, who had at one time comprised a majority of the population of southern France, were all but exterminated by that persecuting Church. The same fate was meted out to the Waldensian Christians as well as to other followers of Christ, such as the Huguenots, of whom several hundred thousand were slain, 70,000 alone at the infamous St. Bartholomew's Massacre in 1572.

The true Christian church has never given its allegiance to the Pope nor been a part of the Roman Catholic Church. For refusing that allegiance, true Christians, who have always existed independently of Rome in large numbers, have been slaughtered by the millions by the Roman Catholic Church.[10] The following excerpt from the "Edict of the Emperors Gratian, Valentinian II, and Theodosius I" of February 27, 380 A.D., refers to the establishment of Roman Catholicism as the state religion and the outlawing of any other form of worship:

> We order those who hold this doctrine [from Rome] to receive the title of Catholic Christians, but others we judge to be mad and raving and worthy of incurring the disgrace of heretical teaching, nor are their assemblies to receive the name of churches. They are to be punished not only by Divine retribution but also by our own measures, which we have decided in accordance with Divine inspiration.[11]

Many other examples could be given from history of how this persecution and slaughter of true Christians took place at the hands of the Roman Catholic Church, but we must limit ourselves to a very few. Consider the letter from Pope Martin V (1417-31) commanding the King of Poland to exterminate the Hussites (those who held the same simple faith as the martyred Jan Hus). It provides insight into the reasons why the popes hated true Christians even more than they hated the Jews:

> Know that the interests of the Holy See [papal Rome], and those of your crown, make it a duty to exterminate

the Hussites. Remember that these impious persons dare proclaim principles of equality; they maintain that all Christians are brethren . . . that Christ came on earth to abolish slavery; they call the people to liberty, that is to the annihilation of kings and priests.

While there is still time, then, turn your forces against Bohemia; burn, massacre, make deserts everywhere, for nothing could be more agreeable to God, or more useful to the cause of kings, than the extermination of the Hussites.[12]

To a Jew, Hitler and Mussolini were Christians. In fact, they were Roman Catholics from birth, and in spite of their horrendous crimes against humanity they were never excommunicated from their Church. The same was true of Himmler and many others in the Nazi hierarchy. Indeed, the Roman Catholic Church has a long history of persecution, expulsion, and slaughter of Jews, to which Hitler referred in justifying the Holocaust. Even the great historian Will Durant was a victim of this misunderstanding that failed to distinguish between Roman Catholics and those true Christians who had never given allegiance to Rome. He writes:

[During the Middle Ages] in every Holy Week, the bitter story of the Passion was related from a thousand pulpits; resentments flared in Christian [Roman Catholic] hearts, and on those days the Israelites shut themselves up in their own quarter . . . fearful that the passions of simple souls might be stirred to a pogrom. . . .

Romans had accused Christians of murdering pagan children to offer their blood in secret sacrifice to the Christian God; Christians [Roman Catholics] of the twelfth century accused the Jews of kidnaping Christian children either to sacrifice them to Jahveh, or to use their blood as medicine or in the making of unleavened bread for the Passover feast. Jews were charged with poisoning the wells . . . and of stealing consecrated wafers to pierce them and draw from them the blood of Christ . . . [and] of draining the wealth of Christendom into Jewish hands.

> ...There were some lucid intervals in this madness ...[and popes and Catholic prelates who at times tried to rescue the Jews].
>
> When in 1095, Pope Urban II proclaimed the First Crusade, some Christians [Catholics] thought it desirable to kill the Jews in Europe before proceeding so far to fight Turks in Jerusalem. Godfrey of Bouillon, having accepted the leadership of the crusade, announced that he would avenge the blood of Jesus upon the Jews ...leav[ing] not one of them alive; and his companions proclaimed their intention to kill all Jews who would not accept Christianity [Roman Catholicism].[13]

Jews were slaughtered by the thousands all across Europe as the Catholic Crusaders made their way to the "Holy Land" to recover it from both Jews and Turks for the Roman Catholic Church, the new people of God who had displaced the Jews as God's chosen people. Durant reminds us that the Second Crusade (1147 A.D.) "threatened to better the example of the first." In spite of individual Catholic bishops who saved Jews in many places, one can only blame the Church for the atrocities. The councils and some popes had confined the Jews to ghettos, had made them wear an identifying color or cloth badge (Hitler would later say he had learned these tactics from the Church), and in many other ways had isolated them and aroused resentment against them on the part of the simple Catholics who saw the need to "avenge the blood of Christ" by killing His murderers.

A Common Factor

The fanaticism that aroused Catholics to murder was often associated with the Eucharist and the wafer (Host), which, according to the Church, literally became the body and blood of Christ at the Mass through the alleged miracle of "transubstantiation." True Christians, independent of Rome, did not accept this doctrine. The Bible clearly taught that Christ had died once for the sins of the world, had risen bodily, and was now alive at the Father's right hand in a glorified body, never to die again. Thus no wafer could become the literal body of Christ and be offered repeatedly on Catholic altars in an alleged repetition of His sacrifice on the cross.

For rejecting the doctrine of transubstantiation, Christians were burned at the stake by Roman Catholics by the hundreds of thousands. Church historian R. Tudor Jones writes that "the majority of the martyrs were ordinary people, including many women. . . . The lengthy interrogations of scores of these people have survived and they concentrate on such topics as their beliefs about the Bible [which Rome claimed it alone could interpret] and its authority [which Rome claimed resided in the Church rather than in Scripture], transubstantiation" and other Catholic doctrines unacceptable to Christians.[14]

John Foxe was an eyewitness and earnest historian of the fierce persecution in England in his day. His *Book of Martyrs* gives detailed accounts of many public trials and executions of those whom the Roman Catholic Church judged to be heretics worthy of death. His descriptions of Christians being burned at the stake tell of their inspiring bravery in the face of such a horrible death and of the determination of Roman Catholicism to exterminate everywhere true Christians who opposed her.

Similar records have come down of the massacres of Jews at the hands of the Roman Church. Often their deaths, like those of Christian martyrs, resulted from the Roman Catholic belief that the Host (tiny wafer) had become the literal body of Christ. In 1243, "the entire Jewish population of Belitz, near Berlin, was burned alive on the charge that some of them had defiled a consecrated Host." In 1298, "every Jew in Rottingen was burned to death on the charge of desecrating a sacramental wafer."[15] In Deggendorf the entire Jewish community was slaughtered for allegedly stealing and "torturing" a consecrated wafer. Who could forget the inscription in the Catholic Church in that quiet town which for centuries, under a picture commemorating that mass murder of Jews, proclaimed in "Christian" triumph, "God grant that our fatherland be forever free from this hellish scum"![16] And who could deny that centuries of such fanaticism would prepare Germany for Hitler's "final solution."

Rindfleisch, a devout Catholic baron, "organized and armed a band of Christians [Roman Catholics] sworn to kill all Jews; they completely exterminated the Jewish community at Wurzburg, and slew 698 Jews in Nuremberg. The persecution spread, and in half a year 140 Jewish congregations were wiped out." In 1236, Crusaders "invaded the Jewish settlements of Anjou and Poitou . . . and bade all Jews be baptized; when the Jews refused, the crusaders trampled 3000 of them to death under their horses' hoofs."[17] With that background, Hitler's treatment of the Jews is less an isolated incident than a continuation of what had been in progress for centuries.

A New Wave

Anti-Semitism, even after the Holocaust shocked the world, has continued unabated into our time. Earlier we quoted Arafat's uncle, Grand Mufti of Jerusalem, on Radio Berlin March 1, 1944, urging all Arabs to "kill the Jews wherever you find them! This pleases God [Allah] and religion [and] saves your honor. God is with you!" Similar slogans calling for the extermination of Jews, ignored by the world now as were Hitler's then, are still being earnestly proclaimed by Muslim leaders in mosques everywhere. The satanic spirit that inspired Hitler's Holocaust continues to call for "peace" as a deceitful step toward Jewish destruction. In spite of his new "peace" posture, Yasser Arafat has never renounced his oft-repeated commitment to the extermination of the Jews as the PLO's sacred Islamic duty.

Anti-Semitism is once more on the rise throughout Europe. Kibbutz-born Yaron Svoray, 40, an ex-paratrooper and former Tel Aviv District Police detective, spent several months (September 1992 to February 1993) infiltrating some of Europe's far-right organizations, including neo-Nazi groups in Germany. In the process he uncovered a frightening amount of resurgent anti-Semitism, which he reported in his book *In Hitler's Shadow: An Israeli's Amazing Journey Inside Germany's*

Neo-Nazi Movement. The Simon Wiesenthal Center in Los Angeles helped fund his investigation and "broke the story in a televised press conference in New York on April 19, 1993." That event led to testimony before a Congressional committee and the eventual admission by the German government that "terrorism from the right is at least as much a problem as terrorism from the left."[18]

Of the Jews in Poland in 1940, about 3 million perished in the Holocaust and only 369,000 survived. Today about 4000 Poles classify themselves as Jewish, though estimates of Jews in Warsaw alone run as high as 10,000 and there is a revival of Jewish culture throughout Poland. There in that land where Poles took over the homes of Jews who had been sent to the camps, then refused to give them up to their rightful owners who had been liberated by Allied troops—and where Poles actually cursed the Jews who were being liberated from Auschwitz and even killed some of them—anti-Semitism is alive and prospering.

Recently in Krakow, Poland, graffiti scrawled on a prominent billboard demanded, "Jews get out!" Earlier someone had spray-painted in large letters on Warsaw's National Jewish Opera House, "Jews to the ovens!" The Polish Tourist Office is trying to introduce Israelis to what it calls "the new Poland," but so far the tens of thousands of Israeli tourists come only to tour the former death camps where their relatives died but do not linger otherwise. The Poles complain that Israelis come to Poland to cry, then go to Germany to enjoy themselves in spite of the fact that Germany was the main instigator of the Holocaust. Apparently Germany has been forgiven, while Poland has not. That anomaly may be at least partially explained by the fact that the renewed wave of anti-Semitism which is sweeping the world seems more open in Poland than elsewhere.

In Poland, Jewish cemeteries are once again being defaced with swastikas. The tense situation is being inflamed by anti-Semitic rhetoric at the highest levels. Poland's President, Lech Walesa, a staunch Roman Catholic, recently declared on TV:

"A gang of Jews took over our resources and exploited our land, and their aim is to destroy us." Hitler made similar accusations to prepare Germany for his "final solution." No wonder that Jacek Kuron, once a minister in Walesa's government and a likely candidate to replace him, has confessed bluntly that "anti-Semitism is a Polish disease."[19]

Growing Apprehension

Of the 2,000,000 Jewish survivors still alive in Europe at the end of World War II, many of them "came to a terrible conclusion: whatever the regime, it was best not to be Jewish at all." Today that fear is awakening again. Rozsa Berend mentions anti-Semitic overtones in recent Hungarian election campaigns and says, "Things seem good now, but no one knows what will happen if the economy keeps going down and people start clamoring for a strongman. The Jews could still end up paying a bitter price."[20]

Just beneath the surface of the optimism of Europe's current revival of Jewishness referred to in an earlier chapter, an oppressive fear lurks. Russian Parliament member Alla Gerber admits, "It is still possible to be frightened. There is a feeling that we are guests who should leave on time." The apprehension is growing. Israel is considering evacuating Poland's Holocaust survivors (estimated to number as many as 7000), remnants of 3.4 million who once lived there, because Poland is becoming unsafe for Jews.

The Peppermint Train: Journey to a German-Jewish Childhood, by Edgar E. Stern, tells how at the age of nine the author fled his native German town of Speyer for America, then returned recently to visit today's Speyer and search for his roots. Back at the scene of his childhood, now so changed, he is haunted by a specter he suspects hides just below the town's idyllic facade. Are some of those who robbed and murdered their Jewish neighbors still alive? What memories do they have? What have they told their children and grandchildren?

It is clear that the Jewish culture which was such a large part of pre-World War II will never be revived. "You cannot revive

Jewish culture here . . . something that is finished," says Gerber. Furthermore, the older generation fears that the revived enthusiasm for Jewishness among the youth has little depth to it. "A lot of them want to be Jewish without the religion," complains Rabbi Jozsef Schweitzer, head of Budapest's Rabbinical Seminary. He wants "synagogue Jews, not club Jews."[21] Is that not perhaps an unreasonable demand, considering that 30 percent of the Jews in Israel today claim to be atheists?

Repentance at Last?

In a rare development, on November 15, 1994, Austrian President Thomas Klestil apologized for his country's role in the Nazi Holocaust and acknowledged that "many of the worst henchmen in the Nazi dictatorship were Austrians." He made the speech before the Israeli parliament during a three-day visit to Israel, the first by an Austrian head of state. "No word of apology can ever expunge the agony of the Holocaust," Klestil said. "On behalf of the Republic of Austria, I bow my head with deep respect and profound emotion in front of the victims." About 15,000 Jews reside in Austria today, compared with 180,000 in 1938. About 70,000 Austrian Jews perished in the Holocaust.[22]

The Roman Catholic Church today claims never to have nurtured anti-Semitism. There has been talk by the present Pope about some kind of confession of past wrongs. Always, however, he intimates that the evil was done by the "sons and daughters of the Church," leaving the Church itself and its leaders innocent. The latter are allegedly infallible and therefore could not admit wrongdoing without destroying the credibility of the Catholic Church itself. Vatican II makes the following deceptive declaration concerning the Jews:

> It is true that the Church is the new people of God, yet the Jews should not be spoken of as rejected or accursed as if this followed from holy Scripture. . . . Indeed, the Church reproves every form of persecution against whomsoever it may be directed. Remembering, then, her

THE MYSTERY OF ANTI-SEMITISM ◆ 165

common heritage with the Jews and moved not by any
political consideration, but solely by the religious motivation of Christian charity, she deplores all hatreds,
persecutions, displays of anti-Semitism leveled at any
time or from any source against the Jews.[23]

Nothing could be more hypocritical than this statement.
The Church strongly condemns "hatreds, persecutions . . .
anti-Semitism," but only by others, not by herself. No mention
is made of the fact that during the many centuries when the
Roman Catholic Church held sway over society, ruling even
kings and emperors, *she* was the inspirer and perpetrator of an
anti-Jewish bias as bad as anything the world has ever seen.
Vatican II makes it sound as though the Church has always
been opposed to anti-Semitism, when in fact the opposite is
true.

At the same time that the Pope is seeming to condemn past
anti-Semitism, powerful elements within that Church are
denouncing such a change in attitude toward the Jews. Consider the following declaration which exudes its own anti-
Semitic odor:

The Roman Catholic Church today is groaning under
the weight of her enemies . . . who work day and night
to destroy her. . . . This Enemy had caused the persecutions, wars, upheavals, revolutions, intellectual
aberrations and the general decadence of human society.
This pest in the Catholic Church and the scourge of all
humanity . . . [is] the Zionist, who is awaiting the future King of Israel . . . [he] is the eternal enemy of all
Christianity. These are Christ-killers even in modern
times. . . .
[W]e must voice our complete disagreement with the
Vatican II Declaration on the Jews . . . [we] are obligated
to reject it as injurious to the following popes who have
issued Encyclicals, statements and warnings against the
Jews: Honorius III, Gregory IX, Innocent IV, Clement
IV, Gregory X, Nicholas III, Nicholas IV, John XXII,
Urban V, Martin V, Eugene IV, Calixtus III, Paul III,

Julius III, Paul IV, Pius IV, Pius V, Gregory XIII, Sixtus V, Clement VIII, Paul V, Urban VIII, Alexander VII, Alexander VIII, Innocent XII, Clement XI, Innocent XIII, Benedict XIII, Benedict XIV, Clement XII, Clement XIII, Pius VIII, Gregory XVI, Pius IX, Leo XIII, Pius X, Pius XI.

... those powerful few Jews have succeeded to subvert our Divine Institution to serve their own ends. ... Why don't they cease to blaspheme the name of Jesus? ... They do not mention how they instigated the Roman persecutions; and the murder of millions upon millions upon millions of Christians in the Communist countries. They do not mention their hateful desecrations of the holy places in Palestine. ...

The Jewish plot against our holy Mother Church is reaching its culmination by their penetration and influence among the high Catholic clergy and in the Vatican.[24]

The Most Subtle and Persuasive Form

Anti-Semitism takes many forms. One of the most subtle is the falsification of history in the media and even in school textbooks. One of the most widely used college textbooks in America on the topic of the Middle East, *Politics in the Middle East* (to which we referred earlier), provides a shocking example. As one reviewer has said, "Its description of Israel adheres closely to that found in the most blatant type of PLO propaganda."[25] Yet *Politics* is accepted as authoritative by millions of university students.

The Anti-Defamation League recently reported "a record number of anti-Semitic incidents ... a jump of more than 10 percent during 1994 [2066, up from 1867 in 1993] in the reported acts of violence, threats or harassment against Jews or Jewish institutions in the United States."[26] At the same time there has been an increase in libelous accusations against the Jews from a historical standpoint. Coming to their defense, the American Historical Association condemned as false recent allegations that Jews played a disproportionate role in the

African slave trade. Only twice in its 111-year history has the Washington-based group taken such a public position on a historical issue. Both times it felt compelled to come to the defense of the Jewish people.

The AHA represents 18,000 historians and groups involved in documenting historical events. In 1991 it condemned as false the statements that the Holocaust never happened or that it has been greatly exaggerated. The latest resolution declared that statements charging Jews with a major involvement in the African slave trade—

> so misrepresent the historical record . . . that we believe them only to be a part of a long anti-Semitic tradition that presents Jews as negative central actors in human history. . . .
>
> Unfortunately, the media have given the latest charges wide currency, while failing to dismiss them as spurious. As professional historians, who have closely examined and assessed the empirical evidence, we cannot remain silent while the historical record is so grossly violated.[27]

God's Reward to His Chosen?

So anti-Semitism not only persists, but astonishingly it even grows in a world where equality of the sexes and races is promoted and discrimination on the basis of race or color is supposedly being wiped out. Is the astounding persecution which the Jews continue to experience their reward for being God's "chosen people"? In a sense it is.

As God's special people, so near to His heart, the Jews might well expect that He would protect His own. And so He does. But He also disciplines those whom He loves until they repent, something which the Jews as a whole have not yet learned to do. They have been experiencing God's chastisement for 2500 years, yet continue to rebel against Him.

Does this mean that the Jews are morally more culpable than the Germans or Portuguese or Swedes or Chinese or other people? No. Why then should they suffer, as no others do, the chastisement of God?

We must repeat: The fact of Jewish suffering in itself proves once more that what the Bible says of this people's uniqueness is true. They are God's "chosen people," and as such they have failed to be the example to the world of the holiness for which God chose them. They have failed to love and serve God with their whole being, as commanded, and they are being chastised for their own good and for the world's enlightenment.

The Only Rational Explanation

Moreover, in addition to God's chastisement, there is another explanation for anti-Semitism: to wipe out the Jews so that the Messiah, who the prophets said would be a Jew, couldn't come into the world to rescue mankind and defeat Satan. God allows anti-Semitism because, up to a point, it fits His purposes for His people. Satan is the instigator of anti-Semitism because he hopes it will result in the extermination of the Jews.

God promised Abraham and Jacob that through their "seed" a blessing would come to "all the nations of the earth." Here was a confirmation of that wonderful promise which God gave to Adam and Eve that one day the Messiah, born of a virgin (the seed of the woman), would come to this earth to bring mankind back to God:

> I will put enmity between thee [Satan] and the woman, and between thy seed [those who follow Satan] and her seed [the Messiah]; it [the woman's seed, i.e. the Messiah] shall bruise thy head [i.e. a deadly wound destroying Satan], and thou shalt bruise his heel (Genesis 3:15).

At last we uncover the most compelling explanation for anti-Semitism: Satan himself is the author of this incredible genocidal fervor. He must destroy the Jews through whom the Messiah is to come or his cause is doomed. Moreover, even if the Messiah did come, by destroying the Jews at any time thereafter Satan could still prevent God from fulfilling the many biblical prophecies which declare that the Messiah will one day rule over the descendants of Abraham, Isaac, and

Israel on the throne of His father David in Jerusalem. Obviously, if Hitler had succeeded in his "final solution to the Jewish problem" or if Satan even today could wipe out the Jews, he would have proved that God lied in making such promises as the following:

> I have sworn unto David my servant, Thy seed [the Messiah] will I establish forever, and build up thy throne to all generations. . . . I will not lie unto David. His seed shall endure forever, and his throne as the sun before me (Psalm 89:3,4,35,36).

Anti-Semitism is clearly too universal and enduring throughout history to have its source in any human agency. The effort to destroy the descendants of Isaac and Jacob has been consistently pursued for thousands of years. That time period is so far beyond the lifespan of any human being that no mortal could be behind it. In confronting this evil, one must realize that its inspiration and strength originates in that very being who has made himself the enemy of good and God.

Those who oppose Israel and her people are on Satan's side against God, whether they realize it or not. This statement is not made out of prejudicial favor toward the Jews. We have shown that the Bible makes it clear that God did not choose them because of favoritism.

Jerusalem stands as a signpost to all mankind. Those who love her and pray for her peace are on God's side. Those who try to take Jerusalem out of Israel's hands are on Satan's side. And God's curse rests upon those who attempt to prevent the Jews from possessing all of the land that was promised to them. So says the Bible in language that cannot be misunderstood. Therefore, those who disagree with this view of Israel have an argument with God and His Word, not with the Jews themselves.

Such is the importance of Jerusalem, as we shall see, that it occupies the very center of a conflict between God and Satan for control of the entire universe. Anti-Semitism is not politics, nor is it religion. While it affects both, it is far more than either. It is a powerful satanic weapon in the battle between good and evil. While anti-Semitism is aimed directly at the Jews, it is designed to pervert the moral character of those who become its advocates—and ultimately to influence the eternal destiny of mankind.

If this explanation of the mystery of anti-Semitism seems melodramatic, we challenge the reader to provide some other rationale. Remember, anti-Semitism is only part of a package that includes the scattering of the Jews throughout the entire world, their preservation as an identifiable people in spite of repeated attempts at their extermination, their return to the promised land after 2500 years of dispersion, and the importance of Jerusalem for world peace out of all proportion to the miniscule size of that land of which it is the disputed capital. There is no central explanation for these phenomena except the unpopular one which the Bible presents.

[T]he world has had to hear a story it would have preferred not to hear—the story of how a cultured people turned to genocide, and how the rest of the world, also composed of cultured people, remained silent. . . . [W]e would much prefer to disbelieve, treating it as the product of a diseased mind, perhaps. And there are those today who—feeding on that wish, and on the anti-Semitism that lurks near the surface of the lives of even cultured people—are trying to persuade the world that the story is not true, urging us to treat it as the product of diseased minds, indeed.

—Robert McAfee Brown[1]

Never shall I forget that night, the first night in camp, which has turned my life into one long night. . . . Never shall I forget the little faces of the children, whose bodies I saw turned into wreaths of smoke beneath a silent blue sky. Never shall I forget those flames which consumed [my mother and little sister and] my Faith forever. Never shall I forget that nocturnal silence which deprived me, for all eternity, of the desire to live. Never shall I forget those moments which murdered God and my soul and turned my dreams to dust. Never shall I forget these things. . . . The student of the Talmud, the child that I was, had been consumed in the flames. There remained only a shape that looked like me. A dark flame had entered into my soul and devoured it.

—Elie Wiesel[2]

10

The "Final Solution"

◆

The immensity of the Holocaust's horror cannot be communicated through mere statistics, overwhelming as they are. Yes, the awesome fact that about 6 million of the approximately 8 million Jews in Europe in 1941 were systematically murdered is horrifying enough. That this greatest act of genocide in human history resulted from the efficient execution of a carefully laid plan by perhaps the best-educated and most culturally advanced civilization the world had seen to that date raises the level of repugnance beyond one's capacity for feeling. But to gain a clearer understanding of what has been called the greatest of crimes in human history, one needs to look behind the grim statistics and the cold-blooded efficiency with which it was planned and carried out by a relatively few Nazi leaders.

It is only within the context of the widespread anti-Semitism which had been practiced for centuries (to which we have referred briefly in earlier chapters) and the acquiescence (sometimes silent, sometimes enthusiastic) of a multitude of solid German citizens that one begins to comprehend the resident evil which found its full expression through Adolf Hitler. The methodical extermination of a race is far more horrible when it is seen as an act of cultured European society rather than the obsession of one madman. And that was indeed the case, despite the popularly held misconception of Hitler and his cohorts as the sole instigators and perpetrators.

The Cautious Approach

In fact, Hitler "proceeded quite cautiously, as if testing whether his passion for persecuting Jews would meet with any significant reprisal at home and abroad. He said as much to a meeting of party cell leaders on 29 April 1937, when he explained that he was biding his time on the Jewish question until he could resolve it without risk to himself:

> The final aim of our policy is crystal clear to all of us. All that concerns me is never to take a step that I might later have to retrace and never to take a step that could damage us in any way.
>
> You must understand that I always go as far as I dare and never further. It is vital to have a sixth sense that tells you, broadly, what you can do and what you cannot do.[3]

Harriett Chamberlain helped Lucille Eichengreen (born Cecilia Landau in Hamburg in 1925) write her story, *From Ashes to Life: My Memories of the Holocaust*. It was a life-changing experience. Chamberlain now admits: "Before researching and working through the painful, yet inspiring, realities of Cecelia's life, I could view the Holocaust as an anomaly, an erratic, irrational eruption of abhorrent group behavior. I now understand the Holocaust as the result of nationally determined government policies, rationally acted upon by ordinary individuals."

The organizational genius of the Nazi state reached into every facet of life. There was the National Socialist Student Association, which put university students into brown uniforms and had them singing crude party songs. Consider these astounding lines: "Sharpen the long knives on the pavements . . . when the hour of retribution strikes, we'll be ready for every sort of mass murder!" Teachers were required to belong to a National Socialist organization, as were lawyers and physicians and journalists to their appropriate groups as well. There were also, of course, the mass rallies designed to capture in mindless hysteria the emotions of a whole nation.

The posters were everywhere, depicting the handsome features of blond, blue-eyed Aryan youth and praising the wholesome lifestyle of the new order. Contrasted with those clean-cut faces were the caricatured likenesses of the hated Jew—dark-visaged, scowling, morally depraved, shrewd, calculating. National textbooks beginning with the lowest grades taught the schoolchildren the proper attitude toward the Jew. One typical page in a primary school textbook contrasted the proud, blond Aryan pictured there "who can work and fight," with an ugly, dark Jew, described as "the greatest scoundrel in the whole Reich." The instruction to the young minds was, "Trust no fox and no Jew!"

Reviving Old Hatreds

It must be emphasized again, however, that such ideas were not new. The Nazi regime was only reinforcing in a more systematic and general way a traditional anti-Semitism that had been fermenting in the European mindset for centuries. The only difference was that this nascent hatred of the "parasite Jew" would be given a bolder expression under a leader who was all but worshiped. Hitler, who would lead the Aryans in freeing Germany from the "Jewish yoke," was elevated to the level of a god. Consider the following dictation assignment from a Munich primary school in 1934:

> Just as Jesus saved people from sin and from Hell, Hitler saves the German "Volk" from ruin. Jesus and Hitler were persecuted, but while Jesus was crucified, Hitler was raised to the Chancellorship. While the disciples of Jesus denied their master and deserted Him, the sixteen comrades of Hitler died for their leader. The apostles completed the work of their lord. We hope that Hitler will be able to complete his work himself. Jesus built for heaven; Hitler for the German earth.[4]

The Germans didn't need to accept Hitler as a god, but they did so because it helped them meet an inner need for transcendence after the shame of Versailles. Worshiping Hitler elevated his followers to the Aryan superiority he promised them was theirs. That superiority would find its justifiable expression in demonstrating to the whole world the inferiority of the Jew. Once again, however, such thinking could not have swept up Germany in its power without centuries of preparation. And much of that preparation had come through the religious upbringing which a large percentage of the German people had in common. The same was true throughout Europe. Fifty years before Hitler came into power, *La Croix* boasted that it was "the most anti-Jewish Catholic paper in France" and condemned "the Jewish enemy betraying France."[5] With this atmosphere so well-established and of such duration, wouldn't there be an outpouring of gratitude among the French for the Nazi extermination of her 80,000 Jews?

Far from standing up against Hitler's evil, the Roman Catholic Church, the dominant spiritual force in Germany at the time, supported it. Curate Roth, who became an official in the Nazi Ministry of Ecclesiastical Affairs, called the Jews "a morally inferior race who would have to be eliminated from public life." Dr. Haeuser, in a book with the *imprimatur* of the diocese of Regensburg, called the Jews "Germany's cross, a people disowned by God and under their own curse [who] carried much of the blame for Germany having lost the [First World] War." A popular priest, Father Senn, called Hitler "the tool of God, called upon to overcome Judaism." Nazism, he said, provided "the last big opportunity to throw off the Jewish Yoke."[6] Another influential cleric, Father Franjo Kralik, stated enthusiastically in a Zagreb Catholic newspaper in 1941:

> The [Nazi] movement for freeing the world from the Jews is a movement for the renaissance of human dignity. The all-wise and Almighty God is behind this movement.[7]

With such a point of view presented by their religious leaders, there was good reason for the average German to participate willingly when Hitler began his moves against the Jews. For many Germans, conscience remained stronger than conditioning; but for the vast majority it was all too easy to ignore the inner voice, especially when given the encouragement to do so that was extended not only by religious but by civic leaders as well. After all, the Jews had been publicly maligned and mistreated for centuries all over Europe.

The General Public's Involvement

So long as the Holocaust is seen as the isolated, demented act of Adolf Hitler and his few henchmen, its loathsomeness is not fully realized. Nor is it comprehended in terms of the Germanic penchant for following orders, nor excused by the necessity to do so in wartime. One needs to confront the extent of the willing and even enthusiastic cooperation of the average citizen in Germany, Poland, Hungary, and other countries having a significant Jewish population. Far from catching Europe by surprise, the Holocaust was in actual fact the culmination of centuries of anti-Semitism without which this "Final Solution" would not have been possible.

Attempts have been made to excuse the citizens of those countries where the Holocaust took place on the grounds that they were ignorant of what was happening. If we are only speaking of the actual manner of death in cattle cars transporting the Jews to the camps, or in the extermination camps themselves, then it is true that there was much ignorance. Of course, the distinctive smell of burning flesh was carried by the wind to those living nearby and word of what was really occurring spread rapidly. It didn't take much thought to make the connection between those smoking chimneys and the Jews who were being rounded up and "relocated."

Rudolph Hoess, the commandant of Auschwitz, should know. He wrote in his autobiography, "When a strong wind was blowing, the stench of burning flesh was carried for many miles and caused the whole neighborhood to talk about the burning of the Jews."[8] Nevertheless, for those not so close to the camps, less than direct knowledge could always be dismissed as originating from "unreliable rumors." There is no excuse, however, for the undeniable direct involvement on the part of the vast majority of the German people and others in the many vital steps which led to the ultimate destruction of 6 million Jews.

Remember, Hitler did not pull the Jews out of their homes and shove them into the ovens in one sudden move. The participation of ordinary citizens was required during years of preparation as the new anti-Jewish laws were put into effect and which gradually tightened the noose around the necks of the intended victims. Here again was irresistible justification in the form of civil ordinances which citizens must obey and which the police and highest courts enforced. Who was to object except those few who, because of a tender conscience, were themselves willing to share the Jews' fate rather than participate in their destruction? The vast majority of good German folk obediently performed to Hitler's satisfaction. In the brutal anti-Semitic behavior of millions of Germans, Hitler received all the help he needed to bring his plan to its successful conclusion.

Past Persecutions

From Russia to Spain and Portugal, from Scandinavia to the toe of Italy's boot, Europe was no stranger to anti-Semitism. Martin Luther had declared that the Jews' synagogues should be burned down and their homes destroyed, and that the Jews themselves should be put to the most menial labor, deprived of their property, and, if need be, driven from the country.[9] Many of the popes had treated the Jews in the same manner: confiscating their property, including even their Scriptures, shutting down their synagogues, confining them to ghettos, and making them wear an identifying badge.

As we have already pointed out, the Roman Catholic Church had intermittently been in the Jewish genocide business for centuries. Inasmuch as that Church had dominated Europe for

1500 years, an anti-Semitic mentality was widespread among the people. One eminent author, Martin Gilbert, reminds us in his monumental work of the background which made the Holocaust possible:

> Even [in the nineteenth century] when Jews were allowed growing participation in national life, no decade passed without Jews in one European state or another being accused of murdering Christian children, in order to use their blood in the baking of Passover bread. The "blood libel," coming as it did with outbursts of popular violence against Jews, reflected deep prejudices which no amount of modernity or liberal education seemed able to overcome. Jew-hatred, with its two-thousand-year-old history, could arise both as a spontaneous outburst of popular instincts, and as a deliberately fanned instrument of scapegoat politics. . . .
>
> Even as the First World War ended on the western front, more than fifty Jews were killed by local Ukrainians in the eastern Polish city of Lvov. In the then independent Ukrainian town of Proskurov, seventeen hundred Jews were murdered on 15 February 1919 by followers of the Ukrainian nationalist leader, Simon Petlura, and by the end of the year, Petlura's gangs had killed at least sixty thousand Jews.
>
> These Jews were victims of local hatreds reminiscent of Tsarist days, but on a scale unheard of in the previous century. In the city of Vilna, the "Jerusalem of Lithuania," eighty Jews were murdered during April 1919; in Galicia, five hundred perished.
>
> "Terrible news is reaching us from Poland," the Zionist leader Chaim Weizmann wrote to a friend on 29 November 1918. "The newly liberated Poles there are trying to get rid of the Jews by the old and familiar method which they learnt from the Russians [i.e. murder]. Heart-rending cries are reaching us. We are doing all we can, but we are so weak!"[10]

Instances without number of the persecution and murder of Jews all over Europe, such as the massacres in the Ukraine in

1918 and 1919, proved that Hitler was neither the inventor of anti-Semitism nor the first to set about to exterminate God's chosen people. The only difference was that through the conquests of the German army Hitler gained control over most of Europe and even deep into Russia. Thus he was able to arouse and organize and put to work a universal and innate anti-Semitism and thereby effect on a grand scale what had for so long been confined to isolated outbreaks in widely scattered localities. Hitler simply intended to finish the job of doing away with the Jews systematically and efficiently, a job which the citizenry of Europe had been sporadically engaged in for centuries without sufficient determination and coordination to carry it to a conclusion.

Furthermore, for this monumental task, Hitler expected Europe's gratitude. Generations to come would remember him as the genius who had effected a "Final Solution to the Jewish Problem." As Gilbert has pointed out:

> The preparations for mass murder were made possible by Germany's military successes in the months following the invasion of Poland in 1939. But from the moment that Adolf Hitler had come to power in Germany in 1933, the devastating process had begun. It was a process which depended upon the rousing of historic hatreds and ancient prejudice. . . .[11]

Europe was ripe for this new adventure, ready to free itself from the Jewish burden once and for all. Hitler proved that fact by involving the ordinary citizens, step by step, in the escalating persecution and, finally, in the elimination of all Jews everywhere in the countries under his heel. It was a shrewd exploitation of that universal hatred of Jews which he knew was resident just below the surface in almost every person.

Public Knowledge and Cooperation

The first tiny step began as early as 1920 with the publication of the embryonic Nazi Party's 25-point program. It had several anti-Semitic clauses, among them the demand that all

Jews who had come to Germany since 1914 must leave. Hitler's speeches often focused on the need to break free from the power of the Jews. These diatribes were sprinkled with such slogans as "Anti-Semites of the world, unite! People of Europe, free yourselves!" Such speeches found a ready audience.

Hitler's manifesto, *Mein Kampf*, published in 1925, was filled with anti-Jewish rhetoric and should have left no doubt in anyone's mind concerning his plans once he came to power. Far from hiding his intentions, he openly declared them for all the world to read. Yet there was no outcry from decent German citizens that such hatred, humiliation, and mistreatment of any race or individual was unbecoming of civilized people. Nor was there much of an outcry from other "civilized" nations.

Upon coming to power, Hitler moved swiftly to put his plan into action and to involve the German people in its execution. On April 7, 1933, came the forcible "retirement" of all non-Aryans. Some Germans were shocked, but no general opposition was voiced. Almost no one came to the defense of Jewish friends and neighbors. Most Germans seemed happy to be identified as "Aryans" of superior lineage and to take over the important jobs vacated by Jews. In fact, "German cities competed in zealous pursuit of the new 'Aryan' ideal.

"In Frankfurt, on the day of this first 'Aryan law,' German Jewish teachers were forbidden to teach in the universities, German Jewish actors to perform on the stage, and German Jewish musicians to play in concerts. . . . On April 13 . . . at Berlin University, notices appeared . . . 'Our most dangerous opponent is the Jew. . . .' Expulsion of Jews from the universities was rapid and total [including even Nobel prize winners]. Albert Einstein was forced into exile."[12] Germany had responded positively to the first step and Hitler's diabolical plan was assured of success.

Concentration camps were set up for those who failed to comply with the new orders. There were relatively few Germans, however, who opposed the now-official anti-Semitism. Jews were being beaten, mutilated, and killed throughout

Germany. Notices began to appear "on thousands of cafes, sports stadiums, shops, and roads leading to towns and villages: 'Jews not wanted.' "[13] No German court found the laws objectionable or a violation of basic decency that was owed to every human being.

Tightening the Noose

The next phase was a more widespread humiliation by public beatings and destruction of property. Everywhere Jewish homes, businesses, and synagogues were forcibly entered and furnishings and valuables thrown into the street and destroyed. In this methodical manner Jews were openly and brutally driven from village after village, creating what became known as "Jew-free" towns. What had happened throughout history in isolated villages was now being pursued with calculated deliberation everywhere. Some Germans were shocked, but most realized the benefits to themselves and were caught up in what became a national fervor. Even the medieval myth of Jews sucking the blood of Christian children and of their ritual murder was revived all over Germany.

Many Jews fled to Palestine to begin life anew in the land of their forebears and amid Arab neighbors. Radio broadcasts from Germany pursued the refugees even there. Beamed into the Middle East, the frenzied voices incited Arabs to riot against the Jews and to follow the example of Germany by making Palestine "Jew-free" once again.

On September 15, 1935, Hitler signed the "Nuremburg Laws." Anti-Semitism was now the official way of life throughout Germany. Jews could no longer be citizens and were forbidden to fly the German flag. Marriages of Jews to Aryans were forbidden. Germany was being purged of all Jews and Jewish influence. A Jewish doctor who had given a transfusion of his own blood to save a patient's life was sentenced to a concentration camp for "race defilement." Anti-Jewish riots were now springing up across Germany and spilling over into neighboring countries. In despair, Jews began committing suicide in ever-increasing numbers, while tens of thousands fled to other countries, many to Poland and Hungary. The refuge they found there would prove to be temporary. It was now only a matter of time until the end of European Jewry (except for a few thousand survivors) would be an accomplished fact.

Worldwide Guilt

Events in Germany were not hidden from the rest of the world. Eyewitness accounts of the increasing horror being meted out to Jews throughout Germany as well as the growing number of riots against them in neighboring countries were carried in the world's media. In July of 1938 an international conference was held in Evian, France, to discuss the problems posed by the growing numbers of Jews desperately trying to escape Germany. In the face of a shameful rising need, the level of international sympathy was dropping. The whole world would have to bear its share of the guilt for the Holocaust. The heartlessness of other nations in the face of the impending extermination of European Jewry is without excuse. Here was one Australian official's explanation for his country's rejection of Jewish refugees:

> It will no doubt be appreciated that as we have no
> racial problem, we are not desirous of importing one.[14]

As the number of Jews wishing to emigrate from Germany grew, "the restrictions against them also grew: Britain, Palestine and the United States each tightened their rules for admission. Four South American countries, Argentine, Chile, Uruguay and Mexico, adopted laws severely restricting the number of Jews who could enter, in the case of Mexico to a hundred a year."[15] Entrance restrictions were tightened in Australia and Scandinavia. Refugees were cruelly turned back to certain destruction even at the border of Switzerland, headquarters for the International Red Cross. Those who managed to escape into such countries were caught by the Swiss, the Dutch, or the French police, arrested, and sent back across the borders into Germany to be consumed by Hitler's efficient engine of death.

Those fortunate few thousands of German Jews who had been able to emigrate before the regulations had been tightened spent their first anxious months and years of freedom in the United States, England, Australia, Mexico, and other countries, trying desperately to obtain visas for their relatives still in Germany. They found themselves confronting an ever-growing barrier of unreasonable rules and restrictions deliberately designed to make it almost impossible for additional Jews to immigrate. The flow of refugees was cut to a trickle, leaving hundreds of thousands who were seeking escape to be shipped to the East and eliminated at last.

Nor did the world at large share Germany's guilt in the Holocaust only by the subtle means of hidden regulations. There were so many incidents, well-publicized at the time, of deliberately turning refugees back to destruction that pretended innocence is in itself a crime. Who can forget the ocean liner *St. Louis*? Its 1128 German Jewish refugees had set out with high hopes of finding a haven in any number of countries. Instead, they were turned away at port after port in North, Central, and South America and forced back across the Atlantic! Yes, the United States and its President, Franklin D. Roosevelt, refused to receive them, even though 700 had valid papers for entering the USA, but in the near future. Other than the 288 admitted by Britain, few of the remainder escaped Hitler's ovens.

In multiplied similar incidents fathers, mothers, children, husbands, and wives hoped, wept, pleaded, and died needlessly. Typical of these innumerable tragedies is the following:

> On August 17 [1938], fifty-three Austrian Jews reached Helsinki by sea. They were refused permission to disembark, and the boat which had brought them was ordered [back] to Germany. Several of the passengers had the necessary papers to enter the United States, and sought only transit rights through Finland. But no exceptions were made to the new policy.
>
> A pregnant Jewess, who was about to have her baby, was allowed to leave the ship and go to a hospital, but

after the birth, the mother and child had to rejoin the other passengers. On the way back to Germany . . . three of the rejected refugees threw themselves overboard and were drowned.[16]

Accelerating Public Involvement

The night of November 9-10, 1938, thereafter remembered as *Kristallnacht* or the "Night of the Broken Glass," marked a terrifying intensification of Hitler's pogrom along the road to the planned extermination of the Jews. In Germany, Austria, and the Sudetenland about 1300 synagogues were vandalized (of which about 270 were burned down or demolished), and about 10,000 homes, businesses, and offices owned by Jews were robbed and wrecked. More than 90 Jews were murdered in cold blood, about 30,000 were arrested for no other reason but their Jewishness, and thousands of the latter later died in the extermination camps.

A secret report by the Nazi Party's chief judge, Walther Buch, explained that those who murdered Jews could not be punished because they were simply carrying out orders. Those who raped Jews, however, were "expelled from the party and turned over to civil courts"—not for rape, but for having "violated the Nuremberg racial laws which forbade sexual intercourse between Gentiles and Jews."[17]

No longer could the murder of Jews and the plunder of their goods be blamed on a few rowdy Brown Shirts. Now all the world had seen the horror of a pogrom planned and directed by governments themselves. It was, as Hitler had planned and we now know, only the beginning of the systematic "final solution to the Jewish problem" which would eventually see the murder of more than 6,000,000 Jews.

Those who had a conscience appealed to the only moral authority which they thought might intervene. In *Min Hameitzar*, Rabbi Weissmandl tells how the civil government of Slovakia appealed to the Vatican to stop the shipments of Jews to the death camps. The Vatican replied that Jews who had converted to Christianity (i.e. Catholicism) were not to be shipped, and as for the rest, families should not be broken up in shipment. In other words, ship them out unless they convert to Catholicism, but ship entire families together!

That the Catholic Church, from the Vatican on down, knew what was happening has been documented in many places so need not be repeated here. When the Jews still thought that expulsion merely meant relocation, a Slovakian archbishop retorted: "This is not just expulsion . . . they will slaughter all of you together . . . and this is the punishment you deserve for the death of our Redeemer. You have only one hope: Convert to our religion, and then I will act to have the decree canceled." Weissmandl gives a further horrifying example of an appeal to the papal nuncio in Slovakia to prevent the slaughter of innocent Jewish lives. The nuncio retorted, "There is no such thing as the blood of innocent Jewish children! All Jewish blood is guilty, and they must die. This is the punishment that awaits them for that sin."[18]

A Truth Too Horrible to Face

The first move of the Nazis to exterminate the Jews in Hungary came when they expelled all foreign Jews. Elie Wiesel's cabbala instructor, "Moshe the Beadle," was a foreigner and was among those who left the village of Sighet crammed into cattle cars. Everyone wanted to believe that the deportees had simply been taken to another area to do work helpful to the war effort. With that comforting assumption, they were soon forgotten—until one day Moshe returned. He had a gun wound in his leg and told a wild tale of the deportees having to dig their own graves in the forest of Galicia, near Kolomaye, of babies thrown into the air as targets and machine-gunned, of everyone else being shot and dumped in the mass grave. He was the lone survivor through a miraculous escape. No one wanted to believe the truth. Elie Wiesel writes:

> Through long days and nights, he went from one Jewish house to another, telling the story of Malka, the young girl who had taken three days to die, and of To-

bias, the tailor, who had begged to be killed before his sons. . . .

Moshe had changed. There was no longer any joy in his eyes. He no longer sang. He no longer talked to me of God or of the cabbala, but only of what he had seen. People refused not only to believe his stories, but even to listen to them.

"He's just trying to make us pity him. What an imagination he has!" they said. Or even: "Poor fellow. He's gone mad."

As for Moshe, he wept.

"Jews, listen to me. It's all I ask of you. I don't want money or pity. Only listen to me," he would cry between prayers at dusk and the evening prayers.

I did not believe him myself. . . .

That was toward the end of 1942. . . . At that time it was still possible to obtain emigration permits for Palestine. I had asked my father to sell out, liquidate his business, and leave.

"I'm too old, my son," he replied. "I'm too old to start a new life . . . from scratch again in a country so far away. . . ."[19]

For some it is equally difficult to face the truth even in our own day. Such booklets as *The Truth of Auschwitz* attempt to deny the Holocaust. Its author, Thies Christophersen, claims to have been a German soldier on duty at Auschwitz during the entire year of 1944 and writes, "After the war I heard about the alleged mass murders of Jews . . . I know such atrocities were never committed."[20] Another book, *The Auschwitz Myth*, is by Wilhelm Staglich, a Doctor of Jurisprudence, who after the war served 20 years as a judge in Hamburg. He claims to have been an officer with the 12th Paratroop-Anti-aircraft Battery "stationed in the vicinity of Auschwitz [in 1944] for the protection of industrial plants employing inmates of the camp." He made a number of visits to the camp and he too claims to have observed no indication that the inmates were in fear or were mistreated and denies the presence of any gas chambers or crematoria.[21]

188 ♦ THE "FINAL SOLUTION"

Fact or Fable?

The Christian News, an evangelical Lutheran newspaper, has repeatedly published accounts that purport to prove the Holocaust a myth. The paper has requested (again as recently as January 1995) a response from anyone able to disprove such accounts as those of Christophersen and Staglich and claims to have received no refutations.[22] Perhaps those with such evidence consider it futile to offer it to those whose minds must be closed to maintain such a posture in the face of the mountains of evidence available. A visit to *Yad Vashem* in Jerusalem or the newer Holocaust Museum in Washington D.C. should satisfy any honest person seeking the facts. Or there are scores of books, such as *The Holocaust*, by Martin Gilbert, whose 828 pages of testimony are backed by another 66 pages of "Notes and Sources." One of the newest books, written since the opening of Eastern Europe made previously secret archives available for study, is titled *Anatomy of the Auschwitz Death Camp* and contains the documentation of a number of researchers.[23]

Of course, there were thousands of survivors of the Holocaust whose eyewitness accounts tell the story. Unfortunately, these witnesses are slowly dying and soon none of them will be left to remind us. In June of 1981, more than 6000 Holocaust survivors from around the world gathered in Jerusalem "to seek long-lost friends, and to make one last desperate search for relatives who might, possibly, have survived."[24] Over 3000 survivors of Auschwitz itself gathered together on January 22, 1995, at ceremonies commemorating the fiftieth anniversary of its liberation.[25] Most of them had never met one another, yet their independent testimonies tell the same story.

If need be, however, there are numerous non-Jewish witnesses of the Holocaust. The mistake of Christophersen and Staglich is apparently a sincere one and is easily explained. During the time they were there, neither gas chamber nor crematorium existed in Auschwitz itself but in nearby Birkenau. Consider the testimony (hundreds of others could be cited) recorded in the diary of another German, Dr. Johan

Kremer, brought to Auschwitz as a physician: "Was present for the first time at a special action at 3 A.M. By comparison, Dante's inferno seems almost a comedy. Auschwitz is justly called an extermination camp!" Questioned after the war, Dr. Kremer testified:

> These mass murders [in 1942] took place in small cottages situated outside the Birkenau camp in a wood. The cottages were called "bunkers" in the SS men's slang. All SS physicians on duty in the camp took turns to participate in the gassings, which were called *Sonderaction*, "special action." My part as physician at the gassing consisted in remaining in readiness near the bunker . . . in case any [of the SS men] should succumb to the poisonous fumes.
>
> When the transport with people who were destined to be gassed arrived at the railway ramp, the SS officers selected, from among the new arrivals, persons fit to work, while the rest—old people, all children, women with children in their arms and other persons not deemed fit to work—were loaded onto lorries and driven to the gas-chambers.
>
> I used to follow behind the transport till we reached the bunker. There people were first driven into the barrack huts where the victims undressed and then went naked to the gas-chambers . . . the SS men kept people quiet, maintaining that they were to bathe and be deloused.[26]

Facing the Awful Truth Today

It is not only the past, however, that many find difficult to face, but the present as well. That fact is clear in the numerous statements by Catholic Church leaders and government officials around the world hypocritically denouncing the Holocaust in the past while at the same time closing their eyes to the same anti-Semitism in the world today. Observing the fiftieth anniversary of the liberation of Auschwitz-Birkenau, where between 1.1 and 1.5 million prisoners perished, 90 percent of them Jews, Pope John Paul II declared:

> Never again anti-Semitism. Never again the ar-
> rogance of nationalism. Never again genocide. [The
> Holocaust] was one of the darkest and most tragic hours
> of our history . . . a darkening of reason, of conscience,
> of the heart [especially for] the Jewish people, for whom
> the Nazi regime had planned a systematic extermina-
> tion. . . .[27]

Those are fine words, but they are hollow without the
necessary acknowledgment of his Church's anti-Semitism, its
slaughter of Jews through the centuries, and the supporting
role it played in the Holocaust. There is also a denial in those
words of the present reality. The same spirit that drove Hitler
to genocide is alive today and is represented in such documents
as the PLO Charter, which continues to call for the extermination of Israel. Yet the Pope receives Arafat at the Vatican as a
statesman. When Kaddafi screams, "The battle with Israel
must be such that after it Israel will cease to exist!" he cannot
be dismissed as an isolated fanatic. Such Hitlerian threats pour
continuously from the mouths of Muslim religious and political leaders over radios and loudspeakers and TV in every Arab
country. They are taught in the mosques and underly the
religion of Islam.

If the Pope really means "never again," why doesn't he
rebuke such obvious anti-Semitism instead of encouraging it
by the Vatican's friendship with Arafat? The Holocaust is not
an event in the distant past to remind us of a mentality which
we have now outlived. Its evil spirit is alive and active today,
and yet, as in Hitler's time, all too few people are willing to
face the facts.

If Germany today made the statements about annihilating
Jews that Arabs regularly make, the world would rise up in
condemnation. Yet the venom of annihilation directed continuously at Israel by Arabs is acceptable because of the specious
claim that Israel has been the aggressor in its conflicts with its
neighbors. A safe haven from the rising anti-Semitism worldwide is needed today as it was in Hitler's day; and as then, so
now, that safe haven is being refused to the Jews who need it.

The whole world is demanding a halt to construction of Jewish housing in what it calls "the occupied territories." Then where are Jewish refugees to be housed? Isn't it cause for concern that Vladimir Zhirinovsky, who openly declares, "I'll act as Hitler did," captured 25 percent of the Russian vote?

History Being Repeated

In Slovakia, the popular weekly *Zmena* declares that "the Jews manipulated the lie of the Holocaust to get their own state, Israel, and that Holocaust chronicler Elie Wiesel received the Nobel Prize for 'the biggest lie of the century,' " and blames Communism on Jews. A recent survey in Slovakia showed that anti-Semitism is strongest among the Catholics, who make up about 65 percent of the population. A drive is underway by his open admirers to rehabilitate Catholic priest Fr. Jozef Tiso, ruler of Slovakia's Nazi puppet regime of 1939-45, which sent that tiny country's Jewish population of 70,000 to the extermination camps in Poland. With the desecration of Jewish cemeteries and the resurgence of its Fascist past, the outlook for Slovakia's 3000 Jews is not good.[28] Is Israel to be closed to them?

Saddam Hussein's ravings against Israel are no less pointed than Hitler's against the Jews. Yet he is the great hero of the Muslim masses because of his promise to "destroy Israel" and to "liberate Palestine." Even *after* Kuwait's rape, Jordan's King Hussein said that "to the majority of the Arab world [Saddam] is a patriotic man who... [treats] others on the basis of mutual respect." Evil becomes good when dedicated to the "just cause" of Jewish extermination! So it was in Hitler's day and so it is today, and the world remains as unsympathetic to current problems as it did then. A *Jerusalem Post* columnist writes with all-too-accurate insight:

> Needless to say, the 50-years-later sympathy for Holocaust victims does not extend to endangered Jews today, particularly if they happen to be Israelis.
> The most recent massacre was a case in point. Expressing little sympathy for Israel, most papers' editorials

were devoted to sanctimonious lectures on why "the pressure for peace needs to be maintained and not slowed down," as *The Guardian*, tonesetter for the politically correct, put it on January 23 [1995] . . . mak[ing] it clear why the [Beit Lid] massacre was particularly objectionable: such terrorist attacks made it "harder to meet legitimate Palestinian expectations, without which the process is doomed."

An even more offensive editorial appeared in *The Washington Post* on the same day [blaming the attack upon] Israeli settlement activity. . . .[29]

Once again the Jew is made the scapegoat, blamed for the world's troubles. It is the intransigence of Israel that is holding up the peace process in the Middle East. It is her desire for more land than she deserves that stands in the way of peace. Forgotten is the need for that land, the same need as in Hitler's day, to provide a safe haven for Jews to escape the escalating anti-Semitism around the world. But this desperate need is declared to be illegitimate and, as in the past, a limit is being imposed upon the numbers of immigrants allowed into Israel.

How amazing that the world is still confronted with the need for a final solution to the Jewish problem! Various alternatives are being attempted. We have no doubt that a temporary "peace" will be achieved, for that is what the Bible declares, as we shall see. Eventually, however, under Antichrist, there will seem to be no other route than the one which Hitler took. That kind of "final solution" will be put into effect in a desperate move to achieve a lasting world peace.

What we are saying is not sensationalism; we are simply repeating what the Bible says. The same prophets who with 100 percent accuracy declared what would happen to Israel to this point in history are the ones who also tell us what is yet to come. The world will either believe their word, which is the Word of God, and conduct itself accordingly, or suffer the horrible consequences. Israel, too, must heed her prophets.

The mosque is often the starting place for demonstration and political revolution, and the Friday sermon is not only a religious practice but it often fervently calls upon the faithful to take political action in the name of Allah.

—Abd-al-Masih, Islamic scholar[1]

. . . slay the idolaters [those who do not worship Allah] wherever ye find them, and take them (captive), and besiege them, and prepare for them each ambush. But if they repent and establish worship [i.e. convert to Islam] and pay the poor-due, then leave their way free. Lo! Allah is Forgiving, Merciful [to Muslims].

—Surah 9:5

Fight in the way of Allah against those who fight against you, but begin not hostilities. Lo! Allah loveth not aggressors. And slay them wherever ye find them, and drive them out of the places whence they drove you out. . . . But if they desist, then lo! Allah is forgiving, Merciful.

—Surah 2:190-92

Fight against such of those who have been given the Scripture as believe not in Allah nor the Last Day. . . . Go forth, light-armed and heavy-armed, and strive with your wealth and your lives in the way of Allah!

—Surah 9:29,41

Those who believe do battle for the cause of Allah; and those who disbelieve do battle for the cause of idols. So fight the minions of the devil.

—Surah 4:76

11

Islam and Terrorism

◆

One of the most intensive international manhunts ever conducted culminated on February 7, 1995, when Pakistani and American agents burst into Room 16 of Islamabad's Su-Casa guest house and surprised Ramzi Ahmed Yousef on his bed, whisking him away before he could offer any resistance. The young fugitive, in his late twenties, for whom the U.S. State Department was offering a 2-million-dollar reward, had evaded a worldwide dragnet for almost two years. Hands and feet tied and eyes blindfolded, he was hustled out of Pakistan and within a few hours was locked up in a secure wing of New York's Metropolitan Correction Center, charged with being the evil genius behind the February 26, 1993, bombing of the World Trade Center that killed six people and wounded more than a thousand. It is suspected that he had the connections and financial backing of at least one country, and his arrest may lead to other highly placed individuals involved in terrorism worldwide.[2]

In spite of bomb-making chemicals and a suitcase of explosives hidden in toy cars discovered in his room in the Holiday Inn in Islamabad, Yousef pleaded innocent when arraigned in Federal Court in New York on February 9. American officials

say, however, that they have evidence that he not only master-
minded the Trade Center bombing but that he "was planning
attacks on other U.S. targets worldwide, including the embassy in Pakistan, and diplomats and airlines in the Philippines." Pakistani officials claim that Yousef admitted to them
his involvement in the Trade Center blast. It is also reported
that he has implicated Iraq as the power that ordered the
bombing. Yousef had fled the United States the very night of
the Trade Center blast.[3]

According to Federal prosecutors:

> Bombing the World Trade Center. Gunning down a
> radical rabbi. Plots to blow up U.N. headquarters and
> assassinate Egypt's president at a Park Avenue hotel. All
> were parts of a conspiracy . . . to wage *holy war* against
> the U.S. government—proof that Mideast terror had
> taken root in America. At least since 1989 . . . a radical
> *Islamic group* has targeted the United States as an *infidel*
> government supporting other *infidels* such as Egypt and
> Israel. . . .[4] (Emphasis added.)

The "Holy" Role of Islam

Notice the words which we have italicized: *holy war, Islamic
group, infidel,* and *infidels.* Islam is fighting a *holy war* for
control of the world! That war was begun by Mohammed
himself in the seventh century and is still carried on today by
his faithful followers through terrorism. The terrorists are not
radicals or *extremists,* as the media continually labels them.
Instead, these are Islamic *fundamentalists* who are true to their
religion and the teachings of the Koran and who follow faithfully in the footsteps of their great Prophet, Mohammed. As
one former Muslim and Islamic scholar has said:

> We must never imagine that such Muslims are being
> unnecessarily wicked. They are simply being faithful to
> their religion. The fact is never hidden as to the attitude a
> good Muslim should have towards Christians and Jews.
> In fact, much of the incitement to violence and war in the

whole of the Quran is directed against the Jews and Christians who rejected what they felt to be the strange god Mohammed was trying to preach.[5]

The prosecution of those connected with the World Trade Center bombing still continues more than two years after that infamous act in the same courtroom where already four men have been sentenced to life in prison without parole for their part in it.[6] The 12 additional defendants are charged with seditious conspiracy in an alleged larger plot to blow up not only the World Trade Center but also the United Nations building, the New York FBI headquarters, and two tunnels and a bridge, as well as to assassinate Egyptian President Hosni Mubarak and a number of other political figures.[7]

Sheik Omar Abdel Rahman, a blind Muslim cleric, has been charged with being the spiritual leader in the alleged conspiracy. Former Attorney General Ramsey Clark is part of the team of legal experts defending Rahman. Of his client, Clark said, "I think he's being prosecuted for the exercising of his religious views and faith."[8] Apparently Clark doesn't realize that his client's "religious views and faith" advocate mayhem and murder in order to spread Islam. Religion cannot justify the murder of those who do not accept it, but that has been the practice throughout Islam's bloody history.

Some of the defendants in the terrorism conspiracy trial accused of obeying Rahman's religious directives in executing their evil plans had been under surveillance by the FBI as long ago as 1989. At that early date law-enforcement officials had photographed two of the currently accused men engaging in target practice on Long Island with three of the men who have already been convicted in the World Trade Center bombing. The government thereby established a long-standing relationship between the parties in building its case that a "jihad organization" existed, headed by Abdel Rahman, which "aimed at waging 'a [holy] war of urban terrorism against the United States' by plotting to blow up buildings, tunnels and bridges in the New York metropolitan area."[9]

In a startling development, one of the defendants, Siddig Ibrahim Siddig Ali, the alleged chief conspirator, changed his plea from not guilty to guilty and presented to the court a detailed confession. The broader conspiracy's plans for "holy war" also included numerous assassinations. The results of the plot were to have been destructive and terrifying beyond anything "this world has ever seen."[10] Ali's confession implicated his fellow defendants, including Sheik Omar Abdel-Rahman. According to Ali, the plot was to have shown Americans that "we can get you anytime!"[11]

A Schizophrenic Denial

Arabs themselves are often the targets of Islamic terrorism. As we have noted, there is not a democracy among the 21 Arab governments in the world. Yet these dictatorial Arab regimes, while professing allegiance to Islam, all fear a takeover by the even more oppressive Islamic fundamentalists. Early in February 1995, the Algerian government removed leaders of the militant Islamic Salvation Front from house arrest and put them back into prison. A deadly war of terror is being waged against that government by the Islamic opposition—a war in which 30,000 people have been killed (most of them Algerians, but many foreigners as well) since January 1992. An authority on the Middle East writes:

> Today there is not a government in the Arab world, including Saudi Arabia's ultrareligious one, that does not fear militant Islam as the major challenge to its stability.[12]

In a schizophrenic attempt to deny the truth, many Muslims, especially those in civil leadership, insist that Islam is a peaceful religion. Yet the terrorism directed at Arab nations in order to pressure them to adopt Islamic law is in complete agreement with the tactics that Mohammed himself employed to enforce obedience to the Koran. At a three-day global summit in Casablanca, Morocco, early in 1995, Muslim leaders, while calling for "Islamic unity," also vowed to stick together in order to resist what they called "religious fanaticism." The 52-member Organization of Islamic Conference condemned terrorism against its members and at the same time warned of a "ferocious campaign to tarnish Islam."[13]

Tarnish Islam? In fact, it is Islam which inspires a large part of terrorism worldwide. As we have seen, violence and terrorism have been the means of spreading Islam from the very beginning by Mohammed and his successors. That is the teaching of the Koran. The teachings of Islam, in fact, inspire Arab terrorism around the world, terrorism which is directed by such Islamic groups as the Palestinian Liberation Organization (PLO), Hamas, Islamic Jihad, Hizbullah, and others.

The bombings and murders come from a sincere religious motivation: the destruction of Israel and eventual subjugation of the entire world to Islamic law. And yet, somehow, it is all blamed upon Israel. It is her fault that she is the target of terrorist attack and thus that those friendly to her suffer the same onslaught. As George Will put it in his syndicated column:

> The "blame Israel first (and last, and in between)" brigade is large and growing, here and abroad. . . . Today it is especially apparent that Israel is the all-purpose but implausible alibi for the various pathologies that convulse many Arab nations and the [strained] relations between them.

Terrorism and Double Cross

Yasser Arafat's PLO, backed to the hilt with Arab oil money and with the blessing of Islamic religious leaders, has been the best-known of the Arab terrorist organizations and at the forefront of worldwide terrorism for many years. Who can forget the ferocious faces by which the world came to know the Palestinians as terrorists, "the black-hooded murderers at the Munich Olympics, the hijackers of Entebbe, the killers of the *Achille Lauro*"?[14] David Lamb writes concerning Yasser Arafat's al-Fatah, which took over the PLO after the 1967 war:

> The vehicle they [Arafat and al-Fatah] chose to carry their case to the world was terrorism, and at that they became real pros. Their hijackings and killings earned headlines around the globe, and soon no one asked anymore who the Palestinians were. Everyone knew. They were "terrorists." . . .
>
> The problem was that the P.L.O.'s platform was based upon . . . the destruction of Israel, a country universally admired in the West. The goal itself became obscured in the rhetoric and bloodshed of accomplishing [it]. . . .
>
> Under Arafat the P.L.O. became the world's best-known, best-armed, wealthiest guerrilla organization. Upward of $1 billion a year . . . swelled its treasury during the peak oil-rich years. . . . President Reagan characterized the entire organization as a "gang of thugs."[15]

And now that the PLO has, for tactical reasons, adopted the new stance of peaceful coexistence with Israel, it finds itself at odds with other Islamic terrorist groups. Westerners tend to think of the Arab world as united when in fact great divisions, animosities, suspicions, and centuries-old conflicts divide them. Even the fundamentalist movement is divided into some 200 or more independent groups which differ in their manner and methods of revolution and terror, a fact which greatly complicates the task of understanding and countering Islamic terrorism. Of course all of the groups are united in their hatred of Israel and their passion to establish Islamic rule everywhere.

The Islamic world is one of constant unrest, double crosses, uprisings, and wars. Arab leaders distrust one another and fight among themselves. Only Islam and the passion to destroy Israel unite them. Though friendly with Western nations, Saudi Arabia's fulminations against Israel have been no less extreme than those of Saddam Hussein or Yasser Arafat. Typical was the following from Saudi King Fahd: "The media must urge the Muslims to launch *Jihad* [Holy War] . . . united in the confrontation with the Jews and those who support them."[16]

Islamic fundamentalism is on the rise throughout the Middle East. It even reaches into the West, where Islam is the fastest-growing religion. Its mosques are being constructed in increasing numbers throughout Europe, Britain, and the United States. That fact has ominous implications for world-wide terrorism. A Middle East expert comments:

> In fact, during each of the three Ramadans I spent in the Middle East, there seemed to be a marked, progressive increase in the number of Arabs who unflinchingly abided by all the restrictions the Koran set forth for observing the holy month . . . even diplomats, professors and businessmen had fallen in with the pack—for public consumption, at least. And that movement toward complete religious obedience is, I think, the most significant trend in the Arab world today. The Middle East is becoming . . . in the process, less tolerant. . . .[17]

Even Arab governments which have supported Islamic terrorism can find themselves the target of aggression. Kuwait was the PLO's chief paymaster during its most destructive days. The PLO terrorists had vowed to "fight Israel" by killing civilians, including those of any nation friendly to Israel. After a number of diplomats, including a U.S. Ambassador, were assassinated, the Emir of Kuwait was asked whether he would continue to finance the PLO. He replied that he would indeed, "with unlimited funds."

How did the PLO repay Kuwait and Saudi Arabia for the billions of dollars they had given it in support of its terrorism over the years? By providing intelligence data to Iraq for its invasion of Kuwait on its way to take over Saudi Arabia. With Saddam Hussein's armies poised on Saudi Arabia's border, Arafat, confident that Iraq would be victorious, declared: "We say to the brother and leader Saddam Hussein, 'Go forward with Allah's blessing!' "

Promise of Paradise

Behold a brotherhood of murderers! What "god" could bless terrorism and the slaughter of innocents? Islamic terrorists believe they are following the instructions of, and have the blessings of, Allah. It is that faith which gives Islamic terror- ists such zeal and makes them willing even to sacrifice them- selves to the cause of worldwide Islamic conquest.

Indeed, the slaughter of innocents is an honorable Islamic practice. In its war against Iraq, the Islamic republic of Iran, under the direction of religious leaders, cleared minefields by using thousands of young schoolboys to walk along in front of troops and tanks. In one minefield alone, in 1982, about 5000 children were torn to bits exploding the mines so that the army could move across the cleared path.[18] Such fanatical sacrifice of life is considered to be the highest achievement in Islam. As the Ayatollah Khomeini explained, "The purest joy in Islam is to kill and be killed for God." Both options hold promise of paradise.

To the Western mind it is unthinkable that "God" should encourage such slaughter. To the Muslim, however, violence and bloodshed are the highest expression of religion and the sure way to eternal reward. No wonder, then, that in the United States far more is being spent on increased security measures to ward off terrorism than on all of the standard police forces.

That Islam offers those who die in Jihad assurance of para- dise encourages the most effective terrorists: suicide bombers. By concealing explosives on their own bodies and sacrificing themselves, these zealots for Islam present the most difficult kind of terrorism to detect and to stop. David Lamb reminds us of an incredible example which illustrates the vast gulf between Islamic and Judeo-Christian morals:

> When an Egyptian soldier named Suleiman Khater went berserk in the Sinai and killed five Israeli tourists, what did Iran do? It declared him a hero, named a street after him and set aside a day honoring him. . . .
>
> Fanatics in the Middle East regard terrorists as Spain does its matadors. They are young and glamorous and nationalistic and daring. They face death stoically, even seek out death . . . [for the] recognition [it brings]. The faces of [these] martyred [heroes] stare down at you from a thousand postered walls in Beirut and Tehran. . . .[19]

Islamic Jihad has been responsible for most of the suicide attacks upon Israel. It has been directed by Fathi Shkaki from Damascus since 1989. Interviewed after the January 19, 1995, Beit Lid suicide bombing that killed 21 people, Shkaki expressed his pleasure at its successful completion. He was especially pleased at the competent execution by two young Gaza suicide bombers of a carefully planned new type of attack. Explained Shkaki proudly:

> At the appointed time, they went from Gaza to Tel Aviv, and from Tel Aviv to the military bus station, which was well protected. Beside the military station there was a small coffee shop where soldiers go. The two men coordinated between them: the first was to enter the shop and blow himself up, while the second was to stay outside, wait for the soldiers to run out, then rush into the crowd and blow himself up.[20]

One of the most spectacular suicide missions, had it been successful, began with the hijacking of Air France Flight 8969 as it prepared to fly with its 227 passengers from Algiers' Houari-Boumediene Airport to Paris. The four Muslim hijackers belonging to the Armed Islamic Group, all in their mid-twenties, led by 25-year-old Abdul Abdullah Yahia, took control while the plane was still on the ground. They placed explosives at strategic locations throughout the plane, explosives which they planned to detonate over Paris, killing themselves and all passengers and crew and raining fiery debris and 15 tons of burning jet fuel on the capital city of France. However, antiterrorist gendarmes stormed the plane when it stopped to refuel at Marseilles. All four hijackers were killed in the battle and 16 passengers and crew were wounded, but the suicide mission was stopped and hundreds, perhaps thousands, of lives were saved. No one knows when a similar mission will be attempted, but it is certain that there will be more.

Trust Arafat?

Jewish religious law requires that the deceased's entire body must be given proper burial. Viewers on Israeli TV in January 1995 saw that law in action as they watched bearded representatives of the rabbinate using paint scrapers to recover bits of human flesh at the scene of the Beit Lid junction suicide bombing. All but one of the 21 victims were soldiers between the ages of 18 and 24. As much as by the deaths, Israelis were shocked by the fact that these were the very elite troops who are assigned to protect the rest of the nation from just such attacks. The reaction of Israelis was more than anger and anguish; it was clear that they had had enough.[21]

Israel is insisting that Arafat crack down on Islamic militants operating out of its territories, and Washington is pressuring Arafat to condemn such terrorism. But how can he condemn methods which he has so long employed himself? The situation would be laughable were it not so tragic. Suppose Arafat condemned terrorism; how could any Arab take that condemnation seriously when Arafat himself was the world's major practitioner of terrorism for years (and still supports it secretly)? And if he were taken seriously, he would lose the support of the Arab world.

Arafat has never apologized to Israel or to the rest of the world for those he killed and maimed. Furthermore, the PLO charter retains the statement that Israel must be destroyed. Incredible! How can Israel possibly imagine that the PLO is serious about a just and lasting "peace"? This is simply part of a long-established plan to gain a foothold in Israel from which better to launch her final destruction.

As part of the agreement to give control of the West Bank and Gaza to the PLO, Arafat pledged to remove from the PLO Charter the clause calling for Israel's destruction. Now that the PLO has that control, however, Israel is being told that the charter cannot be changed! The chief PLO negotiator, Nabil Shaath, stated early in January 1995 that "it is not possible under current conditions to change the Palestinian charter, which calls for the elimination of Israel." Six months earlier he had expressed confidence that "the Palestinian Council would soon meet in Gaza to change the charter."[22] Israeli leaders should have anticipated such foot-dragging from the beginning. To back away from the goal of eliminating Israel would be to renounce Islam and to admit that its teaching, which says that land belongs to the Muslims, was not inspired by the true God after all. No Muslim could ever consent to such heresy.

A Huge Difference

Israel herself, of course, is not without guilt. One cannot automatically condone everything the Israelis have done. As one writer states:

> I have in my files a photostat of a WANTED poster issued by the British colonial authorities about 1943. It shows the mug shots of ten men hunted as terrorists, pictured in alphabetical order; the first is that of a Police Clerk whose "peculiarities" are listed as "wears spectacles, flat footed, bad teeth." His name was Menachem Begin, and he and his colleague, Yitzhak Shamir, also a suspected terrorist, were to become future prime ministers of Israel. Begin would also become a winner of the Nobel Peace Prize, sharing the award in 1978 with President Sadat.[23]

The Israeli Mossad, like almost every other national secret service, is not above torture and cruelty and even the support of terrorism for its own protection and goals. Such tactics are normal in the world of international intrigue, and any nation not using them would find itself at a serious disadvantage. Exactly at this point, however, one observes a huge difference between Israel and her Arab neighbors.

The destruction of Israel is openly stated, even trumpeted, as an official Arab policy. It is part of their religion. One hears the cry for Jihad in every mosque and from loudspeakers blaring in the streets of Arab countries. Yet one never hears a comparable cry from Israel. She wants only to be left in peace, to be accepted among her neighbors as having a legitimate right to exist within secure borders.

Obeying the Koran

It is no accident that so much international terrorism is practiced by Muslims or that they have no qualms about the murder of innocent women and children. After all, the victims are all seen as infidels. Nor can it be denied that it is the Koran which gives a young Muslim the courage to strap a bomb to himself and detonate it to kill Jews in Israel. Such a deed, though infamous by any other standard, earns for the Muslim the highest reward in heaven. It is said that when Abu Dharr asked Mohammed what action was most excellent, the Prophet replied, "Faith in God and Jihad in His path."

Surah 9:19 clearly declares that believing in Allah and the Last Day and striving "in the way of Allah" give more reward than anything else in Islam. Jihad is the struggle to advance Islam by any means and is the obligation of all Muslims. Moreover, it was used by Mohammed for material gain. Surah 61:10-12 makes it clear that striving for the cause of Allah is not only a religious duty but a means of acquiring wealth, as in a business. The Hadith calls Jihad—

> the best method of earning [blessings] both spiritual and temporal. If victory is won, there is enormous booty of a country, which cannot be equalled to any other source of income. If there is defeat or death, there is everlasting paradise.[24]

Examples of the requirement of violence against non-Muslims are so numerous both in the Koran and in Islamic tradition that the point is beyond question. For example, Mohammed says:

> He who dies without having fought, or having felt it to be his duty, will die guilty of a kind of hypocrisy. ... There is no emigration after the Conquest, but only jihad ... so when you are summoned to fight, go forth. ... The last hour will not come before the Muslims fight the Jews and the Muslims kill them.[25]

Remember, this is Mohammed speaking. This is the law of

Islam. This is the religion of those who now, under the pretense of desiring peace, are gaining land in Israel and positioning themselves for the final kill. How can Israeli leaders ignore the obvious?

Revival of Religious Zeal

The rise of Islamic fundamentalism can be traced back to the terrible defeat suffered by Arabs at the hands of Israel in the 1967 war. Nasser had built up the Arabs' confidence that victory, after 19 years of preparation, was assured. The devastating defeat was therefore doubly humiliating. It was that defeat, however, which brought about the current revival of Islam.

Islamic religious leaders began to preach that Allah had punished the Arab states for the secularization of society. The only hope for victory against Israel would be to return wholeheartedly to the devout practice of Islam, in obedience to the Koran. Mosques began to fill with worshipers trying to rid themselves of the guilt of their former lack of faithfulness and the defeat by Israel that had presumably resulted therefrom.

Out of this revival of religious zeal much of today's terrorism was birthed. The names which terrorist groups thereafter adopted reveal their religious motivation and the deep faith that they are on Mohammed's team effecting Allah's will. Consider these groups: Islamic Jihad (Holy War), al-Dawa (The Calling), and Hezbollah (Party of God). As one writer who has made a study of Islam and Arab culture has pointed out:

> A few summers ago the grand mufti of Jerusalem, Sheik Saadeddin Alami, issued a religious order for the killing of President Assad of Syria, saying his assassin would be assured a place in paradise. Such a call by a spiritual leader anywhere else in the world would be considered extraordinary; in the Middle East it caused not a ripple.[26]

Misdirected Hatred

These terrorists who are willing to give their lives to take the lives of others are motivated by a deep sense of injustice nurtured by years of Islamic hatred against the Jews for "stealing the Promised Land." Anyone who has supported Israel is also a fair target. These terrorists' victims more often than not are innocent civilians, including women and children, who cannot even in the remotest way be blamed for the real or imagined injustices being fought against.

What possible connection could there be between Israel's alleged takeover of Palestine and the massacre of tourists in the airports of Rome or Vienna or elsewhere? Found on the body of one of the attackers in Rome's international airport was this note which reflected the twisted thinking produced by years of religious propaganda:

> As you have violated our land, our honor, our people, we will hit you everywhere, even your children, so that you should feel the sorrow of our children. The tears that we have shed will be washed away by your blood.[27]

One struggles to understand such demented thinking. How could randomly targeted and slain strangers from distant lands, who had probably never even visited the Middle East, be blamed for having "violated our land, our honor, our people"? Such is the misdirected hatred bred by Islam. Most of those recruited for such causes have been raised in the horrible conditions present in the Palestinian refugee camps, whose inhabitants are taught from childhood that the entire blame for their plight rests upon Israel and its supporters in the West.

The truth is, however, that Jordan took over more Palestinian land than did Israel. Furthermore, these unfortunate people have been kept in such camps by Arab nations who, from their vast oil revenues, certainly had the monetary resources to give them a better life. Instead, the displaced Palestinians have been held hostage under these pitiful conditions to be used as pawns to gain worldwide sympathy in the battle against Israel. Author David Lamb tells of his frustration when the head of a Palestinian delegation in its Washington D.C. office failed to show up for a scheduled interview and his assistant "sidestepped the one question put to him: 'With so much money in the Arab world, why are the Palestinians still living in refugee camps?' "[28] The reason is quite clear.

Widespread Support for Terrorism

Arab terrorism is often excused as the fault of a tiny minority of Islamic fundamentalist fanatics who are out of step with mainstream Islam and the educated Arab world. However, this does not explain the fact that so many Arab nations provide shelter and financial backing for these terrorists. During the Gulf War, while some Arab states joined in fighting Saddam Hussein, many others, such as Jordan and Syria, gave him their support and expressed their approval of his infamous conduct, conduct that included the unconscionable murder of thousands of civilians and the deliberate creation, by setting Kuwait's oil wells on fire, of the worst ecological disaster in history.

In fact, Hussein was viewed as a hero by most Arabs, including even those living in the United States. A *USA Today* poll found that only 18 percent of Arab Muslims living in the U.S. were willing to have a son or daughter participate in America's war effort against Saddam, while 62 percent disapproved of President Bush's handling of the situation.[29]

Libya's Moammar Kadafi speaks for millions of Muslims when he says, "The solution to all human problems is Islam." And when Kadafi urges Muslims in Zaire to engage in Jihad to overthrow the government and says, "He who kills this man [Mobutu] will go to paradise,"[30] he is not merely expressing one man's fanaticism but the teaching of Islam itself.

Islam is not merely a religion but a way of life. The idea of the separation of church and state, taken for granted in the West, is anathema in Islam. A secular government is a scandal to a Muslim, and Islamic fundamentalists are actively trying to overthrow such governments in Arab nations and install Shari'a (Islamic law) in their place. As Islamic scholar Abd-al-Masih explains:

> Islam not only means a religion for man's head, soul and heart; it is an all-encompassing culture, a theo-centric society in which every area of life, education, economy, family, and politics relate to Allah. There is no question of separation between throne and pulpit or between politics and religion.[31]

Playing into Islam's Hands

More than ignorance of the true nature of Islam causes the West to play into its hands. Often the commercial benefits and profits derived from partnership with Arabs entice Westerners into supporting terrorism for selfish gain. In 1986, when President Reagan was appealing to European allies not to do business with Libya's Moammar Kadafi because of his support for international terrorism, "five American oil companies with upward of a thousand American employees were based in Libya and were pumping 42 percent of Libya's oil. . . . And where did Kadafi get the deadly materials needed to launch attacks on Americans, Europeans and Arabs? They came from none other than the United States. Edwin Wilson, an American entrepreneur and former C.I.A. operative, had provided him with twenty-one tons of C-4 explosives, thousands of miniature detonators and experts to train Libyans in the art of terrorism."[32]

The misinformation presented by Western media also contributes to the confusion. In spite of the Koran's call to kill infidels and the example of Mohammed himself of spreading Islam by the sword, well-meaning commentators persist in denying Islam's basic violence. Consider the following by popular American newspaper columnist, Charley Reese:

> For reasons ranging from ignorance and sloppiness to malice and political scheming, various people are trying

to brainwash the American public into equating Islamic fundamentalism with terrorism. Don't let them do it. . . .

There is nothing in Islamic teaching that should cause any American to be fearful. . . . Islam worships the same God as Christianity and Judaism. . . . The concept of jihad, or holy war, is no different than the Christian concept of just war. Muslims are obligated to go to war only if Islam itself is attacked. . . .

Our political conflicts in the Middle East have nothing to do with religion, so don't let some disinformation specialist dupe you.[33]

Reese himself, like so many others in positions of influence, is the one who has been propagandized. He couldn't be more wrong! Both the Koran and Mohammed called for war against all non-Muslims. Surah 5:33 (see also 47:4) says that all those who oppose Allah (i.e. non-Muslims or infidels) are to be "killed or crucified, or have their hands and feet on alternate sides cut off, or will be expelled out of the land . . . and in the Hereafter theirs will be an awful doom. . . ." We have already quoted the Koran as saying:

Slay the idolaters [non-Muslims] wherever ye find them, and take them (captive), and besiege them, and prepare for them each ambush. . . . Fight against such of those who have been given the Scripture as believe not in Allah nor the Last Day. . . . Go forth, light-armed and heavy-armed, and strive with your wealth and your lives in the way of Allah! (Surah 9:5,29,41).

Although Surah 2:190 says, ". . . but begin not hostilities. Lo! Allah loveth not aggressors," other passages in the Koran justify aggression in spreading Islam. Mohammed himself frequently led his followers in the most naked and unprovoked aggression against caravans and tribes and cities. Muslims have been the aggressors in battles all over North Africa and far into Europe. What were the forces of Islam doing conquering Spain and France if it wasn't aggression? It was surely not self-defense! Seemingly, merely to reject Islam is to be the aggressor against Allah and thus to justify one's death.

As we have already noted, Islamic terrorists are usually viewed as radicals or extremists, when in fact they are simply obeying the tenets of Islam. A typical news report in January 1995 stated:

> More than 500 people have been killed in the radicals' 3-year-old campaign to overthrow the secular government of President Hosni Mubarak and impose an Islamic theocracy. . . . Monday's attacks [January 2, 1995, which killed eight policemen and three civilians] appeared to be coordinated, police said. They began when attackers stopped a minibus and fired at the occupants, killing five police officers and two civilians. In a second attack, assailants killed a policeman and a civilian in a truck and wounded a second civilian. Two other police were killed in attacks on a bus and another truck.[34]

Such terrorist attacks are increasing, yet the media continues to avoid the fact that Islam itself is what inspires the determination to destroy Israel and all who support her. Terrorism will persist in obedience to the Koran, which demands the conversion or forceful subjugation of all non-Muslims. The situation is only made that much worse when the truth is suppressed and misinformation is promoted.

The Great Media Whitewash

The American media's bias against Israel and for the Arabs is demonstrated almost daily. Consider the sanitization of the terrorist organization, Hamas, after one of its agents on a suicide mission blew himself up on a bus in Tel Aviv, killing 22 people and wounding many others.[35] That very afternoon CNN news commentator Hilary Bowker interviewed an "expert," Rosemary Hollis, to shed light on the incident. Bowker commented that while most people think of a terrorist organization when they hear the word "Hamas," in reality "the group actually does quite a bit more than that. . . ."

Hollis eagerly caught the pass and ran for a touchdown: "They are part of the community. Many professionals of

Hamas . . . will perform functions for the wider community
. . . in the schools, or in the clinics or through the mosques,
general support for the needs of the poor people." Bowker
responded that in its early days when it was involved only in
charity, Israel helped to support Hamas in order to divide the
Arab community. The implication was that Israel was therefore to blame at least as much as those who did the foul deed
because she had stopped funding Hamas and had begun to
make deals with the PLO.

Other networks continued the whitewash. Two days later a
similar slant was presented on America's most-watched news
program, ABC's *World News Tonight* with Peter Jennings. *The
Jerusalem Post* has said, "In turning a massacre of Israelis into
pro-Palestinian propaganda, no one is a greater virtuoso than
ABC-TV's Peter Jennings."[36] There was not a word that anyone had been killed in the bus bombing, which Jennings
explained as an act of revenge for an earlier attack upon a
mosque by an Israeli settler. Of course, Jennings failed
to distinguish between an impulsive outburst by a deranged
individual acting on his own and a carefully planned and
coordinated attack by an organization which has devoted itself
year after year to coldly calculated terrorism with the support
and blessing of the Arab/Islamic world.

Jennings had a lengthy interview with Arafat but none with
any Israeli representatives. Much of the program was devoted
to justifying Hamas, which Jennings said first came into prominence "when the Israeli government expelled 400 of its
members to southern Lebanon in the fall of 1992." These
"devout and politically aware Moslems" were praised as
heroes who endured the cold winter in tents and returned in
triumph "when the Israelis were pressured into letting them
come home. . . ."

No blame was leveled at Hamas. Its terrorist attacks, kid-
nappings and murders were referred to obliquely as "attacks
on Israeli Border Police," with no mention of Israeli casualties. Israel was even blamed for the death of one of its own
soldiers, Nahshon Wachsman, who was kidnapped by Hamas

and who, said Jennings, "subsequently died when the Israelis tried to rescue him by force." The acts of Israelis in self-defense were put in the same category as attacks by terrorists bent upon murder; the moral was that Israel's repressive measures in response to the terrorism only served to strengthen these dedicated freedom fighters.

Tom Brokaw was not to be outdone. He went to Jerusalem, from where he broadcast a program called "The Story of the Israeli Fathers." It "featured interviews with Nahshon Wachsman's father, Yehuda Wachsman, and Tyassir Natsche, a 'wealthy Arab merchant,' the father of one of Nahshon's kidnappers. [Commented Brokaw], 'Two fathers in the Middle East, both grieving . . . religious men, joined, for now, only in the deaths of their sons.' "[37]

One wonders by what rationale the death of the one murdered could be placed on the same level as the death of the one who kidnapped and then killed him. Try to make the parents of the victim of any murderer adopt those values and then understand what a masterful deception Brokaw engineered! Nor could Hamas be likened even to a serial killer here in the U.S. who stalks his victims one by one to satisfy some perverted passion. Hamas, in the covenant it released in 1988, has made it clear that the very existence of Israel is illegitimate and that every Muslim is under obligation to aid in its destruction.

A False Promise of "No Compulsion"

While in the early parts of the Koran it says, "There is no compulsion in religion" (Surah 2:256), these words were written when Mohammed did not have the forces to use violence against Christians and Jews. At that time the Prophet claimed to believe the Bible—indeed that he was preaching the same message, not some new religion. Later, however, when he had acquired enough military might, Mohammed began to wage war against those who refused to accept his religion. The same aggressive behavior toward non-Muslims is supported repeatedly in the Hadith (Islamic tradition), and without that background one cannot understand the motive behind most Islamic terrorism.

Furthermore, there is no freedom of religion for non-Muslims in Arab countries, and other elementary rights are often denied to them. One must be a Muslim, for example, to be a citizen in Saudi Arabia. Christian meetings, public or private, are forbidden. Five Christians from the Philippines were recently imprisoned in Saudi Arabia for holding a home Bible meeting.[38] Yet Muslims living in the West demand the freedom here that is refused to non-Muslims in Arab countries. At the same time, however, Muslims even in the West don't want to allow anyone to critize Islam. Consider Salman Rushdie, who, because he wrote a book critical of Islam, was put on the international hit list with a price on his head. Islam is thus a religion of terror which not only forces itself upon its victims but takes awful revenge against those who disagree with its tenets.

So it has been from the very beginning. Asma, a Medinese poetess who attacked Mohammed in her rhymes, was driven through with a sword in her sleep; 100-year-old Afak, who wrote a satire on the prophet, was slain in his sleep. Of a third Medinese poet, Kab ibn al-Ashraf, who wrote insulting verses, Mohammed asked, "Who will ease me of this man?" "That evening the poet's severed head was laid at the Prophet's feet."[39]

A Seventh-Century Mentality Imposed

Wherever Islam is in power there is no freedom of conscience, of the press, of speech, or of religion. In America, thousands of its citizens, including Muslims, protested its participation in the Gulf War; but in Saudi Arabia, one of our allies for whose freedom we were fighting, there was no freedom to protest. The government warned that anyone opposing the war effort would have a hand and a leg cut off or be executed.[40] As one author has stated:

> Because there was no concept of personal freedom or
> civil rights in the tribal life of seventh-century Arabia,
> Islamic law does not recognize freedom of speech, free-
> dom of religion, freedom of assembly, or freedom of the

press. This is why non-Muslims, such as Christians or Bahais, are routinely denied even the most basic civil rights.

The despots of the Ottoman Empire, and the present dictators of Libya, Jordan, Iran, Iraq, Syria, Sudan, Yemen, etc. are merely examples of seventh-century Arabian tyranny transplanted into modern times. . . .

Incarceration without due process; the use of torture; political assassination; the cutting off of hands, feet, ears, tongues, and heads; and the gouging out of eyes— all of these things are part of Islamic law today because they were part of seventh-century Arabian culture.

To Westerners, such things are barbaric and should not have any place in the modern world.

Islam is a distinctively Arabian cultural religion. Unless this is firmly grasped, no real understanding of Islam is possible . . . [and Westerners] will never understand why Muslims think and act the way they do. . . .

The denial of civil rights to women which is clearly in the text of the Quran itself is reflective of seventh-century Arabian culture and its low view of women.

Even today, Muslim women can be kept prisoners in their own home. They can be denied the right to go outside the house if the husband so orders. They are still denied the right to vote in Islamic countries such as Kuwait.

In Islamic countries such as Iran, women must carry written permission from their husband to be out of the house! Women are even denied the right to drive a car in such places as Saudi Arabia.[41]

That terrorism is practiced by Muslim zealots today to further the cause of Allah is only reflective of the fact that violence has been an integral part of Islam since its beginning. "During his ten years in Medina, Muhammad planned sixty-five campaigns and raids, and personally led twenty-seven."[42] Following the Prophet's example, his first successor, Abu Bekr, led his followers into many a victorious battle to spread the new faith. Those who refused either to become Muslims or to pay tribute were slain. Will Durant writes:

[A]s the triumphant Arab armies swelled with hungry or ambitious recruits, the problem arose of giving them new lands to conquer, if only to provide them with food and pay. The advance created its own momentum; each victory required another, until the Arab conquests— more rapid than the Roman, more lasting than the Mongol—summed up to the most amazing feat in military history. . . .

In 635 Damascus was taken, in 636 Antioch, in 638 Jerusalem; by 640 all Syria was in Moslem hands; by 641 Persia and Egypt were conquered.[43]

There is no way that the Arab conquests can be explained as "self-defense"! This was aggression of the most vicious kind. But with victory came division, intrigue, and intertribal and intercity wars as rival factions fought among themselves for the leadership of Islam. More than one Caliph's brief reign was cut short by his assassination: Omar I (Umar Abn al-Khattab) by a Persian slave while he led prayers in the mosque; Othman ibn Affan at the hands of 500 followers of a rebel Muslim sect from Egypt as he sat reading the Koran in his Medina palace; Ali, son-in-law of Mohammed (married to the Prophet's favorite daughter, Fatima), when a Kharijite pierced his brain with a poisoned sword. Shia sect pilgrims journey to his grave as well as to Mecca to this day.

Ali's son, Hasan, who had married 100 times, was poisoned, perhaps by a jealous wife. Again, not a man to hold up as an example of high moral character. Perhaps, at this point, we have said enough about this litany of evil.

*Forever, O LORD, thy word is settled in heaven.
. . . Thy word is a lamp unto my feet and a light unto
my path.*

—Psalm 119:89,105

*He [God] humbled thee . . . that he might make thee
know that man doth not live by bread only, but by
every word that proceedeth out of the mouth of the
LORD doth man live.*

—Deuteronomy 8:3

*Many people shall go and say, Come ye, and let us go
up to the mountain of the LORD, to the house of the
God of Jacob; and he will teach us of his ways, and
we will walk in his paths; for out of Zion shall go
forth the law, and the word of the LORD from Jerusalem.*

—Isaiah 2:3

*The grass withereth, the flower fadeth, but the word
of our God shall stand forever.*

—Isaiah 40:8

*The Word of God is living and powerful, and sharper
than any two-edged sword, piercing even to the dividing asunder of soul and spirit . . . and is a discerner
of the thoughts and intents of the heart.*

—Hebrews 4:12

12

The Bible or the Koran?

◆

Whether the Israeli government or the Arab governments opposing Israel like it or not, the controversy in which they are embroiled is at its heart a religious one and can only have a religious solution. That solution, if it is ever reached, will not depend upon a vote in the United Nations. It will depend upon which religious authority is accepted as having the last word. Will it be the Immams, the Ayatollahs, the Rabbis, the Pope, or the Scriptures of these religions? In the latter case, will it be the Bible or the Koran?

The Vatican leaders are convinced that their Church will eventually provide the authoritative answer to the world's dilemma regarding Jerusalem. That is why Rome has involved itself in its recent accord with Israel. The Roman Pontiff hopes one day to preside over an ecumenical partnership between Judaism, Islam, and Roman Catholicism (as the "true Christianity")—a partnership in which all three will coexist peacefully around the world. The plan is for these religions to have worldwide centers in Jerusalem under the direction of the Vatican. Israeli leaders, apparently ignorant of the Vatican's true intentions, are unfortunately going right along with its scheme.

The Need for Open Discussion

We must therefore make a brief but careful comparison of Islam, Judaism, and Christianity, including the distinction between Roman Catholicism and biblical Christianity. The issues involved are indeed controversial and volatile, but they must be faced without prejudice. To do so there must be an openness which comes only with freedom from fear of being attacked by those who might take offense at an opinion forthrightly expressed which is unfavorable to their religion.

There is little danger of the cruel depredations of past Protestant/Catholic religious wars being presently repeated. The emphasis today is rather upon ecumenism, though for deceitful reasons. Muslims, however, still openly threaten with death those who cannot accept their religion; and the danger of falling victim to Islamic fundamentalists who practice worldwide terrorism is very real today. One who has studied Islam for years and engaged frequently in discussions and debates with Muslims has wisely said:

> After years of dealing with Muslims, we have found it essential at the outset to get their agreement to the fact that in the West we have religious freedom, which means that we have the right to criticize the Bible, the Quran, the Hadith, the Vedas, the Book of Mormon and any other "holy" book.
>
> Such discussions should not be viewed as a personal attack or slur. They should be carried out in an objective and scholarly manner in order that the truth may be discovered.
>
> Any religion which refuses to allow people to examine its sacred book using the normal rules of research and logic evidently has something to hide.[1]

A Few Basic Distinctions

Muslims follow the Koran and Jews the Old Testament. Christians acknowledge both the Old and New Testaments as inspired of God and infallible, the final and sufficient authority in all matters of the faith. Muslims have added the "Hadith," or tradition as equal in authority to the Koran and follow it even when it contradicts the Koran. Roman Catholicism, likewise, has added its own traditions as equal in authority to the Bible and follows them even when they contradict God's Word. The Roman Catholic Church, with its popes, cardinals, and bishops, claims to represent Christ in the world, insists that it alone can interpret the Bible, and requires obedience to its own peculiar rules and rituals.

Its claim of infallibility prevents the Roman Catholic Church from publicly confessing and repenting of its anti-Semitic stance throughout history, its support of Hitler and Mussolini, and its policy of genocide through the centuries toward independent Christians who would not bow to its authority. We have thoroughly documented the historical facts and the danger which the Vatican poses both to Israel and to the world in *A Woman Rides the Beast,* so will not go into details here.

Islam acknowledges Jesus Christ as a virgin-born (Surah 3:47; 21:91; etc.) great prophet who lived a perfect life, while Jews, on the other hand, tend rather to view Him as a charlatan. The Koran, however, is ambivalent regarding both the Old and New Testaments, at times seeming to endorse them and at other times to contradict them, which in itself is a contradiction within the pages of the Koran. Both Jews and Christians reject the claim that the Koran was inspired of God and see it rather as having been composed by Mohammed himself and written down by those who heard him.

Islam's Ambivalence Toward the Bible

In Surah 3:48 ("And he [Allah] will teach him [Jesus] the Scripture and wisdom, and the Torah and the Gospel"); in Surah 5:44 ("We did reveal the Torah, wherein is guidance and a light"); in Surah 5:46 ("We bestowed on him [Jesus] the Gospel wherein is guidance and a light"); and in Surah 5:48 ("We revealed the Scripture with the truth, confirming whatever Scripture was before it") the Koran seems to accept the Jewish and Christian Scriptures. Surah 40:53 clearly declares:

"And We verily gave Moses the guidance, and We caused the Children of Israel to inherit the Scripture."

However, Islam actually accepts only the Torah (first five books of the Bible—Surah 2:87), the Psalms of David, and the four Gospels. Then later, to avoid the obvious conflict between the Bible and Islam, the Koran claims that these Jewish and Christian Scriptures have been perverted and are replaced by the new divine revelation recorded in the Koran.

Yet the archaeological evidence is overwhelming that the Bible we have today, both Old and New Testaments, is exactly the same as when it was originally written and that it, not the Koran, is the reliable record. Certainly there were no changes in the Bible during Mohammed's lifetime and thus no justification for his at first endorsing the Bible and later rejecting or contradicting it.

Changes in the Koran

Moreover, it is a well-known fact and even acknowledged by Islamic scholars that numerous changes have been made in the Koran. Ali Dashti explains that one of Mohammed's followers, Abdollah Sarh, made many suggestions to the Prophet about improving the Koran by rephrasing it, adding to it, or deleting from it, suggestions which Mohammed followed. Eventually, however, Sarh defected from Islam, having at last faced the obvious fact that if the Koran were truly from God it would need no improvement in its wording and concepts and could not be changed. When Mecca was conquered, Abdollah Sarh was one of the first put to death by Mohammed, a fate which the Koran imposes upon all who defect from Islam. In Sarh's case, however, there was a compelling reason for his death: He knew too much.

It was Caliph Uthman who, with great labor, put together the standardized text of the Koran generally accepted today. There was no "original manuscript" of the Koran, as Muslims generally believe. In fact, there were many versions which had been copied from the notes on scraps of leaves, bark, bones, and stones. These versions contradicted one another in places, were of varying lengths, and contained confusing variations in the wording. As one author has pointed out:

> As to the labor of Caliph Uthman, the following historical questions must be asked:
>
> 1. Why did he have to standardize a common text if a standard [original] text was already in existence?
> 2. Why did he try to destroy all the "other" manuscripts if there were no other conflicting manuscripts?
> 3. Why did he have to use the threat of death to force people to accept his text if everyone had the same text?
> 4. Why did many people reject his text in favor of their own texts?

These four questions reveal the utter state of confusion and contradiction that existed in the time of Uthman over the text of the Quran.

The fact that he ordered all of the older copies of the Quran destroyed reveals his fear that such copies would show that his own text was deficient either by addition to or subtraction from what Muhammad actually said.

Thankfully, some of these older materials have survived and have been recovered by such scholars as Arthur Jeffery.

Western scholars have shown beyond all reasonable doubt that Uthman's text did not contain all of the Quran. Neither was what it did contain correct in all of its wording.

As to the Muslim claim that the Quran cannot be translated, it is amazing to us that the English Muslim Mohammed Pickthal could state, "The Koran cannot be translated" (p. vii), in the very introduction to his excellent translation of it! . . .

The true history of the collection and the creation of the text of the Quran reveals that the Muslim claims [of perfection] are indeed fictitious and not in accord with the facts. The fingerprints of Muhammad can be seen on every page as a witness to its human origin.[2]

A Sinful Revealer of God's Word?

Even the Muslim who denies that Mohammed *wrote* the Koran himself but believes that he was the inspired Prophet through whom Allah revealed this new revelation must be concerned about the admitted moral imperfections of Mohammed. Why wouldn't Allah choose a holy instrument through whom to speak to the world? The Bible declares that its pages were not written "by the will of man, but *holy* men of God spoke as they were moved by the Holy Spirit" (2 Peter 1:21). That was obviously not the case with the Koran.

Arab historians candidly admit that, in contrast to Christ's perfect life, Mohammed lied, cheated, lusted, deceived, robbed, and killed, and often did it all *in the name of Allah.* He had numerous wives (at least 16 are named—besides concubines—four times the four wives allowed by the Koran). In fact, one of Mohammed's wives was only eight years old and still playing with childish toys (according to the Hadith) when he took her from her parents to his bed. One could hardly suggest that Mohammed set an admirable example of good morals for his followers! In fact, the Koran makes it clear that Mohammed was a sinner who needed forgiveness from Allah (Surah 40:55; etc).

Contradictions, Contradictions...

In any comparison between the Bible and the Koran one immediately notices numerous contradictions and serious conflicts on some of the most important issues. The obvious fact that both cannot be correct forces the investigator to make a choice between them. The Koran tells some of the same stories as the Bible, but often with an entirely different twist. For example, whereas the Bible in both the Old and New Testaments makes it clear that Noah's entire family was saved to repopulate the earth after the flood, the Koran claims that one of Noah's sons refused to enter the ark and was drowned:

> Noah cried unto his son . . . O my son! Come ride with
> us, and be not with the disbelievers. He said: I shall

betake me to some mountain that will save me from the
water . . . so he was among the drowned (Surah 11:42,43).

According to the Bible, however, "Noah went in, and his
sons, and his wife, and his sons' wives with him, into the ark"
(Genesis 7:7). Both the Koran and the Bible cannot be true.
How do we decide between them? The answer to that question
is not difficult.

In its sketchy account, from which the details given in the
Bible are missing, the Koran doesn't even give us the name of
the son who was allegedly drowned. In contrast, the Bible
gives not only the names of all three of Noah's sons but a
complete genealogy and historically verifiable record of their
descendants (who repopulated the earth) for many generations
after the flood, including names, locations, and national char-
acteristics:

> Now these are the generations of the sons of Noah,
> Shem, Ham, and Japheth, and unto them were sons born
> after the flood . . . these are the families of the sons of
> Noah . . . and by these were the nations divided in the
> earth after the flood [followed by the details] (Genesis
> 10:1,32).

It is unreasonable to imagine that the Bible made up an
entire postflood genealogy and history of one of Noah's sons
who actually died in the flood. It is far more likely that
Mohammed's continual twisting of Bible stories reflects the
fact that he was illiterate (Surah 7:158) and therefore had never
read the Bible for himself. His faulty knowledge is believed to
have resulted from confused or partial memories of conversa-
tions with Christians and Jews, some of whom may themselves
have garbled the Bible stories which they told to Mohammed.
The *Encyclopedia Britannica* suggests that the twisting of
biblical narrative—

> can in most cases be traced back to the legendary anec-
> dotes of the Jewish Haggada and the Apocryphal Gos-
> pels. . . . [T]here is no evidence that [Mohammed] was

able to read, and his dependence on oral communication may explain some of his misconceptions [and] confusion. . . .[3]

Numerous other contradictions demonstrate that the Koran is in error. We have already dealt with some of the Koran's many obvious mistakes, such as its claim that Abraham and Ishmael had a part in building the Kaaba, an idol temple. This claim is clearly not true in view of the condemnation of idolatry by the God whom Abraham knew and worshiped. We also noted that the Koran's claim that Abraham and his offspring lived in the Valley of Mecca (Surah 14:37) is unquestionably false inasmuch as the Promised Land was Canaan, far removed from Saudi Arabia. Even Muslims acknowledge that Abraham, Sarah, and other relatives were buried in the Cave of Machpelah in the land of Israel. All the evidence indicates that the Bible account is the accurate one. It has Abraham living and dying in the Promised Land of Canaan, where he was buried beside the bones of Sarah (Genesis 23:19).

Mohammed's Misconceptions

There are numerous indications in the Koran of Mohammed's misconceptions regarding Christianity. For example, Mary the mother of Jesus is confused with Miriam the sister of Moses (Surah 19:28). There is also confusion between the circumstances of the birth of Jesus and the tragic plight of Hagar when she was expelled from the household of Abraham. The Koran has Mary giving birth to Jesus, alone without her husband, Joseph, under a palm tree, starving and thirsty (Surah 19:22-28), but doesn't explain how or why an expectant mother became the victim of such unusual circumstances.

The Bible, on the other hand, not only tells us that at the birth of Jesus his mother, Mary, was in the company of her husband, Joseph, in a stable in Bethlehem, but it explains why. A decree had gone out from Augustus Caesar that all the world should be taxed. Joseph had to return to the city of his lineage for registration and taxation, as did multitudes of others, leaving Bethlehem's small inn unable to accommodate them all. The date and actual occurrence of this taxing is historically verifiable from independent sources, whereas the vague and unlikely account in the Koran has no such support.

Obviously both the Koran and the Bible cannot be correct. The many clear contradictions between the two records force us to make a choice as to which one to believe. A major consideration is the fact that the Koran was orally recounted by Mohammed about 600 years after Christ, whereas the Old Testament account was written more than a thousand years (and in some cases 2000 years) earlier. It is only logical to assume, barring other evidence to the contrary, that the record written nearest to the events would be the most accurate.

What Evidence of Validity?

It is not only its greater antiquity, however, that points to the Old Testament as the more reliable record. Its perfect accuracy and authenticity are guaranteed in a unique manner which is unknown anywhere else in the world of literature or sacred writings. The Old Testament contains hundreds of specific prophecies concerning the Jews, their land, and their Messiah which (as we have already noted briefly and have dealt with in detail in other books) have been precisely fulfilled hundreds and in some cases thousands of years after they were first recorded.

The mathematical impossibility of these prophecies having come to pass by chance proves that they were inspired of God. Such evidence provides assurance that the rest of the Bible was divinely inspired as well and is thus equally reliable.

The Koran, on the other hand (like the Hindu Vedas or the writings of Confucius or Buddha or of any other religion), has no valid prophecies at all and thus no proof of its inspiration. In fact, in its conflict not only with the Bible but with established history as well, the Koran itself proves that it is not of God. It cannot be verified by other means and thus lacks the proof of its veracity through irrefutable evidence such as the Bible offers. As a consequence, Islam has consistently found it necessary to force itself upon its "converts" by the sword and by terror, as it is attempting to do even today.

Might does not make right. Nevertheless, Islamic fundamentalists are determined to subject not only Arab countries but the entire world to the Koran under the threat of violence and death. While Mohammed generously called upon Christians and Jews to unite with the Muslims in one religion (Surah 3:64), it had to be in obedience to Allah and acceptance of the Koran as the latest revelation that superseded the Bible of either Christians or Jews.

A Basic Problem

Unlike the Old and New Testaments of the Bible, there were no original manuscripts from which the Koran was derived. That serious deficiency quite naturally led to confusion. Mohammed, being illiterate, certainly did not write down his visions and revelations as they occurred. He claimed that the Koran existed in heaven and that installments of it were revealed to him by the angel Gabriel, who made him memorize what he was told. He then repeated these revelations orally to others, who wrote down what they heard.

It was only after Mohammed's death that the Koran was finally assembled. This was accomplished by relying upon the memories of those who had heard him speak and by gathering together the "parchment, leather...leaves of date-palms, barks of trees, bones, etc." on which his avid listeners had written Mohammed's revelations.[4] That mode of preservation may partially explain why the Koran presents biblical characters and events in obviously fictional tales.

The definitive text of the Koran was eventually established in 933, *three centuries* after Mohammed's death. The Sunnites played the major role in that process. They developed, too, and became the followers of Hadith (Islamic tradition gathered from the memorized oral testimony and applications of Koranic texts) passed down from those who had known the Prophet. The Sunnites themselves are divided into several schools of interpretation today.

The Shi'ites, the next-largest sect, renounce Sunnite tradition and are fanatical in their worship of Ali (the first caliph), whom they came to revere as a blessed martyr, sinless and infallible, and believed by some to be an incarnation of Allah. "The eighth Immam was Riza, whose tomb at Mashhad, in northeastern Persia, is accounted the 'Glory of the Shia World.' In 873 the twelfth Imam—Muhammad ibn Hasan— disappeared in the twelfth year of his age; in Shia belief, he did not die but bides his time to reappear and lead the Shia Moslems to universal supremacy and bliss."[5]

Internal Contradictions

The shadow of doubt falling across the Koran is deepened by the fact that, in addition to contradicting the Bible, it often and seriously contradicts itself. These discrepancies are of such a nature that they can neither be explained away nor reconciled by any rationalization. For example, Surah 54:49,50 says that Allah "created everything . . . as the twinkling of an eye." Yet according to Surah 41:9,12, Allah "created the earth in two Days . . . [and] seven heavens in two Days. . . ." Verse 10 adds to the confusion by saying that Allah "blessed it [the earth] and measured therein its sustenance in four Days. . . ."

In further contradiction, Surahs 7:54; 10:4; and 32:4 declare, "Lo! your Lord is Allah Who created the heavens and the earth in six Days . . . and that which is between them, in six Days." Surah 32:5 explains that a day is actually "a thousand years of that ye reckon," while Surah 70:4 declares that a day with Allah "is fifty thousand years." We are left to wonder, in these cases and others, what the Koran really means.

There are too many contradictions in the Koran to deal with them all here: errors of history, of place and time, of the wrong names being given to many biblical characters. For example, the Koran says Abraham's father was Azar (Surah 6:75), whereas the Bible says his name was Terah (Genesis 11:26,31). There are many scientific errors in the Koran as well, whereas none can be found in the Bible. Even Arabian legends are recounted as though they actually happened to real people. To make matters worse, many of the errors in the Koran have been deceptively covered up by the translators. Robert Morey has noted:

> Muhammad made up fictional speeches of people in the Bible using such words as "Muslim" and "Islam" [Surah 5:3; 61:7; etc.] which were not in the languages of the people supposedly quoted at that time.
>
> This would be as ridiculous as claiming that Muhammad said, "I like Kentucky Fried Chicken best."
>
> Obviously, such terminology did not exist in Muhammad's time! And neither did the terminology Muhammad put into the mouths of biblical figures [exist in their times].
>
> All of the speeches attributed to Abraham, Isaac, Jacob, Noah, Moses, Mary, Jesus, etc. contain words and phrases which clearly reveal that [these alleged conversations] are frauds. . . .[6]

The Most Serious Conflict

There is a particular contradiction between the Koran and the Bible which deserves our special attention because it is of such great importance, involving as it does the question of Christ's identity, crucifixion, and resurrection. The Koran admits Christ's virgin birth (Surah 3:47; 19:20; 21:91; etc.) and that this miraculous event was by the Spirit of God (19:17,21). Inasmuch as there was no human father, and God caused Mary to conceive, the Bible calls Jesus the Son of God. It tells us that the angel Gabriel said to Mary, "He [Jesus] shall be great, and shall be called the Son of the Highest [i.e. of God] . . ." (Luke 1:32). Yet the Koran denies that Jesus is the Son of God (Surah 4:171), a denial which seems to contradict Surah 19:17-21.

The cornerstone belief in Christianity is that Christ died for our sins on the cross. The Koran rejects this key doctrine. Surah 4:157 declares that Jesus was not crucified: "They slew him not nor crucified, but it appeared so unto them . . . they slew him not for certain." The next verse seems to indicate that Jesus didn't die at all but was taken alive by God into heaven:

"But Allah took him up unto Himself." Yet Surah 19:33 has Jesus speaking (amazingly, as a babe in the cradle—see verses 29-33) of the day of His *death* and *resurrection*: "Peace on me the day I was born, and the day I die, and the day I shall be raised alive!" Again, the Koran leaves us in confusion on a major point on which the Bible and history give clear and confirming testimony.

What was the significance of the Old Testament sacrifices? Obviously, the blood of animals could never atone for sin. Those sacrifices, therefore, had to be pictures of a true future sacrifice that would justly pay the penalty for sin. What could this sacrifice be? As we have seen, the biblical prophets foretold the coming of the Messiah and His suffering and death on our behalf. He would be the Lamb which Abraham said God would provide.

Did Jesus die on the cross or didn't He? Even in its denial of the cross, Islam contradicts itself. If Christ is still alive in heaven, then how could Mohammed be His successor? Some Muslim scholars believe that Surahs 3:55 and 19:33 indicate that Christ must return to this earth to die a natural death before the day of resurrection. Even if that were true, it obviously hasn't happened yet, which again raises the question of how Mohammed (who himself is unquestionably dead) could be the successor of Christ, who has not yet died. Unlike the empty tomb of Jesus outside Jerusalem, the grave of Mohammed in Medina, to which devout Muslims make pilgrimages, contains the dead Prophet's remains.

What About Miracles?

Miracles provide another interesting comparison. The Bible is filled with accounts of numerous miracles which the Koran acknowledges occurred. Yet there is not one miracle recorded in the Koran. Though he was the original Prophet of Islam, Mohammed did not foresee his own death and made no provision for it by appointing a successor. Moreover, the Koran itself makes it clear that Mohammed was unable to perform miracles (Surah 17:90-96; 29:50-52; etc.).

Yes, later tradition attributes some miracles to Mohammed, but even Islamic scholars, such as Ali Dashti, admit they were belated inventions with no foundation in historical fact. Dashti calls these accounts of miracles "myth-making and history-fabrication of Moslems."[7] Nevertheless, Islam claims superiority over Christianity and is as unalterably opposed to it as it is to Judaism. One Arab writer declares:

> Muslims claim they respect Jesus. Yet many of us know by experience that Islam is the most anti-Christian religion on earth. It is more antagonistic to the Christian faith than Communism ever was. . . . With all the persecutions Christians suffered in the former Soviet Union, the Church of Christ still continued, though underground. In Communist China today, Christianity still thrives. But confession of Christ by a national in an Islamic country is regarded as high treason [for which the penalty is death]. No Church is allowed—not even an official Church that a Communist government could allow is permitted to operate openly in an Islamic country![8]

A Choice to Make

The Bible or the Koran—which one is the authoritative revelation from the true God who created the universe and mankind and to whom we are all accountable? This question obviously holds the key to peace both in the Middle East and in the world at large. Conflicts of all kinds, whether within a family, city, or nation, or wars between religious, ethnic, or national groups, are all caused by the pursuit of selfish interests.

For a husband and wife to agree on a fifty-fifty arrangement is no solution to domestic conflicts when natural selfishness causes quarrels in defining what is fifty-fifty. Only when each loves the other enough to prefer the other's good over one's own desires will there be real harmony in the home. So it is with brothers and sisters, parents and children, neighbors and friends.

According to the Bible, love is not only an emotion but it is commanded by God. Thus one decides, in obedience to God, to love even one's enemies, and all mankind as oneself, as the Bible commands. Without the recognition of a supreme authority by all mankind and the willingness to obey His commands, diplomatic efforts to achieve peace are obviously doomed to failure.

To which authority will this world bow? Will it be to Allah or to the God of the Bible? These two are not the same "God" any more than the Koran through whom Allah speaks and the Bible through whom Jehovah speaks are the same book. Shall we obey the Koran or the Bible—or neither?

If we submit to neither rival authority, then we are pursuing our own way and the world is doomed. If we submit to the Koran, then the essential ingredient of love is missing, for such a relationship, as we shall see, is utterly absent from Islam. If all mankind, however, would obey the Bible's twin commands—to love God with one's whole heart and mind and to love one's neighbor as oneself—there would assuredly be peace, and only then.

Allah! There is no God save Him, the Alive, the Eternal. . . . Unto Him belongeth whatsoever is in the heavens and whatsoever is in the earth.

—Surah 2:255

Say: O Allah! . . . Lo! Thou art Able to do all things.

—Surah 3:26

He [Allah] punisheth whom He will, and forgiveth whom He will.

—Surah 5:40

Allah is the Light of the heavens and the earth. . . . Allah guideth unto His light whom He will.

—Surah 24:35

The LORD [Jahweh/Jehovah], he is God; there is none else beside him.

—Deuteronomy 4:35

When all the people saw it [the fire come from heaven and consume the sacrifice that Elijah had placed on the altar], they said, The LORD [Jahweh/Jehovah], he is the God; the LORD [Jahweh/Jehovah], he is the God!

—1 Kings 18:39

The LORD [Jahweh/Jehovah] is the true God, he is the living God and an everlasting King; at his wrath the earth shall tremble, and the nations shall not be able to abide his indignation.

—Jeremiah 10:10

13

Allah or Yahweh?

◆

Muslims, Christians, and Jews all claim to be the followers of the one true God. The Koran says: "Your God is one God; there is no god save Him, the Beneficent, the Merciful" (Surah 2:163). Likewise, the God of Abraham, Isaac, and Jacob, the God of the Bible, declares repeatedly: "Look unto me and be ye saved . . . for I am God and there is none else" (Isaiah 45:22; etc.). Allah claims to be the one who alone can save mankind; but so says the God of the Bible: "I, even I, am the LORD; and beside me there is no savior" (Isaiah 43:11; etc.).

Is Allah the same as Jahweh/Jehovah of the Old Testament, which Muslims claim to accept? Is the Jewish concept of the God of Abraham, Isaac, and Jacob the same as that of the Christian who believes in Father, Son, and Holy Spirit? In an apparent attempt to seduce Muslims, the Roman Catholic Church teaches that Allah is the God of the Bible:

> The plan of salvation also includes those who acknowledge the Creator, in the first place amongst whom are the Moslems: these profess to hold the faith of Abraham, and together with us they adore the one, merciful God, mankind's judge on the last day.[1]

235

That Muslim, Christian, and Jew each has a different view of God, however, is clear in spite of attempts by ecumenists to claim otherwise. Both Muslims and Jews would deny that they worship the God of the Roman Catholics, who is a trinity. There are, as we shall see, serious differences between the understandings that Muslims, Jews, and Christians have regarding the "God" each embraces. Obviously only one of these three can be the one true God. Which is it? There is no more important question than this.

Every religion claims to offer the revelations of the true god or gods. Yet even in their basic concepts of deity there are sharp contradictions among the world's religions, which means that all cannot be right. Hinduism, for example, embraces multitudes of gods and involves the worship of idols that supposedly represent these gods, since everything is god. By contrast, Islam denounces idol worship and pantheism/ polytheism and claims that its Allah is the only true God. Buddhism, which has conflicting philosophies ranging from "all exists" to "neither the self nor the dharmas exist," generally involves no god and centers upon "enlightenment."

Some Distinctions

That Allah and the God of Abraham, Isaac, and Jacob, the God of the Bible and of the apostle Paul, are not one and the same is quite clear. The Christian God is a triune being of Father, Son, and Holy Spirit, while Allah is a single, individual entity who destroys rather than saves sinners as does the God of the Bible. Allah has compassion on only the righteous, does not deal in grace, but rewards only good deeds, and, unlike the God of the Bible, has no way to redeem the lost. Allah is clearly *not* the God of the Bible.

The God of the Bible condemns idolatry. Yet Allah was the chief god in the Kaabah, the pagan temple that Mohammed "purged" by destroying the more than 300 idols it contained. Why then did Mohammed call the god of his new religion by that same name, Allah? More than likely he kept the name of this ancient pagan moon god because it would help to convert idolaters to his new religion if they could be offered something familiar. Yet today's Muslims see no contradiction in this strategy.

The God of the Bible can be known (1 Chronicles 28:9; Isaiah 19:21; 43:10; Jeremiah 24:7; 31:34; John 17:3; etc.); Allah is unknowable. Thus Allah cannot be personal in the true sense inasmuch as that would bring him down to the level of acquaintance with other personal beings, such as man. The further consequence is that while the Koran attributes compassion and mercy to Allah, those emotions are without rational explanation. Allah may forgive, or he may condemn, as he pleases and without rational reason.

The God of the Bible, on the other hand, is a God of justice whose forgiveness must have a righteous basis. The penalty which His justice demands must be paid before God can forgive; and, because no human could pay that penalty, God Himself came into the world as a man through the virgin birth and suffered the full penalty deserved by a world of sinners. His motivation is always purest love.

There are many other differences between Allah and the God of the Bible, but the above-mentioned are sufficient to prove that the two beings are not one and the same, as is so often mistakenly imagined. How very dishonest and dishonoring to the biblical God to claim that "Jews, Christians, and Moslems all worship the One God"!

Love That Will Not Let Me Go

One of the most obvious qualities lacking in Islam is love. There isn't even one listing for "love" in the index of the popular Marmaduke Pickthall translation of the Koran. Obviously, love is of no great importance in Islam, although it does say that "Allah loveth those who battle for His cause..." (Surah 61:4).

The Koran also says that Allah loves "the beneficent" (Surah 2:195), "those who have a care for cleanness" (2:222), "the steadfast [and] those whose deeds are good" (3:146-7), etc., but never that he loves all mankind, much less sinners. In contrast, love is the crowning attribute of the God of the Bible, who loves the whole world of sinners, and of whom it is said that He *is* love. And He proves that love by *personally* stepping into history to share our suffering. Allah, on the other hand, acts only through angels and prophets.

Love is the major element in true Christianity. The word "love" occurs 310 times in 280 verses in the Bible, while the words "loves," "loved," "loving," and "loveth" occur another 179 times. Love is the very essence of the biblical God's character: "God is love" (1 John 4:8). God's love for mankind is a major theme of the Bible, which is filled with abundant evidence of that love. For example:

> For God so loved the world that he gave his only begotten Son, that whosoever believeth in him should not perish [in hell] but have everlasting life (John 3:16).

> In this was manifested the love of God toward us, because that God sent his only begotten Son into the world that we might live through him.
> Herein is love, not that we loved God but that he loved us, and sent his Son to be the propitiation [cleansing/forgiveness] for our sins (1 John 4:9,10).

According to the Bible, the very first commandment given to Israel and to all mankind was, "Thou shalt love the LORD thy God with all thine heart, and with all thy soul, and with all thy might" (Deuteronomy 6:5). Jesus called this "the first and great[est] commandment" (Matthew 22:38) and declared that all other commandments could be summarized as "Thou shalt love thy neighbor as thyself" (verse 39). He went on to say, "On these two commandments hang all the law and the prophets" (verse 40). So said the Old Testament as well: "Thou shalt love thy neighbor as thyself" (Leviticus 19:18).

There can be no doubt that just as love is the essence of God's character, so it is also the essence of all that the Bible teaches and requires. First Corinthians 13 is known as the love chapter, and there is nothing in all of world literature to match it for beauty, as this excerpt reveals:

> Though I speak with the tongues of men and of angels,
> and have not love, I am become as sounding brass or a
> clanging cymbal.
>
> And though I have the gift of prophecy, and under-
> stand all mysteries and all knowledge, and though I have
> all faith, so that I could remove mountains, and have not
> love, I am nothing.
>
> And though I bestow all my goods to feed the poor,
> and though I give my body to be burned, and have not
> love, it profiteth me nothing.
>
> Love suffereth long and is kind . . . is not easily pro-
> voked, thinketh no evil . . . beareth all things . . . en-
> dureth all things. Love never faileth. . . .
>
> And now abide faith, hope, love, these three; but the
> greatest of these is love.

Christianity is much more than the practice of certain
religious teachings. It involves a loving personal relationship
with God through Jesus Christ, who, by His Spirit, literally
lives in those who open their hearts to Him. Consequently, the
love of God through Christ is expected to be expressed in all
that a Christian thinks, says, and does. Inasmuch as God loved
us when we were His enemies, a Christian is expected—
indeed, commanded—by Christ to love his enemies also:

> Ye have heard that it hath been said, Thou shalt love
> thy neighbor and hate thine enemy. But I say unto you,
> Love your enemies, bless them that curse you, do good to
> them that hate you, and pray for them which despitefully
> use you and persecute you (Matthew 5:43,44).

The Bible declares unequivocally: "He that loveth not
knoweth not God, for God is love" (1 John 4:8). Such is the
God of the Bible (in stark contrast to Allah), and such is to be
the behavior of the Christian. In contrast to the Muslim, who
is to spread the message of Islam with the sword, the Christian
is to lay down his life to bring the message of God's love, a
message that mankind is free to accept or reject, for love does
not force itself upon the one loved:

Beloved, if God so loved us, we ought also to love one another. . . . If we love one another, God dwelleth in us . . . because he hath given us of his Spirit. . . .

And we have known and believed the love that God hath to us. God is love, and he that dwelleth in love dwelleth in God, and God in him. . . .

We love him because he first loved us.

If a man say, I love God, and hateth his brother, he is a liar. . . .

And this commandment have we from him, that he who loveth God love his brother also (1 John 4:11-21).

This love relationship which the Christian enjoys with God is unknown in Islam or any other religion. The following verses of a song present a typical expression of this wonderful intimacy which the Christian enjoys with God through Christ:

O Love that wilt not let me go,
I rest my weary soul in Thee;
I give Thee back the life I owe,
That in Thine ocean depths its flow
May richer, fuller be.

O Cross that liftest up my head,
I dare not ask to fly from Thee;
I lay in dust life's glory dead,
And from the ground there blossoms red,
Life that shall endless be.

The Pagan Connection

It is commonly imagined by non-Muslims that Allah is simply the Arabic word for God, like *Dieu* in French or *Dios* in Spanish. Not so. Allah is a contraction of *al-Ilah*, the personal name of the moon god, chief of the gods in the ancient Kaaba. That fact is still reflected in the crescent moon on the minarets and shrines and mosques and national flags of Islamic countries. If Allah were merely the Arabic word for God, then the Muslims would not hesitate to use the word for God in other languages. But in each language it is insisted that the name

Allah be used; it would be blasphemy to call the Muslims' god anything but Allah.

After a number of visions, Mohammed began openly to announce himself as the prophet of Allah and to preach against worshiping the other gods in the Kaaba. This radical message brought Mohammed into great conflict with his own tribesmen, who profited from the fact that the Kaaba held the favorite gods of all of the surrounding tribes so that those traveling with the merchant caravans through Mecca could worship there.

A cornerstone of Islam today is its rejection of idol worship. How strange, then, that its god is Allah, the onetime favorite god of the Quraish tribe long before Islam was invented. Furthermore, kissing the sacred Black Stone, for centuries an act that was at the very heart of the Kaaba's idolatry, remains an integral part of Islam and of the pilgrimage that each Muslim is obliged to make to Mecca at least once in a lifetime.

The Kaaba also contained enough other deities to satisfy the religious impulses of the many travelers passing through Mecca in the trade caravans. Mohammed smashed all of these idols. Yet he kept the Black Stone, which is still kissed today by Muslims. And he kept, too, the *name* Allah for the god of Islam (its sign was the crescent moon) in order to appeal to his own tribe.

The God of the Bible states unequivocally: "Before me there was no God formed, neither shall there be after me. I, even I, am the Lord; and beside me there is no savior" (Isaiah 43:10,11). Nor does Jahweh simply ignore the gods of other religions. He denounces them all—every one (including Allah) represented by the idols in the Kaaba, and all others— as impostors who actually represent Satan or his demons: "They sacrificed unto devils, not to God" (Deuteronomy 32:17). The New Testament is in agreement: "The things which the Gentiles [non-Jews] sacrifice [to their gods] they sacrifice to devils" (1 Corinthians 10:20).

One wonders what the long-established pagan custom of kissing the Black Stone could possibly have to do with what

Mohammed claimed was an entirely new religion that replaced the old. In pre-Islamic days each tribe adopted for its protection a sacred stone which was believed to hold magical powers. The Black Stone of today's Kaaba was the one which Mohammed's Quraish tribe had adopted long before his birth. Its retention proves that much of Islam, contrary to what Muslims believe, was not received as a new revelation from heaven, as Mohammed claimed, but was simply carried over from long-established pagan customs.

Predating Mohammed

The same holds true in other areas of Islam. For example, much of the dietary laws and dress requirements still imposed upon today's Muslims, 1300 years after Islam's beginning, did not grow out of the new religion or come as revelations from Allah but had for centuries been the custom of Arabs living at that time. Yet these requirements are given strict religious significance by fundamentalist Muslims today. The same is true of the status of women in Islam: It reflects the low view accorded them in pre-Islamic Arab society, a view already established before Mohammed's birth. Such treatment of women is considered by non-Muslims to be not only demeaning but cruel and barbaric by today's standards.

That Allah was a pagan deity that had been for centuries worshiped by Mohammed's ancestors, and that human sacrifices were also offered to it, is even admitted by Ibn Ishaq, the earliest biographer of Mohammed. In his 768 A.D. work, *Surahtu'l*, Ishaq tells how Mohammed's grandfather, Abdul Muttalib, after praying to Allah, was about to sacrifice one of his sons, Abdullah. It was a sorceress in Hijaz who told him that it was not Allah's will for the boy to be sacrificed to him, but that several camels should be offered in his place.[2] Abdullah, his life spared, became Mohammed's father.

The very name of the Prophet's father, Abdullah (Abd ul allah), means "servant of Allah." That fact provides further proof that Allah as a pagan deity was worshiped by Mohammed's ancestors before he was born. Yet for thousands of years the God of the Bible and of Israel, whose name is Jahweh or Jehovah, had forbidden the worship of any other god. Surely Allah and Jahweh are not the same!

Irreconcilable Conflict

Far from being a virtue or kindness, it is pure cynicism and a denial of the meaning of language to suggest that all religions are the same. It is an affront to Muslims, for example, to suggest that Allah is the equivalent of the many gods in Hinduism, or to tell a Christian that his God, who gave His Son to die for our sins, is the same as Allah, of whom it is specifically stated that he has no son:

> So believe in Allah and His messengers, and say not "Three"—Cease! (it is) better for you!—Allah is only One God. Far is it removed from His transcendent majesty that he should have a son (Surah 4:171).

Nor can one deny the irreconcilable conflict between the belief that Christ died for our sins and was resurrected (which is the very heart of Christianity), and the Muslim claim that someone else died in Christ's place. To sweep such differences under an ecumenical rug (as Roman Catholicism attempts to do) is hardly a kindness. Nor is it possible to reconcile the claim of all non-Christian religions that sin is countered by good works (a belief that Catholicism also shares) with the Bible's declaration: "Not by works of righteousness which we have done, but according to his mercy he saved us" (Titus 3:5); "For by grace are ye saved...not of works, lest any man should boast" (Ephesians 2:8,9).

In fact, biblical Christianity (as distinguished from Roman Catholicism's traditions) stands on one side of a theological chasm, with all other religions on the other side. That chasm, in fact, renders any ecumenical union impossible without destroying Christianity itself. At the heart of Christianity is the claim that Jesus Christ stands absolutely alone, without rival, in His perfect, sinless life, His death for our sins, His resurrection, and His coming again.

The promise of Christ's second coming presents another unique aspect of Christianity which separates it from all of the world's religions by a chasm that cannot be bridged by any ecumenical sleight-of-hand. Mohammed never promised to return, nor did Buddha or any other religious leader. Only Christ dared to make this promise. Nor would such a claim by anyone except Christ be given any credence, for the decayed remains of all the founders of the world's religions occupy graves. There they remain until the last judgment.

It is Christ alone who left behind an empty tomb. That undeniable fact, which we have demonstrated fully in other writings, is reason enough to accept His claim to deity and to take seriously His assertion that He would return to this earth in power and glory to execute judgment upon His enemies. Christ's unique claim, "I am the way, the truth, and the life; no man cometh unto the Father but by me" (John 14:6), is the strongest possible rejection of all other religions as counterfeits.

What's in a Name?

Confusion has been caused by some Bible translations (into the Hausa language in northern Nigeria, for example) using Allah as a designation for the God of the Bible. The translators, by using a term familiar to the Muslims in northern Nigeria, no doubt thought they were being helpful. But by using Allah for God in the Hausa Bible, they have succeeded instead in creating confusion.

Allah is not a generic linguistic designation for God. Allah is the *name* of the god of Islam, a name which, as we have noted, once designated the chief god among the numerous idols in the Kaaba in Mecca.

The God of Israel, too, has a *name*: YHWH, now pronounced Jehovah but more anciently as Yahweh. Most Christians are unaware of God's *name* because the Old Testament substitutes LORD for YHWH. In Exodus 6:3 God says, "By my name YHWH was I not known to them"; and at the burning bush when Moses asked His *name*, God explained the meaning of it by saying I AM THAT I AM. Thus YHWH means not just one who *is,* but the self-existent One who *is in and of Himself* (Exodus 3:13,14).

Unity and Diversity

There are two general concepts of God: 1) pantheism/ naturalism, that the universe itself is God; and 2) supernaturalism, that the Creator is separate and distinct from His creation. Within the second concept are two further ways of understanding God: 1) polytheism, that there are many gods; and 2) monotheism, that there is only one true God. Monotheism itself is divided into two more rival concepts of God: 1) that God is a single being; and 2) that God has always existed in three Persons (not three different Gods but three personal Beings who are separate and distinct yet one). Obviously, Christians are the only ones who hold the latter view (though even some who call themselves Christians reject it). Still, it is the only logically and philosophically coherent view of God possible.

There are obvious and insurmountable problems with any other concept of God than the Christian view. Pantheism has fatal flaws. If everything is God, then God is evil as well as good, sickness as well as health, death as well as life. Such a "God" does as much or more evil as it does good and is no more than nature itself, to which no appeal can be made for help. To pray to pantheism's god would be to pray to a tree or volcano or the wind or to oneself—obviously the utmost folly.

Polytheism's problem's are equally obvious. There is no real God who is in charge, so the many gods fight wars, steal one another's wives, and quarrel endlessly among themselves. There is no peace in heaven and thus no basis for peace upon earth. Polytheism's basic problem is *diversity without unity.*

At the other end of the scale is the belief in one God and that He is a single being. This view is held not only by Muslims but also, through a basic misunderstanding of their own Scriptures, by Jews as well. Thus Allah and Jehovah, though different in other respects, are each seen by Muslims and Jews as single entities. A similar view is also held by several pseudo-Christian cults, such as the Jehovah's Witnesses and Mormons, who reject the doctrine of the trinity, and by various aberrant Christian groups who deny the deity of Christ. The belief that God is a singular being poses the opposite problem from polytheism: *unity without diversity.* This is also a fatal flaw.

That God must encompass *both unity and diversity* is quite easy to see. For example, Allah, being a single entity, would by very definition be an incomplete being. As a single entity all alone, Allah would be unable to experience love, fellowship, and communion before he created beings with whom he could share these experiences. The same is true of the false Jehovah of Judaism's imperfect understanding, as well as of the Jehovah's Witnesses and the United Pentecostal Church.

The Bible makes it very clear that in and of Himself "God *is* love" (1 John 4:8,16). The God of Islam and Judaism could not be love in and of himself. He would have to create other beings in order to have the experience either of loving or of being loved. Yet consistently, from Genesis through Revelation, the Bible presents a God who did not need to create any beings to experience love, communion, and fellowship. *This God is fully complete in Himself,* being three Persons—Father, Son, and Holy Spirit—who are separate and distinct yet at the same time eternally one God. They loved and communed and fellowshiped with each other and took counsel together before the universe, angels, or mankind were brought into existence. Even the Old Testament acknowledged by Jews declares this.

Plurality and Unity

Moses revealed the intimate relationship within the Godhead when he wrote, "God said, Let *us* make man in *our* image, after *our* likeness . . ." (Genesis 1:26); and again, "Let *us* go down and there confound their language" (Genesis 11:7). Who is this *us* and to whom is God speaking if God is a single entity? Why does God say, "The man is become as one of *us*" (Genesis 3:22)?

Moreover, if God is a single being, then why is the Hebrew word *Elohim* used for God? *Elohim* is a plural noun that literally means "Gods." Another question confronts us: Inasmuch as Elohim is plural, why do both Jews and Christians believe in one God, not in Gods? And why does the Bible in every language translate Elohim, a plural Hebrew noun, as God and not Gods? Unitarianism, of course, has no answer for such questions; indeed, it doesn't even dare to ask them.

The answer is found in the ancient Hebrew language. Throughout the Hebrew Old Testament we almost always find the strange anomaly of a singular verb and a singular pronoun being used with *Elohim*, a plural noun. At the burning bush, for example, it was *Elohim* (Gods) who spoke to Moses and said, not *"We are that we are,"* but *"I AM THAT I AM"* (Exodus 3:14). No one can escape the fact that all through the Bible, and just as plainly in the Old Testament as in the New, God is presented as a plurality and yet as one, as having both diversity and unity. This concept of God is unique among all the world's religions!

The same anomaly is presented in the *shema*. Israel's famous confession of God's *oneness* is also at the same time a clear and undeniable declaration of His *plurality*: "Hear, O Israel: The LORD [*Jahweh/Jehovah*] our God [*Elohim*] is one [*echad*] LORD [*Jahweh/Jehovah*]" (Deuteronomy 6:4; cf. Mark 12:29). There is that plural noun, *Elohim/Gods*, right in the center of the declaration of God's oneness! How can that be?

One must understand that the Hebrew word for "one" (*echad*) does not designate singularity but a *unity comprised of several becoming one*. For example, *echad* is used in Genesis 2:24, where man and woman become *one* flesh; in Exodus 36:13, when its various parts "became *one* tabernacle"; in 2 Samuel 2:25, when many soldiers "became *one* troop"; and in Ezekiel 37:17, when two sticks became "*one* stick."

Unitarianism or Trinitarianism?

Unitarianism has no explanation for this consistent presentation of God's plurality in singularity, not only in the New

Testament but throughout the Old Testament as well. Only trinitarianism can explain it. The actual word "trinity" does not occur in the Bible, but the concept is clearly there and cannot be explained away. In fact, this concept of the triune God is the only possible explanation for the unity and diversity that makes possible the love, fellowship, and communion within the Godhead.

The heresy that God is a single entity and not three Persons existing eternally in one God was first introduced into the early church around 220 A.D. by a Libyan theologian named Sabellius. Of course he had a problem trying to salvage biblical language concerning Father, Son, and Holy Spirit without acknowledging the triune nature of God. Sabellius claimed that God existed as a single Being who manifested Himself in three activities, modes, or aspects: as Father in the creation, as Son in redemption, and as Holy Spirit in prophecy and sanctification. This view was condemned as heresy by the vast majority of Christian leaders and has been so considered ever since, except among aberrant groups such as the United Pentecostals.

Jesus said, "The Father loveth the Son and hath given all things into his hand" (John 3:35), and again in John 5:20, "The Father loveth the Son. . . ." The God of the Bible truly *is* love, not just toward mankind but preeminently among the three Members of the Godhead. And three *personal Beings* they must be. It is meaningless to suggest that the Father, Son, and Holy Spirit are mere offices or titles or modes in which God manifests Himself. Offices or titles or modes don't love, consult, and fellowship together. Not only Jesus Christ, the Son, is presented as a Person, but the Father and the Holy Spirit are presented as equally personal in the New Testament.

The Old Testament agrees. For example, consider the following: "Hearken unto me, O Jacob and Israel, my called; I am he; I am the first, I also am the last. Mine hand also hath laid the foundation of the earth, and my right hand hath spanned the heavens. . . . I, even I, have spoken. . . . Come ye near unto me, hear ye this: I have not spoken in secret from the beginning; from the time that it was, there am I; and the Lord GOD, and his Spirit, hath sent me" (Isaiah 48:12,15,16).

Note that the One who is speaking through Isaiah the prophet refers to Himself as "the first and the last" and the One who created all things (verse 13), so He must be God. But He speaks of two Others in the same passage who must also be God: "the Lord God, and his Spirit . . ." (verse 16). These two, who must be God, "sent me," says the Speaker, who also must be God. The New Testament explains this passage, for which Judaism has no explanation: "The Father sent the Son to be the Savior of the world" (1 John 4:14).

In Matthew 22:41-46 Jesus presented a similar passage to the Pharisees: "The LORD said unto my Lord, Sit thou on my right hand till I make thine enemies thy footstool" (quoting from Psalm 110:1). In reference to this verse and in response to their statement that the Messiah was the son of David, Jesus asked the rabbis: "If David then call him Lord, how is he his son?" The Pharisees were speechless. How could the Messiah be David's Lord if He isn't God?

An Instructive Analogy

Yes, it is a mystery how God can exist in three Persons yet be one God; but it is also a mystery that God could have no beginning and create everything out of nothing. It is true that no mortal can explain the Trinity; but neither can anyone explain the human soul or spirit or love or beauty or justice. The fact that God's person and power are beyond human comprehension is not sufficient reason for being an atheist. Nor does the fact that we cannot understand how the one true God could comprise three separate personal beings serve as a valid reason for rejecting what the Bible so clearly presents to us from Genesis through Revelation.

The Bible declares that the universe reveals God's glory. In fact, it reflects His triune nature. We see this, first of all, in the fact that the cosmos is tripartite. It consists of space, matter, and time. Furthermore, each of these is divided into three.

Space, for instance, is comprised of length, breadth, and height, each separate and distinct in itself, yet the three make up one unified space. Length, breadth, and width are not three spaces, nor are they modes of manifestation of space, but a unity of three dimensions that together comprise one space. Run enough lines lengthwise and one takes in all of space; the same is true widthwise or heightwise. Each is separate and distinct from the others, yet the three are one—just as the Father, Son, and Holy Spirit are one God.

Time also is a trinity. Consider its elements: past, present, and future. Here again each is separate and distinct, yet each is the whole and together they comprise a unity that is one. Past, present, and future are not three times. Each is all of time. And just as the Father and Holy Spirit are invisible and the Son is visible, so the future and past are invisible and the present is visible. We could pursue the analogy further, but it shouldn't be necessary. Nor is any analogy complete, especially one dealing with God.

The "God" Who Failed

The great Jewish author and Holocaust survivor Elie Wiesel tells how he spent his youth in earnest search for God and in fasting "to hasten the coming of the Messiah. . . ."[3] As a young boy, Wiesel had believed that the God of Israel existed and had sought to know Him. Unfortunately, he had pursued that knowledge not through God's Word but in tradition through the study of Jewish mysticism, particularly as taught in the Cabala.

In response to the eager young pupil's persistent questions, Wiesel's teacher had told him, "You will find the true answers, Eliezer, only within yourself!"

"And why do you pray, Moshe?" Elie had asked him. It was a logical question in view of the statement that all answers were already within everyone.

"I pray to the God within me . . ." had come the mystical reply.[4]

The theory that God is within everyone presents the same problem as pantheism's belief that God is all. If God is everything—poison as well as nutrition, evil as well as good, death as well as life, inanimate objects as well as animate—then the very concept of God has lost its meaning and nothing is God. The same incongruity prevails if God is within everyone—within those who murder as well as those who save lives, within those who rob and plunder as well as those who are helpful and generous, within those who love as well as those who hate, within helpless invalids as well as within the healthy and strong, within imbeciles as well as within geniuses. If that is the case, then no one can point out what it means that God is within anyone. Thus the very concept of God has lost its meaning and ultimately nothing is God. If God is within everyone, then we would have to blame this "god" for all aberrant behavior and thus for all the evil in the world. Who needs such a god?

That "god" to whom Elie Wiesel had been introduced in his youth, who allegedly resides innately in every human being, was not able to survive the Holocaust. Wiesel testifies that it was upon first entering Birkenau, reception center for Auschwitz, that his faith died when he saw women and children being thrown alive into a flaming pit. It is understandable that Wiesel's god could not survive those flames.

The God Who Cares

In the foreword to Elie Wiesel's powerful book *Night*, Francois Mauriac refers to the time when he had first met Wiesel. The young man told Mauriac how the God he had once believed in had died in his soul, even as the victims of the flames at Birkenau had been immolated.

Wiesel had lost father, mother, sister, relatives, and friends in the Holocaust. As a consequence, he could no longer believe in the God who had supposedly chosen the Jews as His special people yet had abandoned them to such a horrible fate. Mauriac's reaction is worth pondering:

> And I, who believe that God is love, what answer
> could I give my young questioner, whose dark eyes still

252 ◆ ALLAH OR YAHWEH?

held the reflection of that angelic sadness which had appeared one day upon the face of the hanged child [that the inmates had been forced to view]? What did I say to him? Did I speak of that other Jew, his brother, who may have resembled him—the Crucified, whose Cross has conquered the world?

Did I affirm that the stumbling block to his faith was the cornerstone of mine, and that the conformity between the Cross and the suffering of men was in my eyes the key to that impenetrable mystery whereon the faith of his childhood had perished . . . ? We do not know the worth of one single drop of blood, one single tear.

All is grace. If the Eternal is the Eternal, the last word for each one of us belongs to Him. This is what I should have told this Jewish child. But I could only embrace him, weeping.[5]

Here we encounter the great difference between all gods and the God of the Bible. He does not stand aloof from our suffering, but has in fact entered into it, becoming a man, suffering crucifixion at the hands of His creatures and dying in their place to save them from the penalty which His own justice demands for their sin.

*They came to the place which God had told him of;
and Abraham built an altar there . . . and bound
Isaac his son, and laid him on the altar. . . .*

—Genesis 22:9

*Thou shalt offer every day . . . a sin offering for
atonement. . . .*

—Exodus 29:36

*Behold, I [Solomon] purpose to build an house
[Temple] unto the name of the LORD my God, as the
LORD spoke unto David my father, saying, Thy son,
whom I will set upon thy throne in thy room [stead],
he shall build an house [Temple] unto my name [in
Jerusalem].*

—1 Kings 5:5

*When We made the House [Kaaba] (at Mecca) a
resort for mankind and a sanctuary, (saying): Take
as your place of worship the place where Abraham
stood (to pray). And we imposed a duty upon Abraham and Ishmael, (saying): Purify My house for
those who go around and those who meditate therein
and those who bow down and prostrate themselves (in
worship).*

—Surah 2:125

*Let Christ the King of Israel descend now from the
cross, that we may see and believe.*

—Mark 15:32

*Being found in fashion as a man, he [Christ] humbled
himself and became obedient unto death, even the
death of the cross.*

—Philippians 2:8

14

Altars, Temples, and a Cross

◆

Neither Christian, Muslim, Jew, nor atheist can deny that numerous Scriptures in the Old Testament (some of which we have previously quoted) plainly declare that God promised the land of Israel (and much more territory than Israel occupies today) to the descendants of Abraham, Isaac, and Jacob. The Mideast crisis confronting the world arises from the fact that both Jews (who are undoubtedly descended from Isaac and Jacob) and Arabs (who ignore the qualification that descent must be through Isaac and Jacob) claim Abraham as their father. It is this common claim which creates an impasse concerning Jerusalem and the land of Israel that threatens the world with its most destructive war to date.

History and Scripture record that Abraham had two sons during his wife Sarah's lifetime: Ishmael and Isaac. The second son God had promised, while the first one He had not. God's solemn promise seemed hopeless because Sarah, Abraham's wife, was barren. Therefore, to help fulfill the promise, Abraham and Sarah took matters into their own hands. Sarah suggested that Abraham have a child through her Egyptian maid, Hagar, in order to provide the heir who would inherit God's promises. The result of that act of unbelief, one of the very few of which Abraham, "the father of all them that believe" (Romans 4:11), was guilty, was the birth of Ishmael. From him the Arabs, in spite of evidence to the contrary, claim to be descended.

Isaac, the promised son, was born by a miracle to Sarah and Abraham 14 years after Ishmael's birth. At that time, in addition to being barren all her life, it had "ceased to be with Sarah after the manner of women" (Genesis 18:11). Only then, when it was physically too late for her to have a child, and thus seemingly impossible for God's promise to be fulfilled, was Isaac born. Here was another indication that the birth of the Messiah, who would be descended from Abraham, would be miraculous, though in an even more remarkable and meaningful way than Isaac's birth. As the prophets declared, the Messiah would be born of a virgin.

A Strange Altar

After the birth of Isaac, we have one of the strangest stories in the Bible. In order to test Abraham's faith, God commanded him to offer Isaac in blood sacrifice upon an altar at a special site in the Promised Land. Again it was an indication that the Messiah, who would be God's Son as Isaac was Abraham's, would be sacrificed at His Father's hand for mankind:

> It came to pass . . . that God did tempt [test] Abraham and said unto him . . . Take now thy son, thine only son Isaac, whom thou lovest, and get thee into the land of Moriah, and offer him there for a burnt offering upon one of the mountains which I will tell thee of.
> And Abraham rose up early in the morning, and saddled his ass, and took . . . Isaac his son . . . [and] wood for the burnt offering, and . . . went unto the place of which God had told him . . . (Genesis 22:1-3).

It is quite clear that Abraham knew that God was testing both his obedience and his faith. All of God's promises for the future were contained in Isaac, the miraculous son of promise. If Isaac were to die before children were born of him, God's promises would fail. Therefore Abraham was confident that

Isaac would somehow, by God's grace, be brought back to life: "Accounting that God was able to raise him up, even from the dead" (Hebrews 11:19). Here was another picture of the Messiah, who, after being given up as a sacrifice by His Father, would be resurrected from the dead:

> Isaac . . . said, My father . . . behold the fire and the wood, but where is the lamb for a burnt offering? And Abraham said, My son, God will provide himself a lamb for a burnt offering. . . .
>
> And they came to the place . . . and Abraham built an altar there, and laid the wood in order, and bound Isaac his son, and laid him on the altar upon the wood. And Abraham stretched forth his hand, and took the knife to slay his son. And the angel of the LORD called unto him . . . Lay not thine hand upon the lad . . . for now I know that thou fearest God, seeing thou hast not withheld thy son. . . .
>
> And Abraham . . . looked, and behold, behind him a ram caught in a thicket by his horns [a picture of God's Lamb, who alone had the infinite power to pay sin's penalty]; and Abraham went and took the ram, and offered him up for a burnt offering in the stead of his son (Genesis 22:7-13).

The Unique Temple Site

God later decreed that the Temple with its animal sacrifices, each one of which also looked forward to the Messiah's sacrifice for the sins of the world, would be built on the very same site where Abraham had offered Isaac. That site, however, was not owned by Abraham and for centuries remained in the hands of the Jebusites, who occupied the fortress on Mount Zion, a stronghold which the Israelites were unable to conquer after their entrance into the Promised Land. It was left for David to capture Mount Zion about 400 years later, establishing Jerusalem as the City of David. How the site for the Temple at the top of Mount Zion was subsequently pointed out to David and was purchased by him is another instructive story.

Because, toward the end of King David's reign, he (and Israel with him) had boastfully begun to trust in the numerical strength and capability of Israel's warriors instead of in God alone, an angel came to execute judgment upon David and Israel for their pride. David saw the angel with its drawn sword in its hand standing over that very place where Isaac had been offered on an altar. It was being used as a threshing floor by Ornan, a survivor of the Jebusites whom David had defeated in capturing the fortress of Zion.

David fell on his face before the angel, confessed his sin, and pleaded for his people to be spared. The angel commanded him to "set up an altar unto the LORD in the threshing floor of Ornan" and offer a sacrifice there. In order to do so, David had to purchase the site, teaching us that true worship is costly:

> David said to Ornan, Grant me the place of this threshing floor, that I may build an altar therein unto the LORD. . . . So David gave to Ornan for the place six hundred shekels of gold by weight. And David built there an altar unto the LORD, and offered burnt offerings and peace offerings, and called upon the LORD; and he [God] answered him from heaven by fire upon the altar. . .
> (1 Chronicles 21:22,25,26).

God later revealed to David that he had unwittingly purchased the site where the Temple would be built by his son, Solomon. Animal sacrifices would continue thereafter in the Temple, with brief interruptions during periods when the Temple was rendered unusable by invading forces, until its final destruction in 70 A.D.

A thick curtain blocked normal access to the Temple's inner sanctuary, known as the "Holiest of all" (Hebrews 9:3). Within that veil the high priest alone could go, and then only once a year (Exodus 30:10; Hebrews 9:25). When Christ died upon the cross, that separating shroud was ripped apart miraculously by the hand of God "from the top to the bottom" (Mark 15:38). The miracle was a clear sign from God that Christ's sacrifice had opened once and for all the way into

God's very presence in heaven. The animal sacrifices, now fulfilled in Christ, were no longer needed, though the priests continued to offer them until the Temple was destroyed.

A Rival Temple in Mecca

Islam, as we have already seen, teaches that God's Temple, rather than being built originally by Solomon in Jerusalem, was actually the Kaaba in Mecca. That structure was supposedly built by God's command and rebuilt and cleansed by Abraham and Ishmael centuries before Solomon's birth: "And when Abraham and Ishmael were raising the foundations of the House, (Abraham prayed): Our Lord! Accept from us (this duty)" (Surah 2:127). The historical fact, however, is that the Kaaba was always a pagan temple filled with idols, the worship of which was an abomination to God and forbidden to Abraham and his descendants. Nor was Abraham ever within hundreds of miles of Mecca.

The Koran claims to present the same revelation as that given in the Bible: "We inspired Abraham and Ishmael and Isaac and Jacob and the tribes [of Israel], and Jesus . . . and Solomon, and as we imparted unto David the Psalms" (Surah 4:163); "Lo! We did reveal the Torah, wherein is guidance and a light" (Surah 5:44); "(We guided) David and Solomon . . . and Moses and Aaron . . . and Zachariah and John and Jesus and Elias" (Surah 6:85,86). Yet Islam has made itself the enemy of both Jews and Christians, whom the Koran designates as "the People of the Scripture [Bible]" (Surah 2:105,144; 3:23,64ff.,110ff.,186; 4:123; etc.).

Moreover, claiming that an idol temple in Mecca is the Temple of God, Islam deliberately stands in the way of rebuilding the Temple in Jerusalem, a Temple which Solomon built, for which David provided most of the materials, for which Moses in the Torah provided the worship instructions, in which Aaron served as the first high priest, and in which Zachariah served and Jesus taught. All of these men the Koran says Allah inspired, yet it opposes that inspiration. The contradiction could not be greater!

We have earlier quoted some of the many verses in the Bible which make it clear that in Jerusalem and especially in its Temple God has placed His name forever: "Jerusalem which I have chosen and the house [Temple] of which I said, My name shall be there . . . forever" (2 Kings 21:7; 23:27; 2 Chronicles 6:34; 7:12,16; 33:7; etc.). That is the Temple which will be rebuilt in spite of every Muslim effort to prevent its reconstruction. Unfortunately for the Jews and the world, Antichrist will desecrate the Temple with his image and cause the world to worship him as God (Daniel 9:27; 12:11; Mark 13:14; 2 Thessalonians 2:4; Revelation 13:6,14,15).

Mystery, Babylon

The Old Testament sacrifices had to be offered in the Temple according to God's precise instructions that pointed forward to the redemption which God would Himself effect in the Messiah's sacrificial death upon the cross. The God of the Bible, unlike Allah, does not act capriciously but only in harmony with His divine nature and His perfect justice and laws. Exodus 20:24-26 required that no stone used in an altar could be fashioned nor was the altar to be approached by steps. In other words, no human effort could be involved in man's redemption; it must be provided solely by God's power and grace.

The Tower of Babel was the ultimate rejection of this requirement: "Let us build us . . . a tower, whose top may reach unto heaven" (Genesis 11:4). Man would attempt, by steps of his own making, to climb into heaven itself. Babel later became Babylon and represents man's religion of works. "MYSTERY, BABYLON" is emblazoned on the forehead of the woman riding the beast in Revelation 17, showing the persistence in the last days of human effort to achieve salvation.

Identifying itself with Babylon, Roman Catholicism teaches in Vatican II that the "saints" by their good deeds "attained their own salvation and at the same time cooperated in saving their brothers. . . ." This Post-Conciliar document signed by Pope Paul VI goes on to declare the official Roman Catholic doctrine of attaining heaven by human works:

> From the most ancient times in the Church good
> works were also offered to God for the salvation of
> sinners, particularly the works which human weakness
> finds hard. . . . Indeed, the prayers and good works of
> holy people were regarded as of such great value that it
> could be asserted that the penitent was washed, cleansed
> and redeemed with the help of the entire Christian
> people.[1]

This Church, which claims to represent true Christianity, could not state more clearly that it carries on the works religion of MYSTERY, BABYLON! Judaism, too, forced to function without the Temple sacrifices for 1900 years, and having rejected their fulfillment in Christ's sacrifice on the cross, has fallen back upon a religion of good works. And the same has always been true of Islam, for the Koran imposes rules and duties upon the Muslim from daily prayer and the Ramadan fast to the Meccan pilgrimage, the keeping of which earn Allah's blessing. The ultimate work, of course, is Jihad. To "kill or be killed" in the service of Allah is the surest road to Paradise, providing the fanatical motivation, as we have seen, behind much of the terrorism plaguing the world.

Islamic Law and Forgiveness

Not many Muslims die in Jihad and none lives the perfect life. So the Koran declares that Allah is ever merciful and forgiving. In contrast to the God of the Bible, however, Allah forgives not on the basis of satisfied justice, but simply by deciding to do so. That sin's penalty must be paid in order for the sinner to be forgiven is a foreign idea in Islam. There being no objective reason why he should or should not forgive, Allah's forgiveness as presented in the Koran breeds uncertainty and confusion:

> Forgiveness is only incumbent on Allah toward those
> who do evil in ignorance [how is that defined?] (and) then
> turn quickly [how quickly?] (in repentance) to Allah.
> These are they toward whom Allah relenteth.

And seek forgiveness of Allah. Lo! Allah is ever Forgiving, Merciful [even to those who did not sin in ignorance?]. And plead not on behalf of (people) who deceive themselves. Lo! Allah loveth not one who is treacherous and sinful. . . .

Yet whoso doeth evil or wrongeth his own soul, then seeketh pardon of Allah, will find Allah Forgiving, Merciful [even those who don't sin in ignorance, deceive themselves, and are treacherous?]. Whoso committeth sin committeth it only against himself [not against Allah?]. . . .

Lo! Allah pardoneth . . . all save [except] that to whom he will [not—why not?] (Surah 4:17,106,107,110,116).

As for the thief, both male and female, cut off their hands. It is the reward of their own deeds, an exemplary punishment from Allah. . . . But whoso repenteth after his wrongdoing and amendeth [his way], lo! Allah will relent toward him. Lo! Allah is forgiving, Merciful . . . [but no hand is restored!]. He punisheth whom He will, and forgiveth whom He will [on what basis?] (Surah 5:38-40).

Islam ignores entirely the necessity of sin's penalty being paid in order for the sinner to be forgiven. Allah simply forgives or refuses to forgive, however he is inclined. While the Koran declares repeatedly that Allah is ever gracious and merciful, there is neither a rational nor a righteous basis upon which his mercy is granted. No reason is ever given why Allah forgives or doesn't forgive.

Furthermore, the Koran is inconsistent. We are told that Allah forgives only those who sin through ignorance—and even then only if they repent quickly. But neither "ignorance" nor "quickly" are defined; and later we are told that Allah can forgive anyone whom he decides to forgive. That presumably means *anyone*, no matter what the sin or circumstances—simply if Allah wills it.

In real life, however, Allah's forgiveness never comes in time to rescue the accused from having a hand or foot or ear cut off. The practice of Shari'a (Islamic law) is particularly cruel in Iraq, where U.N. sanctions have driven Iraqis to crime in order to supply themselves with the bare necessities of life. At the end of January 1995, Baghdad TV showed the graphic details of Shari'a to its viewers: "a close-up of a severed human hand, then one of a man clutching the bloody stump of his forearm, a black cross branded on his forehead. The newscaster said the man had been punished for stealing. . . . According to U.N. and U.S. State Department sources, hundreds and perhaps thousands of Iraqis have had hands, feet or ears amputated, without anesthetic . . . [and] are showing up regularly at camps along the border with Iran."[2]

A Religion of Fear

Muslims justify the mutilations called for by Shari'a as a means of lowering the crime rate. In the Western view, however, severing a thief's hand and branding him on the forehead is considered to be a "cruel and unusual punishment," a callous and malicious violation of human rights. It is beyond all reason to brand for life one who might otherwise be rehabilitated. Certainly such treatment is not helpful in restoring the criminal as a useful member of society.

The Muslim is left in uncertainty and fear, not knowing whether he will ever be forgiven by Allah and thus reach Paradise. How Allah can forgive at all without justice having been satisfied through the payment of sin's penalty remains an unanswered and unanswerable question for the Muslim. The concept of grace, therefore, rather than being a source of assurance and hope in Islam, brings uncertainty and dread. How can one be assured of attaining to this grace? And if it is really grace, one cannot earn it. Yet Allah offers his grace only to those who merit it.

Islam is clearly a religion of fear: the fear of offending Allah, of breaking a commandment, of being damned by failure to live up to its standards, and of being maimed or killed if one dares to follow one's conscience and the gospel taught by Jesus Christ, whom the Koran claims to honor. Islam is a religion without a sure hope. Any rational person knows that no amount of good deeds can ever make up for past misdeeds. The law, once broken, cannot be mended by keeping it, even perfectly, in the future. Passing by a bank without robbing it tomorrow cannot recompense for having robbed it today. Nor can the sinful deed be annulled even if complete restitution were made in cases where that might be possible.

Forgiveness and Justice

The Bible plainly declares what the Koran completely overlooks: "By the deeds of the law there shall no flesh be justified in his [God's] sight" (Romans 3:20). That is why Christ had to die: The penalty had to be paid in full. Yet it is not what man did to Christ that procures our salvation. The mocking and spitting and hatred, the scourging and pounding of nails into His hands and feet, the spear thrust into His side—all these only demonstrated how great is the evil of the human heart. Far from saving mankind, those crimes against the Son of God only proved that mankind merited God's eternal judgment.

Amazingly, however, at the same time that the cross of Christ reveals the horror of sin in the human heart, it also reveals the greatness of God's love and mercy. How wonderful that the very nails and spear driven into the Messiah in anger, contempt, and hatred drew forth the blood that saves us! At the same time that man was venting his hostility against his Creator, Yahweh made the Messiah bear the infinite punishment for our sins, as the Hebrew prophets had foretold:

He was wounded for our transgressions, he was bruised for our iniquities; the chastisement of our peace was upon him, and with his stripes we are healed.

All we like sheep have gone astray; we have turned every one to his own way; and the LORD hath laid on him the iniquity of us all. . . .

Yet it pleased the LORD to bruise him; he hath put him to grief; when thou shalt make his soul an offering for sin . . . (Isaiah 53:5,6,10).

As with Judaism, so with Islam: Christ's crucifixion doesn't fit the moral concepts held by either. No wonder, then, that Muslim writers are in great confusion on the subject of Christ's death and resurrection. Some believe that Christ was miraculously taken from the cross into heaven by Allah and that another person who was made to look like Him (perhaps Judas) was instantly put there and died in His place. Others say that Jesus only fainted on the cross, regained consciousness in the grave, and made His escape to India, where he died of old age.

Like the Jews, the Muslims have no understanding of the many Old Testament prophecies that the Messiah would die for the sins of the world and that His death would be in fulfillment of the animal sacrifices. Thus there is no place either in Islam or in Judaism for Christ's payment of sin's penalty upon the cross. And that is why so many Jews turned against the God they didn't understand when confronted by the Holocaust.

In contrast to the Koran, which declares that sin is only against the individual sinning, the Bible says that sin is an offense first of all against God (Genesis 39:9; Deuteronomy 20:18; 1 Samuel 12:23; Psalm 51:4; etc.). It must be so, for it is *God's* laws which are being broken, and *His* perfect character and sinless purity which sin offends. Thus it is *God alone* who can be man's Savior, as the Bible in both Old and New Testaments repeatedly declares. Only He can pay the penalty demanded by His law.

God's holy character requires that the penalty for sin must be paid in full for sin to be forgiven. This penalty is eternal death to the soul and spirit as well as to the body: "The soul that sinneth, it shall die" (Ezekiel 18:4). The epistle to the Romans is like a lawyer's brief in which the whole world is declared guilty before God and then is offered pardon, but only because Christ has satisfied the righteous claims of the law:

> Being justified freely by his [God's] grace through the redemption that is in Christ Jesus . . . to declare at this time his righteousness: that he [God] might be just, and the justifier of him that believeth in Jesus (Romans 3:24,26).

An Infinite Penalty Paid

That another person of perfect holiness and infinite power must die in man's place to pay for his sins was the obvious message in the Old Testament animal sacrifice: "The life of the flesh is in the blood; and I have given it to you upon the altar to make an atonement for your souls, for it is the blood that maketh an atonement for the soul" (Leviticus 17:11). The New Testament agrees: "Without shedding of blood is no remission [of sin]" (Hebrews 9:22). That no *animal's* blood could pay the penalty for man's sins, however, was evident, or those sacrifices would not have needed to be repeated day after day:

> For the law having a shadow of good things to come, and not the very image of the things, can never with those sacrifices which they offered year by year continually make the comers thereunto perfect.
> For then would they not have ceased to be offered? Because the worshipers once purged should have had no more conscience of sins. . . .
> But this man [Christ], after he had offered one sacrifice for sins forever, sat down on the right hand of God . . . for by one offering he hath perfected forever them that are sanctified. . . .
> Now where remission of these [sins] is, there is no more offering for sin (Hebrews 10:1,2,12,14,18).

By revelation from God, John the Baptist introduced Jesus to Israel with these astonishing words: "Behold, the Lamb of God, which taketh away the sin of the world" (John 1:29). Here was God's promised sacrificial Lamb. As the prophets had foretold, God had come at last in human flesh through a virgin birth to pay sin's penalty. The crucifixion of Christ was that one great cosmic Event toward which all Old Testament altars and Temple sacrifices had pointed. It was at one and the same time history's ultimate crime and the complete redemption of sinners, no matter how evil. That His creatures would nail the Creator to a cross was an outrage of unfathomable proportions. Yet Christ cried from the cross, "Father, forgive them, for they know not what they do" (Luke 23:34)—and His offering of Himself a sinless sacrifice made that forgiveness possible.

It was their sin of disobedience to His command not to eat of the Tree of the Knowledge of Good and Evil that caused God to cast Adam and Eve out of the Garden Paradise in which He had so lovingly placed them. That one sin also began the process of physical death: "Wherefore, as by one man sin entered into the world, and death by sin, so death passed upon all men, for all have sinned" (Romans 5:12).

Sin's horrible consequence—the separation of soul and spirit from the body and from God—could not be set aside even by God's command. To do so would be a contradiction of the judgment God had decreed and would thus violate both His character and His justice. The penalty must be paid in full. Sinful man, being finite and unable to pay an infinite penalty, would be separated from God forever in eternal death.

God Alone Can Save

That God alone could become mankind's Savior was clearly and repeatedly stated in the Old Testament in such verses as the following:

> I am the LORD thy God, the Holy One of Israel, thy Savior ... (Isaiah 43:3).

> I, even I, am the LORD; and beside me there is no savior ... (Isaiah 43:11).

> ... there is no God beside me, a just God and a Savior; there is none beside me. Look unto me and be ye saved, all the ends of the earth; for I am God, and there is none else (Isaiah 45:21,22).

> ... and all flesh shall know that I the LORD am thy Savior and thy Redeemer, the mighty One of Jacob (Isaiah 49:26).

God, being infinite, was the only One who could pay the infinite penalty His own justice demanded. For God to make that payment, however, would not be just because He is not one of us. To save us, God would have to become a man. And that is exactly what the Old Testament prophets foretold. The promised Messiah would be God Himself come to earth as a member of the human race to bear the judgment we all deserved because of sin. The prophet Isaiah, for example, declared concerning the Messiah:

> Therefore the Lord himself shall give you a sign: Behold, a virgin shall conceive and bear a son, and shall call his name Immanuel (Isaiah 7:14).

> For unto us a child is born [son of man], unto us a son is given [Son of God]; and the government shall be upon his shoulder; and his name shall be called Wonderful, Counselor, the mighty God, the everlasting Father, the Prince of Peace.
> Of the increase of his government and peace there shall be no end, upon the throne of David and upon his kingdom, to order it and to establish it with judgment and with justice from henceforth even forever (Isaiah 9:6,7).

"Immanuel" is a Hebrew word which literally means "with us is God." That the "child born" is also "the mighty God, the everlasting Father," is plainly stated by Isaiah. And that this promised One is the Messiah cannot be argued inasmuch as He will sit upon the throne of David and "of his kingdom and peace there will be no end." That the Messiah, the Savior, must be God is clearly stated in these verses as well as others. Furthermore, that God has a Son is evident from the following Old Testament Scriptures:

> I will declare the decree: The LORD hath said unto me, Thou art my Son. . . . Kiss the Son, lest he be angry, and ye perish from the way, when his wrath is kindled but a little. Blessed are all they that put their trust in him (Psalm 2:7,12).

> Who hath gathered the wind in his fists? Who hath bound the waters in a garment? Who hath established all

the ends of the earth [obviously God alone has such power]? What is his name, and what is his son's name . . . ? (Proverbs 30:4).

Another Perplexing Problem

In some ways the Koran goes even beyond the New Testament in its praise of Christ. Whereas the latter attributes no miracles to Christ until after He was baptized by John the Baptist ("This *beginning* of miracles did Jesus in Cana of Galilee"—John 2:11), the Koran has Him speaking as a babe in the crib (Surah 3:46; 19:29ff.) and even doing miracles as an infant.

The Koran commends Christ as a great prophet of God who lived a better life than Mohammed. The latter is presented as an ordinary man (Surah 18:111; etc.) who needed to repent of his sins (Surah 40:55; 48:1,2; etc.). Yet in its denial that Christ died on the cross for our sins, the Koran rejects mankind's only hope, the very salvation which God offers.

There was another obvious problem involved in man's salvation: Even if God forgave the sinner, would he not eventually sin again and thus merit God's judgment . . . again and again? God had the answer for that as well. The death of Christ would not merely be *substitutionary* but the means whereby those who believed in Him would by faith be put to death as well and come forth in resurrection with Him. Thereafter He would be their new life. Faith in Christ means to accept His death as one's own and henceforth to depend upon Him completely for one's life now and eternally. Paul put it like this:

. . . if one died for all, then have all died [in Him]; and . . . he died for all, that they which live should not henceforth live unto themselves, but unto him which died for them and rose again. . . .

Therefore if any man be in Christ, he is a new creature; old things are passed away; behold, all things are become new. And all things are of God, who hath reconciled us to himself by Jesus Christ . . . (2 Corinthians 5:14-18).

> I am crucified with Christ; nevertheless I live, yet not
> I, but Christ liveth in me; and the life that I now live in
> the flesh I live by the faith of the Son of God, who loved
> me and gave himself for me (Galatians 2:20).

Messianic Prophecies Fulfilled

The four Gospels and first chapter of the book of Acts provide the detailed account of the coming of the prophesied Messiah into this world at precisely the time foretold by the prophets. Paul, former rabbi turned apostle of Jesus Christ after meeting the resurrected Savior on the road to Damascus, preached what he called "the gospel of God, which he had promised before by his prophets in the Holy Scriptures" (Romans 1:1,2). And he preached this gospel in the Jewish synagogues by opening their own Scriptures, pointing to what the prophets had said about the Messiah and demonstrating that it had all been fulfilled in the minutest detail in the life, death, and resurrection of Jesus of Nazareth. Here was complete proof that Jesus was the Messiah foretold by the prophets.

Seventy years after the destruction of the City of Jerusalem and its Temple by Nebuchadnezzar in 587 B.C., the Jewish captives began to return to Israel, the Temple was rebuilt, and the city was restored, as God had mercifully promised. At the same time He gave that promise, however, God warned His people that the Temple and city would be destroyed yet again. This time it would be caused by their rejection and murder of the Messiah. Though so long promised and so long awaited, His own people would have the Messiah crucified, and because of that rejection God's judgment would fall once again. Daniel's prophecy was clear:

> Know therefore and understand that from the going
> forth of the commandment to restore and to build Jerusa-
> lem unto the Messiah the Prince shall be seven weeks [of
> years], and threescore and two weeks [of years—a total
> of 69 weeks of years, or 483 years]. . . .

> And after threescore and two weeks [i.e. at the end of
> the 62 weeks that follow the 7] shall Messiah be cut off,
> but not for himself (Daniel 9:25,26).

We have dealt with this prophecy in detail in other books. In brief, the command authorizing the rebuilding of Jerusalem was given to Nehemiah on Nisan 1, 445 B.C. (the twentieth year of the reign of Artaxerxes Longimanus, who ruled from 465 B.C. to 425 B.C.—see Nehemiah 2:1-8). From that date to April 6, 32 A.D., the day Jesus rode into Jerusalem on the colt of an ass and was hailed as the Messiah as prophesied by Zechariah (9:9)—now celebrated as Palm Sunday—was exactly 69 weeks of years, or 483 years! Four days later, at the same time that the Passover lambs were being slain all over Israel, Jesus, "the Lamb of God that taketh away the sin of the world" (John 1:29), was on the cross, rejected and scorned by the Jews exactly as prophesied: "The whole assembly of the congregation of Israel shall take it [that special lamb] and kill it in the evening" (Exodus 12:6).

There He died for the sins of Jews, Arabs, and the entire world—not just at the hands of those who crucified Him, but at the hands of God Himself:

> He is despised and rejected of men, a man of sorrows
> and acquainted with grief; and . . . we esteemed him not.
> Surely he hath borne our griefs and carried our sor-
> rows. . . . He was wounded for our transgressions, he was
> bruised for our iniquities . . . and with his stripes we are
> healed.
>
> All we like sheep have gone astray; we have turned
> every one to his own way; and the LORD hath laid on him
> the iniquity of us all. . . . It pleased the LORD to bruise
> him . . . [to] make his soul an offering for sin (Isaiah
> 53:3-10).

We have documented the many specific prophecies which were fulfilled in the life, death, burial, and resurrection of Jesus elsewhere, so we will not go into those details again here. Suffice it to say that among those many Old Testament prophecies fulfilled in Jesus Christ were the following: that the

Messiah would be betrayed for 30 pieces of silver and that the bribe would be thrown down in the Temple and used to buy a potter's field for burying strangers (Zechariah 11:12,13; Matthew 27:3-10); that the soldiers would divide up his clothes and gamble for his seamless robe (Psalm 22:18; Matthew 27:35); that His crucifiers would give Him to drink in His thirst vinegar mixed with gall (Psalm 69:21; Matthew 27:34); that instead of breaking his legs, as was always done to victims of crucifixion, they would pierce His side with a spear (Exodus 12:46; Numbers 9:12; Psalm 34:20; Zechariah 12:10; John 19:31-37).

Undeniable Proof

One cannot deny that the evidence proves that Jesus is the Messiah whom the prophets promised to Israel. The very place and time of the Messiah's coming was foretold. It would be in Bethlehem (Micah 5:2) and had to occur before the scepter departed from Judah (Genesis 49:10), while the Temple was still standing ("The Lord, whom ye seek, shall suddenly come to his temple"—Malachi 3:1), while the genealogical records were available to prove His lineage (2 Samuel 7:12; Psalm 89; etc.), and shortly before the Temple and Jerusalem would be destroyed: "[Then] shall Messiah be cut off [killed], but not for himself; and the people of the prince [Antichrist] that shall come shall destroy the city and the sanctuary" (Daniel 9:26).

That Jesus Christ was born in Bethlehem and lived during this narrow window of time is a matter of history. The scepter departed from Judah about 7 A.D., when the rabbis lost the right to exact the death penalty (John 18:31), a right which was vital to the practice of Judaism. The Temple was in operation during Christ's lifetime, but within the same generation, 70 A.D., Jerusalem and the Temple were destroyed and with them the genealogical records. It is now too late for any would-be Messiah to prove himself of the lineage of David, as the New Testament proves Jesus Christ to be.

The narrow window of time in which the Messiah had to come is long past. No wonder Paul wrote, "When the fullness

of time [the exact time] was come, God sent forth his Son . . ."
(Galatians 4:4)! Yet tragically His people, Israel, rejected Him
exactly as the prophets with one voice had said they would—
and continue to reject Him to this day. A few Jews still await
the Messiah, ignoring the Scriptures which make it clear that
He has already come, but most Jews have long ago given up on
that vigil.

No honest critic, whether atheist, Buddhist, Muslim, or
Jew, can deny that the life, death, and resurrection of Jesus of
Nazareth fulfilled in precise detail all that was foretold of the
first coming of the Messiah in the Old Testament. Mathe-
matically, all of these specific prophecies could not possibly
have been fulfilled in one individual. Yet they were. Therefore
no one can remain an honest atheist nor can anyone deny that
Jesus is the Son of God, the Savior of sinners, and that through
Him alone forgiveness of sins and eternal life in the presence of
God are offered freely to all who will believe in Him.

God and Evil

Many a Jew has lost his faith in the God of Abraham and
become an atheist because of the suffering and death of relatives in the Holocaust. How could a loving God allow 6 million
of His chosen people to be slaughtered by Hitler? Without the
cross of Christ, and in the face of the Holocaust, one could no
longer believe in God. How could a God worthy of one's trust
remain silent and aloof while His chosen people were tortured
and slaughtered? Indeed, it would seem that God stood by and
did nothing as the entire world He had made was filled with
violence and injustice. Such a God, even if he existed, would
surely not merit our faith and trust.

The God of the Bible, however, in contrast to Allah or any
other god of any religion, is not aloof from human suffering.
Indeed, through a virgin birth, He Himself came into the world
as a man to die for our sins. In spite of suffering at the hands of
His creatures and their rejection of Him, He paid the infinite
penalty which His own justice decreed for sin. This God, who
alone is both light and love, is the only One who merits

mankind's faith and trust and love. Yet most Muslims (and many Jews as well) respond to that love with the most virulent hatred imaginable.

Persecution and Martyrdom Today

It is common knowledge that in Muslim countries becoming a Christian is tantamount to accepting a death sentence, which will often be carried out by one's own family members in order to purge the reproach from the family name. To embrace Judaism is equally unthinkable. Such a change of faith is legally impossible in fully Islamic countries; and in those where Islam is coming into power, though not yet in complete control, the results have been tragic. Consider the following evidence from Nigeria alone:

> [There was] the 1980 Maitatsine Islamic uproar in Kano during which 4,177 people were officially reported as slaughtered with property worth millions of dollars destroyed. Two years later, on October 30, 1982, eight big churches were burnt in Kano. That same year the Muslims struck in Kaduna and 400 people were officially reported as killed. . . . In 1984, Muslims in Yola and Jimeta . . . killed 700 including policemen, and 5,913 people were rendered homeless. They also besieged Gombe and more than 100 people were killed. . . .
>
> [On] March 6, 1987 . . . Muslims [again] went on a rampage. . . . Of all the 150 churches in Zaria alone, only one escaped being burnt down in three days of Jihad in that town. Many Christians were slain in cold blood while some were burnt alive. . . . The immediate cause of the riot: A female Muslim student accused . . . a former Muslim of "misinterpreting the Quran" during his preaching. No non-Muslim must quote from the Quran, even though a Muslim can quote from the Bible. . . .
>
> In 1991 and 1992 there were three more riots by Muslims in Katsina, Bauchi and Kano during which thousands lost their lives. [We couldn't begin to report the many atrocities committed in the name of Allah against non-Muslims!][3]

In the Sudan, Christians are being literally crucified by Muslims. The news of five more crucifixions comes as these lines are being written. More than 100,000 Christian refugees have been forced out of Khartoum by the Islamic government and into makeshift camps in the first few months of 1995.[4] Fanaticism? No, this is what Allah commands in the Koran: "If they turn back (to enmity) [from Islam] then take them and kill them wherever ye find them..." (Surah 4:89). No wonder Muslims are afraid to leave Islam even when they can no longer believe in it! A former Muslim writes:

> In plain terms, therefore, Mohammed or Allah (or whoever is speaking in the Quran) says: "O ye who believe! Take not the Jews and Christians as friends. They are but friends to one another. And he amongst you who takes them (as friends) then surely he is one of them. (Surah 5:51, Al Hil-ali. Verse 54, Jusuf Ali.)[5]

And Israel expects to make a just and lasting peace with Muslims? It is a delusion that can only lead to greater bloodshed! Peace with Islam requires total submission to Allah. Respect for the rights of others is nonexistent. There are no rights—only submission to Allah.

Of course, right now the PLO is not demanding such submission, but is only asking for "reasonable rights." Yet that has always been true in the beginning stages of Islamic takeover. Even Mohammed didn't reveal his total agenda until he had the power to effect complete submission. Those who mouth the well-intentioned but pitifully naive slogan "Just give peace a chance" are woefully ignorant, and perhaps intentionally so, of the true teachings of Islam.

The South African Muslim Jihadist Ahmed Deedat urges today's Muslims to return faithfully to Mohammed's original Islamic principles as found in the Koran: "Our armour, sword and shield in this battle of Faiths are in the Koran, we have been chanting it for centuries... now we must bring them forth into the battlefield.[6] A former Muslim author whom we quote several times is forced to write under a pen name to

protect himself. He reminds Westerners of what they should
know but blithely ignore:

> There are so many incitements against Christians and
> non-Muslims running through the pages of the Quran
> that we find it hard to believe that anybody can be a real
> practising Muslim . . . and not hate Christians [and
> Jews]. It is impossible. Any Muslim who is not violent
> (secretly or openly) [against non-Muslims] is hardly a
> real Muslim, at least not in the Quranic sense. . . .
>
> If words have meaning, then we can confidently
> say . . . that submission to Allah (Islam) is not just in
> prayers and zakat as some would want us to believe, but
> in obedience to the order for killing in order to spread
> Islam. That is the Islam of Mohammed. We have an
> overwhelming monument of evidence from both the
> Quran and the Hadith to prove our claims here.[7]

Islam in Daily Practice

It is instructive to observe Islam in practice in a nation such
as Saudi Arabia, where that religion is so important that about
10,000 religious elders play a key role in running the country.
This, the world's twelfth-largest nation geographically, was
created through unifying previously warring tribes under the
leadership of Ibn Saud. He declared this coalition to be the
kingdom of Saudi Arabia in 1932, with himself as king. A
devout Muslim, Saud confessed that his "three greatest pleasures in life were women, perfume and prayers. . . ."[8] He
proved the first two by marrying more than 120 women, but
kept within the letter of the Koran's limitation of four wives by
divorcing and sending back to her village each new mother
after she had borne him a son.

A man may have "four wives and still keep concubines; even
today it is the women who are to remain chaste, not men."[9]
And a woman who fails to meet that standard (perhaps is only
seen holding hands, or may even have been raped) will likely be
killed by father or brothers to save "family honor."[10]

Such is the practice of Islam in a country where no other
religion is allowed. It is the death penalty in Saudi Arabia to

convert from Islam to another faith. It takes little common sense, however, to realize that faith must come willingly, from the heart. Those who are forced to profess faith in Allah through fear of reprisal or death are not true believers. Yet Islam was spread by the sword from the very beginning, and millions of people remain Muslims in name only for fear of their lives. In contrast, multitudes are won to Christ by the drawing power of His love as demonstrated in the cross.

Consider the multitudes of the "enemies of Islam" who were slaughtered by the Ayatollah Khomeini in the name of Allah. Of these massacres the Ayatollah declared, "In Persia [Iran] no people have been killed so far—only beasts!" Anwar Sadat was also killed by Muslim militants because he ordered the arrest of the Muslims who had killed 50 Coptic Christians. The same Islamic fundamentalist groups are killing Western tourists visiting Egypt: In mid-October 1992, a British tourist was machine-gunned, a Nile cruise ship carrying 140 German tourists was fired upon, three Russian tourists were stabbed, and on and on it goes. These are not the acts of deranged individuals but the concerted, carefully planned and executed program of Muslims who are faithful to the instructions given in the Koran and to the example set by their great Prophet Mohammed.

A Revealing Contrast

What a contrast Islam presents to Christ's love and to His command that Christians are to "love your enemies, bless them that curse you, do good to them that hate you, and pray for them which despitefully use you and persecute you" (Matthew 5:44)! The apostle Paul wrote, "All the law is fulfilled in one word, even in this: Thou shalt love thy neighbor as thyself" (Galatians 5:14). Nothing of that nature is found in the Koran! What a contradiction the teachings and example of Mohammed present to the Torah, which it claims to honor, and which enjoins upon us all:

> Thou shalt not avenge nor bear any grudge . . . but thou shalt love thy neighbor as thyself: I am the LORD. . . .

> And if a stranger sojourn with thee in your land, ye
> shall not vex him. But the stranger that dwelleth with you
> shall be unto you as one born among you, and thou shalt
> love him as thyself (Leviticus 19:18,33,34).

How different were the actions of Mohammed and his followers toward those who did not submit to their tyranny! We
have already noted that Mohammed had several writers of his
day killed for disagreeing with his new religion. The same
pattern of threats and violence continues today. We also
referred to Salman Rushdie, who has been in hiding for years,
under threat of death, for casting Islam in an unfavorable light
in one of his books. Early in 1992, Farag Fouda, an Egyptian
writer, was murdered by Muslims for criticizing Islamic militancy. Two years earlier the Speaker of Egypt's Parliament was
assassinated for taking an anti-Islamic stance.[11] That Islam
must continue such measures suggests a fear that its numbers
might diminish if everyone were allowed to make a free choice.
How tragic!

Muslims demand freedom to practice their religion in other
countries while denying the same right to non-Muslims
in Arab countries. Taking advantage of the freedom in non-
Muslim countries, Islam has become the world's fastest-
growing religion. There are more Muslims than Methodists in
Chicago. According to a new study, the most accurate in
history (conducted by the Islamic Resource Institute), there
are presently more than a thousand Islamic centers in the
United States and Canada. Nearly half a million followers of
Mohammed are active in those centers and their numbers are
growing rapidly. The total number of Muslims in North America is estimated at nearly 5 million and is expected to surpass
the estimated 6 million Jews in North America sometime early
in the next century.[12]

Altars, temples, and a cross. Only the cross can reconcile
God and man. And only through the cross of Christ can
Christian, Jew, and Muslim meet in brotherhood and recon-
ciliation.

Pray for the peace of Jerusalem; they shall prosper that love thee.

—Psalm 122:6

They have healed the hurt of the daughter of my people slightly, saying, Peace, peace, when there is no peace.

—Jeremiah 8:11

By peace shall [Antichrist] destroy many. . . .

—Daniel 8:25

When they shall say, Peace and safety, then sudden destruction cometh upon them, as travail upon a woman with child; and they shall not escape.

—1 Thessalonians 5:3

The real cause of the never-ending turmoil in the Middle East is the unremitting desire of most of the Arab Moslem states to destroy Israel, their inability to come to terms with its very existence. That hatred and that intolerance are fueled by Arab-Moslem fanaticism and intransigence and unwillingness to accept diversity in the region. Only when that will be overcome can peace and tranquility come to the Middle East.

—FLAME (Facts and Logic about the Middle East)[1]

15

Peace, Peace...

♦

Peace in the Middle East? Will the seemingly impossible dream be realized at last? Yes, in spite of difficult roadblocks along the way, in the not-too-distant future a peace agreement involving all parties in the Middle East will be established. Moreover, that achievement will prove to be a major step toward worldwide peace, which will be established as well! Both the Old and New Testaments bear witness that these goals will be reached.

Unfortunately, both parts of the Bible also agree that instead of looking to Israel's Messiah, under whose reign alone true peace can be established, the world will forge a pseudo-peace of its own making, a deceitful peace that will be guaranteed by Antichrist and will eventually explode in Armageddon, the most destructive war in human history. Yet hardly any of the world leaders involved in the current peace process believe the Bible's prophecies, so they plunge on to disaster in proud but well-meaning unbelief.

According to a poll conducted by the Nablus-based Center for Palestinian Research and Studies at the end of March 1995, "support for the peace process among Palestinians has reached its highest level since the signing of the Oslo agreement.... The poll...showed that 67% support continuing negotiations, far higher than the 50% or less in recent months."[2] Does that mean that 67 percent of the Palestinians now have a sincere desire for real peace with Israel? Or does it mean that more Palestinians are finally recognizing what many Israelis suspect—that PLO leader Yasser Arafat hasn't betrayed the Muslim cause of exterminating Israel after all?

A Deadly Deceit

As we have already shown, the current Israeli-Palestinian peace process is a subterfuge that Arafat is using as a pathway to the ultimate destruction of Israel. Even since Oslo, Arafat's own Al Fatah has been involved in continued terrorist attacks.[3] This terrorist-turned-peacemaker has not only convinced Israel's leaders of his good intentions but has managed to deceive most Arabs as well. Islam allows lying in order to achieve its goals, and that is precisely what Arafat is doing. He has deceived the world to such an extent that he was awarded the Nobel Peace Prize in 1994.

Kaare Kristiansen, former leader of Norway's Christian People's Party and long a staunch supporter of Israel, resigned from the Nobel Peace Prize committee after serving only three years of his six-year term. He did so immediately after it was announced that PLO Chairman Yasser Arafat would receive the Peace Prize along with Israeli Prime Minister Yitzhak Rabin and Foreign Minister Shimon Peres. Said Kristiansen, "[My resignation] was the only argument left to me. Arafat's past is too tainted with violence, terrorism and bloodshed and his future too unpredictable to make him a Nobel Peace Prize winner. It is a degradation [of the prize] to give it to someone so disqualified."[4]

As *U.S. News & World Report* commented, "Yitzhak Rabin, Shimon Peres and Yassir Arafat picked up their Nobel Prizes just in time, for their 'process' for peace is fast coming unglued. Arafat has failed to meet the most essential part of his bargain with the Israelis: to restrain terrorism and increase the sense of Israeli security. So lax is his border screening that a Palestinian suicide bomber wrapped in explosives was let through several Palestinian checkpoints on December 4 [1994] and was foiled only by the Israelis at the main Israel-Gaza border. Even worse, Arafat has allowed the radical Hamas to operate right under his nose in Gaza. He still refers to Israel as 'the enemy' and still talks about the 1974 phased plan of the Arabs to make 'peace' for any piece of land that would provide a base for destroying Israel."⁵ On the other hand, Arafat is angry at terrorist organizations other than his own Fatah because their operations undermine his authority in working out the current deal with Israel.

While it is clear from the historical record that the only reason the PLO is involved in the so-called "peace process" is to gain control over territory within Israel from which to launch further terrorism and eventually to destroy her, nevertheless other Muslims are fearful that a genuine peace may be achieved and thus weaken their solemnly sworn war of extermination against Israel. In an October 1994 speech, Iranian religious leader Ayatollah Sayed Alit Khamenei warned that any Arab leaders making peace with Israel would be assassinated. He called upon the people to rise up against their leaders and deal with them as the Egyptians did with Anwar Sadat in October 1981. Following the Ayatollah's lead, the English-language *Tehran Times* wrote, "No doubt, the traitor Sadat awaits his counterparts in hell. Any Arab ruler who shakes hands with the Zionists should be aware of the fate that befell Sadat."⁶

A Partnership of Deception

Arafat's deceptive public statements have indeed given his fellow Arabs and Muslims reason to believe he was betraying their cause. At the signing of the Oslo agreement and on several occasions since, Arafat promised to abolish the long-standing articles in the PLO Covenant that call for the destruction of the State of Israel. The changes, of course, have not been made. His latest excuse for the failure of his solemn promises came at the end of March 1995, when he said the changes couldn't be made until "the Palestinian Authority is elected in Judea, Samaria and Gaza."

In fact, Arafat cannot make such a promise, and he knows it. Any change must be approved by a majority vote of the more than 500 members of the Palestinian National Council. They would have to renounce Islam in order to allow the Jews to have sovereignty over any part of Israel. After all, Islam teaches, in direct contradiction to the Torah, that all of that land was given to the Arabs by Allah.

The Declaration of Principles signed with the PLO late in 1993 at the beginning of negotiations established two objectives for the peace process: 1) The Palestinians would achieve eventual self-determination and thus liberation from Israeli rule; and 2) in exchange, the Israelis would achieve security and no longer be subjected to terrorism. Quite clearly, Arafat has little intention of working conscientiously toward the second point.

The Israeli government has gone along with Arafat's deception and followed a course of compromise and dishonesty of its own in which it has withheld from the public certain information in its possession showing that all was not as Arafat has represented it. As former army commander Ariel Sharon complained recently, "For more than a year intelligence reports said Yasser Arafat wouldn't fight terror, and that attacks on Israelis would continue. But what did the government tell the public? That Arafat would fight terror. . . . Yet terror has increased, taking a heavy toll." Sharon went on to state:

> Intelligence reports indicated Arafat did not intend to, or couldn't abrogate the Palestinian Covenant calling for Israel's destruction. But what did the premier and foreign minister tell the people? That Arafat had promised he would do away with the covenant very soon. They not only ignored information from the intelligence services, but, in addition, gave the public a dishonest picture.
>
> Instead of presenting the facts as they are, some intelligence officers are likely to omit facts or simply not pass them on, for fear of harming our leaders' party-political needs. Or . . . they match evaluations to situations, without recourse to the facts, to suit the politicians' mood.[7]

The Hard Facts

Increasing numbers of Israelis are appalled by the hard facts of what has actually happened since the Oslo agreement. Eli Landau, a local mayor who had supported the peace process, declared, "If the peace process is paved on the bodies of dead Jews, then I take it back." As *Time* magazine reported in February 1995:

> When he took the brave step of entering into a self-rule agreement with Yasser Arafat and the Palestine Liberation Organization 16 months ago, Prime Minister Yitzhak Rabin promised his countrymen peace with security. Ever since, Israelis have enjoyed little peace and less security. Rabin's political stock has plummeted, and many citizens question whether the experiment in peacemaking should go on. . . . As the terrorists take the psychological initiative, the maneuvering room for both Rabin and Arafat is fast running out. . . .
>
> Since Rabin and Arafat signed the first accord in September 1993, 112 Israelis have been killed by Palestinian radicals bent on wrecking the settlement. In the same period, 195 Palestinians have died at the hands of Israelis. Many of them too were innocent civilians, such as 14-year-old Mohamed Abed Ghani, who died last week in the West Bank city of Nablus when Israeli soldiers fired into a crowd of students who were jeering at them. . . .
>
> As he has done after every attack, [Rabin] temporarily shut Israel's borders to Palestinian workers, barring 40,000 of them from crossing daily from the West Bank and Gaza Strip—a form of collective punishment that serves only to inflame Palestinian anger.[8]

The stepped-up terrorism proves that the terrorist element has no intention of stopping short of the annihilation of Israel. It also proves that there is no unity among the Arabs, and that the many factions working for Israel's destruction are also each working for their own domination. There can be no real peace with Israel so long as the Arabs are divided among themselves.

Indeed, the Arabs have always fought one another. The Gulf War was only one example. The conflict between Arab states existed long before and continues today.

There are moderates among the Arabs, but the fundamentalists seem to have the greater power. That is because of the Muslim religion's hold upon the people—and that religion puts the Muslims not only against Israel but against all mankind. Islam calls for submission of all peoples to Allah and to Shari'a (the holy law of Islam). It is a pursuit that must be carried on until Islam finally triumphs worldwide. Thus any "peace" with Israel is established only as a step in the direction of its ultimate destruction.

As Shlomo Gazit, a former IDF Intelligence chief and now a senior research fellow at the Jaffee Center for Strategic Studies at Tel Aviv University, recently pointed out:

> Many Israelis, I know, are not ready for compromise. They want the whole cake. . . . The Palestinian camp, too, contains many extremists . . . they want nothing to do with compromise. They too want the whole cake . . . all of Mandatory Palestine, from the Jordan to the sea. . . .
>
> What they must understand are the consequences. The peace process cannot continue if it means that only the Arab side attains its goals. In such a case, no political compromise would be possible. There would be no alternative to total warfare, to a struggle which would leave one side holding the entire cake.[9]

The Fundamental Disagreement

Since the signing of the Oslo and later the Cairo agreement, the Palestinian Authority overseeing the territories which will eventually achieve autonomy and independence from Israel has "failed to anchor its conduct in the rule of law." Such is the conclusion of Human Rights Watch, a New-York-based organization set up to monitor human-rights violations. According to its most recent report, the PA "has often acted in an arbitrary and repressive fashion . . . [and] the perilous state of human rights in the Palestinian self-rule areas poses a grave threat to prospects for a durable peace in the region." The report stated that "Palestinian authorities beat and mistreat detainees during interrogations, especially those accused of collaborating with Israel."[10]

The Palestinian Authority was established to carry out the Oslo agreement. Instead, it has continuously violated numerous provisions contained therein. With so many breaches of the agreement already, why should anyone imagine that the promise to remove the provisions calling for Israel's destruction from the PLO Covenant would be kept? The destruction of Israel is so deeply rooted in Palestinian consciousness and resolve that it would take a miracle to reverse that attitude. Consider these few excerpts from the original Palestinian Covenant of 1968:

> The partition of Palestine in 1947 and the establishment of the State of Israel are entirely illegal, regardless of the passage of time, because they were contrary to the will of the Palestinian people and to their natural right in their homeland, and inconsistent with the principles embodied in the Charter of the United Nations, particularly the right to self-determination.
>
> The Balfour Declaration, the Mandate for Palestine and everything that has been based upon them, are deemed null and void....
>
> Claims of historical or religious ties of Jews with Palestine are incompatible with the facts of history and the true conception of what constitutes statehood. Judaism, being a religion, is not an independent nationality. Nor do Jews constitute a single nation with an identity of its own; they are citizens of the states to which they belong.[11]

No matter how many peace accords are signed, this fundamental disagreement between Jews and Arabs on the basic facts remains, a disagreement which has caused 47 years of bloodshed. Echoing Islamic doctrine, the PLO denies that the Jews ever had possession of the Promised Land even under Joshua and David and claims that it always belonged to the

Arabs. No wonder Islam finds it necessary to claim that the Old Testament has been changed, for it is filled with the details of Israel's conquest of the Promised Land and 15 centuries of living there until the Diaspora of 70 A.D.!

Yet this incredible denial of the incontrovertible facts of history has been so deeply implanted in Arab consciousness that only a miracle could exchange it for the truth. Even that the Jews ever existed as a nation is denied! They are not acknowledged to be a national, ethnic group of people at all, but merely followers of a religion. Therefore they can never claim a state of their own but can only be citizens of whatever country they individually inhabit. Here we have a disagreement so fundamental that it would seem to be an insurmountable obstacle in the way of a genuine peace in the Middle East.

A Return to the Post-Holocaust Dilemma?

The Arabs really intend to put the Jews back where they were right after the Holocaust, with no national home. In recent months there has been a wave of "attacks against Jews in several South American countries" by Islamic terrorists.[12] Are these and other Jews who face similar conditions to have no national home on this earth? If being a Jew is not a national identity but only a religion in nature, then what is the status of the 30 percent of Israelis who claim to be atheists? They must not be Jews at all. The idea, of course, is utterly absurd, yet this fraud is taken seriously by millions of Arabs. Consider the following from Article 4 in the 1968 covenant:

> The Palestinian identity is a genuine, essential and inherent characteristic; it is transmitted from parent to children. The Zionist occupation and the dispersal of the Palestinian Arab people, through the disasters which befell them, do not make them lose their Palestinian identity and their membership in the Palestinian community, nor do they negate them.[13]

So any Jewish claim that their ancestors were citizens of the nation of Israel, a nation that existed under a series of kings for

1500 years in the very land which God had given to them, is rejected as though it had never happened. Arabs, however, who subsequently occupied that land alongside Jews when neither had sovereignty but both were guests of foreign powers, are declared to be its true owners. And today they claim sovereignty over it, a sovereignty which they never actually had. Remember, there was *never* a Palestinian state. The Israelis are "restoring" to the Palestinians something which was never theirs.

The situation regarding the Golan Heights is similar. This region lies within the boundaries of the "Promised Land" given by God to the descendants of Abraham, Isaac, and Jacob and has historically been part of Israel. Thus Israel's claim to the Golan goes back more than 3000 years, while Syria's claim is of very recent origin and is tenuous at best. In fact, Syria didn't even exist as a political entity until after the First World War. As FLAME has pointed out:

> Until then it was just another province in the Ottoman empire, with ill-defined borders. In 1923, in an Anglo/French great power play, the border between Syria and Israel was established. The Golan Heights were ceded to Syria. . . .
>
> The Golan is the size of the New York borough of Queens, about 10 miles wide, with a plateau on either side of a ridge. If it were part of Syria it would be less than 1% of its territory. But it is of supreme strategic importance to Israel.[14]

Key to Peace, Key to War

That strategic importance is the only reason Israel captured the Golan. It was not because she was greedy for territory; she was attacked and had to strengthen her defensive lines. Even before Israel became a state in 1948, the Syrians were already lobbing shells almost daily from the heavily fortified Golan onto Jewish villages below, making normal life impossible. In both the 1967 Six-Day War and the 1973 Yom Kippur War hundreds of Syrian tanks poured over the Golan into Israel, but were pushed back at great cost in Israeli and Syrian lives. Israel occupied the captured territory and in 1981 annexed it to keep the Syrians back from strategic high ground overlooking Israel and also in order to keep its forces farther away to give time to react in case of another attack. FLAME comments further:

> So in giving back the Golan, Israel will be placing itself in a dangerously vulnerable position. Its high ground provides early-warning capability, without which Israel—just as in 1948, 1967 and 1973—would be subject to surprise attack by the Syrians. Its loss would obligate Israel to stay on constant alert and to maintain a state of readiness and mobilization that would be economically and socially untenable.
>
> The Golan, which ranges up to a height of 2300 feet, dominates the Jordan Valley, the lowest point on earth, about 700 feet below sea level. On the Golan itself there are two natural terrain bottlenecks through which tanks can advance. Those choke points are defensible and made possible the repulse of the 1400 Syrian tanks that attacked Israel in the 1973 war.
>
> But with the Golan in Syrian hands, and without the radar installations that would give Israel warning of any military movements, thousands of tanks—backed by missiles and airplanes—could overrun Israel in a matter of hours. It would be a strategically impossible situation, especially for a country as small as Israel—smaller than Lake Michigan, smaller by half than San Bernardino County in California. The Golan does not make for perfect defense, but it gives Israel a small breathing space for mobilization.
>
> The Golan is the source of over one-third of Israel's fresh water. In 1964, with the Golan in Syrian hands, Syria attempted to divert these headwaters and to cripple Israel's water supply. It is more than likely that, given another opportunity, Syria would once again attempt to destroy Israel's water supply.[15]

Polls have consistently shown that "more than two-thirds of the Israeli public opposes withdrawal from the Golan.

...More than 30 retired IDF commanders and senior officers... said at a news conference at Kibbutz Merom Golan
[early in January 1995] that retaining the Heights was the best
and only way of ensuring the country's security.... [Yitzhak
Hofi] stressed that it would be impossible to defend the north
from the base of the Golan, especially after a surprise attack.
The Syrians have over 4,000 tanks and huge numbers of mobile
artillery pieces, he added."[16]
An influential Jewish organization in the United States has
expressed grave concern over the possibility of giving up the
Golan:

> The current Israeli government, in its keen desire to
> bring peace to its people, after almost fifty years of war
> and bloodshed, would seem prepared to give up the
> limited strategic security it now enjoys by virtue of its
> possession of the high ground—the ridges of Judea/
> Samaria (the 'West Bank') and of the Golan Heights. But
> Israel should not return to the 'death trap' borders of
> 1967 or anything close to it.
> In order to survive within such borders, Israel would
> have to rely on the goodwill of the Arab states, all of
> which—except for the cold peace with Egypt—are still
> in a declared state of war with Israel. An aggressor will
> attack only if confident of victory. With the Golan in
> Israeli hands, attacking Arabs could be confident of
> defeat and peace would be preserved. To hand the Golan
> to Syria is a prescription for war and for Israel's destruc-
> tion....
> The Israeli public perceives Syria to be its most fe-
> rocious opponent in the last 50 years and fears that
> evacuating the Golan would give President Assad a war
> option he does not now have. After 25 years of being told
> how important the Golan is, not only as a defensive
> barrier but as a deterrent to a Syrian buildup, the Israeli
> public is reluctant to take more risks.[17]

Small wonder, then, that Israel is cautious in her dealings
with Syrian President Hafez Assad regarding the return of the

292 ◆ PEACE, PEACE . . .

Golan. There are other compelling reasons as well. As the same Jewish organization with expertise in the Middle East has warned: "Syria is the most destabilizing influence in the Middle East. It is classified by the U.S. State Department as a narcotic-dealing and terrorist state. Its main fury is directed against Israel, which is perceived as a bulwark of Western influence and civilization, both of which Syria totally rejects."[18]

Beware Hafez Assad!

It should be clear to any observer of the Middle East over the past few years that "Syria's President, Hafez Assad, is a tyrant, every bit as ruthless and cunning as his Iraqi counterpart, Saddam Hussein. Under Assad, Syria is a world center for terrorism. It still harbors Nazi bigwigs, who found welcome there after the World War. Few doubt that he [Assad] was the mastermind and final authority in the suicide attack on the Marine barracks in Beirut in which 241 Americans died, and in the explosion of Pan Am Flight 103 in which 270 people lost their lives. He oversees one of the largest narcotics operations in the world."[19]

Israeli Foreign Minister Shimon Peres recently "accused Syria of harboring 10 terrorist organizations opposed to Middle East peacemaking. 'How can Syria advance toward peace while permitting terrorist operations?' Peres said in Washington."[20] In spite of the obvious evil intentions of Syria, Israel continues its negotiations for withdrawing from the Golan. Rabin, in fact, has committed Israel to a withdrawal in stages over four years "to the international border" on the Heights.[21]

As for the true intentions of Assad, Arafat, and other Arab leaders, there should be no question at all in view of the teachings of Islam. In keeping with Islam, Assad, Arafat, and numerous other Arab leaders have repeatedly declared down through the years that their unflinching goal is the destruction of Israel. There has been no apology for those statements (not even by Arafat since signing the Oslo and Cairo agreements) nor for the past aggression and current terrorism.

In fact, there is no indication whatsoever of a change in the ultimate goal. What we are seeing in the peace process is merely a strategic adjustment in how Israel's destruction is to be achieved. As recently as January 1995, Iraqi President Saddam Hussein once again "called on Arab countries to begin missile attacks on Israel similar to Iraq's attacks during the Gulf War.... [Said Saddam], 'The Arab countries should be asking themselves who will fire the 40th missile against Israel!' Iraq fired 39 Scud missiles at Israel during the [Gulf] war."[22]

Even while he has been negotiating with Israel to take back the Golan, Assad has stepped up his support of the Hizbullah terrorists. It is no secret that their operations are directed from bases in Beirut and the Beka'a Valley, which are fully under Syrian control. While Iran is the main supporter of Hizbullah with funds and military hardware, that support could not reach Hizbullah for its attacks against Israel without Syria's full agreement and cooperation. Nor is it a secret that the entire passion of Hizbullah's existence is not merely the disruption of "the peace process" but the utter destruction of Israel. Assad's duplicity is obvious, yet Israel goes ahead in negotiations as though the Syrian President were acting in good faith even though he has never renounced his oft-repeated intention of destroying Israel.

It seems even more astonishing that Israeli defense forces commanders cannot agree whether Assad is "sincere about making peace with Israel or [is] using the negotiations to win the Golan and acquire strategic superiority.... Intelligence Chief Maj.-Gen. Uri Saguy believes Assad has changed, but his chief aide, Brig.-Gen. Ya'acov Amidror, believes Assad is continuing to prepare for war."[23] Even if Assad is sincere, as Yitzhak Hofi, former head of the Mossad, points out, Assad is not immortal, and when the inevitable "changes in the Syrian regime" come, "that would turn everything upside down."

Denial and Cover-Up

In its plans and negotiations regarding the Golan, the Israeli leadership has been less than candid with the public. On the eve of the Knesset elections in 1992, no doubt to gain votes, Yitzhak Rabin declared that "whoever withdrew from the Golan would abandon Israel's security." Then rumors began to fly shortly after the elections that a secret deal had been made to abandon the Golan. On his first trip to the Golan after the elections, Rabin met with leaders in the dining room of Kibbutz Ortal. The expectation that the Prime Minister would dispel the rumors was shattered. An Ortal member, Uri Heitner, quoted Rabin as saying, "[W]hoever said you can have peace with all the Golan [still in Israeli hands] is lying. I look at you and I say there will be a painful withdrawal, but it won't be a full withdrawal."[24]

Rabin still publicly maintains his opposition to a full withdrawal. However, reliable diplomatic sources within not only Syria but Egypt and the United States and even Israel all agree that during secret talks held with Syria as early as 1992, Rabin agreed to a full withdrawal in exchange for recognition and genuine peace, even as Israeli officials continued to deny it. In secret meetings in Cairo, Israeli representatives assured the Egyptian hosts and Syrian representatives that the new Labor-led government, unlike the Likud-led coalition it had defeated, "viewed Israel as being committed by UN resolutions 242 and 338 to a withdrawal from the Golan Heights."[25] What then has held up the deal? Apparently, in spite of Israel agreeing to nearly everything Syria demanded, that country is still not willing to define what it means by "peace."

Former senior U.S. diplomats and defense officials have formed and remained in active leadership of an organization in Washington D.C. called Search for Common Ground which for some years has been "trying to recruit leading Arabs and Israelis with close ties to their governments for dialogue on solving the Middle East conflict." One of the key figures in behind-the-scenes dialogue has been Tahsin Bashir, a senior Egyptian diplomat who helped negotiate the Camp David Accords. Without detailing the long and arduous road thus far traveled and the many disappointments along the way, it can be said, despite denials from Syrian President Assad and high level Israelis, that slow progress is being made toward full Israeli withdrawal from the Golan and full peace and diplomatic relations between Syria and Israel.

Necessity or Deadly Delusion?

In spite of the dangers, Israel would seem at first glance to have no better option than to seek peace with its neighbors. Former Israeli foreign minister Abba Eban argues: "Far from deterring other wars, our victory in [the Six-Day War of] 1967 was followed by three more wars, which ended without our achieving security."[26] But is the current so-called peace process really a necessity or a deadly delusion?

One Israeli columnist has likened the "peace process" to a false Messiah that has captured the imagination of Prime Minister Yitzhak Rabin and foreign Minister Shimon Peres and mesmerized much of Jewry worldwide. He recently wrote:

> Our Arab pseudo-partners know that in the name of this process, Rabin/Peres, Ltd. are ignoring Jewish history and aspirations, ignoring the history of classical Islamic and modern Arab attitudes to Jews and Judaism in general and Jewish sovereignty in particular; and letting themselves be mesmerized by occasional Arab smiles.
>
> Rabin/Peres, Ltd. are also ignoring the long history of Arab statesmen as expert practitioners of the art, rooted in Islamic religious thought, of lying to and smiling at the enemy in order to throw him off his guard, divert him from his goals, weaken and destroy him.
>
> Rabin/Peres, Ltd. are leading the Jewish state across the wasteland of Moslem/Arab hate to a *fata morgana* land that our foreign minister seems to get an erotic thrill out of calling "New Middle East."
>
> Our purported Arab partners relish the thought that whereas common mirages stand, as it were, on solid ground or sea, this *fata morgana* hovers over an abyss, beyond the precipice, and every step forward brings us closer to the edge and, eventually, God forbid, hurtling over the edge into the abyss.[27]

It should be clear by now that the so-called peace process is a fraud that can only lead, in the long run, to war. While the Israelis are sincere in their desire for peaceful coexistence with their Arab neighbors, the latter have sworn themselves to the destruction of an Israeli state of no matter what proportions because they believe its existence to be fundamentally unjust. The Oslo and Cairo agreements are merely steps toward the eventual destruction of the State of Israel. As a recent *Jerusalem Post* editorial accurately stated:

> [A]s long as the danger of Islamic militancy looms, all talk of a positive, significant change in the attitudes of the Arab and Moslem world toward Israel is recklessly, dangerously premature.[28]

Israel Also at Fault

Nor can we place the blame only upon the Arabs. Israel, through her unbelief and disobedience, has brought the present impossible circumstances upon herself. While most of them have a sense of tradition, only a tiny fraction of today's Jews worldwide truly believe that the Bible is God's Word. And an even smaller fraction believe that Yahweh, the God of Israel and the only true God, personally gave the land of Israel to His "chosen people" *forever*—and that they are this people. And an even smaller and very tiny fraction literally believes that the boundaries of the land they have been given are described in Genesis 15:18-21 ("from the river of Egypt unto . . . the river Euphrates," etc.).

We have seen documented the Bible's claim that this land was promised by God to Israel *forever*. It was *never* to be sold, much less given away. God was the One who would by His grace and power give the land to Israel. She would neither attain it nor retain it by her own might or ingenuity, but if she would obey her Lord, He would protect her.

It is clear that modern Israel, like her ancestors, has violated the Torah not only morally but regarding the Promised Land. In disobedience and unbelief, instead of relying upon God's promises and protection, she is bartering land for "peace." She gave part of the Promised Land back to Egypt for the peace pact with that nation; she is in the process of giving land to the PLO for peace with that terrorist organization; she most recently gave land to Jordan in return for promised improved relations with that neighbor; and she is in the process of working out a deal to give the strategic Golan Heights back to Syria in exchange for the promise of peace with that sworn enemy.

Obviously, God's "chosen people" are not trusting in the Lord who said He would bring them into the land and that He would protect and establish them. There seems to be a total absence of any faith in God's promises on the part of Israel's leaders. They needn't make a deal with anyone if they would only remain true to God and His Word. Unfortunately, they will suffer the consequences of their disobedience and unbelief.

"Peace," Destruction, and Prayer

The world wants "peace," and will have it. The reason this peace will not last, however, but will eventually lead to worldwide destruction, is clear. The policy of the United States and other Western nations toward Israel ignores the fact that the Jews are God's chosen people and that the land of Israel is their lawful heritage. While many people in the West, and even some national leaders, profess to be Christians, what the Bible clearly has to say about the Middle East is ignored as impractical.

However, we are moving in the direction which the Bible says will be taken. It is the road to disaster, to Armageddon, but on the way it detours through temporary peace. "When they say 'Peace and safety,' then cometh sudden destruction," wrote Paul. That statement tells us that the world must reach a point where it believes that peace has been achieved—and, of course, that must involve the Middle East. Centuries earlier, Daniel, inspired of the Holy Spirit, wrote that it would be through *peace* that the Antichrist would destroy many. Obviously it would not be genuine peace, but a pseudopeace that would weaken Israel's defenses and strategic protection, making her vulnerable to destruction and encouraging her enemies to attack.

God's promise to Abraham is still in force: "I will bless them that bless thee and curse him that curseth thee" (Genesis 12:3). Since his defeat in the Gulf War and subsequent boycotts imposed upon Iraq, Saddam Hussein, though not yet as fully as Hitler, now knows what that means.

Let us do all in our power to bless Israel in obedience to God. That tiny country needs our prayers. She will surely shrink even further in the days ahead as the Arabs get their Palestinian state and the Israelis quarrel among themselves over how to respond to worldwide pressure to make dangerous concessions. And let us continue to "pray for the peace of Jerusalem" (Psalm 122:6), as God has commanded.

*Behold, I will make Jerusalem a cup of trembling
unto all the people round about, when they shall be in
the siege both against Judah and against Jerusalem.
And in that day will I make Jerusalem a burdensome
stone for all people; all that burden themselves with it
shall be cut in pieces, though all the people of the
earth be gathered together against it. . . .*

*In that day will I [Yahweh] make the governors of
Judah like an hearth of fire among the wood, and
like a torch of fire in a sheaf; and they shall devour all
the people round about, on the right hand and on the
left. . . . The* LORD *[Yahweh] shall defend the inhabitants of Jerusalem . . . he that is feeble among them at
that day shall be as David. . . . I [Yahweh] will seek
to destroy all the nations that come against Jerusalem.*

—Zechariah 12:2,3,6,8,9

*For then shall be great tribulation, such as was not
since the beginning of the world to this time, no, nor
ever shall be. And except those days should be shortened, there should no flesh be saved; but for the elect's
sake those days shall be shortened.*

—Matthew 24:21,22

*I will also gather all nations, and will bring them
down into the valley of Jehoshaphat, and will plead
with them there for my people and for my heritage
Israel, whom they have scattered among the nations,
and parted my land.*

—Joel 3:2

16

A Cup of Trembling

◆

After being scattered for 2500 years to every nation on earth, hated, hounded, persecuted, and perpetually made the object of history's most systematic attempts at genocide, the Jewish people have astonishingly survived as an identifiable ethnic, national group of people and have returned to their ancient land! That would be miracle enough, but the prophets had more to say: that in the last days just before the Messiah's return to earth, Jerusalem would be a "cup of trembling... a burdensome stone" for all nations of the earth. We have documented a number of prophecies being fulfilled in our day, but this is undoubtedly one of the most astonishing of all.

In the fulfillment of the prophecies we have earlier documented, we see miracles that no one can deny. The daily news reminds us that the prophecies concerning Israel becoming "a cup of trembling" and "a burdensome stone" are still in the process of being more fully realized. One would hope that the other prophecies about great tribulation and all nations of the earth coming against Jerusalem in mutual destruction would not come to pass. However, the 100 percent accuracy of biblical prophecies pertaining to the past warns us that the yet-future events must surely also take place. In fact, one would have to be blind not to realize that we are heading in that direction.

It is true that no full-scale war has been fought over Jerusalem in more than 20 years, while there are enough additional trouble spots in the world from Bosnia to Africa to Southeast Asia to take the focus from Jerusalem. Here again, however, precisely as Jesus foretold, these conflicts are being waged by "ethnic group against ethnic group" (Matthew 24:7; Mark 13:8; Luke 21:10) and pose a grave danger to the world. Nevertheless, the weightiest millstone around the necks of the United Nations is without doubt Jerusalem. What shall be done about that city and the State of Israel? That haunting question must be settled to prevent the outbreak of the most destructive war in world history.

A Shocking Insight

While the PLO *talk* peace with Israel, their actions speak louder than words. In the last chapter we quoted some provisions of the 1968 PLO Covenant which called for the destruction of the State of Israel and which Yasser Arafat has promised to abolish. Instead, "the PLO has prepared a new version of its covenant, and it is no less vicious than the original."[1] The new, official version was published in March 1995 in both English and Arabic by the Ministry of Information of the Palestinian National Authority. But instead of moving in the direction that Arafat has promised, it reaffirms in even clearer and tougher language all that the 1968 Covenant declared. Consider this from the new version:

> The 1947 Resolution on the partition of Palestine came only to complement the unjust laws and military orders enacted by the British mandate government. The Palestinian people didn't accept the Balfour Declaration at any time. Britain promised under this declaration to give the Jews land not belonging to her [Britain], in order to establish a Jewish state, an illegal and morally unacceptable act.
>
> The partition of Palestine was also groundless and illegal, because it failed to consult the majority of the Palestinians, estimated at that time at 90% of the total population. . . .

The goal of the Zionist movement towards these initiatives, was to establish their own state at the expense of the original inhabitants of Palestine. The Jews refused all the Arab appeals for peaceful coexistence and for a self-autonomy rule in Palestine and Jordan. All the Arab and international attempts sought to convince the Jews to accept self autonomy rule in Palestine were doomed to failure.[2]

The Arabs are the *"original* inhabitants of Palestine"? The Jews refused "Arab appeals for peaceful coexistence" and for Palestinian self-rule? The Palestinians were given 82 percent of the land. They had their Palestinian state. It was not the Jews who attacked the Arabs, but the Arabs who attacked the Jews. How is it possible to have a reasonable discussion with those who so blatantly disregard the truth?

One current deception is the false impression being given that the grievance of the Palestinians against the Jews extends only to the so-called "occupied" areas of the West Bank and Gaza. The truth is that the Arabs actually intend to recover the entire land of Israel. That fact is made clear repeatedly in the new version just as it was in the old. Note the following commentary on the above:

In view of the above facts and figures, it is now apparent that the Palestinian refugee is deeply rooted to his land—a land he was forced to abandon, to a life of living in camps.

The Palestinian refugee has demonstrated through more than *four decades of Israeli occupation* his unshakeable conviction that he will achieve his legitimate rights [emphasis added].[3]

The meaning could not be clearer. If anything, the new PLO covenant, rather than backing away from those articles which in the 1968 covenant called for the destruction of the State of Israel, argues even more explicitly to the same end. As Ze'ev Begin, a member of the Likud Party in the Israeli Knesset, declared in comment upon this new covenant: "Judea, Samaria, and Gaza have been under Israeli control for less than three decades. But for the PLO, it is the State of Israel within its 1949 lines, which has constituted injustice for 'more than four decades of Israeli occupation.' As far as the PLO is concerned, such injustice must be removed, and the Oslo agreement is just one phase in the struggle toward achieving this goal."[4]

One gains an insight into the falseness of the PLO peace agreement by the fact that since the so-called "peace process" began, an estimated 5000 to 10,000 Palestinians have fled the PLO and Hamas and moved into Israel. Most have become Israeli citizens and are hiding out all over Israel. These so-called "collaborators" had made a real peace pact with Israel years before the Oslo accords and are now being hunted by their fellow Arabs in spite of the provision in that agreement that collaborators be pardoned. The reality has been summarized as follows:

> At least 73 alleged collaborators have been killed since the Oslo accords 18 months ago [some by their own families]. . . . More than 830 have died as alleged collaborators since the intifada began seven years ago.
>
> Some Israelis are worried that the proximity of the state's endangered agents from the territories now endangers them. "What if the 18-year-old son of a collaborator decides to purify his name by killing a Jew?" asked a Jerusalem resident who found such a family living anonymously upstairs. "What if Hamas attacks the kindergarten attended by the child of a suspected collaborator?" asked a parents' committee in Afula. . . .
>
> "If I work on a building site and one of the Arab workers recognizes me, I'm finished," [says a collaborator who moved to Jerusalem from Jericho].[5]

Dividing the Promised Land

Of course, the world believes that the PLO's goal is a genuine peace, and the U.N. is doing what it can to bring the parties to that point. Unfortunately, the nations of the world are going about the establishment of peace in the wrong way and are doing it, again, precisely as the Bible said it would happen. God has given Israel a Promised Land, but the Arabs and the other nations of the world will not admit that fact. Instead of acknowledging Israel's ownership over the land God has given her, the nations of the world, in defiance of God, are dividing the land of Israel, that land which God said was not to be divided.

Zechariah foretold that Jerusalem would become a burdensome weight upon all the nations of the world (12:3). Consider how remarkable even this one prophecy is. Who could have imagined when the Old Testament was written that all the nations of the world would be involved in deciding the fate of Israel? That would have been impossible until the formation of the League of Nations after World War I, and then its successor, The United Nations, after World War II. And this involvement of all nations in dividing Israel has occurred exactly as prophesied and is still in the process of being implemented. Antichrist himself will have the final say in "divid[ing] the land for gain" (Daniel 11:39).

Remember, it was the United Nations which in November 1947 voted to partition the "land of Palestine," as they called it (not the "land of Israel," as the Bible designates it), giving a small portion to Israel instead of what God had promised to her. The new and tiny nation of Israel was immediately attacked viciously by overwhelming Arab forces. As previously explained, she defended herself against threatened annihilation at that time, and in a series of later wars which were fought to preserve her very existence, Israel took additional territory because of its strategic necessity for self-defense. She desperately needed that land because of the constant fear of surprise attack by her Arab neighbors who continued to threaten her with extermination.

The United Nations immediately demanded that Israel return the lands she had taken. Following the Six-Day War in 1967, the U.N. Security Council unanimously passed its Resolution 242. It called for a return by Israel of the captured territories in exchange for recognition by the Arabs of Israel's right to live in peace, a recognition which the Arabs refused to give. After the 1973 Yom Kippur war came Resolution 338, calling once again for Arab recognition of Israel's right to exist and for Israel's recognition of the Palestinian's right to some form of self-expression in at least part of their homeland.

Understandably, Israel has been reluctant to obey the U.N. as long as her neighbors denied her right to live among them in peace and continued to threaten her with annihilation. She returned land to Egypt as part of the peace agreement with that nation, early in 1995 gave back land to Jordan, and is now in the process of returning additional land to the Palestinians. Article I of the "Declaration of Principles on Interim Self-Government Arrangements" between Israel and the PLO states:

> It is understood that the interim arrangements are an integral part of the whole peace process and that the negotiations on the permanent status will lead to the implementation of Security Council Resolutions 242 and 338.[6]

The prophecies pertaining to Israel have been in the Bible for thousands of years. The Bible is read daily by millions of Christians and at least each Sunday in thousands of churches around the world. Many members of the United States Congress and military leaders, and even some leaders in the United Nations and NATO, claim to believe the Bible. Nevertheless, as the prophets foretold, the nations of the world, in defiance of God and His Word, are proceeding to divide the land of Israel. It is as though they are daring God to judge them—and He surely will, precisely as His prophets have warned.

All parties involved in this unbiblical giveaway, including Israel herself for her consent, will be punished severely. So say the prophets. We are not suggesting that the Arabs or Palestinians should be put out of the land; that must not be the intention of Israel. What the Bible says is that the land which was given to her by God should be under the *government* of Israel and open to Jewish immigrants from around the world, who face increasing anti-Semitism and need a place of refuge.

No Rational Explanation

To understand how amazing these prophecies are, one must realize that 2500 years ago, when Zechariah under the inspiration of God made the astonishing allusion to Jerusalem as a "cup of trembling" and "burdensome stone," that ancient capital of Israel lay in ruins and was surrounded by wilderness. It remained in desolation for centuries, and even when rebuilt it never again attained its former glory for the Jews. Only a prophet inspired of the true God who knows the future could have made such a prediction concerning Jerusalem's central role in today's search for peace! This would have been an astounding prophecy even 50 years ago. It cannot even be explained rationally on the basis of information we have today.

Jerusalem is of minor commercial or scientific importance. It has neither strategic location, natural resources, nor unusual beauty (in comparison with other cities) to attract tourists. Each of the Disneylands in California and Florida attracts far more tourists annually (as do several Roman Catholic shrines to Mary) than does the entire country of Israel. Nevertheless, precisely as Zechariah foretold, today's world of 5.6 billion people has its eyes on Jerusalem in fear and trembling, knowing that when the next world war breaks out it will be over this seemingly insignificant capital of one of earth's tiniest countries. An incredible prophecy is indeed being fulfilled before our eyes!

A Consuming Fire

Even more remarkable, however, was Zechariah's explanation of *why* Jerusalem would be a cup of trembling: "In that day will I make the governors of Judah like an hearth of fire among the wood and like a torch of fire in a sheaf; and they shall devour all the people round about, on the right hand and on the left . . . the Lord shall defend the inhabitants of Jerusalem . . . he that is feeble among them at that day shall be as David [Israel's mightiest warrior and military leader] . . ." (Zechariah 12:6,8).

If Israel were a pushover, it would not be a "cup of trembling." But this tiny nation has repeatedly and decisively defeated Arab forces of overwhelming numerical superiority backed by Soviet might, leaving the Arabs—and the rest of the world—no alternative at this point but negotiations.

It cannot be denied that tiny Israel, as Zechariah remarkably foretold, against insurmountable odds has been and still is like a devouring fire to the nations around her. In contrast to the United States, the most powerful nation on earth (whose attempt to rescue its hostages in Iran turned into an embarrassing debacle), Israel successfully and decisively brought its hostages back from the heart of Africa with the loss of only one man. When Iraq built a nuclear facility, Israel, acting on its own for self-preservation, sent its planes in and with precision bombed Iraq's nuclear hopes out of existence. As George Will has said, "The West should remember with gratitude recent history's single most effective and beneficial act of arms control, Israel's 1981 bombing of Iraq's embryonic nuclear weapons program."

In one air battle, about 200 Syrian advanced MIG fighters were shot down while Israel lost a handful. There is no doubt that in the wars with her neighbors the Israeli air force could have bombed Cairo and Damascus, and the Israeli army could have captured these cities had they so desired. The Arabs have learned the hard way that Zechariah's unbelievable declaration of 2500 years ago has come true to haunt them. They do indeed have a "consuming fire" in their midst which neither Allah nor the combined Arab military might can control.

Having rejected what the Old Testament prophets have said, the only strategy left to the Arabs is subterfuge and false promises of peace in preparation for one final attack to exterminate Israel when the time is ripe. And at that time, as we shall see, under Antichrist's leadership, the entire world will join the Arabs in the ultimate "final solution" to the Jewish question.

The Military Imbalance

When one considers the statistics of the military imbalance in the Middle East, it again makes no sense that Israel should have ever been victorious, much less that she should today be a "cup of trembling" to the nations of the world and a "consuming fire" to her Arab neighbors. At the present time Israel's combined regular army and reserves, numbering 500,000, are surrounded by Arab armies numbering nearly 2,500,000, a ratio of 5 to 1. Her 3850 tanks are outnumbered by 15,000 Arab tanks, an impossible ratio of about 4 to 1. In surface-to-surface missiles and rockets Israel is outnumbered about 20 to 1, and in total combat aircraft she is outnumbered more than 3 to 1 (750 against 2350).[7]

Based upon the numbers, and with the thousands of Soviet military experts to advise and train them, the Arabs should have been able to defeat Israel easily. But they could not. This tiny nation has the third-most-powerful armed forces in the world and no doubt the most efficient and effective. Certainly the former Soviet Union didn't care to take on Israel, nor would the United States want to engage Israel single-handedly. She is indeed a "fire among the wood" and capable of devouring all the nations around her, as the biblical prophets amazingly foretold.

It is, in fact, the efficiency of the Israel Defense Forces (IDF) that has stabilized the region and brought the Arabs to the bargaining table. Israel is blamed for starting the Six-Day War in 1967, but the facts are that she only launched a preemptive strike because she was about to be attacked from all sides. "In the four months prior to the 1967 Six-Day War, Gamal Nasser launched 37 attacks into Israel, while the Syrians shelled Israeli tractors on the shore of the Sea of Galilee from their perfect military perches atop the Golan Heights. Emboldened by his success, Nasser closed down Israeli shipping through the international Straits of Tiran. . . ."[8] Israel had no choice but to surprise the Arabs before they executed their well-planned strike.

The Nuclear Factor

Another reason for Jerusalem being a "cup of trembling" to the entire world today is her nuclear capability. Exactly what that capability is remains a secret, but no one doubts that it is there and ready to be used if needed. That fact gives further insight into Zechariah's prophecy concerning Israel being a consuming fire! As a consequence, she is under pressure to sign a nonproliferation treaty with the other nations in that region. Syria has threatened not to sign any peace treaty with Israel until the latter signs the nuclear pact. Egypt has also put pressure on Israel to do so. Said Egyptian President Hosni Mubarak early in 1995, "If we are to sign an agreement [nonproliferation], we must all [including Israel] sign."[9]

That statement stems from Egyptian President Mubarak's recent hard-line position in partnership with Assad of Syria. Mubarak and Assad had a secret meeting in Damascus in November of 1993 which Western intelligence sources "now consider the most important encounter between the two countries since the Yom Kippur War" of 20 years earlier. Egypt and Syria are seeking to bring new leadership to the Arab world and are forging "new alliances with Europe, Japan, China, and Russia." The result has been a hardening of Syria's position, as well, in negotiations with Israel.[10]

Israel, for obvious reasons, refuses to give up her nuclear capabilities until her Arab neighbors have acknowledged her right to exist and have sworn to live at peace with her. Standing next to American Vice-President Al Gore at a press conference during the latter's March 1995 visit to Israel, Rabin declared that Israel "will only begin negotiations on a Middle East nuclear-free zone when it has signed peace treaties with all its Arab neighbors and Iran," a decision which Gore hinted was justified.[11]

There are other reasons for Israel's reluctance to weaken its defense capabilities. The Arab nations have not been known for candor. Islam allows one to lie and cheat in the cause of Allah, and there is no greater Islamic cause than Israel's destruction. Nor is it easy to monitor whether a nation is complying with a nuclear ban. In spite of teams from the victorious Gulf War nations making numerous on-site inspections of Iraq, we are still not certain that she doesn't have a secret nuclear program underway that has defied detection.

The Threat from Iran

Iran poses an even greater threat than Iraq in the Middle East, and specifically to Israel. Nor is it easy to determine the precise extent of that threat. Israel and the U.S. are currently engaged in a debate on that very subject. Israel has requested certain kinds of assistance based upon its assessment of the Iranian threat, while the U.S. is inclined to reject such requests because of its different appraisal of Iran's capabilities. "CIA director James Woolsey estimated in testimony before a U.S. Senate committee that Iran is spending over $1 billion per year on its nuclear program."[12] The Israelis believe this figure will steadily increase.

The best American guess based upon information supplied by the CIA is that Iran is 7 to 15 years from developing operational nuclear weapons on her own. In fact, however, she is receiving assistance in this effort from China, North Korea, and Russia, and civilian technology adaptable to military uses provided by Germany, assistance which Israel believes will move that deadly date up to mid-1996. At that time Iran will likely have operational Hiroshima-type nuclear bombs.

Even U.S. officials have admitted at last that "Teheran has received the medium-range Nodong missile from North Korea, capable of striking Israel from Iran . . . [and that] the smuggling of nuclear materiel from the former Soviet Union to Iran and [to] other countries with nuclear ambitions has been easier than expected . . . [and that] their efforts to stop even an ally such as Germany from supplying dual technology to Iran have failed."[13] Other intelligence indicates that under North Korea's tutelage Iran is now self-producing long-range Nodong-1 surface-to-surface missiles with an estimated range of more than 1000 kilometers.[14]

Scud missiles have been operational in the region for ten years, and not only in Iraq. Iran launched Scuds against Iraq as early as March 1985, and in 1988 rained about 325 missiles upon a dozen Iraqi cities, including 61 Scuds that struck Baghdad. Ominously, such missiles are back in use. South Yemen used them in its civil war early in 1994 and Iran launched several "against the *mujahideen* operating in northern Iraq against the fundamentalist Iranian government." These recent events reveal the fact that dictatorships are not only able but increasingly willing to use missiles in pursuit of their policies.[15]

The new Republican majority in the U.S. House and Senate has promised to take steps to meet this threat. Item six in its "Contract With America" calls for "a missile defense system against rogue dictatorships." Israel has had under development since the mid-1980s its Arrow missile interceptor, and commitments from the United States provide continued long-term funding. It is anticipated that the system will be operational sometime in 1997.[16]

Needless to say, the outlook for the Middle East is not encouraging. While Israel's immediate neighbors are at least going through the motions of acknowledging her right to exist and are entering the "peace process," Iran remains inflexible in its determination to obliterate the insult to Allah and Islam which Israel's very existence presents.

The Israelis have concluded that they must very soon, on their own once again, deliver a blow to Iran similar to the one they struck against Iraq's nuclear reactor in Osirak in 1981. Otherwise Iran will have weapons with which to threaten the entire region. The stakes are high and the game is exceedingly complex.

Iran and Terrorism

Iran is also backing to the hilt the terrorist organizations which operate out of Lebanon with Syria's blessing. IDF commanders call the situation with Lebanon "a constant, ceaseless war. Ambushes, mortar and artillery shellings, rocket firings, assaults on army positions and roadside bomb explosions are almost daily occurrences." According to Peace Watch, "Terror claimed the lives of 123 Israelis during the 18 months since the Oslo accords were signed—85% more than during the 18-month period preceding the accords. . . ."[17]

Ordinarily, Israel would go after the terrorist positions in Lebanon, but now she cannot for fear that "an effective offensive against Hizbullah would undermine the prospects of an agreement with Syria."[18] Surely Israel knows better than to allow herself to be in such a position, one which Syria is exploiting to its own advantage. Why negotiate at all with Hafez Assad, knowing his real motive? One can only conclude that Israel finds itself with no other choice due to pressure from the U.N., the U.S., and Europe.

Iran provides about 80 million dollars per year to Hizbullah and about 30 million dollars annually each to Hamas and Islamic Jihad. "Algerian and Sudanese fundamentalists receive even more, and fulfill Iran's objectives in undermining the regimes [of those nations]," according to an Israeli Foreign Ministry source. Early in December 1994 General John Shalikashvili, chairman of the U.S. Joint Chiefs of Staff, accompanied by an unnamed high CIA official, visited Israel to discuss with Prime Minister Rabin and top IDF brass what to do about the failing policy. The Israelis told the U.S. in clear language that Iran must be contained at all cost before it completely destabilizes the entire Middle East.

Iran's latest move has been to deploy 6000 troops armed with anti-ship missiles on islands in the Straits of Hormuz, through which much of the world's supply of oil must pass. These troops are also equipped with chemical weapons, a further ominous sign. Concerning the role of Iran, a recent editorial in *The Jerusalem Post* had this to say:

> Like the early USSR, which exported revolution by assuming patronage of the world's oppressed, Teheran exports Islamic militancy by pretending to uphold the integrity of Islam and to champion the cause of Moslem masses. The passion and fervor it has inspired in its followers are not unlike those the early Communists evoked in theirs.
>
> And, like the Communists, Iranian-led Islamic militants seem to believe their goal sanctifies all means. Even Libya's Muammar Gaddafi and the PLO's Yasser Arafat

have not been responsible for as much bloodshed as the [Iranian] ayatollahs. Only Saddam Hussein and Hafez Assad are worthy competitors. . . .

And while at this point such grandiose dreams of global influence may seem laughable, the fact is that Algeria is in the throes of a civil war whose outcome may well be the triumph of the militant fundamentalists. And other North African countries, from Morocco to Egypt, are not immune to developments in the same direction.

Iran has also inherited the Soviet Union's mantle as the capital of international terrorism. Through Hizbullah and Hamas (both of which are financed by Teheran) and with the help of fanatics in large Moslem centers [worldwide], the long arm of Islamic militancy already reaches into virtually all Western cities. The various bombings in the West in the past two years: of the Israeli Embassy and the Jewish center in Buenos Aires, the World Trade Center in New York, and the Israeli Embassy and the Jewish center in London, were all operations of Iranian-sponsored terrorism.[19]

Iran's basic objectives are twofold: to build up its military to make it the dominant power in the region and thereby step into the vacuum created by Iraq's defeat in the Gulf War, and "to control oil policy in the Gulf, which is why Iran is perceived by the Gulf states, especially Saudi Arabia, as a threat."[20] Iran's major military suppliers are Russia, Czechoslovakia, and Poland, each of which is desperate for hard currency and obtains it from such sales.

In the February 1994 edition of *Foreign Affairs*, Anthony Lake, President Clinton's national security adviser, called for establishing a "dual containment" policy to rein in both Iraq and Iran at the same time. He criticized former presidents Reagan and Bush for attempting to work through "moderates" in Iran, where it was impossible for such to exist. "These same 'moderates' are responsible for the very policies [of aggression and terrorism] we find so objectionable," wrote Lake. Lake proposed cooperation between the United States and its allies "to keep material for chemical and nuclear weapons out of

Iran . . . [and to] prevent Iran from receiving surface-to-air missiles from such suppliers as North Korea." Israel's reaction to these remarks was enthusiastic, but she subsequently "watched as Iran continued its military buildup uninterrupted and implemented its policy by subversion through such proxies as Hizbullah, Hamas and Islamic Jihad."[21]

A Hopeful Alternative

One hope for peace is to develop trade between Israel, which is much more advanced agriculturally and industrially, and her Arab neighbors, to the advantage of all parties. This would encourage friendly contact between former enemies and provide a profit motive for continued stability in the region. At the end of October 1994, 1200 participants from 80 nations gathered in Casablanca, Morocco, for the Middle East-North Africa Economic Summit. That gathering was by far the "largest effort yet by Israelis and Arabs to strengthen regional stability through investment and development."[22]

So dependent are the Palestinians upon Israel's economy that they could not survive without it. Terrorist activity causes Israel to close her borders to thousands of Palestinians who work inside Israel, and these closures are very costly to the meager Palestinian economy. Therefore, "Palestinians in the Hebron area have been divorcing their wives and marrying Israeli Arab women to get permits to work in Israel. Sheikh Taysir Tamimi, superintendent of the Islamic Courts, told Hebron journalists that 'a group of men have divorced their wives to marry girls inside the Green Line to get work permits.' He said the men did so 'only on paper,' as polygamy is permitted in Islamic law, but the 'divorce' was necessary in order to marry according to Israeli law, which does not allow polygamy."[23]

The dependence of Palestinians upon the Israeli economy is a problem that must be overcome in any peaceful settlement. In fact, Israel is taking steps to replace the Palestinians with non-Arab foreign laborers. Israel feels that if the Palestinians are to have an independent state, they should show their independence by creating jobs for their own people. Israelis are already arguing that there should be no "right of return" to Israel for Palestinians. "When the Palestinians have their own state, they'll have to absorb their brethren in it. They cannot demand self-determination while exiling Palestinians to Israel."[24]

Early in February 1995, because of a wave of Muslim fundamentalist terrorist attacks against Israel which originated in Gaza, and because of Israel's retaliatory sealing off of the Gaza strip, the peace process bogged down. With the encouragement of the United States, the parties came back together. Foreign Minister Shimon Peres and PLO leader Yasser Arafat's adviser, Nabil Shaath, pledged once again to proceed with the peace process and Palestinian self-rule of the West Bank. U.S. Secretary of State Warren Christopher, who had arranged the meeting, said that both parties "made clear that there would be no turning back from the search for peace," though everyone acknowledged it would be a difficult process. The three-hour meeting, which was also attended by Amre Mousa of Egypt and Karim al-Kabariti of Jordan, "produced an agreement to establish new industrial free-trade zones in the region."[25]

Prophecies About the "Many"

Israel exports many of her products outside the Middle East—about 15 billion dollars annually to Western Europe. She even sells flowers to Holland and electronics to Japan! Obviously, a major source of pressure upon Israel to barter land for "peace" is found in the fact that she depends upon these exports for her economic survival. When the nations to whom she sells her products pressure her behind the scenes to make "peace" with the Palestinians, Israel has little choice. She cannot stand alone in the world.

Once again we see the accuracy of Bible prophecy. At the beginning of his seizure of power, the Antichrist will guarantee "peace" for Israel and even allow the Temple to be rebuilt and the Temple sacrifices to resume. We will return to these remarkable events in a later chapter. Of particular interest now is the fact that the prophecy dealing with these occurrences states, "He shall confirm the covenant with many . . ." (Daniel 9:27). Why with *many?* Why didn't the prophets say that Antichrist would confirm the covenant with Israel, since she is the principal party?

Only recently did the circumstances develop to clarify that prophecy, a prophecy which had puzzled Bible scholars for centuries. It is now quite clear that any deal affecting Jerusalem and the Temple must involve *many* parties beside Israel herself. Her Arab neighbors, of course, would be involved, as would NATO and The United Nations. Yes, because of her strategic importance to world peace, any important covenant with Israel, like the current agreements involved in the Middle East peace process as well as those promoting regional stability through trade, can only be with *many*—exactly as the prophets foretold.

The Forty-Seven-Year War

How amazing it is that the rivalry for this "Holy Land," for this "Promised Land," continues today with dogged ferocity. The Arabs call it a war, and it has continued without armistice since it began in 1948. As stated earlier, when our family was traveling in Egypt in May of 1967 just before the Six-Day War broke out, we were puzzled at hearing an oft-repeated phrase: "the 19-year war." We finally realized that 1967 was 19 years since the outbreak of hostilities in 1948. To the Arab world, that war had never ended and was still in progress 19 years later. Today it is the 47-Year War and next year it will be the 48-Year War. How can it ever be settled without the extermination of Israel? In fact, that extermination is precisely what the Antichrist will eventually attempt.

Most of the casualties in this war without armistice which continues to this day are innocent civilians, including women and children, whom the Arabs view as legitimate though random targets. Consider, for example, Alisa Flatow, 20-year-old American studying at a Jerusalem seminary, one of the victims riding in a bus in Gaza that was rammed in early April 1995 by a van loaded with explosives and driven by an Islamic suicide bomber. Ironically, her death saved several Israeli lives to whom her family donated her heart, lungs, liver, and kidneys.[26] Ofra Felix was another 20-year-old student victim. Her car, an apparently random target, was riddled with terrorist bullets which killed her and wounded her brother-in-law, Amichai Remer, but somehow missed Remer's two small children. The heartbreaking list goes on and on.

"Credit" for Ofra's unconscionable and barbarous murder was taken by George Habash's Popular Front for the Liberation of Palestine. The reason? It was in "revenge for the killing of four of its members by the IDF a week earlier."[27] Of course those four had not been shot in cold blood as was Felix, but had been apprehended in an act of terrorism and fought back with their weapons. Had they surrendered when called upon to do so they would not have been killed.

Anti-Israel Propaganda in Western Media

Terrorists who attack Israelis are heroes in the Arab world. Even the Western media goes along with this skewed thinking. *Time* magazine of December 5, 1994, listed the names of what it called "The Global 100 . . . leaders of tomorrow" with a brief biographical sketch for each. Among those listed were Syrian dictator Hafez Assad's son, Bashar; Ali Belhadj, leader of the Islamic fundamentalist movement in Algeria responsible for hijackings and the murder of thousands of innocents; Mohammed Dahlan, mastermind of various terrorist strikes; and other plotters of evil. Comments by the *Jerusalem Post* on this infamous list and on *Time* magazine's gentle treatment and even praise was on the mark:

> Yet in all the 15,000 words *Time* devotes to these 100 future leaders, the word "terrorist" appears only once— in describing [Israeli Likud leader Tzahi] Hanegbi's parents [as] . . . [having been] members of the terrorist Stern Group. . . .
> On the other hand, Dahlan . . . is described as an avuncular former boy scout: "Reputed nice guys are rarities

atop most internal-security agencies. Dahlan is one of them—an affable, even gracious former guerrilla fighter . . . trustworthy and fair."

The description of the intifada is just as sweet. It is "the stone-throwing youth uprising that ultimately helped persuade Israel to begin a withdrawal from the occupied territories." Amazing how this "youth uprising" managed to kill more than 1,000 Arabs and 300 Jews with nothing but stones. Must be because affable guys like Dahlan led it so graciously.[28]

In any war, propaganda plays a vital role. In the current war of words over who has the right to the Holy Land, the world media seems deaf to Israel and overly sympathetic to whatever complaints the Palestinians may make. Israel is the ogre that stole their land and grinds them down in poverty. The fact is, as we have already noted, that in spite of billions of dollars in oil revenues, it was the Arab states that kept the Palestinians in squalid camps and would not integrate them into society. Forgotten too are the benefits Israel has brought to this land.

Misinformation is continually promoted in the international press to prejudice the world against Israel's claim upon Jerusalem. Recently *The Guardian* reported that Israel had built its new Supreme Court "in East Jerusalem . . . where the Palestinians are keen to make their capital." It was suggested that this had been done in defiance of the 1993 Oslo accord. In fact, the Supreme Court building had been built *before* the Oslo accords—and in the western part of Jerusalem. When it comes to Jerusalem, fiction is more acceptable than fact—and certainly more useful in maintaining and escalating prejudices.

One would not expect to find examples of the lies promoted by the media in such places as *Worldview*, a quarterly publication of The National Peace Corps Association. However, that proves to be as fruitful a source of misinformation as any. As David Bar-Illan pointed out recently, in just one issue of *Worldview* there were numerous errors: that Israeli law has maliciously imposed a prohibition on growing the Palestinian national herb, *za'atar* (in fact the Arabs had practically wiped out *za'atar,* so the Israeli law prohibits picking the plant in the wild and encourages its cultivation); that "excavation of 'sites of Palestinian heritage' is prohibited by law" (in fact, the meticulous care with which Israel has preserved archaeological sites and encouraged proper digging is second to none); that Palestine was a primordial paradise before Israeli "occupation" destroyed the environment and especially the farming. Bar-Illan deals with the latter accusation in detail:

> [Actually], before the Zionist era, Palestinian agriculture was so primitive that the country could never sustain more than 200,000 people. Life expectancy was under 50. Under the Jordanians, one third of the Judea-Samaria population and half of Jerusalem's Arabs left the country. There were no schools of higher learning and no industry.
>
> Israel has transformed a poverty-stricken, disease-ridden, backward population into a thriving, industrious, educated, computerized, agriculturally sophisticated, immigration-drawing, television-owning society. It is a crime for which Israel will never be forgiven.[29]

United Nations "Peacekeepers"?

It is astonishing that Prime Minister Rabin has tried to quell the fears of Israelis regarding withdrawal from the Golan Heights by assuring them that it won't be done without a guarantee that United Nations peacekeeping forces will be stationed there for Israel's protection. That such "peacekeepers" have a poor record doesn't seem to concern Rabin. It is the propaganda value of invoking their presence that he is after.

In a letter to *The Jerusalem Post,* a Jewish physician living in America reminds Rabin that just before the Six-Day War in 1967, Nasser "ordered the UN Emergency Force stationed in the Sinai to withdraw from their observation posts along the Israeli-Egyptian border. Without even bringing the matter to the attention of the General Assembly, Secretary-General U Thant complied with the demand and the UN forces were gone within 48 hours, leaving Israel on its own." His letter continues:

What might be of interest to Mr. Rabin is the action of the Serbs [in the Bosnia-Herzegovina-Sarajevo war] *vis-a-vis* the great power of NATO and the UN. They have treated them with utter contempt. Despite all the dire warnings coming from these august and all-powerful bodies, the Serbs have persisted in their lethal objectives. They have, within the last few days, added insult to injury and actually taken over 400 UN peace-keepers as political hostages. Of course, the US role in these proceedings has been even less distinguished.

Are these the world forces that Mr. Rabin is expecting to protect Israel from Syria, Palestinian Arabs, Iraq, Iran and Saudi Arabia once Mr. Rabin has given up Israel's vital defensive positions on the Golan Heights and in the mountains of Judea and Samaria?[30]

Eyes on Jerusalem

Jerusalem is the prize in an irreconcilable conflict between the Jews and Arabs for the "land of promise." As one expert on Islam, Professor Gideon Kressel of Beersheba's Ben Gurion University, has said, a Muslim is convinced by his religion that "once land has been controlled by Islam it must be returned to Islam." That religious conviction demands total Islamic ownership and therefore cannot be satisfied by dividing up the land.

Genuine peace will not be achieved, no matter how much of Israel is placed under Arab control, so long as a State of Israel exists. FLAME (Facts and Logic about the Middle East) explains:

> The obsession of the Moslem Arabs with Israel is totally irrational. To have Israel, an advanced, highly civilized Western outpost, as an independent country in the middle of the Arab-Moslem world is utterly intolerable to them. That is the reason that, making allowance for the very cold peace with Egypt and the recently concluded peace with Jordan, the 21 Arab states, among them the richest countries in the world, with a combined

population of more than 200 million and with a land area greater than that of the U.S., have since the beginning of the century concentrated obsessive ferocity by military, economic, ideological, political, diplomatic, and any other means to destroy the tiny Jewish community of Palestine, and its successor, the Jewish state of Israel. . . .

The insincere focus on the Palestinian plight is designed to divert attention from the many domestic problems and inter-Arab conflicts, and to direct the Moslem Arab frustration against Israel, the "infidel Western outsider." [For] Israel [to] divest itself from its historic heartland, the 2,362 sq. mi. "West Bank" and from the Golan Heights would be . . . strategic suicide.[31]

Many of the biblical prophecies seemed ludicrous when they were made. Certainly the prophecies of Jerusalem's ultimate importance seemed akin to madness as Jerusalem was repeatedly destroyed and then lay in ruins and all but abandoned for centuries. Yet today, in continuing fulfillment as further prophecies unfold, Jerusalem has indeed become a "cup of trembling" and a "burdensome stone" around the necks of all nations. The eyes of the world are upon Jerusalem, knowing that no matter how preposterous it may seem, that small city, with its roots so deep in the past, holds the key to future world peace. Who except God alone could have foreseen that remarkable development 2500 years ago?

What one nation in the earth is like thy people, even like Israel, whom God went to redeem for a people to himself, and to make him a name, and to do for thee great things and terrible, for thy land, before thy people, which thou redeemedst to thee from Egypt, from the nations and their gods? For thou hast confirmed to thyself thy people Israel to be a people unto thee forever; and thou, LORD, art become their God.

—2 Samuel 7:23,24

Thus saith the LORD, which giveth the sun for a light by day and the ordinances of the moon and of the stars for a light by night, which divideth the sea when the waves thereof roar; The LORD of hosts is his name: If those ordinances [of nature] depart from before me, saith the LORD, then the seed of Israel also shall cease from being a nation before me forever.

Thus saith the LORD, If heaven above can be measured [which can't be done], and the foundations of the earth searched out beneath [which can't be done], I will also cast off all the seed of Israel for all that they have done, saith the LORD.

Behold, the days come, saith the LORD, that the city [Jerusalem] shall be built to the LORD. . . . It shall not be plucked up nor thrown down anymore forever.

—Jeremiah 31:35-40

He saved others; himself he cannot save. If he be the King of Israel, let him now come down from the cross, and we will believe him.

—Matthew 27:42

Which Israel? The Israel—the church. . . . That's the Israel of God, not that garlic one over on the Mediterranean Sea!

—Rick Godwin, popular Charismatic leader[1]

17

Christians For—and Against—Israel

◆
────────────────────

J esus of Nazareth was born a Jew of the tribe of Judah and of
the household of David, according to the genealogy of His
mother (given through Joseph's father-in-law, i.e. Mary's
father—Luke 3:23-31). The genealogy back to David of
Joseph, who, though not Christ's father, was head of the
household, is given in Matthew 1:6-16. Like Jesus Himself, the
original 12 disciples were all genuinely Jewish, as was the early
church.

The first Gentiles were not converted until some years after
Pentecost (Acts 10). Nor did significant numbers of Gentiles
come into the church until even later, when "a great number [of
Greeks] believed and turned to the Lord" in the city of Antioch. It was these Gentile believers who were first called
"Christians" (Acts 11:19-26). Even then, for many years the
leadership of the church remained Jewish and was centered in
Jerusalem. In view of these facts, it seems odd that Jews
generally consider Christianity to be anti-Jewish and look
upon Jews who believe in Jesus as traitors to their people.

A Plea for Jewish Tolerance

A Jew who, on the basis of what the Hebrew prophets said
and the testimony of those who knew Jesus the best, decides

that Jesus was indeed the Messiah is almost always cast out by family and cut off by friends. Why can't a Jew make such a choice without suffering this rejection? In Israel, a country which prides itself on its tolerance, Jews who believe in Jesus have been stoned, had their places of worship burned down, and lost their jobs. At times they have experienced discrimination and persecution rivaling that which the Jews suffered in Nazi Germany prior to the Holocaust. Today a Jew who, in another country, even where anti-Semitism is rampant, has confessed a belief in Jesus is refused the right to immigrate to Israel. Why such prejudice in a land where Jews are fully accepted who embrace almost any other belief from atheism to New Age to Zen Buddhism?

"Well, Jesus wasn't the Messiah" is the offered justification. "He didn't bring peace." Exactly how and when and what kind of peace the Messiah is supposed to bring must be decided on the basis of what the Hebrew prophets have said. Moreover, the prophets foretold much more than a universal peace in reference to the coming Messiah, and, as we have shown, Jesus fulfilled *all* the messianic prophecies. But even if Jesus were not the Messiah, does that justify the rancor displayed by Jews toward their brothers and sisters who believe in Him?

There were a number of Jews, from Judas Maccabee to Judas of Galilee to Theudas to Bar Cochba, whose followers believed them to be the Messiah. Yet none of these obviously false messiahs is remembered with the animosity that Jews express toward Jesus. In fact, many of them are remembered fondly. Why then is Jesus Christ so hated among Jews today? Is it because the numbers of those who believe in Him continue to grow? Is He damned for His success?

There is certainly sufficient reason on the basis of what the Hebrew prophets said about the coming of the Messiah to give at least serious consideration to the claims of Christ and to show respect toward those who sincerely believe that He fulfilled those prophecies in His life, death, and resurrection. Furthermore, only the one statement by Daniel that the coming of the Messiah would be 69 weeks of years (483 years) after the command to rebuild Jerusalem (which occurred in 445 B.C.) would argue that the time for the Messiah has passed by more than 1900 years and there is no point in waiting any longer. If Jesus, who came at that precise time and fulfilled all the prophecies, was not the Messiah, then the prophets lied and the whole idea of a Messiah one day rescuing Israel from her enemies must be abandoned At the very least, Jews ought to give fellow Jews who believe in Jesus credit for their sincerity and drop the hostility toward them!

Common Jewish Misunderstandings

In Jesus' day, "the common people heard him gladly" (Mark 12:37). Multitudes followed Him and, according to the eyewitness testimony of His disciples, were miraculously healed and fed by Him. How then did He come to be crucified? Jealous because His popularity exceeded theirs, the rabbis incited the people to demand His crucifixion. Their theological justification was twofold: 1) He broke the law by healing on the Sabbath day (Luke 13:14; etc.); and 2) He blasphemed by claiming to be God (John 8:58; 10:33; etc.). Yet, as we have seen, the Hebrew prophets had declared that the Messiah must be God (Psalm 110:1; Isaiah 7:14; 9:6; Malachi 3:1; etc.). The rabbis simply couldn't believe that. Nor did they understand the other messianic prophecies or they would have realized that they were fulfilling some of them by rejecting and crucifying Jesus.

The misunderstandings and prejudices about Jesus fostered by the rabbis in His day have been retained by Jewish people ever since. Those misunderstandings motivate such books as *The Myth-Maker,* by Talmudic scholar Hyam Maccoby.[2] The author sets out to prove his prejudices, prejudices which so severely blind him that one could drive a fleet of trucks through the holes in his pitiful arguments. His central thesis is that Paul invented Christianity. Yet Paul himself argued that he preached "the gospel of God" which God Himself had "promised before by his prophets in the holy Scriptures" (Romans 1:1-4). Paul's entire approach was to open the writings of the

328 ◆ CHRISTIANS FOR—AND AGAINST—ISRAEL

Hebrew prophets in the synagogue, to point out what they had prophesied concerning the Messiah, and to prove that Jesus had fulfilled the messianic prophecies. Maccoby fails to deal with Paul on that ground and shows his ignorance of Christianity by proposing ideas and offering arguments which are so ludicrous that we need not waste our time in refuting them.

Goaded by their religious leaders, the Jews persecuted the early Christians just as the pagan Roman emperors did. Remember, for at least the first hundred years it was not the Christians who persecuted the Jews but the Jews who persecuted the Christians. It would be the fourth century before those who called themselves "Christians" would begin to persecute and kill Jews. That mistreatment began only after Roman Catholicism became the only "Christianity" that was officially allowed, as have earlier explained.

It was only at this point, when the Roman Catholic Church began to dominate the empire and the papal system was in place, that the persecution of Jews began by those who claimed to be, and whom the Jews thought were, Christians. We can hardly blame the Jews that as a result of centuries of such persecution a great fear and mistrust of "Christians" became a part of the Jewish psyche, as it is today. For that tragedy Roman Catholicism must take the blame—but it has never apologized or admitted the great evil for which it was responsible. Today's Pope hints that an apology is due, but only because of what some of the Church's overzealous and misguided "sons and daughters" did, leaving the Church itself, which is infallible, without blame. "During his *Angelus* message on Sunday, February 12 [1995], John Paul II referred to the medieval Crusades against Muslims in the Holy Land as 'an inappropriate means for defending the holy sites,' "[3] but he didn't specify the horrors of the Crusades nor mention the crimes against the Jews.

It was the popes themselves, as we have noted, who conceived and executed the "Christian" persecution of the Jews, confining them to ghettos, making them wear an identifying badge or hat, destroying their synagogues, torturing them in the inquisitions, and forcing them to convert or be expelled or killed. Every Jew has heard of the Inquisition in which his ancestors suffered. One Catholic historian writes:

> Of eighty popes in a line from the thirteenth century on, not one of them disapproved of the theology and apparatus of Inquisition. On the contrary, one after another added his own cruel touches to the workings of this deadly machine.[4]

Hitler was a Roman Catholic and was never excommunicated by that Church, so the Holocaust is seen as one more evidence against "Christianity." The Catholic Croatian Ustashi, headed by Ante Pavelic, were responsible for the deaths of tens of thousands of Jews in the early 1940s, but also for the sadistic murders of hundreds of thousands of Serbian Orthodox adherents who also claimed, like the Catholics, to be Christians.

A Confused Notion of Christianity

Most Jews are not aware of the fact that the Inquisition consumed probably 100 times as many Christians as it did Jews. For 15 centuries (for 1200 years *before* the Reformation) the Roman Catholic Church, at the same time it was killing Jews by the thousands, was torturing and killing Christians by the millions. One of the most respected Catholic historians of the nineteenth century wrote:

> Through the . . . unwearied activity of the Popes and their legates . . . the view of the Church had been . . . [that] every departure from the teaching of the Church, and every important opposition to any ecclesiastical ordinances, must be punished with death, and the most cruel of deaths, by fire. . . .
> It was the Popes who compelled bishops and priests to condemn the heterodox to torture, confiscation of their goods, imprisonment, and death, and to enforce the execution of this sentence on the civil authorities, under

330 CHRISTIANS FOR—AND AGAINST—ISRAEL

pain of excommunication. . . . Every Pope confirms
and improves upon the devices of his predecessor . . .
[involving] the Inquisition, which contradicted the
simplest principles of Christian justice and love to our
neighbor, and would have been rejected with universal
horror in the ancient Church.[5]

Most of these victims were the true followers of Christ, who
through the centuries refused allegiance to the Pope or to his
Church and who instead sought to follow the Bible as their
guide in all matters of faith and practice. As a result they were
hated, hunted, persecuted, tortured, and slaughtered by the
Roman Catholic Church *in the name of Christ,* in complete
opposition to all that Christ had taught. This false "Christianity" headquartered in Rome had become as bloodthirsty
as Islam, and in many ways even worse. One must in all
fairness acknowledge that the Moorish occupiers of Israel
were in many instances more honorable and merciful than the
invading "Christian" Crusaders.

Though Jews have heard of the Reformation that occurred
in the sixteenth century under Martin Luther's leadership,
most don't know its significance. Multitudes began to read the
Bible for themselves and as a result were set free from the
delusion that the Roman Catholic Church held the keys to
heaven. Instead of following the Pope, they became the followers of Jesus Christ.

Lovers of Israel and the Jews

As a result of the Reformation, there are millions of Christians today, known as evangelicals, who utterly reject Roman
Catholicism as a false religious system (more pagan than
Christian) of works, ritual, purgatory, indulgences, and the
perpetual sacrifice of Christ in the Mass. Since the Reformation, these followers of Jesus have been persecuted and burned
at the stake by Roman Catholics by the hundreds of thousands.
The persecution of Protestants still continues to whatever
extent possible in today's world wherever Roman Catholicism
is firmly in control.

These non-Catholic followers of Christ love Israel and pray for the peace of Jerusalem. Far from engaging in anti-Semitism or persecution of Jews, they would give their lives for those who by physical birth are the brethren of Jesus Christ. For example, consider Kaare Kristiansen, former leader of Norway's Christian People's Party. When asked about his long-standing love of and support for Israel, he replied, "It came with my mother's milk." He was "born into a deeply religious Evangelical Lutheran family [and] grew up hearing his father read the Bible."[6] Such love for Israel and Jews worldwide is taught not only in the Old Testament but in the New as well and characterizes all true Christians.

Jewish prejudices against Jesus Christ and Christians result to a large extent from the mistaken notion that Roman Catholicism is Christianity and from the failure to recognize that there are millions of Christians who refuse allegiance to Rome. That Church's mistreatment of Jews was fostered by the heretical teaching that the Jews ought to be killed for killing Christ. (No such teaching can be found in the New Testament, nor was it ever practiced by the early church.) Forgotten was the fact that the Romans, not the Jews, were in power and could have released Jesus instead of executing Him. It was taught that the Jews were no longer the Chosen People but were under God's wrath.

The "New" Israel and the "Old"

The belief gradually developed that the Roman Catholic Church was the New Israel and Rome the New Jerusalem. Rome claimed to be the spiritual center of the world and took Jerusalem's place as "the city where God had placed His Name." Catholic Rome claimed every title that had belonged to Jerusalem: the Holy City, the Eternal City, the City of God. The land of Israel was seen as belonging to the Church and the popes organized Crusades to take back the Holy Land not only from the Turks but from the Jews themselves. There would be "holy war" against the Jews until "Christianity" triumphed.

To compete with Islam's promise of Paradise to Muslims who died fighting infidels, Pope Urban II, organizer of the First Crusade, promised a plenary indulgence (instant entrance into heaven without any time in purgatory) for Crusaders who died in that great cause. The knights and knaves who responded with enthusiasm to that deceitful promise left a trail of mayhem, plunder, and murder on the way to Jerusalem, searching out every Jew they could find and giving them the choice of baptism into Roman Catholicism or death. One of the Crusaders' first acts upon "freeing" Jerusalem was to herd the Jews into the synagogue and set it ablaze.

Pope Gregory XIII declared that the guilt of Jews in crucifying Christ "only grows deeper with successive generations, entailing perpetual slavery." A succession of popes continued the persecution up through Pius IX (1846-78). In 1862, *La Civilta*, the semiofficial voice of the Vatican, echoed a belief held for centuries and which remains official Roman Catholic doctrine to this day: "As the Jews were formerly God's people, so are the Romans [Catholics] under the New Covenant."[7] Sickened with the despotic tyranny of the popes, the Italian people finally rose up against them. The forces of the new united Italy fought their way to independence and freed the last of the papal states from Pius IX, taking Rome itself finally and forcing the Pope to take refuge behind the Vatican walls. A former priest turned historian writes:

> Eleven days after Rome fell, on 2 October 1870, the Jews, by a royal decree, were given the freedom which the papacy had denied them for over fifteen hundred years. The last ghetto in Europe [at the time] was dismantled.[8]

When the Jews at last had a national home to call their own, it took the Vatican 46 years to acknowledge Israel's right to exist. Diplomatic relations were established only when it became apparent that Israel was launched on the road to some sort of "peace" with the Palestinians and its Arab neighbors and that the fate of Jerusalem would be part of the deal. Rome needed some official relationship in order to have her say in that process. She is now poised to be the spiritual guardian of

Jerusalem. Israel's current leaders are so intoxicated with the prospect of peace that they close their eyes to the long history of Catholic anti-Semitism and Islamic oaths to destroy Israel. They pretend that both Rome and Mecca have at last decided to let Israel live in peace.

Replacement Theology

Today, more than 400 years after the Reformation and in repudiation of the martyrs who gave their lives to break free from Rome, we are seeing Protestants joining hands with the very Church which sent their ancestors to the flames. As part of that ecumenical togetherness, Protestants in growing numbers are embracing the very Roman Catholic beliefs which were anathema to their forebears. Even the heresy that the Church is Israel, also known as the Identity or Restoration movements, has been embraced by a large part of Protestantism. A letter received from members of a conservative and evangelical church explains:

> The eschatology of the Lutheran Church, Missouri and Wisconsin Synods, is Catholic in nature: no rapture, no millennium. The church is Israel and Scriptures are spiritualized to claim promises to Israel for the church. Israel as a nation has been stripped of any importance.[9]

One influential Charismatic leader, Earl Paulk, has even said that those who say, "If you bless Israel, God will bless you," are promoting "the spirit of antichrist,"[10] attributing what God said ("I will bless them that bless thee, and curse him that curseth thee"—Genesis 12:3) to Satan! Paulk claims that "whatever has been written concerning the law and prophecies about Israel as a nation is now transferred to spiritual Israel, which is the people of God [i.e., the church]...."[11] David Chilton, a popular Reformed theologian and Reconstructionist author, writes, "[With] Israel's final excommunication in A.D. 70, when Jerusalem was destroyed... the Kingdom had been transferred to His new people, the Church.... The Kingdom... will never again be possessed by national Israel."[12] Another influential Christian leader, James McKeever, writes in his newsletter:

> We love the Hebrews who live . . . in the nation of Israel. . . . However, the Lord has shown us clearly that in no way are they Israel. Israel is composed of all believers in Jesus Christ. . . .
>
> It is vitally important for the body of Christ to realize that they *are* Israel and that the unfulfilled prophecies concerning Israel are theirs to participate in. The unfulfilled promises to Israel are for the church to receive.[13]

He couldn't contradict the Bible more clearly. There is no way that the promises given by God to Israel can now be usurped by the church. Nor do these men who want the *promises* that God gave to Israel ever suggest that the church also has inherited the *curses* which the prophets pronounced upon Israel. Nevertheless, another highly regarded evangelical author writes: "[A]ll future promises of glory and blessing for Israel and Zion must belong to the true Israel [the church] and the heavenly Zion."[14] He concludes his study of *The Hope of Israel* with the firm denial that there exists in all of Scripture "the slightest support to the doctrine of the restoration of the Jewish nation in a coming age and its exaltation of lordship over the nations of the world."[15] One further quotation should suffice to document this blatant and growing misapplication of Scripture:

> [M]any people earnestly but mistakenly . . . describe the twentieth-century nation of Israel as "God's chosen people." That may not be believed, however, by those who believe the New Testament. The Authorized or King James version of the Bible uses the word "chosen" 30 times in the New Testament—*but never to refer to the nation of Israel. . . .*
>
> The teaching of the New Testament has not changed in the last 1,900 years, and we ignore its truth at our peril. The church was the Israel of God's choice in the first century and it is still the Israel of his choice today. . . .

It is spiritual Israel alone which he has chosen "to be his peculiar people" (Ex. 19:5; Dt. 26:18; Ti. 2:14; 1 Pet. 2:9).[16]

Distinguishing the Church from Israel

On the contrary, the true church is heavenly, not earthly, and no land on earth was ever promised to her. Christ's promise very clearly was: "In my Father's house [heaven] are many mansions. . . . I will come again and receive you unto myself, that where I am [with the Father], there ye may be also" (John 14:2,3). Paul's understanding by revelation from Christ was equally clear: "The Lord himself shall descend from heaven . . . the dead in Christ shall rise first; then we which are alive and remain shall be caught up together with them in the clouds to meet the Lord in the air; and so shall we ever be with the Lord" (1 Thessalonians 4:16,17).

The major promise to Israel for the last days is that she will be gathered from the nations where God scattered her to dwell once more in the Promised Land and that Christ will rule over her from Jerusalem—a promise that would be meaningless for the church. The church was never cast out of any land, and it was never promised that she would return to the land from which she was cast out, as God promised Israel.

Israel is distinguished from the church for all time by the land which God gave to her. It is those repeated prophecies of a specific land which should prevent Israel from bartering that land away in exchange for a false "peace" promised by those who have sworn eternal enmity against her. Unfortunately, Israel's leaders, and the vast majority of Israelis, do not believe God's promises in the Bible, nor do they heed His warnings.

The "Spiritualizing" Syndrome

In order for the church to take to itself the promises that God gave to Israel, one must deliteralize or "spiritualize" the Old Testament. It thus becomes allegory instead of the factual history of a real people known as Israel. Consider, for example, a large Charismatic conference held in Phoenix, Arizona, a few years ago titled "Take It By Force." The theme verse was God's command to Joshua to "go in to possess the land" (Joshua 1:11).

Month after month, the five-page ads in *Charisma* declared that God was raising up a "Joshua generation" who would "go in and possess the land," i.e. the United States. The application was that Christians needed to stand on God's promises and turn the United States into a Christian country by taking over the media, the school boards, and local, state, and federal government positions—all this because of promises and commands given to Joshua and the people of Israel 3500 years ago. On his Trinity Broadcasting Network "Praise the Lord" show, Paul Crouch told the millions of Christians watching around the world that the church was going to take over the media and the airwaves and do it "by force" if necessary.

If, however, the Israelites were real people who were captives in Egypt and were set free and led across the wilderness by Moses and taken by Joshua into a real place known as the land of Israel, then we must understand these verses in that context. The land that Joshua was to possess had boundaries which are stated in Genesis 15:18-21. It was that specific land, and no other, which Joshua and the people of Israel were told to possess. There was no command to Joshua to take over the United States or any other country—only the land promised to Abraham, Isaac, and Jacob. What a twisting of Scripture to take a promise given to Joshua and Israel concerning the land of Israel and apply it to the church as its mandate to take over the world, and even "by force"! Those who promote these ideas, whether Catholics or Protestants, make Christianity sound like militant Islam, which also is determined to take over the world, and to do so by force.

Consider another favorite passage: "If my people, which are called by my name, shall humble themselves and pray, and seek my face and turn from their wicked ways, then will I hear from heaven, and will forgive their sin and will heal their land" (2 Chronicles 7:14). Once again, it is becoming popular for Christians to take this verse as a formula that the church can apply to Christianize a nation, whether the United States, Canada, England, Germany, or some other. Such a verse can be helpful to Christians in prayer and repentance, but the primary application is to Israel alone, not to the church. Nevertheless, in defiance of logic and commonsense exegesis, both the Roman Catholic Church and many Protestant churches insist today:

> The Old Testament promises and prophecies about the return to, and rebuilding of, the old city of Jerusalem were fulfilled thousands of years ago. . . . All remaining fulfillments of prophecies regarding the city of Jerusalem refer to spiritual Jerusalem, the church.[17]

Such reasoning, of course, dictates the attitude which Christians hold toward Israel and especially toward Jerusalem. Catholics and Protestants are joining together in opposition to Israel. Consider the following disturbing news release in December 1994:

> In a first-ever joint statement, leaders of all the major Christian groups in Jerusalem called for a special "judicial and political" status for Jerusalem. The city is "too precious" to the world to be dependent solely on municipal or national political authorities, "whoever they may be," they said.
> (Israel insists that Jerusalem remain under Israeli sovereignty in any final Arab-Israeli peace agreement. It gave Jordan a say in supervision of religious monuments. Palestinians have demanded that East Jerusalem be placed under their rule.)
> Signers of the statements included Catholic, Orthodox, Anglican, and Lutheran leaders concerned about being left out of a settlement that affects their interests.[18]

The Restoration of Israel

The church was never given the task of establishing an earthly kingdom. After spending 40 days with their risen

Lord, during which time He spoke to them "of the things pertaining to the kingdom of God" (Acts 1:3), the disciples knew the right question to ask: "Lord, wilt *thou* at this *time restore* again the kingdom to *Israel?*" (verse 6). The italicized words set forth four simple truths: 1) It is *Christ* (*thou*), not the church, who will do this special work; 2) it will be done at a *future time* predetermined by the Father (verse 7); 3) a kingdom which once was will be *restored*; and 4) the restoration will be to *Israel* (not to the church) of a kingdom it once had. The church has nothing to do with any of it.

Peter again (Acts 3:19-26) makes the same four points a few days later in his second sermon: 1) There is a future and specific *time* 2) for the "restitution [*restoration*] of all things," 3) and only when it is time for the restoration will Christ, who alone can do the restoring, return from heaven 4) to *restore* to "the children of the prophets" (i.e. the Jews—verse 25) that which "all the prophets . . . have spoken" (i.e. restoring the Davidic kingdom and occupying David's throne—verse 24).

The so-called "Restoration movement" would have these verses teach a last-days restoration of the purity and power of the first-century church. That is again an obvious misapplication. There is nothing about the church in Peter's sermon. He is speaking to *Jews* and makes it clear that the subject of his sermon pertains to them alone as "children of the prophets." That designation disqualifies non-Jews. The subject is not the church nor its restoration at some future time to its first-century status, but the restoration of the kingdom to Israel.

Let it be clearly understood that true Evangelicals, while not overlooking her mistakes and faults, support Israel because they know that the Jews remain God's chosen people, though scattered and under His judgment. These Christians have always looked forward to Israel becoming a nation once again. I remember as a boy in the 1930s the preachers speaking of Israel's rebirth. Even in the nineteenth century, sermons were preached and books were written anticipating the day when God would bring the Jews back into their land and the nation of Israel would exist once again. There was absolute confidence in this event, no matter how unlikely it seemed at the time, because the prophets foretold that the Messiah would return to His people in their land. Indeed He would rescue Israel at Armageddon from the armies of the world about to destroy her, so for the second coming (a central Christian doctrine) to take place the Jews had to be back in their own land.

An Important Difference

Some Muslims attempt to justify their militancy and even terrorism by arguing that Christians attacked them in the Crusades and that Catholic missionaries to the Americas in the early centuries attempted to convert natives under threat of death. Charlemagne and other Roman emperors spread Roman Catholicism by the sword even as the Muslims spread Islam by the same means. Any "Christianity," however, that was spread by the sword was a fraud. Anyone who claimed to be a Christian and acted violently against another person, either to defend or spread the Christian faith, was acting in the clearest opposition to the teachings of the Bible and of Christ and His example. That is not Christianity at all!

There is a clear difference between Islam and Christianity that must be understood. The Muslim who straps explosives to his body and blows himself up in order to kill others, or who hijacks a plane or who kills a former Muslim who has converted to Christianity, is a true Muslim. He is following both the teachings of the Koran and the example set by Mohammed and his successors down to the present day. He is being faithful to the official teachings of Islam in the Koran, and as taught in mosques worldwide.

It is the true teaching of Islam that inspires suicide bombers such as 27-year-old Saleh Abdel Rahim al-Souwi. To the glory of Allah, Souwi detonated a suitcase he carried containing 50 pounds of TNT, blowing up himself and his fellow Tel Aviv bus passengers on October 26, 1994, killing 22 and wounding 47. The next day a videotape released in Nablus by Hamas showed him bidding farewell to family and friends and warning of further Hamas suicide attacks.[19] The Palestinian police who

340 CHRISTIANS FOR—AND AGAINST—ISRAEL

are supposed to prevent such incidents cannot fulfill that task without betraying their religion. When these police first entered Jericho their chant was heard over loudspeakers, "Through violence and blood we shall liberate all Palestine!" As the Palestinian flag was raised for the first time a great cry arose: "Today Gaza and Jericho—tomorrow Jerusalem!"[20] Such must ever be the dream of a true Muslim. That fact reveals the current "peace process" for the fraud it really is.

A "Christian," on the other hand, who joined the Crusades and killed Jews to take the Holy Land for the Church, or who joined an equally violent crusade against the Albigenses, Waldenses, Hussites, or Huguenots, and slaughtered these and other Christians who refused allegiance to the Roman Catholic Church, was not a true Christian at all. Such a person was acting in direct opposition to both the teachings and example of Jesus Christ. Remember the indictment quoted above by that nineteenth-century Catholic historian of his own church for the torture and murder of those who opposed her: "[The Inquisition] contradicted the simplest principles of Christian justice and love to our neighbor, and would have been rejected with universal horror in the ancient Church."[21]

A Christian is motivated by Christ's love toward Israel and toward all mankind. That love, of necessity, desires the best for those who are its object. We are all guilty of the death of Christ because it was our sins that required His death in order to save us. Paul, the former rabbi who met Christ after His resurrection, loved his "kinsmen according to the flesh" so much that he was willing to forfeit his own salvation to save them (Romans 9:1-5). He declared, "Brethren, my heart's desire and prayer to God for Israel is that they might be saved" (Romans 10:1).

Such is the passion of every true Christian toward Jews and Muslims and all mankind. Then let not Jew or Muslim or atheist or the follower of any religion take offense at Christians who attempt to persuade them to believe in Jesus Christ as Savior and Lord. Even those who disagree with them can at least thank Evangelicals for their sincere concern.

Who can read the following words of Christ as He wept over Jerusalem just before His crucifixion without being moved by His love for His people? He knew the awful consequences of their rejection of Him which all the prophets had foretold and which He had reiterated—consequences that came true in part in 70 A.D. when the city was destroyed, and consequences far worse which still lie ahead for Jerusalem and the people of Israel:

> When he was come near, he beheld the city and wept over it, saying, If thou hadst known, even thou, at least in this thy day, the things which belong unto thy peace! But now they are hid from thine eyes.
>
> For the days shall come upon thee that thine enemies shall cast a trench about thee, and compass thee round, and keep thee in on every side, and shall lay thee even with the ground, and thy children within thee; and they shall not leave in thee one stone upon another, because thou knewest not the time of thy visitation (Luke 19:41-44).

> O Jerusalem, Jerusalem, thou that killest the prophets and stonest them which are sent unto thee, how often would I have gathered thy children together, even as a hen gathereth her chickens under her wings, and ye would not!
>
> Behold, your house is left unto you desolate. For I say unto you, Ye shall not see me henceforth till ye shall say, Blessed is he that cometh in the name of the Lord (Matthew 23:37-39).

And he [Antichrist] shall confirm the covenant with many for one week [of years; i.e. seven years]; and in the midst of the week he shall cause the sacrifice and the oblation to cease. . . .

—Daniel 9:27

Let no man deceive you by any means, for that day [of the Lord] shall not come except there come a falling away first, and that man of sin be revealed, the son of perdition [Antichrist], who opposeth and exalteth himself above all that is called God or that is worshipped, so that he as God sitteth in the temple of God, showing himself that he is God. . . .

Even him whose coming is after the working of Satan with all power and signs and lying wonders, and with all deceivableness of unrighteousness in them that perish, because they received not the love of the truth that they might be saved.

And for this cause God shall send them strong delusion, that they should believe a lie, that they all might be damned who believed not the truth but had pleasure in unrighteousness.

—2 Thessalonians 2:3,4,9-12

And they [mankind] worshiped the dragon [Satan] which gave power unto the beast; and they worshiped the beast [Antichrist]. . . . And all that dwell upon the earth shall worship him, whose names are not written in the book of life of the Lamb slain from the foundation of the world. . . .

And he [the false prophet] had power to give life unto the image of the beast [Antichrist] . . . and cause that as many as would not worship the image of the beast should be killed.

—Revelation 13:4,8,15

18

Antichrist and the Temple Rebuilt

◆

The Jewish Temple will be rebuilt on Temple Mount in Jerusalem and the daily sacrifices will begin again! How do we know this? Because both the Old and New Testaments testify to this fact. And on the basis of the 100 percent accuracy which we have documented for past prophecies, we have absolute confidence that those pertaining to the future will also be fulfilled. We don't know *when* this staggering transformation of Temple Mount will take place, but from all indications it should be very soon. In fact, the Temple *must* be rebuilt for certain other prophesied events to occur.

Paul tells us that the Antichrist will "sit in the temple of God" when he declares to the world that he is God. Obviously the Temple must be in existence at that unspecified future time. John tells us that "all the world will worship him" and that all mankind will be required, under pain of death, to bow to his image. Nor can there be any doubt that this image will be placed in the rebuilt Temple in Jerusalem. An image of the world dictator, which the entire world must worship, would surely be displayed in the holiest place in the world, the Temple of Solomon, rebuilt and functioning 1900 years after its destruction.

344 ♦ ANTICHRIST AND THE TEMPLE REBUILT

The ultimate defiance toward the God of Israel, which is intended by this image of a man worshiped as God, could only be effected by placing it in the Temple of the God of Israel. Daniel's prophecy of "the abomination that maketh desolate" could be fulfilled in no other way. No greater abomination could be imagined than polluting the Temple of God with an image made to a man who is both empowered by Satan and who claims to be God. Here is Daniel's warning of that event in the last days:

> . . . and they shall pollute the sanctuary [temple] . . . and shall take away the daily sacrifice, and they shall place the abomination that maketh desolate. . . . And the king shall . . . exalt himself above every god, and shall speak marvelous things against the God of gods. . . .
>
> Go thy way, Daniel, for the words are closed up and sealed till the time of the end. Many shall be purified and made white and tried, but the wicked shall do wickedly; and none of the wicked shall understand, but the wise shall understand. And from the time that the daily sacrifice shall be taken away and the abomination that maketh desolate set up there shall be a thousand two hundred and ninety days [until the end] (Daniel 11:31,36; 12:9-11).

There is no need to seek for a mysterious or complicated interpretation of the above. Daniel's language ("he shall exalt himself above every god") is so similar to Paul's ("who opposeth and exalteth himself above all that is called God, or that is worshipped") that they must be referring to the same man. Nor can there be any doubt that the reference is to Antichrist.

An "Angel of Light"

Probably no concept has been more misrepresented than that of Antichrist. Though he will be the very embodiment of Satan, yet this coming world ruler will not be the easily recognized and obviously evil ogre that is usually portrayed. Rather, he will be a most appealing figure, projecting Satan's "angel of light" image (2 Corinthians 11:14), someone whom the world will not only admire but also worship. He will be embraced by Israel as her Messiah, by Muslims as Islam's long-awaited Immam or Maitreya, and as Christ by professing "Christians" (all *true* Christians will have been taken from the earth in the rapture). In this incredibly charismatic deceiver, all of the world's religions (and governments) will be united.

Could the world be so completely deceived that it would literally worship so evil a man? Hitler provides a preview of the possibilities. In retrospect, his evil is easily recognized except by a few neo-Nazis. But in his time nearly everyone was deceived. William Shirer wrote from Germany in 1934: "A newly arrived observer was somewhat surprised to see that the people of this country did not seem to feel that they were being cowed and held down by an unscrupulous and brutal dictatorship. On the contrary, they supported it with genuine enthusiasm. Somehow it imbued them with a new hope." There were seemingly good reasons for that hope.

Of course, Hitler's rise to power took place 60 years ago, and people are not as easily deceived today. Really? What about the fanatical worship of the Ayatollah Khomeini in Iran and the continued loyalty to him even as conditions worsened? And look at the frenzied mobs not only in Iraq but throughout the Arab world who still take to the streets chanting loyalty to that "Arab Hitler," Saddam Hussein.

Romania's dictator of 24 years until the end of 1989, Nicolae Ceausescu, was likewise as evil as Hitler; he simply lacked the opportunity to operate on as large a scale. Yet he was lauded as the "supreme embodiment of good," "Hero of Heroes," "Worker of Workers," and "First Personage of the World." His equally evil wife, Elena, was called "a model to be followed by all women in our country," the "legendary mother," and "the most just woman on earth." Talk about delusion!

Nor was it the masses alone that were deceived. Even when the Romanian people's eyes were opened and they began quite fittingly to call Ceausescu the "Antichrist," he continued for years to beguile world leaders. Westerners were lavish in their praise of him. As the media reported, "Queen Elizabeth knighted him, and the United States extended to his country most-favored-nation trade status. . . . Former Israeli Prime Minister Menachem Begin credited the Romanian leader with mediating the late Egyptian President Anwar Sadat's historic 1977 peace mission to Jerusalem."[1]

The Cosmic Christ

There is deception even within the word "Antichrist." It is commonly understood that this man will embody the ultimate enmity toward Christ. The Greek prefix *anti,* however, not only means "opposed to or against" but also "in the place of or a substitute for." That Antichrist will embody both meanings is clear. He will indeed oppose Christ, but in the most diabolically clever way possible (anything less wouldn't be worthy of Satan's genius): by pretending to actually *be* Christ.

Thus Daniel, who calls Messiah "the Prince" (Daniel 9:25), refers to Antichrist as "the coming prince" (verse 26), i.e. the pretender prince. Israel rejected her Messiah, even though He came at the exact time foretold and in fulfillment of the dozens of specific messianic prophecies, because He didn't bring the kind of peace she expected. Jews still reject Jesus Christ today on the same basis. Tragically, Israel will embrace the pretender Messiah, the Antichrist, who comes with no biblical credentials but who will seemingly bring peace and make it possible for the Temple to be rebuilt. Anyone who can accomplish that *must* be the Messiah, or so Israel will mistakenly believe in its enthusiasm over the "salvation" he will bring to her.

The Roman emperors presided over the pagan priesthood and pagan festivals and were worshiped as gods under the title *Pontifex Maximus.* When the Emperor Constantine around 313 A.D. decided for tactical reasons to call himself a "Christian" (not a true one, as the evidence makes clear) and gave Christianity preferred status, he was automatically recognized as the head of the Christian church. As such, he took to himself the new title, *Vicarius Christi,* or Vicar of Christ. *Vicarius* is the Latin equivalent of *anti.* When translated into Greek, Vicar of Christ literally means Antichrist.

Of course, Constantine did not mean that he was against Christ. He meant that he was Christ in the sense of taking His place on this earth. The popes have borne both titles for nearly 1500 years: the clearly pagan *Pontifex Maximus* as well as the blasphemous *Vicarius Christi*, titles which they claim to have inherited from Constantine. That fact has caused some critics to say that the Antichrist will be a Pope. In fact, the coming Antichrist will be the new Constantine, the ruler of the revived Roman Empire, which will encompass the entire world. The Pope in office at that time will be his right-hand man, exerting immense power from behind the scenes, a relationship which the popes bore to emperors for centuries.

Covenant for a "Week"

When one takes the prophecies of Daniel as a whole (which space limitations prevent us from doing here), it is clear that there is a double Antichrist application: first of all to Antiochus Epiphanes, who, though he fulfilled much of the prophecy, was not the Antichrist but a prefigure or type; and secondly, to the Antichrist himself, who will fulfill all that is prophesied. Antiochus caused the Temple sacrifices to cease and, in their place, swine's flesh to be offered on a Greek altar erected in the Temple. He rededicated the Temple of God to Zeus and set up an image within it to this chief deity of the Greek pantheon. Here was indeed an "abomination that maketh desolate," as Daniel had foreseen—but not *the* abomination.

What part of the prophecy did Antiochus not fulfill? He did not "confirm the covenant with many for one week" and then "in the midst of the week" put a stop to "the sacrifice and the oblation" (Daniel 9:27). (Nor has anyone else done so, including Nero, Hitler, or any other past tyrant identified by various groups as Antichrist. On the contrary, Antichrist is yet to come.)

The "one week" for which Antichrist will "confirm the covenant" can only be the last of the 70 weeks which Gabriel told Daniel were "determined upon thy people [Israel] and

upon thy holy city [Jerusalem] to finish the transgression, and
to make an end of sins, and to make reconciliation for iniquity,
and to bring in everlasting righteousness, and to seal up the
vision and prophecy, and to anoint the most Holy" (Daniel
9:24). In other words, that time period will see the completion
of every remaining prophecy pertaining to Israel.

Weeks of Years

We understand the "70 weeks" to be weeks of years and thus
to represent not 490 *days* but 490 *years*. There are a number of
reasons for this interpretation. We have noted earlier that
Israel occupied the Promised Land for a period of 490 years (70
weeks of years) prior to the Babylonian captivity. During that
time she failed to keep, as commanded, every seventh year as a
special Sabbath. (Here we clearly have the concept of weeks of
years.) For this disobedience Israel owed the land 70 years of
rest, a debt which was paid while her people languished as
captives in Babylon. It was immediately after Daniel understood the relationship between the Babylonian captivity and
the previous 70 weeks of years that the angel Gabriel revealed
to him that another 70 weeks would wind up God's purposes
for Israel's future. It would be odd if this latter period were not
comprised of weeks of years as well, which indeed it is.

In Revelation 11:3 John indicates that 1260 days (3½ years)
into the great tribulation period Antichrist is able to slay the
"two witnesses" who have been prophesying in Jerusalem.
From that point the non-Jews are in control of Jerusalem, able
to "tread [it] under foot forty and two months" (verse 2), or
another 3½ years, making the total tribulation period seven
years. It is reasonable to assume that this Gentile takeover of
Jerusalem coincides with Antichrist's breaking of the covenant
in the middle of Daniel's seventieth week, thus confirming that
week to be seven years.

In Revelation 11:2,3 and 12:6, John seems to be defining the
midpoint of Daniel's seventieth week in another way. The
woman in chapter 12 obviously represents Israel giving birth to
the Messiah. She (Israel) must flee from Satan for 1260 days

(3½ years). It is again reasonable to associate this turning of Satan's wrath upon Israel with Antichrist's breach of the covenant "in the midst of the week." So again we have 1260 days (3½ years) elapsing from midweek to the end of Antichrist's reign, proving once more that the length of the "week" is seven years.

Daniel's timing is only slightly different. He states in Daniel 12:11 that the end comes "a thousand two hundred and *ninety* days" after Antichrist stops the Levitical Temple sacrifices and sets up "the abomination that maketh desolate" in the Temple. If we assume an additional 30 days after Armageddon for some special purpose, perhaps to cleanse the earth, we are left once again with 1260 days or 3½ years from midweek to the end thereof. In the next verse Daniel mystifies us further: "Blessed is he that waiteth, and cometh to the thousand three hundred and five and thirty days." Prophecy students are puzzled both by the added 30 days in verse 12 and this additional 45 days in verse 13. Neither addition, however, contradicts but rather confirms the conclusion that the seventieth week is a period of seven years rather than seven days.

Viewing both the Old and New Testaments together, it seems clear that Daniel's seventieth week represents a period of seven years which coincides with the seven-year great tribulation period described in detail in the book of Revelation, a period which is yet to come and during most of which the world will be under Antichrist's control.

Messiah Rejected, Blessing Deferred

Furthermore, the Messiah didn't ride into Jerusalem to be hailed by the multitudes at the end of 69 literal weeks (483 *days*) after the command to restore Jerusalem. There wasn't even a would-be Messiah that history records waiting in the wings at that time. But Jesus did ride into Jerusalem on a donkey and was hailed by the multitude as the Messiah precisely 69 weeks of years (483 *years*) to the day from that date given to us in Nehemiah 2. Again, "weeks of years," not literal weeks, fits the prophecy.

Obviously, God's purposes for Israel have not all been fulfilled as yet. The Messiah is certainly not yet reigning on David's throne in Jerusalem. Therefore we know that the 70 weeks have not yet run their course. All that God intended to happen through the end of the first 69 weeks of years, however, was fulfilled in Jesus Christ. If not in Him, there can be no fulfillment because the specified time has passed. Jesus Christ is literally the only candidate for Messiah available to Israel—the *only* one.

Either the book of Daniel lies—and thus the entire Old Testament is not to be trusted—or the Messiah came on schedule. One conclusion or the other must be accepted. There is no third alternative.

There is no question that the blessings which were prophesied to mark the culmination of the seventieth week have not occurred. Here is one more reason for concluding that the seventieth week, having been deferred because Israel rejected her Messiah, will run concurrently with the seven-year tribulation period, which yet lies ahead.

Christ was crucified, and salvation (through His payment of sin's penalty) came to the entire world. As a result the church was formed, a new entity comprised of both Jews and Gentiles (Ephesians 2). The past 1900 years has seen Israel set aside and the church occupying center stage. With Israel at last back in her land, the church is in decline, experiencing a growing apostasy, and must be removed for Daniel's seventieth week (which pertains only to Israel) to run its course at last.

Why the Covenant?

In the meantime we need to understand something more about Antichrist and the nature of the "covenant" which he confirms with "the many." The covenant he makes will undoubtedly allow the Temple to be rebuilt and the animal sacrifices to be reestablished. That fact could not be clearer inasmuch as his breach of the covenant causes the "sacrifice and oblation to cease." One wonders immediately why Antichrist would be interested in allowing the Jewish Temple to be rebuilt. It would seem to be madness.

Antichrist's decision obviously is not made in order to promote worldwide peace, much less to make friends with the billion Arabs who control most of the world's oil. Such a decision would be certain to inflame them. One Middle East expert calls the rulers of the Arab Gulf states "the guardians of the two major forces in the Arab world—Islam and petrodollars...."[2] Arabs who are even moderate Muslims cannot soften their position on Jerusalem. The following recent news report presents the atmosphere which, without some incredible event to transform Arab thinking, the Antichrist would face:

> King Hassan of Morocco has hardened his position on Jerusalem, and has joined forces with Egypt's President Hosni Mubarak and Jordan's King Hussein in a concerted effort to discourage the US from moving its embassy to the [Israeli] capital [i.e. Jerusalem]. Hassan said such a move would have a "serious effect" in the Arab and Islamic world, and would be interpreted as a major change in American policy.[3]

Nor will Antichrist be trying to curry Israel's favor; she is not that important to him. One can only conclude that this emissary of Satan who has suddenly been catapulted into power wants the Temple rebuilt for his own selfish reasons. From the very beginning he has in mind using it to promote himself as God and to get the world to worship him. And here again we are driven to the conclusion that something cataclysmic has occurred to give the Antichrist such power and to make the Arabs amenable to this surprising decree transforming Temple Mount, a decree that would otherwise be resisted by the entire Muslim world.

Certainly any attempt to rebuild the Temple today would bring instant war with the Arabs, a war that would likely engulf the entire world. Islam, the fastest-growing religion in the world, is experiencing a surging revival at the moment. One finds evidence of that fact even among the Bedouin. They have been Israeli citizens from the very beginning and serve their time in the armed forces, and some even rise to the rank of officers. Reflecting the rise of Islam, however, a frightening change has recently been occurring in their attitude toward Israel:

> For the past five years, the Beduin, 50% of whom are under age 18, have been swept up in an Islamic revival. Consider Rahat, for example, the largest Beduin town in the northern Negev. In 1988, the town had one mosque, with barely 50 people attending Friday prayers. Today, Rahat has five mosques packed with worshipers.[4]
>
> And now for the first time Beduin have been implicated in terrorism, an attempt on March 21, 1995 to explode a truck loaded with 200 kg of explosives in the middle of Beersheba.[5]

Again it seems clear that something unforeseen must cause Islam's militant stance to soften if the Temple is to be rebuilt. Inasmuch as Antichrist makes his covenant for "a week," he must be recognized as having that authority by the whole world at the very beginning of Daniel's seventieth week. There are a number of reasons for believing that he comes to power as suddenly as the seventieth week comes upon the world, and for the same mysterious reason.

While some translations say that Antichrist "confirms" the covenant, the Hebrew literally means that he forces it upon the world. The very nature of the covenant, which the Arabs would violently oppose, indicates that some incredible event must have occurred, something so extraordinary and uncanny that even the most fanatical Muslims who would fight the rebuilding of the Jewish Temple to the death are like putty in Antichrist's hands. We will discuss at the end of this chapter what that event might be.

A Staggering Ecumenical Movement

At the same time that Islam is on the rise, we are witnessing the most astonishing ecumenical movement the world has ever seen. A recent news report stated: "Religions are now headed toward what may eventually form a United Religions Organization (URO), structured in much the same way as the United Nations and sharing similar goals. . . . [providing] a conduit for divine power to bring healing and inspiration to Earth." A key article in *The Futurist* revealed that "world religions are increasingly working out the theoretical basis of a world theology. . . . The merging of two or more religious impulses, such as Hinduism and Christianity, is increasingly producing hybrids, such as Christian yoga." The article went on to state:

> World religions are beginning to work together in tackling global problems such as pollution. Some world religions are increasingly using computers to network and develop missions. . . . [T]he Japanese have reclaimed the doctrine of the divinity of the Emperor. We will likely see a major Eastern contribution to the global doctrine of God, or the whole-earth concept of theism, in the twenty-first century. . . .
>
> The Green Movement and the world religions are converging. . . . The feminine is increasingly partnering the masculine in religious thinking, leading to a fully integrated male/female world theology. [6]

In the spirit of the new and growing ecumenism, enthusiastic Catholics and Protestants are uniting worldwide under the banner of "A.D. 2000 Evangelism's" appealing challenge that all Christians should forget their differences and join forces to evangelize the world by the year 2000. Concern for doctrinal purity has been set aside in favor of a "positive gospel" calculated to appeal to a world largely concerned about ecology and peace. Biblical warnings of a false gospel and coming apostasy in the "last days" are considered to be negative hindrances to the new and more attractive "Christianity."

Hailed as "the decade of evangelism," the 1990s are expected to culminate in the presentation "to Jesus Christ on His 2000th birthday" of what Christian leaders boast will be "a mostly Christian world."[7] That this objective may be accomplished by subtly adopting a new definition of "Christian" which will create an apostate bride for the Antichrist seems to be given little thought in the enthusiasm of the new "unity." Robert Runcie, while he was Archbishop of Canterbury, argued that Christians must recognize "the incompleteness of our faith" and enter a New Age of mutual understanding where we acknowledge the truth in all religions. Here is the Antichrist's new "Christianity" acceptable to all religions.

As we have fully documented elsewhere, Pope John Paul II is the leader in this movement to unite the world's religions. He has stated, "It is my profound wish that the world's religious leaders embark on a pilgrimage to Jerusalem to pray together to merciful God for the gift of peace, understanding and collaboration among all the religions of the world."[8] The most amazing ecumenist the world has ever seen, the Pope has traveled to more than 100 countries in his pursuit of ecumenism.[9] His efforts are bearing fruit, as the following news report testifies:

> On November 3, 1994, in the Synod Hall at the Vatican in Rome, Pope John Paul II opened the Sixth Assembly of the World Conference on Religion and Peace [which] . . . gathered 900 religious leaders and delegates for an interreligious dialogue on preventing war and ending injustice. . . .
>
> [S]affron-robed Buddhist monks, white-turbaned Sikhs, Muslim mullahs in flowing capes, and even American Indians in traditional dress listened for three hours, as the Pope welcomed one and all, saying: '*The Vatican is open to you. I hope you will all return soon.*' Agreement—inside and outside the Vatican—was that this was a historic occasion, the first time an official interreligious organization had been convened at the Holy See. . . .
>
> [T]he Holy Father was flanked on the synod hall podium by Cardinal Francis Arinze, President of the Vatican's Interreligious Council, the Secretary of the World Islamic League, Ahmed Muhammed Ali, Rabbi David Rosen from Jerusalem, the Hindu parliamentarian, Dr. M. Aram, and Nikkyo Niwano, a Japanese

Buddhist WCRP founder. Together they listened to Koranic verses, followed by Jewish, Shinto, Buddhist and Hindu invocations for peace.

A new initiative for peace was announced at the conference titled "Service for Religion and Peace-building." It will be funded by the Rockefeller Foundation and will "offer services to local inter-confessional communities: legal training in conflict resolution, research and publication facilities, and structures for on-site interreligious dialogue." [10]

Dialogue with Muslims?

Such efforts may seem impressive, but they could never cause the Arabs to allow the Temple to be rebuilt, even if the Dome of the Rock and the Al Aqsa mosque remained. For 30 years Vatican II has been asking Muslims to forget past quarrels and has been urging all religions to make "a sincere effort to achieve mutual understanding. . . ."[11] It is a noble sentiment, but a vain one. Islam, as we have seen, is a religion that cannot compromise. It must dominate, and it must do so by force if necessary.

Catholics and Jews who enter into hopeful dialogue with Muslims are deceiving themselves. And any Muslims who enter into such dialogue for "mutual understanding" are either not real Muslims or, what is more likely, are pretending to go along with the naive ecumenism of the unsuspecting non-Muslim world until Islam gains the supremacy. Then all "dialogue" and "freedom of conscience and religion" will vanish. We have already quoted the Koran specifically forbidding a Muslim even to make friends with Christians or Jews.

The mere fact that Muslims in the West demand freedom to practice Islam while denying similar freedom in their countries to any faith other than Islam should be sufficient to reveal their true motives in any dialogue. It is clear from Islam's doctrines that there could never be peaceful coexistence among the three religions of Jerusalem (Islam, Judaism, and Christianity). Much less could the Temple and a mosque stand side by side on the same sacred site. Such ecumenism is proved to be impossible by the very injunctions which the Koran lays upon devout Muslims. An Arab observer, knowing well the Koran and the world scene, writes:

> So, all Islamic leaders who come to British and American Church leaders for inter-faith co-operation are either defying the instructions of Allah or they have a hidden agenda. . . . It is the same tactic of "No compulsion in religion" that Mohammad first adapted to Christians and Jews, that Muslims are using in the Western world today.
>
> Migrate to Christian areas because they are tolerant. Pretend to be peaceful, friendly and hospitable; begin to clamour for religious, political and social rights and privileges that you will not allow to Christians in an Islamic country; breed fast there and settle down; there should be no Christian activities in your community; you may speak or write to discredit their religion, but they must not talk about Islam; begin to expand your community; Christian activities would be restricted in all the places you expand to; the moment you have enough military might against these "disbelievers," these trinitarian kaferis, go ahead and eliminate them or suppress them as much as you can, and be in control.[12]

A Persistent Question

Even so, all of the world's religions, including militant Islam, will be united under Antichrist. Furthermore, Antichrist will do what seems absolutely impossible from today's perspective: He will have the Temple rebuilt and will bring worldwide peace at the same time. No wonder the Jews will accept him as their Messiah! Though it will prove to be a false peace that will destroy many (Daniel 8:25), it is "peace" nevertheless, and will last for a period of time, probably most of the first 3½ years after Antichrist takes power.

What could possibly cause a billion Muslims to agree to the construction of the Jewish Temple where the Dome of the Rock now sits, or even alongside it? We know from Scripture that it will happen, so we are driven again to conclude that some cataclysmic occurrence on this planet must take place, an event of such incredible magnitude and awesome consequences that it will in itself unite the world and completely transform the thinking of all mankind. No other conclusion can be reached in view of the otherwise-impossible realization of Antichrist's objectives.

Not only would the Arabs instantly fight to the death to prevent the Temple from being rebuilt anywhere on Temple Mount, but a great many Jews, even religious ones, would give no support to such a project because they see no significance to restoring the ancient Temple and its rituals. Both Conservative and Reformed Jews want Judaism to be progressive, not to regress to past tradition. Moreover, 30 percent of Israelis deny any belief in God or the Bible and would oppose a return to Temple worship. Even the Orthodox rabbis have been forced to downplay the importance of Temple sacrifices in view of their absence from Judaism for the past 1900 years. Certainly, rebuilding the Temple is not vital to Judaism as it is presently practiced.

An Inescapable Intuition

Having said all of the above, there is nevertheless a powerful emotional appeal related to the Temple that overwhelms almost every Jew at times, even the atheists among them. Professor Gershon Salomon of Jerusalem's Hebrew University portrays something of that emotion each time he reminisces about the day the Jews recaptured the old Temple site from the Arabs:

> I was in the first Israeli paratroop unit who made it through to the Temple Mount on the fourth day of the [Six Day] War [in 1967]. My feeling, and every soldier's feeling, was the same upon entering this place for the first time...all of the soldiers...started to cry. We could not stop ourselves.
>
> We stayed on the Temple Mount for long hours—we could not move. You cannot understand this moment for

358 ANTICHRIST AND THE TEMPLE REBUILT

us! This place was the place of the Temple, the heart and soul of the Jewish people.

I felt that I was very close to Abraham, Isaac, Jacob, King David, and the prophets. It was the most important day of my life, and it follows me every moment. . . . I felt that we had completed a special mission that all of the generations since the destruction of the Temple in A.D. 70 asked us to fulfill.[13]

As a result of that experience, Salomon founded and directs to this day the Temple Mount and Eretz Yisrael Faithful Movement, which is dedicated to the rebuilding of the Temple. The plans have been laid, Levites are being trained, and priestly robes are being made, as are the special musical instruments needed for the Temple. *U.S. News & World Report* recently carried a feature article on the subject of the rebuilding of the Temple:

> The rebuilding of Solomon's Temple in Jerusalem's Old City has been so important to Jews that they have prayed for it for centuries and they end each wedding with the breaking of a glass to remind participants of the Temple's destruction—first by Babylonians over 2,500 years ago and then again 656 years later by Rome after it was rebuilt. Its reconstruction [however] is unthinkable because it stands on the same location as the Dome of the Rock Mosque, the site believed by Muslims to be where Mohammed ascended to heaven in the early seventh century.
>
> While stressing that they have no plans to displace the mosque, a small group believes that if proper preparations are made, a miracle will occur, enabling the Temple to be rebuilt. The first step, says Chaim Richman of the Temple Institute, is replication down to the precise detail of Temple objects, half of which have now been made. In addition, a Mississippi cattle farmer has agreed to provide special unblemished red heifers, the ashes of which are required for a purification ritual.
>
> Others also prepare for the miracle. Rabbi Nehman Kahane of the Old City has created a database of all Jews

descended from Aaron, the priestly brother of Moses. They will be called into service if the Temple is rebuilt.

Richman says he is not messianic: "[We hope] the Temple will be again the spiritual center of all mankind."[14]

How about that for an innovative idea—the Temple as an ecumenical center for all religions! God's purpose for the Temple seems to be forgotten. Even if it were possible to rebuild the Temple, however, numerous problems stand in the way.

A Surprising Solution

There is disagreement among the leading rabbis concerning where the ancient Temple was located. Some are convinced that the Dome of the Rock is on the very site and would have to be removed. Others think the Temple was located adjacent to the Dome and could be rebuilt next to it. That idea, however, would not be satisfactory either to the Jews or the Muslims.

Let us end the speculation: Both the Dome of the Rock and the Al-Aqsa Mosque will be moved, and with the Arabs' permission. It cannot be otherwise. The Jews could not allow a Muslim holy place such as the Dome of the Rock or the Al-Aqsa Mosque to be on the Temple site, nor could the Muslims allow a Jewish Temple on the same site as their holy places.

Remember, the Dome of the Rock monument was not originally built there for the reason that is offered today: that this was Al Aqsa, the "far distant place" to which Mohammed in a vision was allegedly "carried by night upon a heavenly steed . . . [and] caught up through the seven heavens to the very presence of God."[15] That this monument to Islam was built primarily to outshine Christian and Jewish monuments in Jerusalem and as a reproof to Judaism and Christianity is clear from the Koranic verses quoted inside the Dome. One finds such denunciations of the God of the Bible as these:

> It befitteth not (the Majesty of) Allah that He should take unto Himself a son. Glory be to Him! (Surah 19:35).

> O People of the Scripture [Christians and Jews]! Do
> not exaggerate in your religion nor utter aught concerning
> Allah save the truth. The Messiah, Jesus son of Mary,
> was only a messenger of Allah. . . . So believe in Allah
> and His messengers, and say not, 'Three'—Cease! (it is)
> better for you!—Allah is only One God. Far is it removed
> from His transcendent majesty that he should have a son.
> (Surah 4:171).

In fact, Surah 17:1, which contains the only mention of Al
Aqsa, the "Far Distant Place," is conspicuous by its absence
among the quotations from the Koran found in abundance
around the interior of this dome today. That verse, which we
have already quoted, is far from conclusive: "Glorified be He
Who carried His Servant by night from the Inviolable Place of
Worship to the Far Distant Place of Worship the neighborhood
whereof We have blessed, that We might show him of Our
tokens. Lo! He, only He, is the Hearer, the Seer." Antichrist
may very well point out another location as being the real Al
Aqsa referred to in the Koran, causing the Arabs to move their
monument there and leaving the Jerusalem site clear for the
rebuilding of the temple.

There may be some significant tempering of Islam on the
horizon as well, which would help prepare for Antichrist. A
serious conflict already exists in the world of Islam. While the
overwhelming percentage of Arabs profess allegiance to Islam,
most of them reject what they call "Islamic fundamentalism"
or "Islamic radicalism/extremism." Iran, for example, is
accused of exporting what the rest of the world calls "Islamic
revolution." That revolution is feared as much by Arab countries professing Islam as it is in the West. Once enough thinking Arabs face the fact that the fundamentalism, or radicalism,
that they fear is in fact exactly what the Koran teaches and
Mohammed exemplified, they may well decide that Islam
itself needs to be revised.

While there are numerous smaller sects, there are two main
divisions in Islam: the Shi'ites and the Sunnis. The former are

predominant in Iran (about 95 percent of its 60 million population) and a majority in Iraq (about 55 percent), while the latter are the majority elsewhere (99 percent in Algeria, 94 percent in Egypt, 98.7 percent in Morocco, 92.1 percent in Saudi Arabia, etc.). The Shi'ites are the major proponents of the Islamic revolution, which is simply fundamental obedience to the Koran. Here again there is hope for some moderation in view of the Sunnis' numerical preponderance.

Favorable Factors

In Antichrist's favor is the fact that the world recognizes its desperate need for unity, peace, and disarmament. Some concrete steps, though small, and many sincere gestures, are already being made in that direction. Addressing the U.N. in late September 1993, President Clinton offered to place U.S. nuclear weapons "under international supervision."[16] The idea of "international supervision" is catching on and is being applied to Jerusalem as well. On November 19, 1994, John Paul II received "Jordan's first ambassador to the Holy See, Mutasim Bilbeisi [and] reiterated the Vatican's insistence on international guarantees for Jerusalem's sacred sites. The Vatican established formal diplomatic ties with Jordan in March [1994], shortly after it did the same with Israel, as part of the drive for a voice in the Middle East process."[17]

The world community would almost certainly favor a Jewish temple on Temple Mount in exchange for internationalization of Jerusalem, thus removing it from Jewish control. To have their temple restored, the Jews might very well be willing to make such a deal. That the first steps are already being taken behind the scenes has been rumored for some time and the evidence is mounting for such an arrangement. An editorial in a Jewish publication recently revealed the contents of a secret letter (to which we earlier referred in part) from Israeli Foreign Minister Shimon Peres:

> According to Mark Halter, a close friend of Peres, who . . . delivered the letter to the Pope, "Peres offered

to hand over sovereignty of Jerusalem's Old City to the Vatican. Jerusalem is to stay the capital of Israel but the Old City will be administered by the Vatican . . . the city would have an Israeli mayor and a Palestinian mayor both under the control of the Vatican. . . ."

The PLO was shown the Vaticanization Plan just before the signing of the Declaration of Principles. At that time Arafat agreed not to oppose the plan. Arafat had also consulted a number of influential Palestinians who were delighted with the plan. . . .

Jerusalem is to become the second Vatican of the world with all three major religions represented under the authority of the Vatican. A Palestinian state is to emerge in confederation with Jordan, its religious capital is to be Jerusalem but its administrative capital would be situated elsewhere, possibly Nablus.

A member of the Foreign Ministry claims the plan is a good one because Israel's ties to the Catholic world will lead to trade, tourism and prosperity. Further, Peres believes with a strong governing authority, future disputes between Arabs and Israelis will be easily resolved.

Despite all this information that has been made public, the Israeli government continues to deny that the future of Jerusalem is being negotiated.[18]

While an image of Antichrist in the Temple would offend Jews, that abomination will not be introduced until the middle of the seven-year tribulation. On the other hand, images are quite acceptable to Roman Catholics and Eastern Orthodox adherents, making an image to Antichrist in the Temple hardly objectionable for at least that large segment of the population. As for worshiping a man as God, that idea, once viewed as the rankest superstition in the West, hardly raises an eyebrow anymore.

A Most Appealing Lie

No one makes the idea of men becoming gods more appealing to the masses than "His Holiness the Dalai Lama," recipient a few years ago of the Nobel Peace Prize. And no one (with the possible exception of Pope John Paul II) is more highly regarded and trusted as a "spiritual leader" working for peace in the world today. The Dalai Lama's main mission, which he is diligently pursuing around the world, is to teach everyone how to become a god. He does this by initiating aspirants into what he calls "Tibetan Tantric Buddhist Deity Yoga." In Los Angeles, for example, in the summer of 1989, he led an audience of 3000, many of whom had come from distant parts of the world, in a "three-day Kalachakra ritual for world peace" at Santa Monica's Civic Auditorium. News reports of that conference stated in all seriousness:

> The Dalai Lama taught in Santa Monica that it was possible for all human beings to eventually become a Buddha, a being of the highest wisdom and compassion and power. Tibetan Buddhism . . . proposes a number of special paths to quickly become a Buddha . . . [which] according to the Dalai Lama generally involve a method called Deity Yoga. . . .
>
> Deity Yoga . . . is a special conscious act of creating, visualizing the illusion that we are already perfect beings, already god-like. If we can . . . *completely be* a seemingly permanent illusion, then we would know the procedures to create our own reality. Beings who are developed enough to create their own reality are Buddhas.[19]

Here we have an astonishing delusion being embraced wholesale around the world, a delusion that is at the heart of most of the self-improvement and positive-mental-attitude courses being taught in the business world today (that by the power of the mind one can create one's own world through visualization and positive thinking). Paul tells us that the Antichrist will seemingly be able to demonstrate to the world such abilities through the power of Satan and that God Himself will help these deluded people to believe the very lie they want to believe and for which they have rejected God and their moral responsibility to Him:

> Even him whose coming is after the working of Satan
> with all power and signs and lying wonders, and with all
> deceivableness of unrighteousness in them that perish,
> because they received not the love of the truth that they
> might be saved. And for this cause God shall send them
> strong delusion, that they should believe a lie (2 Thes-
> salonians 2:9-11).

The spirit realm is very real and fraught with danger.
Science knows nothing about it and has no instruments or
formulas for evaluating it. Today's world is espousing and
seeking "spirituality" while rejecting any guidelines for
assessing it. Spiritual "power" is being sought for selfish
reasons, while the very idea of submitting to the authority of
God is rejected.

Belief in a "higher power" is being embraced, but only as
definable by individual preference (the ecumenical "God as
you conceive him to be" of Alcoholics Anonymous and Free-
masonry, for example). At the same time the God of the Bible
is rejected because He makes moral demands that the power
seekers are unwilling to acknowledge, much less obey. The
only "god" these people desire is one whose power they can
use to their own ends, thus making themselves gods. This
modern openness to the "spiritual" realm for the power it
offers will surely help prepare the world to fall in worship at
the feet of the Antichrist when his incredible satanic powers
are displayed.

A Necessary Catalyst

In spite of all of the current trends, however, from ecumenism to a naive embrace of "spirituality" (which are
undoubtedly laying important groundwork for the coming
world religion and world government), something more is
needed. It is inconceivable that a world so divided could be
suddenly (or even gradually) united by a mere man, no matter
how talented, charismatic, or empowered by Satan. To this the
Bible agrees. It declares that Antichrist cannot be revealed
(i.e., the world won't accept him) until a particular event

known as the rapture takes place: "You know what prevents him from being revealed in his time" (2 Thessalonians 2:6 lit.).

Just before the cross, Jesus told His disciples that He was leaving them to rejoin His Father in heaven ("In my Father's house are many mansions. . . . I go to prepare a place for you"—John 14:2). He assured them, however, that He would return: "I will come again and receive you unto myself [in heaven], that where I am, there ye may be also" (John 14:3). Only Jesus dared to make such a promise. Neither Buddha, Mohammed, Confucius, nor any other religious leader ever promised to return after his death to take his disciples bodily to heaven without their dying. This one facet of Christianity alone separates it from every religion the world has ever known.

Being caught up out of this world into heaven was the "blessed hope" (Titus 2:13) of the early church. Paul tells us that when the pagan idol worshipers in Thessalonica heard the gospel, a great number of them believed it. As a result, they "turned to God from idols to serve the living and true God; and to wait for his Son from heaven" (1 Thessalonians 1:9,10). The Philippian believers considered themselves already to be citizens of heaven, "from whence also," wrote Paul, "we look for the Savior, the Lord Jesus Christ" (Philippians 3:20). The writer of the epistle to the Hebrews assured his readers that "unto them that look for him shall he [Christ] appear the second time without sin unto salvation" (Hebrews 9:28). Paul describes this incredible event, so wonderful for believers but so terrifying for those left behind:

> The Lord himself shall descend from heaven with a shout. . . and the dead in Christ shall rise [be resurrected] first; then we which are alive and remain shall be caught up together with them in the clouds to meet the Lord in the air, and so shall we ever be with the Lord. Wherefore comfort one another with these words (1 Thessalonians 4:16-18).

Very soon, millions upon millions of those living on this earth will be mysteriously snatched away from the planet and taken to heaven! Only then can the Antichrist be revealed. In fact, this event will be the catalyst that will catapult him into power at the very beginning of Daniel's seventieth week. Nothing else could possibly do so.

Terror and Unity

Such an event, involving the sudden mysterious disappearance of perhaps 200 million people, is beyond our ability to imagine. It is not difficult, however, to realize what the world's reaction will be. This world will be absolutely terrorized! The Joint Chiefs of Staff, the President's Cabinet, the Congress, the United Nations, and every responsible government and business and educational body will be meeting in emergency session—stunned, devastated, trying to understand what happened to the missing millions. "Where did they go? Who took them? Who will be next?" will be the queries on trembling lips around the world.

Nothing else but such a disaster could unite the world. Even now, if there are a few survivors of a plane crash isolated in the wilderness, though they may have been enemies before, they become suddenly united in the common pursuit of survival. After the rapture, the "survival" of this event will unite those remaining as nothing else could. Islamic ambitions to take over the world, the mutual hatred of Serbian Orthodox and Croatian Catholics, the animosity and suspicion between North and South Koreans—these and all other enmities will be forgotten in the mutual terror and necessity of cooperating together.

With all the Christians removed, Satan's great opportunity to take over the world has arrived. Terrified and confused, those that remain will worship anyone who can bring order and meaning out of this chaos. Immediately, at the height of this terror, Satan's man, the Antichrist, steps forward. He claims to know where everyone was taken. Some rogue civilization a few light-years away has snatched them as slaves. But he assures the world that he is in negotiations with an intergalactic council to get everyone back. And to show that what he says is not idle talk, be performs seeming miracles by the power of Satan.

Make no mistake—the world will fall at Antichrist's feet. And in its desperation the world will be willing to accept the most tyrannical measures for its survival. Antichrist declares that everyone must take his mark on their hand or forehead in order to buy or sell (Revelation 13:16-18). That will be the sign for alleged space aliens to keep hands off. Moreover, the mass disappearance, which has fouled up insurance and banking records and created financial chaos, necessitates the beginning of a totally new economic order.

This may sound like science fiction, but the rapture of all true Christians has been the great promise of God for nearly 2000 years, and it surely will happen. In fact it could happen at any moment. There is no other conceivable way by which Antichrist could take over as world ruler, no other way in which all of the world's religions, including a billion Muslims whose Scriptures forbid such unity, could be united as one.

While the extraterrestrial aspect of the above is not stated in the Bible, all of the other matters we have discussed in this chapter are clearly taught therein. Will UFOs and extraterrestrial intelligences (ETIs) have any special role to play? We examine this more closely in the next chapter.

*In the beginning God created the heaven and the
earth. . . . [And] God created man in his own image
. . . male and female created he them. And God . . .
said unto them, Be fruitful and multiply, and re-
plenish the earth. . . . And God saw everything that
he had made, and, behold, it was very good.*

—Genesis 1:1,27,28,31

*The LORD hath prepared his throne in the heavens,
and his kingdom ruleth over all. Bless the LORD, ye
his angels, that excel in strength, that do his commandments, hearkening unto the voice of his word.*
    *Bless ye the LORD, all ye his hosts, ye ministers of
his that do his pleasure. Bless the LORD, all his works
in all places of his dominion; bless the LORD, O my
soul.*

—Psalm 103:19-22

*They sang a new song, saying, Thou art worthy
. . . for thou wast slain, and hast redeemed us to God
by thy blood out of every kindred and tongue and
people and nation . . . and every creature which is in
heaven, and on the earth, and under the earth . . .
heard I saying, Blessing and honor and glory and
power be unto him that sitteth upon the throne and
unto the Lamb for ever and ever.*

—Revelation 5:9,13

19

Where Are the Aliens?

◆

Extraterrestrials have snatched millions of people from this earth and taken them to some distant planet? Fantasy? Science fiction? Wild speculation? It is no speculation that very soon millions will vanish from earth in an event called the rapture. The Bible verses quoted in the last chapter (and many others) make that fact very clear. If millions should in fact suddenly vanish, what other explanation could there be? Surely not the rapture, which only a relatively few evangelical Christians are expecting, and which Catholics and most mainline Protestants reject.

Those who were not taken away will consider themselves fortunate to have escaped this horrible fate. Certainly they will not believe that what occurred was the rapture. The only people who took that outrageous Christian-fringe teaching seriously have vanished. Furthermore, those who remain, because they rejected the gospel, have been given a "strong delusion" from God to believe Antichrist's lie. So says the Bible (2 Thessalonians 2:11,12).

An Old Lie Returns

The lie that the world will accept is certainly not a new one. It has its roots in evolution. That theory has long been the

369

required teaching of public schoolteachers and has been force-fed to students even over the objections of concerned parents. Though it cannot be proven by available data and has never been observed to occur, evolution is nevertheless a mainstay of the science curriculum in virtually all public schools in the United States. In those same schools, the possibility that God created the universe is not allowed even as an alternative. Of course, a belief in extraterrestrial intelligences "out there somewhere" follows logically from evolution.

There is no reason to believe that earth is unique unless it was so *created*. If life is merely the product of random forces innate within the universe and requires no Creator, then the same forces at work on earth could be at work everywhere in the cosmos. If life evolved on earth by chance, then it could have developed similarly on other planets as well. Moreover, such beings might even possess science and technology far beyond mankind's capabilities. The possibility that we are not alone in the universe is extremely exciting to most people and is presented in many of the most popular and influential books, films, and TV programs.

What could be more fitting than for this lie to come back to haunt those who rejected God as Creator? Having chosen to believe that life happened by chance, it is only justice that they should face the terror of what that could mean. There is no reason to believe that "highly evolved" beings must be benevolent. Why should they care about the feelings of mere humans? They might consider us to be such lowly creatures as to experiment with us as we do with guinea pigs. Why not, if there is no God who sets the moral standards for His universe? In that case, might makes right.

The New Hope: Highly Evolved ETIs

Robert Jastrow, founder and for many years director of the Goddard Institute for Space Studies (which played a key role in the Pioneer, Voyager, and Galileo space probes), declares that life could have been evolving on some other planets 10 billion years longer than on earth. Jastrow suggests that these beings could therefore be as far beyond man on the evolutionary scale as man is beyond the worm. They would seem like gods to us if we met them—an exciting but also terrifying possibility.

It is astonishing that mankind would rather look for help and advice to other mortal beings, even ones who could be extremely cruel, than to the God of infinite love and justice who created us. Israel's great King David knew better than that. When the prophet Gad gave him, by God's word, the choice between being judged by man or by God for his sin, David replied:

> Let me fall now into the hand of the LORD, for very great are his mercies; but let me not fall into the hand of man (1 Chronicles 21:13).

Today's leaders would rather fall into the hands of extraterrestrial intelligences (ETIs) than trust the mercy of God. Serious international efforts have been underway for years to contact ETIs. In this country the program is titled Search for Extraterrestrial Intelligence (SETI). The United States and other major countries pour huge investments into this search, sending radio signals into space and listening for some coherent message from "out there," convinced that such beings exist and that it is only a matter of time until we make contact to our great benefit.

The Voyager spacecraft, which is steadily making its way deeper into space, carried a message on a gold record affixed to its exterior. It was hoped that some friendly, intelligent life might intercept and decipher the message and as a result contact earth:

> This Voyager spacecraft was constructed by the United States of America. We are a community of 240 million human beings among the more than 4 billion who inhabit the planet Earth . . . still divided into nation states, but . . . rapidly becoming a single global civilization.
>
> We cast this message into the cosmos. . . . Of the 200 million stars in the Milky Way galaxy, some—perhaps

many—may have inhabited planets and spacefaring civilizations. If one such civilization intercepts Voyager ... here is our message:

> This is a present from a small, distant world, a token of our sounds, our science, our images, our music, our thoughts and our feelings. We are attempting to survive our time so we may live into yours. We hope someday, having solved the problems we face, to join a community of galactic civilizations. This record represents our hope and our determination, and our good will in a vast and awesome universe.
>
> Jimmy Carter
> President of the United States of America
> THE WHITE HOUSE, June 16, 1977

Nonphysical Beings?

Taking the theory of evolution the next step, Robert Jastrow suggests that life beyond earth may be "far beyond the flesh-and-blood form that we would recognize. It may [have] ... escaped its mortal flesh to become something that old-fashioned people would call spirits. And so how do we know it's there? Maybe it can materialize and then dematerialize. I'm sure it has magical powers by our standards...."[1] Like many other top scientists today, Jastrow, though an agnostic, repudiates scientific materialism and acknowledges that the universe may very well extend beyond matter into a nonphysical dimension of spirit beings. Nor is he alone in this conviction; Jastrow is joined by many of the world's most eminent scientists from every field.

Philosophy-of-science professor John Gliedman interviewed top scientists throughout Europe and America and as a result reported in *Science Digest*: "From Berkeley to Paris and from London to Princeton, prominent scientists from fields as diverse as neurophysiology and quantum physics are... admitting they believe in the possibility, at least, of...the immortal human spirit and divine creation."[2] In agreement are such celebrated scientists as Nobel Laureate Eugene Wigner, known as "one of the greatest physicists of the century," Sir Karl Popper, who has been called "the most famous philosopher of science of our age," and the late mathematician and quantum mechanics theorist John von Neumann, who has been described as perhaps "the smartest man who ever lived." Nobel Laureate Sir John Eccles has put it rather succinctly:

> But if there are bona fide mental events—events that are not themselves physical or material—then the whole program of philosophical materialism collapses.
>
> The universe is no longer composed of "matter and a void" but now must make (spaceless) room for (massless) entities [i.e. nonphysical intelligences].[3]

In *Science and the Unseen World*, Sir Arthur Eddington, one of the greatest physicists of all time, wrote that to imagine that consciousness is ruled by the laws of physics and chemistry "is as preposterous as the suggestion that a nation could be ruled by . . . the laws of grammar."[4] Ken Wilbur reviewed the writings of the greatest physicists of this century and discovered that they virtually *all* believed in a nonphysical dimension of reality. Based on their writings, he concluded, "There is no longer any major physical-theoretical objection to spiritual realities. . . . [T]his view . . . in all likelihood marks final closure on that most nagging aspect of the age-old debate between the physical sciences and religion. . . ."[5] In complete agreement, Arthur Koestler declared:

> The nineteenth-century clockwork model of the universe is in shambles and, since matter itself has been dematerialized, materialism can no longer claim to be a scientific philosophy.[6]

A Dangerous Application

When one applies these developments to the Search for Extraterrestrial Intelligences, the conclusions are staggering. Not only spirit mediums, psychics, yogis, and kooks but now top scientists are seriously attempting to contact "spirit beings" whom they believe are highly evolved, godlike entities with greater knowledge and powers than humans possess. Surely if contact were made with friendly ETIs, earth's leaders would jump at the chance to benefit from their counsel and help! But how could we know who these spirit beings were, and how could we be assured of their true intentions and motivation? In fact, we could not. It takes little insight to realize that the attempt to contact nonphysical entities opens the door to all kinds of satanic deception that could be used in putting Antichrist in power!

Not only former President Carter but other major political leaders have hopes that contact with ETIs would lead to a solution of earth's problems. In fact, Syrian President Hafez Assad, in an interview with *Time* magazine, expressed the belief that *only* an extraterrestrial power could bring real peace to this world. He has had a long-standing interest in UFOs and takes these unidentified flying objects quite seriously, believing they are space probes from other planets. *Time* asked Assad, "Suppose, as we discussed earlier, there were an extraterrestrial power and it tried to solve the Middle East's problems. What would you want it to do?" Hafez replied, "Certainly it would be a big power, and we would expect it to be unbiased."[7] Unbiased, yes, as far as earth's competing interests are concerned, but why would it be unselfish about its own interests?

The Syrian President, of course, is not alone in his beliefs, though not all are quite as hopeful. Leading figures in many fields from around the world met in Washington D.C. during May 27-29, 1995, in a conference titled "When Cosmic Cultures Meet." The conference attempted to come to grips with the question of what to do when the expected contact with ETIs finally comes about (perhaps sooner than we think).

It is interesting to note that the thought of contact with ETIs used to arouse fear. The radio program *Invasion of the Martians* created nationwide panic in the late 1930s. But since then, popular movies such as *Close Encounters of the Third Kind* and

ET have portrayed ETIs as possessing magical powers but kindly dispositions. Certainly this expectation is held widely by the general public. It would be too terrifying to think otherwise.

An Unexplained Phenomenon

While scientists are almost unanimous in the belief that ETIs are "out there," they disagree as to what UFOs actually represent. Highly credible UFO researchers, however, have accumulated a great deal of evidence which seems to indicate that beings from other planets have been visiting earth for some time in space vehicles. Because our scientists have been unable to identify the composition, method of propulsion, and origin of these mysterious vehicles (if that is what they are), they have been dubbed Unidentified Flying Objects (UFOs). Thousands of sightings are reported annually around the world, the vast majority of which exist only in the imagination or have some earthly explanation. That still leaves, however, numerous sightings which, upon careful investigation, seem to indicate that something "not of this earth" is visiting us for unknown reasons.

There have been several government investigations of UFOs, the exact results of which remain secret. According to files released under the Freedom of Information Act, the FBI even became involved for a time in the search for evidence at alleged crash sites. However, in a letter dated September 27, 1947, FBI Director J. Edgar Hoover wrote to Air Force Major General George C. McDonald: "I am advising the Field Divisions of the Federal Bureau of Investigation to discontinue all investigative activity regarding the reported sightings of flying discs, and am instructing them to refer all complaints received to the appropriate Air Force representative in their area."[8] Nevertheless, the FBI continued to have some involvement, as annual interoffice memorandums, such as the following from W.R. Wannall to W.C. Sullivan and dated 10/2/62, indicate: "There appears to be no necessity for additional instructions for the field or insertion in the FBI

Handbook or Manuals relative to flying saucers. This matter will again be reviewed on or about 10/1/63."[9] The FBI didn't dismiss UFOs out of hand as not worth some attention.

FBI files, in fact, include numerous reports of mysterious flying objects, seen in many parts of the country by competent observers including Air Force pilots and flight instructors as well as FBI personnel. There are references to the great speed of the objects, the absence of any means of propulsion known on earth, and maneuvers impossible for earthcraft, all of which indicate an origin outside of this planet. The reports also include observations of physical evidence on the ground, such as indentations from a heavy object as well as burned and radioactive areas where the object had landed. A CIA memorandum from the Deputy Director to the Director of Central Intelligence (date obliterated) states:

> At this time, the reports of incidents convince us that there is something going on that must have immediate attention. The details of some of these incidents have been discussed by AD/SI with DDCI. Sightings of unexplained objects at great altitudes and travelling at high speeds in the vicinity of major U.S. defense installations are of such nature that they are not attributable to natural phenomena or known types of aerial vehicles.[10]

The Impossible Religion

There are only two possible explanations for intelligent life beyond earth, if it exists. It either evolved by chance (the only view allowed in public schools), or God created it. The first possibility, in spite of its official status, can be quickly dismissed on mathematical grounds alone. Eminent British astronomer Sir Fred Hoyle points out that "even if the whole universe consisted of organic soup" from which life is made, the chance of producing the basic enzymes of life by random processes without intelligent direction would be approximately one in 10 with 40,000 zeros after it.

Such a number is beyond comprehension, but a comparison can be made. The likelihood of reaching out and by chance plucking a particular *atom* out of the *universe* would be about 1 in 10 with 80 zeros after it. If every atom in this universe became another universe, the chance of reaching out at random and plucking a particular atom out of all of those universes would then be 1 in 10 with 160 zeros after it.

Remember that 1 chance in 10 with 40,000 zeros after it (which is clearly impossible) only gets the basic enzymes. As a consequence of the mathematics alone, Hoyle concludes that "Darwinian evolution is most unlikely to get even one polypeptide [sequence] right, let alone the thousands on which living cells depend for survival." But even if that happened, chance would have to go on to develop millions of kinds of cells, each with thousands of complex chemical processes in progress at the same time and in delicate balance with one another. Furthermore, these cells (there are trillions in the human body) must be gathered into nerves, eyes, heart, kidneys, stomach, intestines, lungs, brain, fingernails, etc. all in the right place and each functioning in proper harmony with the rest of the body. The odds that all of this could happen by chance aren't even calculable!

The truth is that evolution is mathematically impossible, and this cold fact can easily be proven. Then why does this theory persist? It should have been abandoned long ago! Hoyle accuses the evolutionists of self-interest, unfair pressure, and dishonesty in keeping their theory alive and in forbidding the only alternative, divine creation, from being heard:

> This situation [mathematical impossibility] is well known to geneticists and yet nobody seems to blow the whistle decisively on the theory. . . .
> Most scientists still cling to Darwinism because of its grip on the educational system. . . . You either have to believe the concepts, or you will be branded a heretic [11]

"Heretic" is an appropriate term, because evolution, like psychotherapy, is a religion—a religion to which Hoyle himself remains strangely committed. While he has defected from the Darwinian camp, Hoyle has simply switched his membership to another "denomination" of evolutionists which has the equally bizarre belief that life came in from outer space. Of course this theory only raises a further question: Where and how did *that* life originate? We are obviously back where we started.

Evolution or Creation: Chance or God

Hoyle does admit that perhaps "God" is the One who sent life in from space, but who or what is "God"? That question cannot be answered by science. Unfortunately, the popularizers of science have convinced our generation that science will ultimately answer every question. That is a delusion which the world's greatest scientists have long denounced, but almost no one has been listening. Sir Arthur Eddington wrote that "'Ought' [morality] takes us outside chemistry and physics."[12] Nobelist Erwin Schroedinger, who played a vital role in giving the world today's new physics, reminds us:

> [Science] is ghastly silent about all . . . that is really near to our heart, that really matters to us. . . . [I]t knows nothing of beautiful and ugly, good or bad, God and eternity. . . .
> Whence came I and whither go I? That is the great unfathomable question, the same for every one of us. Science has no answer to it.[13]

In *Chance and Necessity*, Nobelist molecular biologist Jacques Monod gives a dozen or more reasons why evolution could not possibly occur. He explains, for example, that the essential characteristic of DNA is its perfect replication of itself; that evolution could only occur through a mistake in that operation; and that it is absurd to imagine developing even a single cell, much less the human brain, from a series of random and harmful mistakes in the DNA mechanism. Yet after giving reason after reason why life could not possibly be the product of chance and why evolution couldn't work, Monod concludes that it *must*, nevertheless, have happened that way.

Monod has no valid reason for his "faith." He simply refuses to accept creation by God and trusts "chance" instead.

British Museum of Natural History senior paleontologist Colin Patterson declares: "Evolutionists—like the creationists they periodically do battle with—are nothing more than believers themselves. I had been working on this stuff [evolution] for more than twenty years, and there was not one [factual] thing I knew about it. It's quite a shock to learn that one can be so misled for so long."[14] Speaking before a group of his fellow biologists, D.M.S Watson, popularizer of evolution on British television (as Carl Sagan has been on American TV), reminded them of the common *religious faith* they all shared:

> Evolution itself is accepted by zoologists not because it has been observed to occur or . . . can be proved by logically coherent evidence to be true, but because the only alternative, special creation, is clearly incredible.[15]

The Irrational Consequences

Furthermore, evolutionists cannot live with the consequences of their godless theory. If evolution, not God, is responsible for our existence, then we should shut down all medical facilities and let the weak die naturally. Medically prolonging the lives of those with genetic disabilities or diseases allows such persons to pass on their defects to subsequent generations and thereby weaken the race and undermine the survival of the fittest. We must stop trying to find a cure for AIDS and let its victims die. Since AIDS is largely a homosexual disease, one can only conclude that it is nature's way of eliminating those who practice what is undeniably unnatural and unreproductive sex. The sooner those with deficiencies die, the better for our species. That is the way evolution works!

If stopping all assistance to the ill so that only the fittest survive sounds harsh, then blame nature (that's her way); and blame the theory of evolution (that's how it supposedly works). Nature has neither morals nor compassion but simply involves an inexorable process. Human beings, however, do have concern for the weak, the sick, and the dying; they feel compelled to help the helpless even to their own detriment. That fact cannot be explained by evolution. It proves that man was created by a personal, loving, and gracious Creator who has given us the capacity to be compassionate. Certainly the law of the jungle, of fang and claw, of the survival of the strongest, would never move us with compassion for others.

If nature is god, then let nature take its course without any interference from man. There is nothing more *natural* than disease, pain, death, and those calamities known as "*natural disasters*" (hurricanes, earthquakes, lightning, drought, and famine, to name a few). Gaia or "Mother Nature" is anything but kind. The evolutionist's attempt to have it both ways—denying a personal Creator yet insisting upon morals and compassion which can't come from nature—betrays the lie that is taught as fact in our educational institutions.

Irreconcilable Contradictions

The contradictions that go unnoticed or are deliberately ignored reveal the prejudice of mankind against God. If evolution is true, then man is as much a part of nature as the animals and no complaint can be made against anything he does, any more than against any other part of nature. If it is not "wrong" for a volcano to spew forth poisonous gases, then surely it is not wrong for a man-made factory to do the same. And as for all the furor that is raised over the possible extinction of a species such as the spotted owl, isn't that what evolution has been doing for millions of years? If man wants to cut down trees for making his home, is that any more unnatural than for a bird to pick up grass and sticks to make its nest? Then to stop loggers from felling trees because it might cause the extinction of the spotted owl is to defy the natural forces of evolution!

One cannot believe in both evolution and ecological preservation of species or habitats. If evolution is a fact, then whatever man, as the end product of that process, does is natural. If he, as a result of the evolution of his brain and nervous system and psyche, succeeds in destroying the earth in a nuclear holocaust or some ecological disaster, then in the big picture of the evolving universe that must be accepted as progress, since it was brought about by evolution.

On the other hand, the mere fact that man can reason about and interfere with ecology and survival of species, including himself, indicates that he is not the product of such forces. On the contrary, he must have a higher origin. Obviously he didn't create himself, so he, like all of the universe, must have been made by some intelligent Creator to whom he is accountable. If that is so, then the solution to his problems is not in hugging trees, in getting in touch with nature and in listening to the earth, as we are being told, but in getting in touch with the God who made him and in submitting to His will.

In contrast to all animals, man mourns the death of his fellows for days and years. It is not only that the loved one grieved for is missed, but there is something tangible beyond that. There is an inner anger felt against death, that it is an enemy of life and all that ought to be. At a deeper level, man realizes that death is not natural; it is not the way things ought to be, but is an enemy which has invaded our lives because something has been lost that is beyond our power to recover.

This is where religion comes in—to offer something beyond death—the happy hunting ground of the American Indian, the Paradise of the Muslim filled with beautiful maidens, the Nirvana of the Buddhist or Hindu. Despite these vain hopes, the hereafter is most often a land of shadow and fear that is haunted by an inescapable sense of loss. Something has gone wrong. We were not made to die, and that fact seems to be built into the human psyche. Hope of life after death is vain, however, without a resurrection. And that is what Jesus Christ came to provide.

Hope or Hopelessness

If life evolved by chance, then God, even if there were a God, has no concern for humanity. If He didn't even bother to create man, but simply let him become whatever evolution might make him, then surely He has no interest in man's affairs. The Bible is a fraud, written by men. God didn't choose the Jews, has no interest in Jerusalem or Israel, and couldn't care less whether Arabs or Jews are in control. Let them fight it out and let the world destroy itself, for all that this "God" cares.

The prophecies we have considered, however, prove that God does exist and that He inspired His prophets to write the Bible. That Book's testimony can be relied upon. When it tells us that God gave Israel to the Jews and has a plan for His chosen people, for their land and for Jerusalem, the world needs to behave accordingly. And what God has to say about Jerusalem tells us that there are no ETIs out there. As we have already seen, God repeatedly states that Jerusalem is the city which He has chosen for His Temple and where He has placed His name forever. It is the center of the universe. We will come back to that in the closing chapter.

In spite of the impotence of science where it really matters and the confession of that fact by the world's greatest scientists, religious people continue to bow to this sacred cow and thereby try to gain a certain credibility. In order to be "scientific," a hybrid belief is becoming popular among Christians: that God allowed evolution to proceed, then stepped in to transform an apelike creature into Adam when it had evolved high enough. But evolution is a fraud. And the Bible says that the moment God breathed life into the form He molded from dust, it was a man, Adam (Genesis 2:7), so he couldn't have existed in a previous form. Furthermore, death did not invade earth until Adam sinned ("by one man sin entered into the world, and death by sin"—Romans 5:12), so there could not have been prior species dying and evolving.

What About ETIs?

Yes, but why couldn't God have created intelligent life on other planets as well as here on earth? He could have, but why would He? Any intelligent created beings with the power of choice, being less than God, would seek to do their own will and thus become rebels in God's universe. The Bible calls that rebellion *sin*. God does not need to experiment ("Man sinned, but let me try again on another planet . . . etc."). Thus if there are other sinners scattered throughout the universe, God put them there intentionally. But why? Surely one planet of rebels is enough!

Sinners need redemption and a loving Creator would provide it. In fact, redemption for the entire universe has been provided through the sacrifice of Christ on the cross on this planet. We earthlings have the testimony of eyewitnesses, archaeological evidence, historical evidence, and prophecies fulfilled on this earth. Such proofs would not be available to other beings who had to believe in a Christ who died on a distant planet.

It is to this earth that Satan came to spread his rebellion, and to this earth that Christ came to die for man's sin. The battle between God and Satan for the universe is centered here. Christ's sacrifice on the cross purified heaven itself of sin (Hebrews 9:23). Christ's death and resurrection on this planet fully dealt with sin for the entire universe, as many Scriptures declare:

> In whom we have redemption through his blood. ... That in the dispensation of the fullness of times he might gather together in one all things in Christ, both which are in heaven and which are on earth... (Ephesians 1:7,10).

> That at the name of Jesus every knee should bow, of things in heaven and things in earth... (Philippians 2:10).

> Having made peace through the blood of his cross, by him to reconcile all things unto himself... whether they be things in earth or things in heaven (Colossians 1:20).

> They sung a new song, saying, Thou art worthy ... for thou wast slain, and hast redeemed us to God by thy blood out of every kindred and tongue and people and nation. ...

> And every creature which is in heaven and on the earth, and under the earth... heard I saying, Blessing and honor and glory and power be unto him that sitteth upon the throne and unto the Lamb for ever and ever (Revelation 5:9,13).

> . . . all things shall be subdued under him [Christ]
> . . . that God may be all in all (1 Corinthians 15:28).

From Genesis to Revelation, the Bible makes it clear that in the final consummation of God's purposes the entire universe will be reconciled to Himself through Christ's once-for-all sacrifice on the cross. For Christ to redeem us, He had to become one of us through a virgin birth, a genuine man who died in our place. Likewise, to redeem any other beings "out there" He would have had to become one of them also. But the Bible says that Christ did not die anywhere else. He died only *once*, and here on earth. We know that Christ's sacrifice was not repeated on any other planet:

> . . . by his own blood he entered in *once* into the holy place [heaven], having obtained eternal redemption for us. . . . Now *once* in the end of the world hath he [Christ] appeared to put away sin by the sacrifice of himself. . . .
> This man, after he had offered *one* sacrifice for sins forever, sat down on the right hand of God. . . .
> For by *one* offering he hath perfected forever them that are sanctified [and] . . . there is *no more* offering for sin (Hebrews 9:12,26; 10:12,14,18).

Deception and Disaster

It is upon this earth that Satan will attempt to establish his counterfeit kingdom through Antichrist. As we have seen, it is entirely possible that UFOs and the belief in ETIs may play a role in deceiving mankind to follow Antichrist, though we are not certain what that role might be. We do know, however, both from the testimony of the Bible and from the mathematical impossibility of life happening by chance, that there are no physical ETIs. The only intelligent life, in addition to man, is all in spirit form: God, angels, Satan, and demons.

Spirits, including Satan and his minions, unfortunately, are able to invade the physical realm. The book of Job in the Old Testament makes this clear. Satan put boils on Job, caused Sabeans and Chaldeans to rob Job and kill his servants, and caused a "great wind" to destroy a house and kill Job's children—and in each case one person was left alive to bring the news to Job. Satan took Christ to the top of a mountain and to the pinnacle of the Temple. Jannes and Jambres (2 Timothy 3:8), the magicians in Pharaoh's court, were able to duplicate by the power of Satan many of the miracles Moses and Aaron did by the power of God.

What limits there may be upon the satanic "power and signs and lying wonders" which the Antichrist will use to deceive the world (2 Thessalonians 2:9) we don't know. We do know that the delusion will be sufficient to cause the whole world to worship Antichrist as "God" (Revelation 13:8). And the fact that mankind is now open to contacting and receiving advice and help from ETIs, who can only be masquerading demons, sets the stage for the last-days "strong delusion" (2 Thessalonians 2:11) to which we have earlier referred and concerning which the Bible warns mankind repeatedly.

Tragically, Israel has rejected the testimony of her prophets concerning her Messiah. She is fulfilling those prophecies by that rejection, and will further fulfill them by accepting the Antichrist as her Savior. That alliance will end in destruction for Israel, the worst destruction she has ever experienced. The Hebrew prophets all spoke of it as "the day of the LORD" (Isaiah 2:12; 13:9; Jeremiah 46:10; Ezekiel 30:3; Joel 1:15; Amos 5:18; etc.). The great prophet Jeremiah called it "the time of Jacob's trouble" (30:7). That day lies yet ahead for Israel.

In the latter years [last days] thou shalt come into the land that is brought back from the sword and is gathered out of many people, against the mountains of Israel, which have been always waste; but it is brought forth out of the nations. . . . Thou shalt ascend and come like a storm; thou shalt be like a cloud to cover the land, thou and all thy bands, and many people with thee. . . . To take a spoil and to take a prey; to turn thine hand upon the [formerly] desolate places that are now inhabited, and upon the people that are gathered out of the nations. . . . And thou shalt come up against my people of Israel as a cloud to cover the land; it shall be in the latter days, and I will bring thee against my land, that the heathen may know me . . . and all the men that are upon the face of the earth shall shake at my presence . . . and they shall know that I am the LORD.

—Ezekiel 38:8-23

I will gather all nations against Jerusalem to battle, and the city shall be taken. . . . Then shall the LORD go forth and fight against those nations, as when he fought in the day of battle. And his feet shall stand in that day upon the mount of Olives, which is before Jerusalem on the east. . . .

—Zechariah 14:2-4

I saw the beast [Antichrist], and the kings of the earth, and their armies, gathered together to make war against [Christ returning in power and glory to rescue Israel]. . . . And the beast was taken, and with him the false prophet that wrought miracles before him, with which he deceived them that had received the mark of the beast, and them that worshiped his image. These both were cast alive into a lake of fire. . . .

—Revelation 19:19,20

20

Double Cross and Armageddon!

◆

The prophecies foretelling earth's greatest battle are too specific for their accuracy to be denied. The situation as presented by the prophets some 2500 years ago for the "latter years" (also called the "last days"—Genesis 49:1; Isaiah 2:2; Acts 2:17; etc.) precisely fits our day: The land of Israel, after being desolate for centuries, is once again inhabited by "people that are gathered out of the nations." That surely describes the present situation.

The undeniable and miraculous accuracy of the prophecy to this point requires that we take very seriously everything else it says about things yet to come. What part, if any, the demonic delusion of UFOs may play in the outworking of the prophecies concerning Israel is not specified in Scripture. It is of some interest, however, that recently in a meeting in South Africa, "an international group of UFO-logists urged that an embassy for extraterrestrials be opened—in Jerusalem—to give them 'a safe place' to land."[1] Once again the key role to be played by Jerusalem in coming events seems to be widely recognized.

Moving on into what would seem to be the near future, the prophecy declares that Israel will be in a state of complacency, feeling secure and unthreatened (as those "that are at rest, that

dwell safely"—Ezekiel 38:11). Antichrist's seven-year covenant allowing the Temple to be rebuilt, an unexpected con-
cession to Israel, will have been accepted by a world unified
through disaster. As it puts that horror behind it, still hoping
that Antichrist will be able to effect the return of the scores of
millions missing, the world will move into a time of international prosperity unprecedented in world history. That is when
the judgment of God begins to come upon earth's rebels in a
series of cosmic calamities, as described in the book of Revelation. Israel, however, is like a small island of safety, untouched
by the natural disasters devastating other parts of the planet all
around her.

Ironically, Israel will unwittingly have entered the time of
her gravest danger, "the time of Jacob's trouble" (Jeremiah
30:7). Lulled into a false sense of peace and safety under
treaties with her neighbors (guaranteed by Antichrist as part
of the covenant he confirms with Israel for Daniel's seventieth
week), Israel will be ill-prepared for the overwhelming attack
that will be mounted against her. This time all the nations of
the world will join Israel's Arab neighbors in launching an all-
out attempt at a final solution to the Jewish question.

The Bible calls this war Armageddon. It results from a
double cross by the Antichrist, who breaks his covenant and
turns against Israel. In order to save His people, Christ intervenes from heaven and destroys Antichrist and his armies, thus
preventing them from destroying Israel. Of Antichrist, Paul
wrote: "Whom the Lord shall . . . destroy with the brightness
of his coming" (2 Thessalonians 2:8). We will consider Christ's
salvation of Israel more carefully in the next chapter.

The Rapture Comes First

Christ's intervention at Armageddon is known as "the second coming of Christ," which many Christians mistakenly
believe is the same event as the rapture. At the rapture,
however, Christ comes *for* His saints (His true followers),
while at the second coming He comes *with* His saints and *for
Israel* to rescue her in the midst of Armageddon. We are clearly

told that when Christ's "feet shall stand in that day upon the mount of Olives" (when He intervenes at Armageddon) He will bring "all the saints" from heaven with Him (Zechariah 14:4,5; Jude 14,15). Therefore one can only conclude that He must have previously taken the church, His bride, up to heaven. Thus the rapture, which precedes it, and the second coming are two distinct events.

Separated by seven years, the rapture comes at the beginning of Daniel's seventieth week, and the second coming at the end of it. We know that Christ comes to rescue Israel at the end of the great tribulation in the midst of Armageddon when His people are about to be annihilated. We also know that He comes to rapture His saints to heaven at a time of peace and prosperity. The Bible clearly states that before Armageddon's great "destruction cometh upon them," the world must feel confident that it has achieved "peace and safety" (1 Thessalonians 5:3). At that point the rapture will occur, in a worldwide climate of proud complacency and continuing rebellion against God and with no fear of His judgment—the very attitude of mankind just before the flood in the days of Noah.

Christians, too, will be caught off guard at the rapture, unless they are walking closely with Christ. He has given us fair warning: "Therefore be ye also ready; for in such an hour *as ye think not* [i.e. when the world and the church are at ease and not looking for Christ because everything is going so well] the Son of man cometh" (Matthew 24:44). Surely that is not describing the second coming, for in the midst of Armageddon everyone knows that Christ is about to return. Even Antichrist knows it, and is forced to turn from his attack upon Israel "to make war against him [Christ]" (Revelation 19:19).

Like the Days of Noah and Lot

In contrast to the chaos and destruction at Armageddon, Christ vividly described world conditions at the time of His coming to catch the redeemed from earth into heaven. It will occur not in the midst of war and devastation but at a time of apparent but false "peace and safety":

As it was in the days of Noah, so shall it be also in the days of the Son of man. They did eat, they drank, they married wives, they were given in marriage, until the day that Noah entered into the ark, and the flood came and destroyed them all.

Likewise also as it was in the days of Lot: They did eat, they drank, they bought, they sold, they planted, they built; but the same day that Lot went out of Sodom it rained fire and brimstone from heaven and destroyed them all.

Even thus shall it be in the day when the Son of man is revealed (Luke 17:26-30).

The ease and security, the prosperity, the normal course of life and business described in these verses simply cannot and will not exist at the end of the great tribulation in the midst of Armageddon. In contrast to the rosy picture painted above, as early in Revelation as chapter 6 it states that already a fourth of earth's inhabitants have been killed (verse 8) and there have been devastating meteor showers and earthquakes (verses 12-14) that have even moved mountains and islands out of their places. Earth's inhabitants have such an overpowering sense of God's judgment in these disasters that they cry out—

to the mountains and rocks, Fall on us and hide us from the face of him that sitteth on [heaven's] throne and from the wrath of the Lamb; for the great day of his wrath is come, and who shall be able to stand? (verses 16,17).

There is no way to reconcile the peaceful, pleasure-filled, prosperous world "as it was in the days of Noah . . . [and] Lot" with conditions at the end of the tribulation, when the world is already devasted and is in the midst of the most destructive war in history. A posttribulation rapture doesn't fit this picture at all. Obviously, this catching away to heaven ("Then shall two be in the field; the one shall be taken and the other left"— Matthew 24:40; etc.) must occur at the beginning of Daniel's seventieth week.

As we have seen, the terrorization of the world resulting from the rapture is the only possible catalyst that could suddenly put Antichrist in power as dictator of a unified world. Thus the day of the Lord comes when the world least expects it ("as a thief in the night"—1 Thessalonians 5:2; 2 Peter 3:10) and is ushered in with the mass disappearance of millions upon millions from planet Earth at a time when the world is exulting in the "peace and safety" it has achieved by its own efforts, without "the Prince of Peace."

The Price of Amorality

That Antichrist's rule will be arbitrary, despotic, and completely amoral (an exchange willingly made for "peace") will make it easier for the world to justify the "final solution" at Armageddon when that time comes. One would have to be blind indeed not to realize that we are moving in the direction of an amoral society in preparation for that day. Natan Sharansky looks back to his time as a *refusenik* in the USSR with a certain sense of nostalgia as "a time when there was a clear choice between good and evil."

Sharansky sees today's world as "confused" on moral issues and believes that the principles set forth by the late Senator Henry Jackson when he authored the Jackson amendment should be followed in Israel's pursuit of peace with its Arab neighbors and especially with the PLO. "If Jackson were around today," suggests Sharansky, "he would say that Syria should first open its borders and then discuss its new borders. . . . With the Palestinians, too, we should not discuss details until they have taken care of their internal affairs . . . you do not move forward with the next step of an agreement without ensuring compliance with the previous one."[2]

In failing to follow this advice, Israel has opted for a most dangerous amorality of its own. As a result, the peace process has only created growing problems and mounting casualties. Under Palestinian rule terrorist attacks have increased, such as the suicide mission by Islamic militants against a crowd of Israeli soldiers around a snack bar January 22, 1995 (the fiftieth anniversary of the liberation of Auschwitz), that killed 19 Israelis and wounded about 60 others. A new tactic was applied by the terrorists for the first time: setting off a small blast first and then the major explosion when the rescuers arrived.

In response, Israeli President Ezer Weizman "proposed that Israel stop the peace talks for an extended review before expanding Palestinian self-rule into the West Bank." Predictably, his advice was not followed. As with all the other attacks, the Cabinet meeting in emergency session closed off the occupied territories, "blocking the movement of all Palestinians into Israel [and keeping] tens of thousands of Palestinians away from jobs in Israel."[3] It was a matter of, once again, shutting the barn door after the horse was gone.

Prime Minister Yitzhak Rabin's reaction to Weizman's advice was a starry-eyed avoidance of the real truth: "There is no doubt in my mind that this action now is another attempt by the extreme Islamic terror groups to achieve their dual goal of killing Israelis and halting the peace process."[4] It is astonishing how "the peace process" has mesmerized Israeli leaders and much of the population into believing Arab ploys and lies. So the "militant extremists" want to disrupt the steps toward an alleged normalization of relations with Israel. Yet that "normalization" will eventually leave sworn enemies of Israel—who have vowed her destruction—in charge of territories within her borders from which to launch their final blow!

A Strange Path to "Peace"

In her desperation to make peace with her Arab neighbors, Israel has admitted within her borders not only sworn enemies but trained fighters who have long been mobilized for her destruction. For example, an agreement was reached between Israel and the PLO early in 1995 "to allow 1,500 pro-Arafat fighters to leave refugee camps in Lebanon to join the Palestinian Police in the territories," according to the Beirut daily *Ad-Diyar*. The "first group of 900 fighters [was] due to leave from Sidon Port [in February 1995]."[5]

One of the most obvious dangers in the peace process is that Israel will make so many concessions and finally give the Palestinians and Syria so much territory and power that they will not be able to resist the opportunity to attack Israel in one more attempt to annihilate her. Thus the peace process will eventually lead only to war. The road which Israel is presently traveling has no provision for U-turns, no possibility of reversing direction. It is a road which leads where Israel doesn't want to go and over which she now has no control. As a recent *Jerusalem Post* editorial put it:

> When the Oslo agreement became known, it was wholeheartedly supported by many army officers. Tired of chasing terrorists and stone-throwing youths in Gaza, they said there was little risk in evacuating the [Gaza] Strip. As one of them put it: "If they so much as sneeze the wrong way, we'll get back in there and teach them a lesson they will never forget."
>
> Such bluster is no longer heard. It is finally realized that no matter how flagrantly the PA [Palestinian Authority] violates the agreement, returning in force to Gaza is virtually a political impossibility.[6]

Arafat simply lied when he said he would change the PLO Charter to remove the provision for the destruction of Israel. Paragraph 33 of the Palestinian Covenant (PLO Charter) reads: "This Charter shall not be amended save by [vote of] a majority of two-thirds of the total membership of the national congress of the Palestinian Liberation Organisation [taken] at a special session convened for that purpose." On August 10, 1994, radio Monte Carlo quoted a letter from Yasser Arafat to the representative of Al Fatah: "Never shall I lend my hand to alter just one paragraph of the Palestine Covenant." Why then do Israel's leaders go along with this lie?

Terrorism and Anti-Semitism Renewed

Even when, "in the midst of the week," Antichrist in an obvious double cross and breach of the seven-year covenant places his image in the Temple and demands that the world worship him, Israel's leaders will not catch the scent of danger—or at least will ignore it. Orthodox Jews will fiercely object and many will flee "to the mountains" as some did during the siege of Jerusalem in 70 A.D., perhaps this time to Petra in Jordan (Zechariah 14:5; Mark 13:14; Luke 21:21). As a result, Israel will be seen again as obstreperous and unwilling to fit into the new world religion.

After a brief respite, perhaps even for several years, terrorism against Israel and probably around the world will have begun anew. One of the gravest dangers Israel faces today and in the foreseeable future is from ground-launched ballistic missiles. These weapons are now developed and produced in a number of countries[7] and, for a price, are available to terrorist organizations for launching at Israel from neighboring states. It is true that Israel's sophisticated airpower demonstrated its capabilities by destroying almost every Syrian air defense missile battery in the Beka'a Valley during the 1982 Lebanon War and without the loss of a single attacking aircraft.[8] Tracking down *mobile* launchers, however, is a different story.

In the case of surface-to-surface ballistic missile attacks, Israel's sophisticated air superiority is of little value except in retaliatory strikes against stationary launching sites. The Gulf War proved the difficulty of locating and destroying mobile launchers. And when missiles are launched from a neighbor that has signed a peace treaty and expresses seemingly sincere regrets while at the same time pleading an inability to prevent such terrorist activity, it will be extremely difficult to retaliate. After all, if the United States cannot prevent terrorists from destroying a Federal building in its very heartland, as was demonstrated recently in the Oklahoma City bombing, how could Syria or Lebanon or Jordan be held responsible for like failure to control terrorists who target Israel?

Anti-Semitism will have been stifled temporarily by the peace treaties and Antichrist's covenant allowing the Temple to be rebuilt. The satanic purpose behind anti-Semitism, however, will not have changed, and this evil will be stirred anew in the hearts of millions. Remember, Satan *must* destroy Israel in order to prevent the Messiah from returning to rule the world from David's throne in Jerusalem. With Israel's destruction (and *only* thereby), Satan would have prevented the fulfillment of Bible prophecies, would have proved God to be a liar, and would thus have escaped his own defeat.

The stakes are high for Satan—not only for his own survival but also for control of the universe—and he will use all of his guile and power to destroy Israel. She is at the center of the raging battle between God and Satan for the destiny of planet Earth and the universe. Antichrist's covenant with Israel and the false peace that ultimately will "destroy many" (Daniel 8:25) are merely strategic steps toward the intended annihilation of Israel.

God has said through His prophets that in the last days Jerusalem would be a "cup of trembling" to the entire world. No treaties can change that fact. World leaders will gradually agree in secret meetings that the only way to remove this "cup of trembling" will be to effect the destruction of Israel. Carefully they will begin to lay their plans.

The Vatican, Islam, and the PLO

The Vatican, of course, will be in on the plot. For her it is a simple matter of self-interest involving her high stakes in the Middle East. In spite of Vatican II's claim that Allah is the God of the Bible, Catholic relations with Islam have not been what the Vatican had hoped thus far. Cardinal Achille Silvestrini, one of the Vatican's top diplomats, has said that John Paul II's "most fervent desire" after "ecumenism among Christians" and "a deepening dialogue between Christians and Jews" is "dialogue with Islam." He admits, however, that after many years of attempted dialogue very little progress has been made in smoothing relationships.[9] So too Father Maurice Borrmans, "one of the Vatican's most respected specialists on Islam," categorizes "Christian-Islamic dialogue" as "extremely delicate and difficult."[10]

After the rapture and with Antichrist firmly in power, the

Vatican will at last achieve the close relationship to Islam which it has been pursuing for years. Everything will have changed under the new world religion. John Paul II has been laying the ecumenical foundation for that blending of all religions under Vatican leadership for nearly two decades. Islam and the Vatican will be working in close cooperation with each other and with all the world's religions. Only Israel will be the fly in the ointment of worldwide "spiritual unity."

Pope John Paul II welcomed Yasser Arafat into the Vatican as early as 1982. Their meeting was cordial even though, in those days, Arafat made no attempt to hide the fact that he directed international terrorism of the most brutal kind. After cultivating Arafat's friendship for 12 years, the Vatican established official ties with the PLO on October 25, 1994.[11] The fact that anti-Semitism will not die, as we mentioned above, even with the new promotion of "peace," is seen in Arafat and his lieutenants, such as his right-hand man, Jibril Rajoub. Once imprisoned for multiple murders of Israelis, Rajoub was released by Israel as a good-faith gesture to promote the new "peace process" with Islam.

Earlier we quoted Arafat from his May 15, 1994, speech in which he said, "I call upon every Muslim to wage Jihad against Jerusalem." Remember, this was eight months after the September 13, 1993, good-faith handshake between Israeli Prime Minister Yitzhak Rabin and PLO Chairman Yasser Arafat at the dramatic signing of the Oslo agreement on the White House lawn. Remember, too, that in spite of such statements, Arafat, along with Rabin, was later given the Nobel Peace Prize.

Showing his gratitude for being released from prison, and his commitment to "peace" (and letting the world know that Arafat meant what he said), Rajoub declared defiantly, "The battle over Palestine has come to an end. The battle for Jerusalem has begun."[12] In his call for Jihad, Arafat designated Jerusalem as "the capital of Islam!" The blindness of Israeli officials who nevertheless continue the "peace process" is beyond comprehension!

John Paul II and Mikhail Gorbachev

Antichrist's eventual plot to destroy Israel could hardly move forward to a successful completion without the complicity and full support of the Vatican. Pope John Paul II is the most influential leader on earth, and the Vatican's agents worldwide are as efficient as those of any national secret service anywhere. That fact has been demonstrated on numerous occasions—for example, in the partnership between Reagan and the Pope that unraveled Communism and brought down the Berlin Wall.

The cover of *Time* magazine of February 24, 1993, carried the pictures of former President Ronald Reagan and Pope John Paul II, together with this startling caption: "HOLY ALLIANCE: How Reagan and the Pope conspired to assist Poland's Solidarity movement and hasten the demise of Communism." The lead story told how Reagan had "believed fervently in both the benefits and practical applications of Washington's relationship with the Vatican. One of his earliest goals as President, Reagan says, was to recognize the Vatican as a state 'and make them an ally.'" Antichrist will see the necessity and wisdom of an even closer relationship with the Pope.

Time told the story of the intrigue and cooperation between the CIA and the apparently even more effective agents of the Vatican. A five-part strategy was developed in 1982 "that was aimed at bringing about the collapse of the Soviet economy, fraying the ties that bound the U.S.S.R. to its client states in the Warsaw Pact and forcing reform inside the Soviet empire." In the outworking of the plan, former Secretary of State Alexander Haig acknowledged that "the Vatican's information was absolutely better and quicker than ours [the CIA's] in every respect. [The] Vatican liaison to the White House, Archbishop Pio Laghi, kept reminding American officials, 'Listen to the Holy Father. We have 2000 years' experience of this [international intrigue].'"[13] That experience will be placed at the service of the Antichrist, as Revelation 17 clearly foretells.

Former Soviet President Mikhail Gorbachev has a syndicated column in leading newspapers around the globe. His column of March 3, 1992, carried this heading: "Pope John Paul made change possible." Gorbachev had "sent a copy of his article to the Pope before it appeared in print. In it Gorbachev said, 'Everything that took place in Eastern Europe in recent years would have been impossible without the Pope's efforts.' "[14] In an interview in response to the article, the Pope said of Gorbachev, "He does not profess to be a believer, but with me I recall he spoke of the great importance of prayer and of the inner side of man's life. I truly believe that our meeting was prepared by Providence. . . ."[15]

It is not difficult to imagine a similar justification for the Pope's close relationship with the coming world ruler. Antichrist will also advocate a universal "spirituality" which, like Gorbachev's, will bear no relationship to the Christianity of which the Pope claims to be the head on earth but which he actually undermines while promoting a religion acceptable to all.

Nor is Gorbachev to be counted out of a future world leadership role, in spite of his loss of the Russian presidency. His close friendship with the Pope continues. Gorbachev now heads the Green Cross, which "aspires to be for the environmental crisis what the Red Cross and Red Crescent already are for disaster relief."[16] A three-star U.S. Army General handed Gorbachev the keys to the Gorbachev Foundation USA's new offices overlooking the Golden Gate entrance to San Francisco's harbor. Where were the keys handed over? In the Presidio, a major U.S. military base which is being closed down.[17] Amazingly, Gorbachev, through his foundation, has acted as a major consultant in the closing down of U.S. military bases in 36 communities.[18]

In God's Name

Is it possible that the Vatican, which claims to be the headquarters of the one true Church, and the Pope, who claims to be the Vicar of Christ, could cooperate in Israel's destruction? In fact, that has been the stance of Roman Catholicism throughout history. Having thoroughly documented that fact in *A Woman Rides the Beast*, we will not present further evidence here.

We earlier noted that Hitler, who was praised by Popes Pius XI and XII and other high Roman Catholic clergy, offers some interesting parallels to Antichrist from which we can learn valuable lessons. Hitler claimed to be acting for God and frequently invoked God's blessing. Following are but a few extracts from his speeches showing both the perversity of Hitler and the blindness of those who followed him:

> 1940: We pray our Lord that He would continue to bless us in our battle for freedom.
> 1941: We believe we shall earn the blessing of the supreme leader. The Lord God has given His approval to our battle. He will be with us in our battle. He will be with us in the future.
> 1942: And we will pray the Lord God for that, the salvation of the nation. . . .
> 1943: We will continue to give our whole strength to our nation this year. Only then can we dare, as we usually pray to our Lord God, that He will help us as He always has. . . .

Religion will play a vital role under Antichrist. Remember that the leading Nazis were all convinced that National Socialism was a new religion that was destined to rule the world and thereby establish a golden age comparable to the prophesied biblical millennium. The contradictions were many, yet were seemingly overlooked. Hitler killed Jews but claimed to be a follower of Jesus Christ, whose Jewishness he denied. At the same time he hated Christianity, declaring, "We will wash off the Christian veneer and bring out a religion peculiar to our race!"[19] Yet he also said, "National Socialism is Positive Christianity." Here was a clear example of an Antichrist "Christianity." Of National Socialism, French academician Louis Bertrand said enthusiastically, "This is religion!"[20]

Antichrist will be not only the world's political leader but its religious leader as well. In fact, as already noted, the world will worship him as "God." He will seem at first to be the epitome of humanistic man and will be admired of all. As God's judgment begins to be poured out upon this earth, however, it will become clear to those who have eyes to see that Antichrist is utterly possessed by Satan himself! This man is not repeatedly called a "beast" in the book of Revelation (13:1-4,15,18; 14:9; 15:2; 16:2; 17:3; 19:19; etc.) without cause.

A new Hitler (without, as yet, the former's power) is gaining prominence in Russia. He is a political leader who presents another model for Antichrist: Vladimir Zhirinovsky. He shows once again both the backing which a seemingly fanatical lunatic can arouse and how the promotion of lies about the Jews and anti-Semitic bombast still gains a following. Like Hitler, Zhirinovsky is a study in contradictions. He claims that American Zionists offered him "$100 million to leave politics," and that only Russia can "save the world from the spread of Islam."[21] Consider this vicious anti-Semitism from a 90-minute interview with *Time* editors in New York City in mid-November 1994:

> It's well known that finance and the press in America—and also in Western Europe and Russia—are controlled by Jews. The very difficult economic situation in Russia was the result of activities by these forces. There is no such thing as a poor Jew in Russia . . . a majority of the people who made the [Bolshevik] Revolution possible, as well as perestroika, were of Jewish origin. In fact, the first Soviet government was almost 90% Jewish. Those who first ran the Gulag prison camps were mostly Jewish. . . .
>
> Certain anti-Semitic sentiments have been created because there are people occupying [prominent positions] who are living much better [than ever before] under the present conditions in Russia. . . . There is a great possibility of a military coup in the next six months, and again, the Jews will have a say in it.[22]

Complacency at Such a Time?

Again we must say, anti-Semitism is neither dead nor will it die. In spite of renewed threats and terrorist activity, however, the guarantees of peace and her new acceptance among the family of nations will have lulled Israel into a sense of complacency even as the nations prepare their attack. Could this really happen? Indeed, it has happened before and without the assurances of peace that Israel will have at that time under Antichrist.

Early in January 1995, the Agranat Commission report was released at last to the public. It contains shocking information about Israeli unpreparedness and incompetency that almost cost the loss of the entire land of Israel during the 1973 Yom Kippur War. Legendary war hero Moshe Dayan, then the defense minister, was described by former president Chaim Herzog as "seemingly paralyzed" during the first days of the war. The report quoted Dayan as saying:

> What I am most afraid of in my heart is that, in the end, the State of Israel will not have enough weapons to defend itself. It doesn't matter where the line is. We won't have enough tanks and planes. Nobody will fight this war for us.[23]

Yet prior to the surprise attack, Israel's military leaders, confident of her superiority, had been convinced that the Arabs wouldn't dare to start a war. Three times—in November 1972, January 1973, and then May 1973—Egypt mobilized troops along the Suez Canal. Each time Major-General Eliahu Zeira, then head of Intelligence, insisted that Cairo was bluffing. That there was no attack on those occasions seemed to vindicate this opinion. So "when Syria mobilized tens of thousands of troops and hundreds of tanks along the Golan Heights in mid-September 1973, Zeira was again certain that President Hafez Assad was merely rattling his saber."[24]

Israeli Defense Forces (IDF) Intelligence reported massive Egyptian troop concentrations along the Suez, along with other convincing evidence that a gigantic coordinated attack was imminent. As if that were not enough proof to at least stir Israel's military into preparedness, reports came of the departure from the Middle East of the families of the thousands of Soviet advisers in Egypt and Syria. The Mossad warned that war was imminent.

Nevertheless, Zeira ignored the warnings and even called the Russian evacuation of families "an exercise"! Looking back now, it seems impossible to comprehend the utterly blind and incompetent complacency at such a time:

> Those in IDF who disagreed with Zeira faced reprisals. Aviezer Ya'ari—then a lieutenant-colonel . . . was twice reprimanded for warning the Northern Command . . . of an impending Syrian attack on the Golan Heights. . . .
> The belief that the Arab states were incapable of war led to a sharp decline in IDF preparedness that proved disastrous when troops finally arrived to repulse the Egyptian and Syrian invasions.[25]

The War to End All Life

The prophets declare that a similar complacency will grip Israel again. Whether Israel is prepared or not this time, however, will make little difference upon the outcome. That great battle will have come at last, about which the prophets have warned: Armageddon! Considering the overwhelming odds against her, there is no way that Israel could possibly win. She will have the capability, however, of causing great destruction to her enemies in defending herself.

According to a report in *Jane's Intelligence Review*, Israel may have as many as 200 nuclear weapons. She will not go down in flames at Armageddon without utilizing her nuclear capabilities. That a nuclear exchange will have begun which could envelop the world seems certain from these words of Christ:

> For then shall be great tribulation, such as was not since the beginning of the world to this time, no, nor ever

shall be. And except those days should be shortened, there should no flesh be saved; but for the elect's [Israel's] sake those days shall be shortened (Matthew 24:21,22).

This prophecy mystified students of Scripture for nearly 2000 years. What manner of making war could possibly destroy all flesh? Such destructive capabilities were unknown until our generation. And we now have not only the hydrogen and neutron bombs, but an array of incredible weapons that could destroy this earth many times over, leaving it drifting through space with not even a cockroach or a microbe alive. Again we see the amazing accuracy of Bible prophecy and the fact that our generation fits the description precisely.

Israel will be up against the military might of all the nations of the world in coordinated assault against her. The situation will be hopeless from the very beginning. Nevertheless, Israel will not surrender. She has sworn, "Never again!" She will use her ultimate weapon in self-defense, and Christ will intervene to prevent a nuclear holocaust.

If the Bible is true—and the course of history in fulfillment of prophecy certainly proves that to be the case—then, as the verses we have quoted declare, God Himself will defend Israel from her enemies. He will not allow her to be destroyed, for that would disprove the Bible and discredit God Himself. Not only the Arabs but all the nations of the world need to be reminded of the fact that "he that toucheth you [Israel] toucheth the apple of his [God's] eye" (Zechariah 2:8).

Comfort ye, comfort ye my people, saith your God. Speak ye comfortably to Jerusalem . . . that her warfare is accomplished . . . her iniquity is pardoned. . . . O Jerusalem . . . be not afraid; say unto the cities of Judah, Behold your God! Behold, the LORD God will come with strong hand. . . .
—Isaiah 40:1,2,9,10

I will pour upon the house of David and upon the inhabitants of Jerusalem the spirit of grace and of supplications; and they shall look upon me whom they have pierced, and they shall mourn for him. . . . And one shall say unto him, What are these wounds in thine hands? Then he shall answer, Those with which I was wounded in the house of my friends.
—Zechariah 12:10; 13:6

Therefore the redeemed of the LORD shall return and come with singing unto Zion, and everlasting joy shall be upon their head; they shall obtain gladness and joy, and sorrow and mourning shall flee away.
—Isaiah 51:11

And the cities shall be inhabited and the wastes shall be built . . . and I will . . . do better unto you than at your beginnings, and ye shall know that I am the LORD.
—Ezekiel 36:8-11

It shall come to pass that he that is left in Zion and he that remaineth in Jerusalem shall be called holy, even every one that is written among the living in Jerusalem.
—Isaiah 4:3

But he that shall endure unto the end, the same shall be saved.
—Matthew 24:13

And so all Israel shall be saved. . . .
—Romans 11:26

21

"All Israel Shall Be Saved"

♦

L isten to the glorious declaration: "Behold, the LORD God will come [to rescue Israel] with strong hand" and "*All Israel shall be saved.*" What a wonderful promise and yet how ominous! God's miraculous intervention will be required to prevent Israel's total destruction! The prophecy of Israel's salvation tells us once again that ultimately all of the peace treaties and solemn pledges of goodwill and recognition of Israel, no matter who signs them, will not be worth the paper on which they have been written.

To create a sense of helpless pessimism is not our intent, but to make an appeal to realism. Nor would we attempt to sabotage the peace process, but only to offer a reminder that God and His Word are being ignored. The world's leaders (and that includes Israel's leaders and the Vatican as well) have chosen to ignore what the prophets have clearly said. And they have made this deliberate choice in spite of the fact that the prophets' declarations are supported by overwhelming evidence and common sense.

On the basis of God's Word and abundant proof that only the willfully blind could fail to see, we must declare again that the so-called "peace process" upon which Israel has embarked can only lead eventually to disaster. Not only prophecy but history can be called upon to support that statement. Today's peace process actually began with the historic peace agreement between Egypt and Israel signed by Anwar Sadat and Menachim Begin in 1977. How genuine was Egypt's desire for a true peace? Actions betray the truth which words on paper are crafted to conceal.

As with the PLO today, which has broken its promise to change the Palestinian Covenant calling for Israel's destruction, so Egypt, when it made "peace" with Israel, never renounced having endorsed that Covenant at Rabat in 1974. And in the 18 years of "peace" since 1977, Egypt has scarcely tried to hide its hostility toward Israel's very existence. In spite of repeated and almost groveling invitations to visit Israel, Egyptian President Mubarak has avoided that simple civility for 17 years.

A Revealing Record

A recent editorial in *The Jerusalem Post International* reminded readers of the long-standing "Moslem-Arab assertion that no Jewish (or indeed Christian) state shall exist in the 'Arab world.'" It went on to point out the following:

> [I]n Egyptian eyes the acquisition of Sinai [by Egypt as part of the "peace treaty"] was the consummation of a phase in the dismantling of Israel. . . . Anwar Sadat (yes, the peacemaker) in a Cairo mosque in 1971, referring to the Jews of Medina, said: "The most splendid thing that the prophet Mohammed did was to drive them out of the whole Arabian peninsula. . . . We shall not give up an inch of our territory. . . . We shall not . . . bargain with them over a single one of the rights of the Palestinian people." [He never retracted such statements.]
> . . . [At] the 1975 symposium of the Egyptian intellectual community . . . Boutros Boutros-Ghali (now secretary-general of the UN) said the Jews must give up their status as a nation and Israel as a state, and [be] assimilate[d] as a community in[to] the Arab world. . . . [Again a statement that was never retracted.]

Remember Sadat's ferocious refusal [after "peace"] to allow a single Jew to remain in Sinai? The failure to implement the various agreements that flowed from the peace treaty?... Egyptian support for anti-Israel UN resolutions—which made nonsense of the Camp David agreement and the peace treaty? The continued and uninterrupted Nazi-style propaganda against Israel and the Jewish people in the controlled Egyptian media?...

President Mubarak... put a plane at the disposal of [and gave refuge to] the murderers of Leon Klinghoffer [wheelchair-bound Jewish hostage, dumped overboard by the hijackers of the ocean liner Achille Lauro[1]].
... Told of the cold-blooded murder of seven Israeli tourists in Sinai, he dismissed the incident as a matter of no importance.[2]

The Palestinians long complained that the Israeli police are brutal in their reaction to threats (of course the terrorists are not). Now that the Palestinians have their own police and are running their own show, the shoe is on the other foot. The New York-based Human Rights Watch has warned that "the failure of the... Palestinian Authority to protect human rights in the Gaza Strip seriously threatens the establishment of a Palestinian democracy and prospects for stable peace in the Middle East." It charged the "peace"-keeping body with "sweeping political arrests, mistreatment of prisoners, censorship of the press and failure to curb abuses of power in Gaza and the West Bank town of Jericho." The group charged that "a Palestinian suspected of collaborating with Israel during its 27-year occupation of the Gaza Strip was tortured to death in July [1994]... and a second died under what appear[ed] to be similar circumstances.

"The 50-page report also assailed the Palestinian police's use of lethal measures to control a Gaza City riot Nov. 18 [1994] in which 13 people were killed. The most troubling problem now, according to the report, is the increasing use of mass political arrests by the Authority in response to continuing attacks by Islamic militants on Israeli soldiers and civilians. The arrests are leading to detention without trial and

408 ♦ "ALL ISRAEL SHALL BE SAVED"

to the beating of prisoners, the group charged. Suicide bombers from the Islamic Resistance Movement, known as Hamas,
and from Islamic Jihad, both of which oppose the self-government agreement the PLO signed with Israel in September
1993, have killed more than 50 Israelis in the last year. Eric
Goldstein, the Middle East research director for Human Rights
Watch, said Arafat's order last week [early February 1995]
setting up a state security court staffed by military personnel,
largely in response to Israeli pressure, is worrisome. It is 'a
denial of basic rights and due process, a rejection of the rule of
law,' he said."[3]

One explanation for such blatant and repeated civil rights
violations may lie in the fact that the Palestinian police are
largely made up of men who have been accustomed to violating
the law and the rights of others in their role as "freedom
fighters" and terrorists. For example, Abu Samahdaneh, who
unabashedly killed an alleged "collaborator" "before news
cameras in the Gaza strip" has been given "a senior post in the
Palestinian Police's security service. Hundreds of jubilant residents" welcomed him to Rafiah after he had slipped through
Israeli surveillance.[4] Or consider Ziad Abu Ain, convicted in a
U.S. court of murdering two 16-year-olds with a terrorist
bomb in Israel (defended unsuccessfully by former U.S.
Attorney-General Ramsey Clark) and extradited to Israel.
Released in the Jibril prisoner exchange, Ziad has been ap-
pointed "comptroller of the Palestinian Authority."[5]

A Glimpse into the Islamic World

While first the PLO, then Jordan and perhaps even Syria,
are engaged in establishing "peace" with Israel, observation
of the remainder of the Arab and Islamic world provides
further evidence that nothing has really changed. Iraq and Iran
certainly have not changed their stance toward Israel. Nor has
the hate-filled rhetoric emanating from mosques throughout
the Islamic world, which continues to call for Jihad against
Israel. The fact is that the battle is not between Arab and Jew
but between Islam and the entire world. Israel happens to be

particularly troublesome because it exists in the very heart of Islamic countries.

To understand what Islam means, one needs to look in upon an Islamic society such as Sudan, where Christians are being literally crucified. Sudan is a closed society, totally controlled by its Islamic regime. From January 23 to February 2, 1995, an American-Dutch human rights investigative group from Puebla Institute and Dorkas Aid International uncovered evidence of an Antichrist-like plot. Children of non-Muslim parents are being kidnapped and taken to "high-security, closed camps in remote areas where they are given new Arabic names, indoctrinated in Islam, and forced to undergo military-style training."[6]

Sold out by his supposed friends and supporters, international terrorist leader Ramirez Sanchez (the infamous Carlos) was captured in Khartoum at the end of August 1994. Syrian President Hafez Assad had offered his head to U.S. President Bill Clinton in exchange for U.S. pressure upon Israel to return the Golan. Seeking revenge against former friends who betrayed him, Carlos told the U.S. about a "hitherto-unknown [Islamic] terrorist unit called Allahu Akhbar (God is great) based in an old fort outside Khartoum." An intelligence expert in Paris commented, "It's no secret that the Sudan, funded by Iran, is today's major center for training Hamas, Hizbullah, Islamic Jihad and Egyptian and Algerian fundamentalist recruits. The most intelligent, versatile and fanatical candidates are selected to join Allahu Akhbar. We suspect that they assassinated Egypt's president Sadat and Bashir Jemayel, the Lebanese Christian leader. They led the group which came close to killing George Bush on a visit to Kuwait after the Gulf War."[7]

We could give many more specific examples, though none should be necessary, to demonstrate that peace treaties will never remove the deep-rooted determination to exterminate Jews and to do away with the Jewish State. Such agreements are only phases on the road to those irreversible goals, phases which are dictated by the strength of Israel's military might.

But one day the armies of the entire world will come against Israel to destroy her. Of that coming day Jeremiah wrote, "Alas! for that day is great, so that none is like it; it is even the time of Jacob's trouble, *but he shall be saved out of it*" (Jeremiah 30:7). In spite of the horrible loss of life, Paul declared that "*all Israel shall be saved*." What did he mean?

Resurrection and Salvation of All?

Some Bible interpreters link this prophecy with the one given in Ezekiel 37:1-14, concerning the valley of dry bones coming "together, bone to his bone . . . the sinews and flesh [coming] upon them . . . the breath [coming] into them, and they lived, and stood up upon their feet . . . the whole house of Israel . . . O my people, I will open your graves, and . . . bring you into the land of Israel." Does this mean, as some believe, that every Jewish person who ever lived, no matter how wicked and rebellious against God (even Korah, whom the earth swallowed alive into hell, or Judas, who betrayed Christ), will be resurrected as a saint to dwell eternally in God's presence?

On the contrary, both Old and New Testaments of the Bible make it clear that there are certain conditions for salvation which must be met in this life or it is forever too late. David wrote, "The wicked shall be turned into hell" (Psalm 9:17) and John tells us that "death and hell" shall be "cast into the lake of fire," called the "second death" (Revelation 20:14), from which there is no return. Jesus repeatedly warned of everlasting punishment in hell (Matthew 25:46; Mark 3:29; 9:43-48; etc.). We are clearly told that "it is appointed unto men once to die, but after this the judgment" (Hebrews 9:27).

Of course, there is the almost mystical and tragically empty comfort that some seek in the face of death, typified in the saying "A thing of beauty is a joy forever." Yes, in a sense the deceased live on in the memories and memorabilia they have left behind. Yet no one would suggest that such memories are the same as the person. The loss which death imposes is real in spite of denials such as that of Rabbi Byron Sherwin, director of Chicago's Center for the Study of Eastern European Jewry.

Sherwin comforts fellow Jews with the philosophy that "there are Jewish spirits in Catholic Poland, made from flakes of black ash, sealed in the silent sky with the tears of lost memories. In Poland, a Jew is never alone. The souls of our ancestors encompass us, welcome us, embrace us." Do they? What does this mean? In fact, the ancestors are dead, as is Poland's once-flourishing Jewish culture. Considering that such empty rhetoric is the only comfort their religious leaders can offer, no wonder the Rabbi admits:

> Jews have grown increasingly "secularized" since the Holocaust, and many have lost sense of their special covenant with God and their ethical mission to the world. Instead, many now identify themselves as part of an ethnic group, and commit themselves only to the survival and strengthening of that group and its national expression—the state of Israel.[8]

Who Is a Jew?

Early in 1995, *Parade* magazine asked students the important question, "Do you believe in God?" The confused response of a Jewish girl reflected the futility of the "faith" offered by such rabbis as Byron Sherwin:

> I'm a practicing Jew. Meaning, I do go to temple a lot, and on holidays it's very important to me to take time out to celebrate. . . . I pray a lot . . . because that's a tradition of the Jewish people. But I'm not really sure who I'm praying to.
> I don't necessarily believe in God right now. I'm more devoted to Judaism as a whole. . . . Judaism promotes the making of my own values.
> I'm still very much confused . . . I guess I am praying to God. Yet I don't really know what God is.[9]

"Praying" to a "God" she doesn't know and isn't even sure exists? Judaism, for her, allows her to make her own values? No wonder Paul wrote, "For they are not all Israel which are of Israel" (Romans 9:6)!

The mere fact that a person is a Jew by birth does not mean that every promise given to Israel applies to him or her. The land of Israel was promised to the descendants of Abraham, Isaac, and Jacob. Yet that promise was denied to the entire generation (except Caleb and Joshua) that came out of Egypt because of their sin and unbelief. Paul explained that "he is not a Jew which is one outwardly, neither is that circumcision which is outward in the flesh; but he is a Jew which is one inwardly, and circumcision is that of the heart, in the spirit" (Romans 2:28,29).

Such Scriptures have caused some Christians today, as we have noted, to claim that the church is Israel and that Christians are the only true Jews because of their spiritual relationship with God through Christ. On this point there is much confusion. Make no mistake, there are those who are *physical* Jews because of a *physical* birth. Paul referred to them as "my kinsmen according to the flesh" (Romans 9:3). These physical descendants of Jacob are God's "chosen people" in a way that no Gentile can ever be. Consequently they have certain promises concerning the land of Israel and the restoration of the kingdom to Israel under the Messiah which apply to them alone and to no others.

These promises require a *physical* relationship to Abraham (thus no Gentile can qualify), but that alone is not enough. There must also be that *spiritual* relationship to the God of Israel which Abraham enjoyed. The absence of that *spiritual* relationship of faith in God and obedience to His commands has robbed generations of *physical* Jews of living under the Messiah in the Promised Land.

Two requirements must be met by those who will live in the land of Israel during the millennial reign of Christ: 1) They must be *physical* Jews, and 2) they must have that *spiritual* relationship to God which Abraham had. What then does it mean that *all* Israel shall be saved? When will this happen? Jesus declared that "he that endureth to the end shall be saved" (Matthew 10:22). The end of what? Saved from what?

Armageddon or Not?

The prophet Zechariah explains that in the midst of Armageddon, when Israel is surrounded by the armed forces of all the nations of the world and about to be destroyed, the Messiah suddenly arrives from heaven to rescue her. There are nailprints in His hands and feet and a spear wound in His side. The greatest outcry of mourning in history breaks out as Israel realizes that for 19 centuries, just as her prophets warned they would, Jews have despised and rejected the very One who died for their sins. Nevertheless, His love for them in spite of their hatred and rejection has brought Him to their rescue. That fact breaks their hearts and brings them to repentance and faith in their Savior. *All* Jews who are alive at that time, upon seeing Him, believe and are saved:

> I will pour upon the house of David and upon the inhabitants of Jerusalem the spirit of grace and of supplications; and they shall look upon me whom they have pierced, and they shall mourn for him as one mourneth for his only son, and shall be in bitterness. . . .
> In that day shall there be a great mourning in Jerusalem . . . and the land shall mourn, every family apart . . . [and] there shall be a fountain opened to the house of David and to the inhabitants of Jerusalem for sin and for uncleanness. . . .
> And the LORD shall be king over all the earth; in that day shall there be one LORD (Zechariah 12:10–13:1; 14:9).

This battle of Armageddon, at which the Lord intervenes to save His people, is described in some detail in Ezekiel 38 and 39. On this point again, however, there is disagreement among students of prophecy. The majority view is that Ezekiel 38 and 39 describe a devastating war that precedes Armageddon by several years and probably precedes even the rapture of Christ's true followers. Numerous books and tapes by Bible teachers specializing in prophecy have been declaring for years that an attack upon Israel by Russia and her Arab allies could come at any moment, leading to World War III and a devastating defeat for Russia in the land of Israel. This war is supposed to be the next event to take place in the Bible's prophetic timetable.

The failure of such interpretations to be realized on schedule has bred increasing skepticism, even in conservative evangelical schools such as Dallas Theological Seminary and Moody Bible Institute. In their forthcoming book, *Doomsday Delusions*, Moody Bible Institute Professors C. Marvin Pate and Calvin B. Haines Jr. argue that "passages in Ezekiel that premillennialists say predict a future Armageddon probably refer to the invasion of Israel by Scythian hordes in pre-Christian times, according to the scholars. Imaginative doomsday preachers ignore this."[10] Unfortunately, the professors also ignore the fact that these prophecies contain elements (as we shall see) which could not possibly have applied in the past but which unmistakably point to a future fulfillment.

Gog and Magog

It is true that there has been some unwarranted speculation and even sensationalism in attempts to apply apocalyptic prophecies. That fact, however, does not warrant throwing these prophecies out, but instead calls for care in interpreting them. Ezekiel 38 and 39 list certain leaders, peoples, and nations that will be involved in the future attack upon Israel. "Persia, Ethiopia, and Libya" are specifically named. Others are not so easily identified: "Gog, the land of Magog... Meshech and Tubal... Gomer, and... Togarmah of the north" (38:5,2,6). Some prophecy writers have allegedly traced these names and peoples to Russia and northern Europeans. It is difficult, however, to verify the accuracy of such claims, and it is not necessary.

There is no reason to believe that Ezekiel's listing is intended to name each and every nation that will be involved in the last-days attack upon Israel. Moreover, we find "Gog and Magog" mentioned again in Revelation 20:8, representing *all nations on earth* coming against Jerusalem and Christ at the end of the millennium. Clearly that final battle is not the one mentioned in Ezekiel 38 and 39. If "Gog and Magog" represent *all nations* in Revelation, then we may assume that the same is true in Ezekiel. There are two battles involving all nations: Armageddon just preceding, and the battle in Revelation 20 at the end of Christ's 1000-year reign. This is only one of several reasons for concluding that Ezekiel 38 and 39 refer to Armageddon and not to some earlier World War III.

Another reason for this conclusion is the personal presence of God at the climax of the battle described in Ezekiel precisely as it will be at Armageddon. It is clearly Yahweh, the God of Israel, speaking to His people through His prophet Zechariah, whom we have quoted at the beginning of the chapter: "They [those in Israel alive at that time] shall look upon me whom they have pierced, and they shall mourn for him as one mourneth for his only son" (Zechariah 12:10). This is an amazing prophecy without parallel in any of the world's religions and which Judaism has never been able to explain satisfactorily. Furthermore, this element of the prophecy clearly did not occur at any time in the past.

The Pierced One Returns

The word "pierced" in Zechariah comes from the Hebrew *dawkar*, which means to thrust through with sword or spear, whereas in Psalm 22:16 the Hebrew *aree* is used: "They pierced my hands and my feet." The Bible thus foretells that the Messiah will be pierced in two ways: the piercing of hands and feet in crucifixion (prophesied centuries before crucifixion was known), and the piercing with sword or spear to the death, which was not normally a part of crucifixion, but which Jesus endured.

A major purpose of crucifixion was to torture the criminal with a slow death. The thrust of a spear would end the torment, so the two types of piercing would rarely, if ever, occur together as they did with Jesus. Once again we see how specific the prophecies were concerning the Messiah and how remarkable their fulfillment was in Christ, leaving no doubt that He is the Messiah of Israel. Wounds in hands and feet could be faked, so the prophet made it clear that the One who will rescue Israel at Armageddon will have a deadly spear wound in his side and will have risen from the dead.

The devout Jew, who waits today for the Messiah, must honestly ask himself when his Messiah was pierced. Likewise, the Jehovah's Witness, who denies that Jesus is God, must ask himself when his Jehovah, who is pure Spirit without a body, was pierced with sword or spear. The One whom Zechariah said will appear at Armageddon to rescue Israel has been pierced to the death and yet is alive. Obviously, the resurrected Messiah did not appear to rescue Israel from invading "Scythian hordes in pre-Christian times" before He had yet been crucified, as the two Moody professors mistakenly suggest!

That this One who is speaking through Zechariah is Yahweh, the God of Abraham, Isaac, and Jacob, is clear. Yet He comes to Israel as a man who was crucified for claiming to be Yahweh and has risen from the dead. The "me" who was pierced and the "him" for whom Israel mourns are clearly one and the same. Jesus said, "I and my Father are one" (John 10:30), not just in work and purpose, as the cults teach, but in essence.

Instead of breaking Jesus' legs, the normal procedure in any crucifixion, a soldier thrust his spear into His side. Why this sudden impulse (which fulfilled a prophecy unknown to this Roman)? Perhaps it was in anger because Jesus was already dead long before He should have been and had therefore not suffered all of the physical pain which that means of death was designed to produce. Pilate, in fact, was astonished that Christ was "already dead" (Mark 15:44). Our redemption came not through the physical suffering but through the deeper agony He endured in payment of the eternal punishment that God's infinite justice demanded for our sin.

Jesus had said, "I lay down my life that I might take it again. No man taketh it from me, but I lay it down of myself. I have power to lay it down and I have power to take it again" (John 10:17,18). The apostle John, who witnessed it all, wrote:

He that saw it bore record, and his record is true
...that ye might believe. For these things were done
that the Scripture [Exodus 12:46; Numbers 9:12; Psalm
34:20] should be fulfilled, "A bone of him shall not be
broken." And again another Scripture [Zechariah 12:10]
saith, "They shall look on him whom they pierced"
(John 19:35-37).

Behold, he cometh with clouds [of saints with Him];
and every eye shall see him, and they also which pierced
him; and all kindreds of the earth shall wail because of
him. Even so. Amen. (Revelation 1:7).

The Biblical Proof

There is no doubt, from both Zechariah 12 and Revelation 1
and 19, that this personal coming of Yahweh to rescue His
people and to destroy Antichrist and his armies takes place at
Armageddon. It is significant, then, that similar language
concerning the personal presence of God is found in Ezekiel 38
and 39, thus identifying the event described there as Armageddon also:

All the men that are upon the face of the earth shall
shake at my presence . . . and I will be known in the eyes
of many nations, and they shall know that I am the LORD
(Ezekiel 38:20,23).

I will set my glory among the heathen [nations], and
all the heathen shall see my judgment that I have executed, and my hand that I have laid upon them (Ezekiel
39:21).

Furthermore, we see striking similarity of language between this passage in Ezekiel and John's description of
Armageddon in Revelation 19:17,18. John writes: "An angel
...cried...to all the fowls that fly.... Come and gather
yourselves together unto the supper of the great God, that ye
may eat the flesh of kings, and the flesh of captains, and the
flesh of mighty men...." Obviously referring to the same
event, the Old Testament prophet wrote:

> Speak unto every feathered fowl...gather your-
> selves on every side to my sacrifice...upon the moun-
> tains of Israel....Ye shall eat the flesh of the mighty,
> and drink the blood of the princes of the earth...ye
> shall be filled at my [supper] table with horses...with
> mighty men and with all men of war, saith the Lord God
> (Ezekiel 39:17-20).

In addition to these descriptive similarities, we have the
conclusive statements concerning the results of this battle
upon Israel and the nations. All Israel, now saved through faith
in her Messiah, will never again be abused by the nations, or
displease God or be forsaken of Him or suffer His judgment;
and the nations at last will have come to know that the God of
Abraham, Isaac, and Jacob, the God of the Bible, is the only
true God.

That transformation, as we have seen, both for Israel and
the world, will not take place until the midst of Armageddon,
when Yahweh intervenes from heaven. Yet Ezekiel 38 and 39
depict this very same salvation for Israel and recognition of the
true God by the nations. Both Zechariah and Ezekiel, then,
must be speaking of the same event, an event which very
clearly is yet future, for nothing of this nature has ever occurred in the past.

Until Christ appears and is recognized by His people, Israel
continues to displease God, to be abused by godless nations
(which all finally attack her at Armageddon) and to suffer
God's judgment. Therefore the following statements could not
possibly refer to a previous war but could only describe the
results of Armageddon upon Israel, preparing her and all
nations for Messiah's millennial reign on the throne of His
father David. Notice the finality of the results, which once
again proves that this prophecy is yet future and in fact can only
be fulfilled at the end of the great tribulation, when Christ
returns to rescue Israel and to establish His millennial kingdom:

> So will I make my holy name known in the midst of
> my people Israel; and I will not let them pollute my holy

name anymore, and the heathen shall know that I am the
LORD, the Holy One in Israel. Behold it is come, and it is
done, saith the Lord God; this is the day whereof I have
spoken. . . .

So the house of Israel shall know that I am the LORD
their God from that day and forward. And the heathen
shall know that the house of Israel went into captivity for
their iniquity. . . .

Then shall they [Israel] know that I am the LORD their
God, which caused them to be led into captivity among
the heathen; but I have gathered them unto their own
land, and have left none of them anymore there.

Neither will I hide my face anymore from them, for I
have poured out my Spirit upon the house of Israel, saith
the Lord God (Ezekiel 39:7,8,22,23,28,29).

This pouring out of God's Spirit upon Israel clearly does not
take place until God rescues His people at Armageddon, as
Zechariah 12:10-13:1 tells us. And that it is the God of Israel
Himself who rescues her is specified again for us: "Then shall
the LORD [Yahweh] go forth and fight against those nations
[attacking Israel], as when he fought in the day of battle. And
his feet shall stand in that day upon the Mount of Olives, which
is before Jerusalem" (Zechariah 14:3,4). Another event which
certainly has not happened as yet, but will.

Disillusionment and Skepticism

Obviously, this prophecy could not have been fulfilled until
Israel had come back into her land. Naturally, then, when the
nation Israel came into being again after 1900 years of dis-
persal, there was great excitement among Christians and great
expectation. *U.S. News & World Report* recently focused upon
the world's leading evangelist to remind us how that excitement has died down:

When the United Nations created Israel, premillennialists exulted that the final countdown had begun. In
1950, a youthfully exuberant Billy Graham told a rally in
Los Angeles, "Two years and it's all going to be over."

Since then Graham has become more cautious regarding apocalyptic timetables.[11]

There was no biblical justification for the designation of "two years." Such unwarranted expectations only breed embarrassment and new predictions. In spite of the delay of more than 47 years since Israel's rebirth, there is a growing conviction on the part of a high percentage of people among not only evangelical Christians but the general populace that the end of the world is coming, and perhaps rather soon. According to a recent Market Facts, Inc. poll, nearly 60 percent of Americans think the world will end sometime in the future and almost a third of those think it will end within a few decades. More than 61 percent say they believe in the second coming of Christ and 49 percent believe that a literal Antichrist will arise.[12]

Of course, opinions do not establish truth, since one-third of all Americans doubt there was a Holocaust.[13] There is considerable skepticism as well that an Antichrist figure could arise and that people would worship him. After all, it was 50 years ago that the world was deceived by Hitler. Surely the average citizen is far too sophisticated to be so easily hoodwinked today. Yet we could give many examples from the present. Consider once more Vladimir Zhirinovsky, who captured 25 percent of Russia's vote. His popularity only increased when he said:

> I will say it quite plainly. When I come to power, there will be a dictatorship. . . . I may have to shoot 100,000 people, but the other 300 million will live peacefully.[14]

U.S. News & World Report reported recently, "In almost every generation, Christians have tried to identify the Antichrist from among their contemporary enemies, from the murderous Roman emperor Nero in the first century to Napoleon Bonaparte, Benito Mussolini and Saddam Hussein. More recently some Christians even suspected Ronald Wilson Reagan, in part because each of his names has six letters.

...Professors at such bastions of premillennialism as Dallas Theological Seminary, Moody Bible Institute in Chicago and Wheaton College in Wheaton, Ill., recently have raised strong objections to the literal interpretation of some apocalyptic texts and to the intense search for 'signs of the times' in current events."[15] Yet prophecy is all about coming events!

God Has Spoken Through His Prophets

Pate and Haines argue that "premillennial doomsday preachers often 'misinterpret and misapply' biblical prophecies by ignoring their historical context. . . . The Antichrist in Revelation, for example, says Pate, was no doubt 'intended to signify Nero,' a persecutor of Christians who committed suicide by falling on a sword."[16] On the contrary, the prophecies about the Antichrist specify, as we have seen, definite acts on his part which neither Nero nor any other figure from the past fulfilled: affirming a covenant regarding Israel for seven years, breaking that covenant halfway through that period, setting up in the Temple an image that speaks, a "666 mark" of some kind in hand or forehead without which no one could buy or sell, etc. The suggestion by Pate and Haines is tantamount to denying the inspiration of the Bible, for if John meant Nero, or any other past figure, then he was badly mistaken.

Apparently blind to the full consequences of their skepticism, professors at such bastions of evangelicalism as Wheaton College are joining the ranks of those who reject prophecy as a literal foretelling of events for the last days. *U.S. News* goes on to report that "even at Jerry Falwell's fundamentalist Liberty University in Lynchburg, VA, New Testament Prof. D. Brent Sandy challenges the notion that details of future events can be extracted from the Bible. Prophecy's primary purpose, Sandy writes in the evangelical journal *Christianity Today*, is simply 'to assure readers that God is going to accomplish his plans in unique and amazing ways.' "[17]

What is truly amazing is that such a preposterous contradiction of both the Bible and common sense could be seriously stated by a university professor and then be repeated in *Christianity Today*. How symbolic stories of fictitious events that pretend to foretell the future but never come to pass could "assure readers that God is going to accomplish his plans in unique and amazing ways" is not explained! On the contrary, faith would be destroyed by such means. Furthermore, the Bible is full of specific prophecies concerning future events which *have* come to pass (those concerning Israel, for example, which we have documented), a fact which distinguishes it from all other religious writings. As we have seen, prophecy fulfilled is the major theme of the Bible and the most powerful and effective means which God uses to prove His own existence.

The undeniable fact is that the Bible does warn about Antichrist, and it does give specific prophecies for the last days, some of which have been fulfilled without doubt, while others will yet be fulfilled. Israel's prophets accurately foretold her history and her return to her land in the last days. They warned that Armageddon's destruction is coming. But all of Israel that is alive when Christ returns will see Him for themselves and believe in this pierced and resurrected One and "will be saved."

A poll of 1,000 American adults conducted Dec. 2-4, 1994 revealed that 59% of Americans believe the world will come to an end; 60% believe the Bible should be taken literally when it speaks of a final Judgment Day, 49% when it speaks of the Antichrist, 44% when it speaks of the battle of Armageddon and the Rapture of the church; while a surprising 53% believe that "some world events this century fulfill biblical prophecy." Yet of the latter group, only 6% see the establishment of Israel as a fulfillment of Bible prophecy! [1]

Say unto my servant David, Thus saith the LORD of hosts . . . I will set up thy seed [the Messiah] after thee . . . and I will stablish the throne of his kingdom forever.
—2 Samuel 7:8,12,13

Of the increase of his [Messiah's] government and peace there shall be no end, upon the throne of David and upon his kingdom, to order it and to establish it with judgment and with justice from henceforth even forever. The zeal of the LORD of hosts will perform this.
—Isaiah 9:7

Behold I have taken out of thine hand the cup of trembling, even the dregs of the cup of my fury; thou shalt no more drink it again. . . .

Awake, awake; put on thy strength, O Zion; put on thy beautiful garments, O Jerusalem, the holy city; for henceforth there shall no more come into thee the uncircumcised and the unclean.
—Isaiah 51:22; 52:1

I saw a new heaven and a new earth; for the first heaven and the first earth were passed away. . . . And I John saw the holy city, new Jerusalem, coming down from God out of heaven, prepared as a bride adorned for her husband.
—Revelation 21:1,2

22

The New Jerusalem

---◆---

A new Jerusalem, on a new earth, inhabited by new people, in a new universe! That is God's promise! Furthermore, He has solemnly and repeatedly declared through His prophets that He will Himself see to it that this glorious finale is accomplished. Is this necessary? Indeed it is. That nothing less than God's direct intervention could solve today's Middle East crisis ought to be quite clear by now. One need only have a nodding acquaintance with world history to be convinced of that fact. The Arab-Israeli conflict is but a reflexion of the constant strife endemic to human nature and which has prevailed throughout the world at all times. How astonishing, then, that world leaders continue to pursue the vain hope of themselves establishing a peace upon earth that has eluded mankind for all its thousands of years of history!

On February 23, 1995, Elie Wiesel, winner of the 1986 Nobel Peace Prize, told an appreciative and apparently convinced "standing room only" audience at the University of Houston that "only education offers hope that [the Holocaust] will not happen again."[2] Really? Was it lack of education that caused the German people to follow Hitler? Germany was the most highly educated nation in the world in the 1930s and yet it produced the Holocaust. It has never been shown that education makes anyone more loving and kind or less selfish or delivers anyone from anti-Semitism.

Perhaps by "education" Wiesel means a knowledge and understanding of the true facts. But who knew the facts better than the very Nazis who tortured and killed and fed the flames with Jews? They didn't need a Yad Vashem memorial to tell them what was happening. Nor do the Islamic or Jewish terrorists need anyone to point out to them what they are doing. They know it very well.

Prevention of evil is not a matter of *education* but of *conscience* and the moral integrity to heed it. And from whence does conscience come? It may be warped or dulled or perverted by parental upbringing or by education, but it is not created by such circumstances. In all cultures there is a consistency in the recognition of basic right and wrong. Conscience is implanted in every human being by God just as He has built individual instinct into each species of animals.

Animals automatically follow their instincts, but mankind is free to reject conscience, and does so. Of course, there is always a "good" reason. One can allow a seemingly just *cause,* such as Zionism or anti-Zionism, "black power" or "white power," or some other passion, to override conscience. In the final analysis, however, it is the basic selfishness within the human heart that lies at the root of all of the world's troubles. To put the blame elsewhere is to blind ourselves to the painful truth.

Facing the Truth

The problem is not white oppression of blacks, as so many in the United States attempt to persuade us. Look at what blacks do to blacks in Africa: the despicable slaughter of Hutus by Tutsis and Tutsis by Hutus in Rwanda, for example; or look at what the Zulus and Mandela's African National Congress have done to each other in South Africa. Blacks were selling blacks into slavery, fighting wars with blacks and torturing and killing blacks long before the white man ever set foot on the

African continent. Blacks by the thousands, among them a number of leading sports figures, are converting to Islam in the West as though it were a black man's religion, apparently forgetting that it was the Arabs of North Africa, good Muslims, who were the first traders to export slaves from Africa.

Look at the history of the world. Whites tortured and killed and fought wars against whites long before they had any contact with blacks, and internal violence is prevalent in all cultures and nations. Certainly America is proof of that fact. Nor is the problem in the Middle East to be explained as Jew against Arab. One need only look at the Iran-Iraq war or the recent Gulf War to see what Arabs do to Arabs and Muslims to Muslims. Neither is it helpful for Israel to boast that it has tortured and killed less and has been provoked more than its Arab neighbors. There are evils on both sides. As these lines are being written, a news dispatch has just come across the wire:

> An Islamic militant died today after an interrogation by Israeli security agents, and human rights organizations and relatives contend he was tortured to death. Abdel-Samad Hassan Harizat, 30, was hospitalized at Jerusalem's Hadassah Hospital on Saturday, a day after he was detained by Shin Bet security agents, his family said. He was unconscious and in serious condition, and died in intensive care early today, hospital spokeswoman Eilat Tal said.[3]

Two days later, Israeli media confirmed that Harizat was "tortured to death . . . by five Palestinian collaborators who acted under orders from interrogators of the Sin Bet secret police."[4] Man is against man because he is against himself; and he is against himself because he has rebelled against the God who created him. Inspired of God, the Hebrew prophets said it so well—and one will find nothing like this in the Koran or in the sayings of Buddha or Confucius or in the sacred writings of any other religion:

> The [human] heart is deceitful above all things, and desperately wicked; who can know it? I the LORD search

the heart, I try the reins [secret thoughts], even to give every man according to his ways (Jeremiah 17:9,10).

Behold, the LORD's hand is not shortened that it cannot save, neither his ear heavy that it cannot hear; but your iniquities have separated between you and your God, and your sins have hid his face from you, that he will not hear.

For your hands are defiled with blood, and your fingers with iniquity; your lips have spoken lies, your tongue hath muttered perverseness. None calleth for justice, nor any pleadeth for truth; they trust in vanity and speak lies; they conceive mischief and bring forth iniquity. . . .

Their feet run to evil, and they make haste to shed innocent blood; their thoughts are thoughts of iniquity; wasting and destruction are in their paths. The way of peace they know not, and there is no judgment [against evil] in their goings; they have made them crooked paths; whosoever goeth therein shall not know peace. . . .

In transgressing and lying against the LORD, and departing away from our God, speaking oppression and revolt, conceiving and uttering from the heart words of falsehood. And judgment is turned away backward, and justice standeth afar off; for truth is fallen in the street, and equity cannot enter. Yea, truth faileth . . . (Isaiah 59:1-15).

The wicked are like the troubled sea, when it cannot rest, whose waters cast up mire and dirt. There is no peace, saith my God, to the wicked (Isaiah 57:20,21).

So Many Rationalizations

April 12, 1995, was a historic day for Israel. It saw the successful launching of Israel's first operational spy satellite, Ofek-3. Reportedly capable of reading license plates in Baghdad, the satellite is designed to supply Israel with vital military intelligence for defense purposes.[5] So it goes, a technological race to keep ahead of enemies, at best a temporary prevention of war or a defense in the midst of it, but not the sure path to lasting peace.

The present "peace process" does not even begin to lead in
the right direction. So far it has only increased terrorism.
Responding to criticism to that effect, Shimon Peres told the
Knesset early in April 1995 that the "peace process is to
prevent war, not stop terror" and to preserve the "moral
character" of the Jewish people. "We will make Israel an
island of peace, of truth, of the moral heritage of the Jewish
people," he added. "The Jewish people never believed in
might, but in spirit. But we have the might to maintain the
spirit."[6] What a contradiction!

An *"island"* of peace? Not likely! It is simply more rhetoric
to shore up the walls of self-delusion—to pretend, to hope, but
ultimately in vain. "Might" makes right? That sounds like
Hitler. Israeli "might" may be sufficient to "maintain the
spirit" in the face of threats from her Arab neighbors, but not
enough to stand up to the entire world when that time comes.
And that time will come. The Hebrew prophets have foretold it
and they have never been wrong. Is it not prudent to give heed?

Yet there are so many rationalizations. If only this were
tried or that had been done or not done. The latest is to imagine
that if only Arafat were replaced all would be well. Arab heads
of state visiting Washington recently have reportedly "encouraged the Clinton Administration to dump Yasser Arafat and
support Mahmoud Abbas as the new chairman of the PLO
. . . [because] Arafat has proven to be incapable of transforming himself from a revolutionary into a statesman. . . ."[7]

Does it really matter who heads the PLO? Can the right man
at the helm of that supposedly reformed terrorist organization
be the key to peace? As evil as Arafat has proven himself to be,
his heart only reflects that of every Jew and Arab—indeed, of
all mankind. Solomon, whose heart also was not perfect, said
it so well for all of us, under the inspiration of God:

> As in water face [reflects] . . . face, so the heart of
> man [reflects the heart of] . . . man (Proverbs 27:19).

The world rejoiced that Russia and the United States had
embarked upon a new relationship of mutual trust and, as a

consequence, nuclear arsenals would be shrinking. In the meantime, nuclear capabilities are spreading to fanatical Islamic regimes such as Iraq and Iran and thus to the terrorists whom they sponsor. Between May and August of 1994, German police made four seizures of "smuggled weapons-grade plutonium 239 . . . [and] the threat of nuclear terrorism has entered an alarming phase."[8] *Time* reported that "the first symptoms of the nuclear plague are spreading into Europe. . . . The biggest haul [of smuggled bomb-grade material] came on August 10 [1994], when Lufthansa Flight 3369 from Moscow landed in Munich with 350 grams of [illicit] atomic fuel aboard."[9] What about the smugglers who are not detected?

Many put their hope for ultimate peace in a strong international "United Nations peacekeeping force." Unfortunately, we have more than enough examples of the failure of such forces around the world to prove the inadequacy of such a solution. Even Mikhail Gorbachev admits that peace and social harmony between Palestinians and Israelis "would have to be founded on the spirit of Jesus."[10] That sounds encouraging until one remembers that he has claimed that Communists "promote the cause of Christ."[11] It sounds as though he never read the Bible. Certainly he knows nothing of the biblical Christ.

Betting on a Dead Horse

The Bible presents the only basis for world peace. It must be in concert with righteousness: "Righteousness and peace have kissed each other" (Psalm 85:10); "the kingdom of God is . . . righteousness and peace and joy in the Holy Spirit" (Romans 14:17). True worldwide peace can only be established by "the God of peace" (Romans 15:33; 16:20; 1 Thessalonians 5:23; Hebrews 13:20; etc.) through the transforming power of the "gospel of peace" (Romans 10:15). In no other way can sinful mankind be reconciled to God—and without that reconciliation there can be no genuine peace in one's heart or in the world.

Suppose a person goes to the racetrack daily and every time bets on the same old nag that can hardly stagger out of the starting gate and always finishes last. One could logically conclude that his attachment to that horse far exceeded his common sense. Then what must be said of those who, in spite of the record of thousands of years of man's failure to eliminate war, continue to bet that mankind will somehow solve his problems and bring peace to this planet? That horse is *dead!*

Obviously we need help from outside this world. Like Hafez Assad, many people hope for that help from extraterrestrial intelligences. In the meantime, of course, Assad is not sitting around and waiting for ETIs to arrive. He is taking matters into his own hands. As an editorial in *The Jerusalem Post* recently reminded its readers:

> [Syria] has been arming itself feverishly. Its army, air force and missile force are larger than Israel's. And it has developed an impressive arsenal of chemical and biological weapons.
>
> To assume that the nuclear force allegedly possessed by Israel can serve as a deterrent to Syrian ambitions, particularly when Syria's ally Iran joins the nuclear club, is to indulge in the kind of wishful thinking no responsible leadership can permit itself.[12]

Rabin probably won the election by promising, in June of 1992, that he would never give the strategically essential Golan back to Syria. Now, however, Foreign Minister Shimon Peres declares that "there is not the remotest chance of signing a peace treaty with Syria without leaving the Golan." And that a peace treaty with Syria would be worthless when Syria decided to attack is plain enough from the fact that whenever it has suited him Assad has broken numerous treaties with other Arab states and with Turkey. Nothing has changed.

A Tale of Two Cities

The animosity of the Arabs and their contention that Israel occupies land which belongs to them is clear enough. But there is another, more sinister, rivalry which remains largely behind the scenes, and it hides beneath the veneer of religious zeal.

We refer, of course, to the age-old conflict between Rome and Jerusalem, a conflict which is destined to play an important role in the most destructive war the world has ever seen.

Rome's presumption to replace Jerusalem, and the Catholic Church's claim to be the true Israel, explain the attitude which that Church has maintained toward Israel and Jerusalem through the centuries: the Crusades to take the Holy Land for the Church, the slaughter of Jews periodically throughout history, the Vatican's refusal to admit Israel's right to exist for 46 years after her birth in 1948, the duplicity of the Vatican's interest now, and its continued insistence that Jerusalem be under non-Jewish control.

Catholic Rome claims to be the "Eternal City," the "Holy City," and even "Zion," titles which the Bible has given to Jerusalem alone. Rome also claims to be the "New Jerusalem," putting her in direct conflict with God's promises concerning the true City of David. The Vatican claims to be the headquarters of God's kingdom and to be guided by popes who are God's true representatives on earth. A popular pictorial history of Rome is titled *Rome Eternal*. It presents in text and pictures the "significance of Rome and the Papacy in the history of Christianity and Western civilization," giving it credit for the key role,[13] as though there were something about which to feel justly proud.

With astonishing accuracy, the Bible does not single out Damascus or Cairo, London or Paris, Washington D.C. or Moscow as the centers of action in the last days. It points to two other specific cities: Jerusalem and Rome. They are diverse, have been enemies since the days of the Caesars, and, remarkably, are still rivals today for spiritual supremacy and for the religious devotion, loyalty, and affection of the world.

There have been 2000 years of tension and antagonism between both pagan and "Christian" Rome and Jerusalem. That animosity has not been erased by the recent overtures which the Vatican has found it expedient to make toward Israel. The past supposedly forgiven and forgotten, Israel sent its first envoy to the Vatican in September 1994. Ambassador

Shmuel Hadas was received by the Pope in a ceremony "formally completing the historic establishment of ties between the Holy See and the Jewish state."[14]

A New Relationship at Last?

Why has Rome finally established diplomatic relations with Israel? She wants to influence the future of Jerusalem, which she still insists must not be the capital of Israel or under its control. The Vatican's excuse for this incredible denial of Jerusalem to Israel is that the "holy places" in Jerusalem are so important to Muslims and Christians that freedom of access to these shrines must be guaranteed to the followers of these religions—and presumably only an international body can do so.

The insincerity of the argument is easily proven. Jordanian forces occupied Jerusalem from 1948 to 1967. Under their control Jewish synagogues were destroyed, Jewish holy places were desecrated, and Jews were denied access to eastern Jerusalem. At no time during this period did the Vatican call for international control over Jerusalem. Since Israel took the Old City of Jerusalem in 1967, Christians and Muslims have been guaranteed free access to their holy places and Arabs have been given control of Temple Mount. Yet strangely enough, the Vatican now calls for international guarantees of access to Jerusalem.

Clearly the issue is not free access to the holy places, but the fact that Israel's possession of Jerusalem directly challenges the Vatican's claim of 1500 years' duration that Rome had replaced Jerusalem as the Holy City, the Eternal City, the City of God, earth's true spiritual center. Recently the Vatican has seemed to drop its demands for internationalization of Jerusalem and is supporting the PLO's claim upon that Holy City as the capital of the Palestinian state. That would still leave Israel without the exclusive rights to Jerusalem and would seem to legitimize the claim that Rome has replaced Jerusalem as the spiritual center of the world.

Two Unashamed Whores

Both Jerusalem and Rome have been accused by God of spiritual adultery. Of Jerusalem God said, "How is the faithful city become a harlot!" (Isaiah 1:21). Israel, whom God had set apart from all other peoples to be holy for His purposes, had entered into unholy, adulterous alliances with the idol-worshiping nations about her. She had "committed adultery with stones and with stocks [idols]" (Jeremiah 3:9); "and with their idols have they committed adultery" (Ezekiel 23:37).

Catholic Rome, too, is accused of spiritual immorality. She is the "great whore" riding the beast in Revelation 17, "with whom the kings of the earth have committed fornication" and "the inhabitants of the earth have been made drunk with the wine of her fornication" (verse 2). She claims to be the headquarters of the true church, the bride of Christ, whose kingdom is in heaven; but she, like Jerusalem (which continues its adultery today), has been in unholy alliances with godless nations in her attempt to build an earthly kingdom.

Both Jerusalem and Rome will come in for their share of God's judgment. (Yes, and Damascus and Cairo and all the rest of the world will pay dearly as well for their rebellion against God.) It requires little more than casual attention to the daily news to recognize the accuracy of such ancient prophecies. The falsity of Rome's claim to be the "Eternal City" will be proven with its horrible destruction foretold in Revelation 17 and 18.

Everyone Has Designs

Strange as it may seem, Jerusalem's ultraorthodox Jews, of which there are about 130,000 today, are also opposed to Jerusalem as the capital of Israel. These anti-Zionists, as they are sometimes called, consider the present State of Israel to be a counterfeit established contrary to God's will. They believe that only the Messiah can establish true Israel and that He has not yet come. If they should join with the Palestinian residents of Jerusalem, these two factions could well take over that divided city.

The Protestants, too, want to take Jerusalem out of Jewish hands. The World Council of Churches, a body which represents thousands of Protestant congregations worldwide (about 80 percent of all Christian churches), is the ally of the Roman Catholic Church in the battle for Jerusalem. The WCC opposes Israeli adoption of Jerusalem as its capital, claiming that such action "dangerously undermines all efforts towards the just solution of the Middle East problem and thus jeopardizes regional and world peace."[15] This astonishing opinion was expressed in the "Statement on Jerusalem" adopted in the WCC's August 1980 meeting, which also included the following:

> The Central Committee reiterates the statement on Jerusalem issued by the WCC Assembly in Nairobi, 1975, which stressed that the . . . destiny of Jerusalem should be viewed in terms of . . . Christians as well as Jews and Muslims and . . . considered [as] part of the destiny of the Palestinian people . . . within the general context of the settlement of the Middle East conflict in its totality.
>
> The Central Committee calls the member churches to exert through their respective governments all pressure on Israel to withhold all action on Jerusalem . . . [and] urges the WCC to undertake an active role in expressing the concerted Christian voice and to aid churches in fully assuming their role as partners in deciding the future character of Jerusalem.
>
> The Central Committee also urges the general secretary to explore, in consultation with member churches in the area and the Vatican, possibilities of trying to find the best solution to the problem of Jerusalem through all appropriate and effective means and ways such as convening . . . international consultations . . . on Jerusalem.[16]

Catholics, Protestants, and Muslims are not the only ones with designs on Jerusalem. The entire religious world is obsessed with the Holy City, but so is secular political leadership. How remarkable it is that this small, seemingly insignificant ancient city has taken center stage in the modern world, precisely as the prophets foretold! With no regard to Scripture, even the United Nations recognizes that Jerusalem holds the key to peace. Indeed, for 4000 years this village, then town, then small city has carried the name that means "City of Peace." One might pass this fact off as a coincidence were it not for the many fulfilled prophecies concerning Jerusalem which testify to the unique place it holds in God's plans for the world.

God Has Plans Too

Those plans have the Messiah reigning over His people Israel and the entire world from David's throne in Jerusalem. We have already noted that merely being a physical descendant of Abraham, Isaac, and Jacob will not qualify one to be a citizen of that kingdom. Here again there is confusion as to who will be living on earth during the millennial reign of Christ.

Before the cross, mankind was divided into two groups: Jews and Gentiles. Since the cross, there are three divisions: Jews, Gentiles, and the church (1 Corinthians 10:32). God's plan for each is distinctly different. That third entity, the church, is comprised of both Jews and Gentiles:

> Now in Christ Jesus ye [Gentiles] who sometimes were far off are made nigh by the blood of Christ. For he [Christ] is our peace, who hath made both [Jews and Gentiles] one, and hath broken down the middle wall of partition [between them], having abolished in his [crucified] flesh the enmity, even the law of commandments . . . for to make in himself of two [Jew and Gentile] one new man, so making peace; and that he might reconcile both unto God in one body by the cross, having slain the enmity thereby, and came and preached peace to you [Gentiles] which were afar off and to them [Jews] that were nigh. For through him we both [Jew and Gentile] have access by one Spirit unto the Father (Ephesians 2:13-18).

All who repent of their sins and believe in Christ as the Savior who paid the penalty they deserve are graciously forgiven by God and given eternal life as a free gift. Those who, whether Jew or Gentile, come to faith in Christ before Armageddon are in the church and will reign in their glorified bodies with Christ over this world during His thousand-year millennial kingdom. Those who do not believe on Christ until He intervenes from heaven at Armageddon, but who believe then, will live in their physical bodies upon earth during the millennium. If they are Jews, they will live in Israel; if Gentiles, they will make up the nations that survive around the world.

Zechariah 12-14 ("They shall look upon me whom they have pierced, and they shall mourn . . .") is referring strictly to the Jews alive at that time. Other Scriptures, however, indicate that Gentiles, too, around the world, will witness Christ's miraculous intervention at Armgeddon and will believe: "Behold, he [Christ] cometh . . . every eye [Jew and Gentile] shall see him, and they also which pierced him [Jews]; and all kindreds of the earth [Jew and Gentile] shall wail because of him" (Revelation 1:7).

The mourning equates with repentance and salvation in Zechariah 12-14 and no doubt signifies the same in Revelation. We may thus assume that Gentiles will also be saved at that time. These are seen living upon earth, with access to the New Jerusalem, in the eternal state of the new heavens and earth:

> The nations of them which are saved shall walk in the
> light of it [the New Jerusalem]; and the kings of the earth
> do bring their glory and honor into it (Revelation 21:24).

The PLO's Partnership in "Peace"

The peace of Jerusalem is the key to peace for the world. How much more evidence is needed until the whole world admits that it cannot make that peace through "peace treaties" conceived in its own wisdom and guaranteed by its own integrity and strength? The so-called peace between Israel and the PLO has been in force (on paper) for many months, yet the situation is worse now than before. Terrorist attacks against Israel have only increased and there are no signs of a real peace anywhere in sight.

Having been given self-rule over the West Bank, "the PLO has been exerting its unfettered energies in . . . the establishment of a reign of terror, a police state . . . [and] Fatah hawks [Arafat's own faction in the PLO] have killed dozens of 'collaborators' . . . Arafat banned two newspapers that failed to praise him enthusiastically enough. . . . The emergence of this police state [increases] the threat on Israel's borders, and [makes] the danger of aggression from a Palestinian state in alliance with other dictatorships almost inevitable."[17]

All of the efforts toward peace have only proven the hopelessness of such efforts. Here was a summary of the situation in early April 1995, by an Israeli member of the Knesset who suggests that "awarding the Nobel Peace Prize to Yitzhak Rabin, Shimon Peres and their partner Yasser Arafat was a farce":

> The Oslo agreement is being realized in accordance with our most severe predictions, and . . . darkest fears. Reality has cruelly shattered all assumptions underlying the agreements with the PLO. . . . Mr. Rabin complained to Vice President Gore that the Israelis are accusing him of promising peace, and yet there is still terror. . . .
>
> They also remind the premier of other promises: that the Palestinian Covenant would be abolished (the PLO brought out a new edition last month); that the Arab boycott against Israel would be rescinded (last week the Arab League decided it would continue); and that the issue of Jerusalem would be deferred (the PLO is merrily building its governmental institutions in Jerusalem). . . .
>
> In the Gaza and Jericho areas, Hamas enjoys freedom of action, both in recruiting people and training them. Palestinian Authority activity against this organization is minimal. . . . [Palestinian police won't risk "civil war" by using their authority and arms against Hamas, but will try to "persuade them" to behave.[18]

We were told that Hamas itself would keep the Gaza area quiet, as it would be interested in proving that terror

exists only where Arab rule hasn't yet been established.
However, almost no day passes without a terrorist attack
in the Gaza area. . . .

Even Minister Yossi Sarid [champion of the Palestinian state], confessed in an interview last week that it
would be "impossible to assure the cessation of terror
after the establishment of the Palestinian state."

The debacle of the Gaza-Jericho experiment proves
that extending it to Judea and Samaria can only assure
increased terror. And the premier will be in no position to
claim he didn't know.[19]

This rocky and perilous road, as we have seen from Bible
prophecy, will eventually lead to what will pass for "peace."
The world will boast in "peace and safety" (1 Thessalonians
5:3) and under Antichrist it will seem secure for a time. Then
will come the worst destruction this world has ever known or
could ever know. Still, the world will continue to pursue this
proud delusion.

Misunderstandings Among Christians

Christians in increasing numbers seem to be embracing a
false idea of the peace that Christ will bring to this world and
how it will be accomplished. Trinity Broadcasting Network,
the largest Christian television network in the world, with over
450 stations, has tried unsuccessfully for years to get permission for a TV station in the Middle East. Even after assuring
Israeli leaders and Anwar Sadat that there "would be no
proselytizing" (in spite of Christ's command to "go into all the
world and make disciples"), the request was turned down.

Now Paul Crouch, TBN's head, declares enthusiastically
that he has received PLO leader Yasser Arafat's permission to
build a TV station "to cover the entire Middle East from the
Palestinian territory known as the Westbank!"[20] Reporting on
that meeting with Arafat and "a number of other leaders in the
Palestinian Movement," Crouch writes:

Praise God, there will be peace in the Middle East
according to the Word of God. He loves the Arab and the

Jew equally. He has a blessed plan for both and we are on our way to the Promised Land! . . . Praise the Lord! Peace is coming to the Holy Land and perhaps we may be a small part in seeing it become a blessed reality![21]

How amazing that a Christian leader could become so excited about an alleged "peace" being engineered between a Muslim terrorist organization and an unbelieving Israeli leadership that is disobeying God in bartering land He gave to Israel and which was never to be given up! That Crouch could ever equate this ungodly arrangement with the peace that has been promised in the Bible for Israel under her Messiah shows how far many Christians have departed from what the biblical prophets have so plainly declared. Worst of all is the fact that this delusion is being spread to the millions who regularly watch TBN around the world. One Christian newsletter made this comment:

> While Saudi-Arabia would hang Paul Crouch if he ever dared to speak about Christ in that country and while in Fundamentalist Muslim Sudan . . . Christians are being murdered for their faith and no Christian is safe in Iran and in various other lesser known regions of the world under the control of Islam, Arafat will honor his word to allow the "gospel" to be preached over the radio waves emanating from his territory?
>
> May we suggest . . . that because as a good Muslim, who is according to the Koran not bound to keep his word with an "infidel," Arafat will welcome the station built with Christian money, then create legislation allowing only religious programs . . . promoting the PLO view condemning Israel for its stand on Jerusalem![22]

In contrast to all the schemes of mankind, which are doomed to fail, the Bible says that Jesus Himself must return to this planet—not this time as a Lamb to be crucified but in power and glory to establish His kingdom. And He will indeed do so, but for a different purpose from that which most people imagine.

Answering an Age-Old Complaint

Many people complain that it isn't fair that all the descendants of Adam and Eve should reap the consequences of this guilty pair's sin. After all, it is argued, who can say that the rest of us, had we been in the Garden of Eden, would have disobeyed God? That question will be answered for all eternity by the millennium.

During Christ's thousand-year reign the whole earth will once again be an Edenic paradise. Better yet, Satan will be locked up to free earth's inhabitants from his evil influence. Christ will rule with a "rod of iron" (Psalm 2:9; Revelation 2:27; 12:5; 19:15), thus enforcing His laws. No temptations will be allowed to flourish and the slightest crime will be punished swiftly. Moreover, the saints in their resurrected bodies reigning with Christ will be proof of the salvation that Christ offers. Jerusalem will be a place of joy, the center of both the world and the universe:

> It shall come to pass in the last days that the mountain of the LORD's house shall be established . . . and all nations shall flow unto it . . . for out of Zion shall go forth the law, and the word of the LORD from Jerusalem.
> And he shall judge among the nations . . . and they shall beat their swords into plowshares and their spears into pruninghooks; nation shall not lift up sword against nation, neither shall they learn war anymore (Isaiah 2:2-4).

> And it shall come to pass that everyone that is left of all the nations which came against Jerusalem [at Armageddon] shall even go up from year to year to worship the King, the LORD of hosts. . . . And the LORD shall be king over all the earth; in that day shall there be one LORD, and his name one (Zechariah 14:16,9).

> And he [an angel] laid hold on the dragon, that old serpent, which is the Devil, and Satan, and bound him a thousand years . . . that he should deceive the nations no more till the thousand years should be fulfilled (Revelation 20:2,3).

Even with all of these advantages, however, the human heart will not have changed. Those alive on earth will prove themselves the children of Adam and Eve by rebelling exactly as the progenitors of the race did and under conditions that make those in the millennium even more responsible for their actions. When Satan is loosed at the end of the millennium, earth's paradise will be shattered as the nations of the world, like Adam and Eve, join that deceiver in open rebellion to destroy Christ and the Holy City:

> The nations which are in the four quarters of the earth, Gog and Magog . . . gather . . . together to battle, the number of whom is as the sand of the sea. And they went up . . . and compassed the camp of the saints [Israel], and the beloved city [Jerusalem]; and fire came down from God out of heaven and devoured them (Revelation 20:8,9).

The Final Proof

Those who attack Jerusalem and Christ in earth's last battle will be the believers' offspring born into and raised in the idyllic millennial kingdom! The millennium will be the final proof that education, psychology, sociology, theology, group therapy, promises, and peace treaties—even a strong police force and swift judgment in the courts—can never solve the problems that plague this world. Rather than being the final kingdom of God promised by the prophets, the millennium will be the ultimate proof of the incorrigible nature of the human heart! Until man is individually right with God he cannot be right with himself or his fellows.

It is not enough even for Christ Himself to be present on this earth, ruling it from Jerusalem, enforcing an outward righteousness and meting out judgment swiftly and impartially. Inwardly, man remains under the rule of self in unrepentant rebellion against his Creator. Only when one's faith has been placed in Christ as his Savior who died for his sins, and He has been invited into one's heart to rule there as Lord, can peace come at last.

How tragic that with this final, hopeless, Satan-led rebellion and destruction human history and the present universe itself will come to an end. No further proof will be needed that man's only hope is to be made anew in Christ. Only such new creatures in Christ will be allowed to live in the new universe He creates. Peter wrote:

> The day of the Lord will come as a thief in the night, in which the heavens shall pass away with a great noise and the elements shall melt with fervent heat; the earth also and the works that are therein shall be burned up.
>
> Seeing then that all these things shall be dissolved, what manner of persons ought ye to be in all holy conversation and godliness, looking for . . . the coming of the day of God, wherein the heavens being on fire shall be dissolved, and the elements shall melt with fervent heat?
>
> Nevertheless we, according to his promise, look for new heavens and a new earth, wherein dwelleth righteousness (2 Peter 3:10-13).

Life Out of Death

Yes, the entire human race on earth must die. This world and the universe of which it is part must be completely destroyed. God must start all over again with a new race. But it would do no good merely to create another Adam and Eve and begin the cycle again. The evil and tragedy that inevitably plague any rational beings with the power of choice has already been fully demonstrated. That is why God Himself came to this earth as the man Christ Jesus to die in our place for our sins. Those who accept His death as their own thereby experience what Paul rejoiced in:

> I am crucified with Christ; nevertheless I live, yet not I, but Christ liveth in me; and the life which I now live in the flesh I live by the faith of the Son of God, who loved me and gave himself for me (Galatians 2:20).
>
> Therefore if any man be in Christ he is a new creature [creation]; old things are passed away; behold, all things are become new (2 Corinthians 5:17).

> For by grace are ye saved, through faith . . . not of works . . . for we are his workmanship, created in Christ Jesus unto good works, which God hath before ordained that we should walk in them (Ephesians 2:8-10).

Christ is called the "last Adam" (1 Corinthians 15:45). He is the progenitor of a new race of "born again" people who have died in Him and who now share His resurrection life. The life God offers is through the new and last "Adam." And the life which this new "Adam" possesses and which He gives to those who belong to Him is *resurrection* life. Obviously the only ones who can receive *resurrection* life are dead people—those who have died in Him. Having been made new creations in Christ, they alone will inhabit the new universe that God will make when He destroys this old one. John saw that glorious day in a God-given vision:

> I saw a new heaven and a new earth, for the first heaven and the first earth were passed away; and there was no more sea. And I John saw the holy city, new Jerusalem, coming down from God out of heaven, pre-pared as a bride adorned for her husband.
> And I heard a great voice out of heaven saying, Behold, the tabernacle of God is with men, and he will dwell with them, and they shall be his people, and God himself shall be with them and be their God.
> And God shall wipe away all tears from their eyes; and there shall be no more death, neither sorrow, nor crying; neither shall there be any more pain; for the former things are passed away.
> And he that sat upon the throne said, Behold, I make all things new. . . .
> And the city [new Jerusalem] had no need of the sun, neither of the moon, to shine in it; for the glory of God did lighten it, and the Lamb [that was crucified] is the light thereof. And the nations of them which are saved shall walk in the light of it. . . .
> And there shall in no wise enter into it anything that defileth, neither whatsoever worketh abomination or

maketh a lie, but they which are written in the Lamb's book of life (Revelation 21:1-5,23,24,27).

A Commonsense Appeal

If the Bible is true, then it is the utmost folly for Jew or Arab or Christian not to obey what it says about Israel and Jerusalem. If it is not true, as Israel's leaders, the hierarchy of the Roman Catholic Church, the World Council of Churches, and Muslim leaders would by their actions aver, then what is the point of Catholics and Protestants playing church or of Jews and Muslims going through the motions of synagogue and mosque? Let us abandon this charade.

On the contrary, we have seen in the specific prophecies about Israel and their fulfillment in detail hundreds and even thousands of years later, all the proof anyone needs that God exists and His Word is true. Then let the nations of the world bow to what the Bible says about Israel and Jerusalem—and about Jesus Christ.

God came to this earth as a man to reveal Himself in love and mercy and to bear the hatred and false accusations of His creatures and to die for their sins. Man rejected this overture of love. It is not too late to invite Christ back. He *is* coming, whether the world invites Him or not. Shall it be in judgment or in mercy?

The prophecies do not present a hopeless picture. First of all, for the individual person, whether Jew or Gentile, "repentance toward God and faith toward our Lord Jesus Christ" (Acts 20:21) brings personal salvation. And for the world, repentance would bring peace. There is no more definite, uncompromising prophecy than "Yet forty days and Nineveh shall be overthrown [destroyed]" (Jonah 3:4). That was the determined judgment which God had Jonah cry out against that wicked city. Yet Nineveh was not overthrown in 40 days, nor even in 40 years. It was not until some 250 years later, in 612 B.C., that Nineveh was at last so completely obliterated that its very existence as presented in the Bible was considered a myth. It remained so until the nineteenth century, when archaeologists discovered its ancient ruins.

Why was Nineveh spared in Jonah's day? We are not left in doubt: Nineveh's people repented—not with their lips only, but in deed as well. The king of Nineveh—

> laid his robe from him, and covered [himself] with sack-cloth, and sat in ashes. And he caused it to be proclaimed ... "Let neither man nor beast ... taste anything ... but let man and beast be covered with sackcloth and cry mightily unto God; yea, let them turn every one from his evil way, and from the violence that is in their hands. ...."
>
> And God saw their works, that they turned from their evil way; and God repented of the evil that he had said that he would do unto them, and he did it not (Jonah 3:6-10).

What happened to Nineveh was not a special case that cannot be repeated. Nor was it a contradiction of God's Word, but a fulfillment of it. God has said, "At what instant I shall speak concerning a nation and concerning a kingdom to pluck up and to pull down and to destroy it, if that nation against whom I have pronounced turn from their evil, I will repent of the evil that I thought to do unto them" (Jeremiah 18:7,8). If this is true of a nation, how much more could it be true of Israel and of the whole world!

Israel needs to repent. Its more than a million professing atheists need to repent. The political leaders of Israel and the whole world need to repent of imagining that they could bring peace through their own efforts; they all need to repent of bartering land that God said was never to be traded or sold, and exchanging it for a false peace at that. The Supreme Court of Israel needs to repent of sanctioning homosexual "marriages" and its other unjust judgments. The people of Israel need to repent of their selfishness and wickedness and contempt for God and His Word. The rabbis need to repent of their pride and of voiding the Word of God by their traditions.

The Arabs need to repent of their rejection of God's gift of the Promised Land to the Jews. They need to repent of the hatred in their hearts toward the Jews, of their making heroes out of murderers and of their determination to drive God's chosen people from the land which God gave to them.

The whole world needs to repent of a thousand evils which are practiced daily by earth's billions of rebellious inhabitants. It is not too late. We need to fall on our faces before God, the true God of the Bible—not some vague "higher power" or other god of our own making, but the God of prophecy who has proved who He is by telling us what would happen to His people Israel long before it happened.

There will be a New Jerusalem on a new earth in a new universe that will last for eternity! Its inhabitants will experience boundless joy and endless fulfillment. Inspired of God, King David wrote for the encouragement of us all: "Thou wilt show me the path of life; in thy presence there is fullness of joy; at thy right hand there are pleasures for evermore" (Psalm 16:11). This is God's promise to all who will accept it on His gracious terms.

Notes

Chapter 1—Jerusalem, City of Our God
1. *The Jerusalem Post International Edition*, Week ending February 4, 1995, p. 5.
2. Will Durant, *The Story of Civilization: The Age of Faith* (Simon and Schuster, 1950), Vol. IV, p. 229.
3. *The Jerusalem Post International Edition*, Week ending December 31, 1994, p. 6.
4. *Parade*, April 3, 1994, front cover.
5. *The Jerusalem Post International Edition*, Week ending October 8, 1994, p. 2.
6. *The Jerusalem Post International Edition*, Week ending October 1, 1994, p. 8B.
7. Ibid.
8. *Jerusalem Post International Edition*, Week ending May 27, 1994.

Chapter 2—Land of Promise
1. A compilation of statistics from various sources.
2. *The Jerusalem Post International Edition*, Week ending December 31, 1994, p. 15.
3. *Time*, February 6, 1995, pp. 36-40.
4. Ibid.
5. Ibid. See also *The Jerusalem Post International Edition*, Week ending October 1, 1994, pp. 12-15.
6. *The Jerusalem Post International Edition*, Week ending October 8, 1994, p. 23.
7. *The Jerusalem Post International Edition*, Week ending February 11, 1995.
8. *The Jerusalem Post International Edition*, Week ending November 26, 1994, p. 12A.
9. Elishua Davidson, *Islam, Israel and the Last Days* (Harvest House Publishers, 1991), pp. 92-94.

Chapter 3—The City of David
1. *The Jerusalem Post International Edition*, Week ending January 7, 1995, Moshe Kohn, "Which David?", p. 13.
2. Will Durant, *The Story of Civilization* (Simon and Schuster, 1950), Vol. III, p. 543.
3. Ibid., p. 542.
4. Ibid., pp. 542-45.
5. Ibid., pp. 545-46.
6. Ibid.
7. Ibid., p. 548.

Chapter 4—The Holy Land
1. *The Jerusalem Post International Edition*, Week ending January 21, 1995, "Why do we coddle wife killers?", p. 7.
2. *The Jerusalem Post International Edition*, Week ending February 18, 1995, p. 5.
3. *Israel My Glory*, December 1994/January 1995, p. 19.
4. *The Jerusalem Post International Edition*, Week ending December 24, 1994, p. 6.
5. *The Jerusalem Post International Edition*, Week ending January 7, 1995, p. 16A.
6. Ibid.
7. *The Jerusalem Post International Edition*, Week ending December 24, 1994, p. 6.
8. *The Jerusalem Post International Edition*, Week ending January 7, 1995, p. 24.
9. Herb Keinon, "Deaths from terror up sharply since Oslo accord," in *The Jerusalem Post International Edition*, Week ending September 24, 1994, p. 24.
10. *The Jerusalem Post International Edition*, Week ending February 18, 1995, p. 4.
11. Austin Flannery, O.P., Gen. Ed., *Vatican Council II, The Conciliar and Post Conciliar Documents* (Costello Publishing Company, 1988 Revised Edition), Vol. 1, p. 359.
12. Ibid., p. 360.
13. Ibid., p. 357.
14. *Inside the Vatican*, April 1994, p. 24.
15. Flannery, op. cit., Vol. 1, p. 367.
16. Ibid., p. 740.

17. Rabbi Meir Zlotowitz and Rabbi Nosson Scherman, gen. eds., *SHOAH, A Jewish Perspective on Tragedy in the Context of the Holocaust* (Mesorah Publications, Ltd., 1990), p. 161.
18. *Washington Post*, August 9, 1994.
19. *The Jerusalem Post International Edition*, Week ending October 29, 1994, p. 6.
20. *Spotlight on Israel* as quoted in *UPLOOK*, November 1994, p. 11.

Chapter 5—Conflict and Bitterness
1. Lance Lambert, "Israel and the Nations," a lecture given at Jerusalem in 1986.
2. Robert Morey, *The Islamic Invasion* (Harvest House, 1992), p. 24.
3. See Genesis 50:24; Exodus 2:24; 6:8; 33:1; Leviticus 26:42; Numbers 32:4; Deuteronomy 1:8; 6:10; 9:5,27; 30:20; 34:4; 2 Kings 13:23; etc.
4. See Exodus 3:6,15,16; 4:5; Deuteronomy 29:13; Matthew 22:32; Mark 12:26; Luke 20:37; Acts 3:13; 7:32; etc.
5. John McClintock and James Strong, *Cyclopedia of Biblical, Theological, and Ecclesiastical Literature* (Baker Book House, 1981), I:339.
6. Jon Immanuel, "Feeding the dogs of war," *The Jerusalem Post International Edition*, Week ending February 25, 1995, p. 9.
7. *Toronto Star*, November 8, 1994.
8. *The Koran*, Surahs 125-27.
9. Will Durant, op. cit., Vol. IV, pp. 160-61.
10. Ibid., p. 170. .

Chapter 6—Prophecy Becomes History
1. Guenter Lewy, *The Catholic Church and Nazi Germany* (McGraw-Hill, 1964), p. 274.
2. Will Durant, *The Story of Civilization, The Reformation* (Simon and Schuster, 1950), Vol. IV, p. 727.
3. *The Jerusalem Post International Edition*, Week ending January 7, 1995, p. 24.
4. *National & International Religion Report*, December 26, 1994, p. 2.
5. *The Jerusalem Post International Edition*, Week ending January 14, 1995, p. 12
6. *Time*, April 4, 1988, p. 46.

Chapter 7—The Struggle to Survive
1. David Lamb, *The Arabs* (Vintage Books, 1987), p. 212.
2. *Time*, April 4, 1988, p. 47.
3. *London Economist*, October 2, 1948.
4. *Al Difaa*, September 6, 1948.
5. *Time*, April 4, 1988, p. 50.
6. *The Jerusalem Report*, December 15, 1994, p. 8.
7. *Time*, April 4, 1988, p. 40.
8. *Time*, April 4, 1944, p. 46.
9. *The Jerusalem Post International Edition*, Week ending November 26, 1994, p. 7
10. *Newsweek*, June 5, 1967, p. 48.
11. *The Jerusalem Post International Edition*, Week ending January 14, 1995.
12. *The Orange County Register*, January 4, 1995, NEWS 3.
13. *Newsweek*, June 19, 1967, p. 29.

Chapter 8—A *Chosen* People?
1. Penny Rosenwasser, *Voices From A 'Promised Land': Palestinian and Israeli Peace Activists Speak their Hearts* (Curbstone Press, 1992), p. 100.
2. Ibid., p. 73.
3. Ibid., p. 217.
4. Ibid., p. 204.
5. *The Jerusalem Post International Edition*, Week ending January 7, 1995, p. 24

6. *The Jerusalem Post International Edition*, Week ending November 5, 1994, p. 7.
7. Elie Wiesel, *Night* (Bantam Books, 1986), p. 64.

Chapter 9—The Mystery of Anti-Semitism
1. Will Durant, *The History of Civilization: Part III, Caesar and Christ* (Simon and Schuster, 1944), p. 546.
2. *Time*, February 6, 1995, p. 40.
3. William Whiston, translator, *The Life and Works of Flavius Josephus* (The John C. Winston Company, 1957), p. 607.
4. Will Durant, *The Story of Civilization: Part II, The Life of Greece* (Simon and Schuster, 1966), pp. 582-83.
5. Ibid., p. 584.
6. Ibid.
7. Ibid.
8. Ibid., Vol. III, pp. 542-45.
9. Ibid., Vol. III, pp. 548-49.
10. See Dave Hunt, *A Woman Rides the Beast* (Harvest House, 1994), pp. 243-62.
11. Sidney Z. Ehler and John B. Morrall, trans. and eds. of these ancient documents, *Church and State Through the Centuries* (London, 1954), p. 7.
12. R.W. Thompson, *The Papacy and the Civil Power* (New York, 1876), p. 553.
13. Durant, op. cit., Vol. IV, pp. 385-89.
14. R. Tudor Jones, *The Great Reformation* (InterVarsity Press), p. 164.
15. Durant, op. cit., Vol. IV, p. 391.
16. Guenter Lewy, *The Catholic Church and Nazi Germany* (McGraw-Hill, 1964), pp 272-73.
17. Durant, op. cit., Vol. IV, pp. 391, 393-34.
18. *The Jerusalem Post International Edition*, Week ending December 10, 1994, p. 16.
19. *The Jerusalem Post International Edition*, Week ending November 26, 1994, p. 16A
20. *Time*, February 6, 1995, p. 40.
21. Ibid.
22. From the Associated Press as reported in *This Week in Bible Prophecy*, January 1995, p. 13.
23. Flannery, op. cit., Vol. 1, p. 741.
24. *St. Michael's News, A Publication of St. Michael's Legion*, March 1968, pp. 1-2.
25. John C. Landau, "Textbook case of propaganda," in *The Jerusalem Post International Edition*, Week ending November 5, 1994, p. 13.
26. Religion News Service as reported in *The Christian News*, February 20, 1995, p. 18
27. Ibid.

Chapter 10—The "Final Solution"
1. Elie Wiesel, *Night* (Bantam Books, 1986), from the Preface for the Twenty-fifth Anniversary edition by Robert McAfee Brown, p. v.
2. Ibid., pp. 32, 34.
3. Frederic V. Grunfeld, *The Hitler File: A Social History of Germany and the Nazis, 1918-45* (Bonanza Books, 1979), p. 308.
4. Ibid., p. 165.
5. *National Catholic Reporter*, July 29, 1994, p. 13
6. Lewy, op. cit., pp. 272, 279.
7. Ibid., p. 16.
8. Peter Vierick, *Meta-Politics: The Roots of the Nazi Mind* (Alfred A. Knopf, Inc., 1941, 1961 edition), p. 319.
9. Durant, op. cit., Vol. IV, p. 727; see also Martin Luther, *Von den Juden und ihren Lugen* ("On the Jews and their Lies"), Wittenburg, 1543.
10. Martin Gilbert, *The Holocaust: A History of the Jews of Europe During the Second World War* (Henry Holt and Company, Inc , 1985), pp. 19-22

11. Ibid., p. 18.
12. Ibid., pp. 36-37.
13. Ibid., p. 41.
14. Ibid., p. 64.
15. Ibid.
16. From the *Yad Vashem* archives, as cited in Gilbert, op. cit., p. 65.
17. William L. Shirer, *The Rise and Fall of the Third Reich* (Fawcet Publications, Inc., 1959), pp. 580-87.
18. Cited in Rabbi Yoel Schwartz and Rabbi Yitzchak Goldstein, *SHOAH: A Jewish perspective on tragedy in the context of the Holocaust* (Mesorah Publications, Ltd., 1990), p. 161.
19. Wiesel, op. cit., pp. 4-6.
20. *The Christian News*, January 30, 1995, p. 16.
21. Ibid., p. 17.
22. Ibid., pp. 16-17; see also same paper, February 6, 1995, pp. 9-11.
23. *The Jerusalem Post International Edition*, Week ending January 28, 1995, p. 11.
24. Gilbert, op. cit., pp. 821-22.
25. *The Jerusalem Post International Edition*, Week ending January 28, 1995, p. 5.
26. Gilbert, op. cit., pp. 437-48.
27. *Bend [OR] Bulletin*, January 30, 1995.
28. *National Catholic Reporter*, July 29, 1994, p. 12.
29. *Jerusalem Post International Edition*, Week ending February 18, 1995, p. 13.

Chapter 11—Islam and Terrorism
1. Abd-al-Masih, *Wer Ist Allah im Islam?* (Villach), p. 32, as cited in Elishua Davidson, *Islam, Israel and the Last Days* (Harvest House Publishers, 1991), p. 82.
2. *Times* [St. Petersburg, FL], February 13, 1995, p. 3A; *Newsweek*, February 20, 1995, pp. 36-38; *Time*, February 20, 1995, pp. 24-27.
3. *USA Today*, February 10, 1995, p. 2A.
4. *The Orange County Register*, January 9, 1995, NEWS 8.
5. G.J.O. Moshay, *Who Is This Allah?* (Dorchester House Publications, 1994), p. 24.
6. *The Bulletin* (Bend, OR), from the AP wire, February 6, 1995, front page.
7. *The Orange County Register*, January 9, 1995, NEWS 8.
8. Ibid.
9. *The New York Times*, February 8, 1995, pp. A1, A9.
10. Ibid.
11. *The Bulletin* (Bend, OR), from the AP wire, February 6, 1995, front page
12. Lamb, op. cit., pp. 102-04.
13. *National & International Religion Report*, December 26, 1994, p. 7
14. *Time*, April 4, 1988, p. 47.
15. Lamb, op. cit., pp. 214-17.
16. Ibid., pp. 102-04.
17. Ibid.
18. Ibid., p. 288.
19. Ibid., pp. 87-88.
20. *Time*, February 6, 1995, p. 34.
21. Ibid., pp. 32-33.
22. *Sharek al-Awsat* (a Saudi-owned, London-based weekly newspaper) as quoted in *The Jerusalem Post International Edition*, Week ending January 21, 1995, p. 3.
23. Lamb, op. cit., p. 85.
24. *Mishkat Masabih*, Vol. II, p. 253.
25. See especially Mishkat al Masabih Sh. M Ashsraf (1990), pp. 147, 721, 810-11, 1130 etc.
26. Lamb, op. cit., pp. 87-88.
27. Ibid., p. 92.
28. Ibid., p. x.
29. *USA Today*, February 6, 1991.
30. *Nigerian Sunday Punch*, January 26, 1986

31. Abd-al-Masih, op. cit., p. 32.
32. Lamb, op. cit., p. 71.
33. Charley Reese, "People aren't that different," in *Brandon News & Shopper*, August 4, 1993, pp. 10A, 15A.
34. *The Orange County Register*, January 3, 1995, NEWS 6.
35. *The Messianic Times*, Winter 1995, p. 13.
36. *The Jerusalem Post International Edition*, Week ending November 26, 1994, p. 13.
37. Ibid.
38. *The Baptist Challenge*, December 1994, p. 8.
39. Durant, op. cit., Vol. IV, pp. 168-69.
40. Associated Press, February 2, 1991.
41. Robert Morey, *The Islamic Invasion* (Harvest House Publishers, 1992), pp. 26, 32.
42. Durant, op. cit., Vol. IV, p. 170.
43. Ibid., p. 188.

Chapter 12—The Bible or the Koran?
1. Robert Morey, *The Islamic Invasion: Confronting the World's Fastest Growing Religion* (Harvest House Publishers, 1992), p. 132.
2. Ibid., pp. 125-27.
3. *Encyclopedia Britannica*, Vol. 13, p. 479.
4. Abdullah Mandudi, *The Meaning of the Quran* (Islamic Publications, Ltd., 1967), p. 17; Durant, op. cit., Vol. IV, pp. 164, 175, etc.
5. Durant, op. cit., Vol. IV, pp. 217-18.
6. Morey, op. cit., pp. 142-43.
7. Ali Dashti, *23 years: A Study of the Prophetic Career of Mohammad* (London, 1985), p. 3.
8. Moshay, op. cit., p. 111.

Chapter 13—Allah or Yahweh?
1. Austin Flannery, O.P., general editor, *Vatican Council II, The Conciliar and Post Conciliar Documents* (Costello Publishing Company, 1988 Revised Edition), Vol. I, p. 367.
2. A. Guillaume, *The Life of Muhammad* (Oxford University Press, 1955), pp. 66-68 as cited in Moshay, op. cit., pp. 139-40.
3. Wiesel, op. cit., p. 16.
4. Ibid., pp. 2-3.
5. Ibid., pp. x, xi.

Chapter 14—Altars, Temples, and a Cross
1. Austin Flannery, O.P., general editor, *Vatican Council II, The Conciliar and Post Conciliar Documents* (Costello Publishing Company, 1988 Revised Edition), Vol. 1, pp. 66, 68.
2. *Time*, February 6, 1995, p. 46.
3. Moshay, op. cit., pp. 40-44.
4. *UPLOOK*, November 1994, p. 11.
5. Moshay, op. cit., pp. 24-25.
6. Ahmed Deedat, *What is his Name?* (Islamic Propagation Centre, Durban, 1986), p. 14.
7. Ibid., pp. 25-26.
8. Lamb, op. cit., p. 254.
9. *The Catholic World Report*, February 1995, p. 22.
10. Laura Rosen Cohen, "Death in the family: Killing women who bring 'shame' to their families remains a Mid-Eastern tradition," *The Jerusalem Post International Edition*, Week ending September 10, 1994, p. 14.
11. Moshay, op. cit., pp. 30-31.
12. *National Catholic Reporter*, January 20, 1995, p. 5.

Chapter 15—Peace, Peace...
1. From a FLAME ad in *The Jerusalem Post International Edition*, Week ending April 1, 1995, p. 23.
2. *The Jerusalem Post International Edition*, Week ending April 1, 1995, p. 3.
3. *The Jerusalem Post International Edition*, Week ending February 11, 1995, p. 7.
4. *The Jerusalem Post International Edition*, Week ending December 17, 1994, p. 8B.
5. *U.S. News & World Report*, December 19, 1994, p. 84.
6. *International Herald Tribune*, October 28, 1994.
7. *The Jerusalem Post International Edition*, Week ending April 29, 1995, p. 7.
8. *Time*, February 6, 1995, pp. 32-33.
9. Shlomo Gazit, "Arafat's end of the bargain," in *The Jerusalem Post International Edition*, Week ending November 5, 1994, p. 7.
10. *The Jerusalem Post International Edition*, Week ending February 25, 1995, p. 2.
11. From articles 19 and 20 of the Palestinian Liberation Organization Covenant.
12. David Miller, NNI Correspondent, "Jewish Community In South America Fears Rising Wave of Persecution," in *This Week In Bible Prophecy Magazine*, February 1995, p. 20.
13. From Article 4 of the PLO Covenant.
14. *The Jerusalem Post International Edition*, Week ending November 12, 1994, p. 23.
15. Ibid., from an ad for FLAME (Facts and Logic about the Middle East, P.O. Box 590359, San Francisco, CA 94159).
16. *The Jerusalem Post International Edition*, Week ending January 14, 1995, p. 3.
17. An ad "published and paid for by *FLAME*, Facts and Logic about the Middle East, P.O. Box 590359, San Francisco, CA 94159" in *The Jerusalem Post International Edition*, Week ending November 12, 1994, p. 23.
18. Ibid.
19. Ibid.
20. *The Jerusalem Post International Edition*, Week ending February 18, 1995, p. 2.
21. Ibid.
22. *The Jerusalem Post International Edition*, Week ending January 14, 1995, p. 3.
23. Ibid., p. 9.
24. *The Jerusalem Post International Edition*, Week ending December 10, 1994, p. 10.
25. Ibid.
26. *The Jerusalem Post International Edition*, Week ending November 26, 1994, p. 7.
27. *The Jerusalem Post International Edition*, Week ending January 14, 1995, p. 13.
28. "The Iranian Threat," in *The Jerusalem Post International Edition*, Week ending April 1, 1995, p. 8.

Chapter 16—A Cup of Trembling
1. *The Jerusalem Post International Edition*, Week ending April 1, 1995, p. 6.
2. *Palestinian Refugees and the Right to Return* (Palestinian National Authority, Ministry of Information Publication Number 6, March 1995), pp. 4, 8, as quoted in *The Jerusalem Post International Edition*, Week ending April 1, 1995, p. 6.
3. Ibid.
4. *The Jerusalem Post International Edition*, Week ending April 1, 1995, p. 6, "PLO covenant: alive and snarling," by Ze'ev Begin.
5. *The Jerusalem Post International Edition*, Week ending March 25, 1995, p. 8A.
6. From the Declaration, signed in Washington D.C. on September 13, 1993, by Shimon Peres for the Government of Israel and Mahmoud Abbas for the PLO and witnessed by Warren Christopher of the United States of America and Andrei Kozyrev for The Russian Federation, as cited in Shlomo Gazit-Zeev Eytan, Edited by Shlomo Gazit, *The Middle East Military Balance 1993-94* (Tel Aviv University, Jaffee Center for Strategic Studies, 1994), p. 43.
7. Statistics from Shlomo Gazit-Zeev Eytan, Edited by Shlomo Gazit, *The Middle East Military Balance 1993-1994* (Tel Aviv University, Jaffee Center for Strategic Studies, 1994), pp. 482-87.
8. *The Jerusalem Post International Edition*, Week ending December 31, 1994, p. 22.

9. *Jeruusalem Post International Edition*, Week ending January 21, 1995, p. 1.
10. Shmuel Segev, " 'New Middle East' is dead," *The Jerusalem Post, International Edition*, Week ending January 28, 1995, p. 7.
11. *The Jerusalem Post International Edition*, Week ending April 1, 1995, p. 2.
12. *The Jerusalem Post International Edition*, Week ending December 17, 1994, p. 9.
13. Steve Rodan, "Is it time to worry about a nuclear Iran?", in *The Jerusalem Post International Edition*, Week ending January 21, 1995, p. 16A.
14. Ibid.
15. *The Jerusalem Post International Edition*, Week ending December 17, 1994, p. 7.
16. Ibid.
17. *The Jerusalem Post International Edition*, Week ending March 25, 1995, p. 3.
18. Editorial, "The Lebanon dead-end," in *The Jerusalem Post International Edition*, Week ending December 24, 1994, p. 8.
19. "The Iranian Threat," in *The Jerusalem Post International Edition*, Week ending April 1, 1995, p. 8.
20. Ibid.
21. *The Jerusalem Post International Edition*, Week ending December 17, 1994, p. 9.
22. *The Evansville Courier*, Sunday, October 30, 1994, p. A10.
23. *The Jerusalem Post International Edition*, Week ending April 1, 1995. p. 4.
24. Ibid., p. 7.
25. Associated Press dispatch as reported in *St. Petersburg Times*, February 13, 1995, p. 2A.
26. *The Bulletin* (Bend, Oregon), April 11, 1995, p. 1A.
27. *The Jerusalem Post International Edition*, Week ending January 14, 1995, p. 3.
28. Ibid., p. 13.
29. David Bar-Illan, "Peace Corps message of hate," in *The Jerusalem Post International Edition*, Week ending March 11, 1995, p. 14.
30. Dr. J.S. Kaufman, Bloomfield, Michigan, "The Bosnian Lesson," in *The Jerusalem Post International Edition*, Week ending December 31, 1994, p. 22.
31. From a FLAME ad in *The Jerusalem Post International Edition*, Week ending April 1, 1955, p. 23.

Chapter 17—Christians For—and Against—Israel

1. Rick Godwin, Sunday evening sermon at Metro Church, Edmond, Oklahoma, April 11, 1988; "Rick Godwin No. 2" audiotape.
2. Hyam Maccoby, *The Myth-Maker, Paul and the Invention of Christianity* (Harper & Row, 1986).
3. *Inside the Vatican*, March 1995, p. 7.
4. Peter de Rosa, *Vicars of Christ: The Dark Side of the Papacy* (Crown Publishers, 1988), pp. 175-76.
5. J.H. Ignaz von Dollinger, *The Pope and the Council* (London, 1869), pp. 190-93.
6. *The Jerusalem Post International Edition*, Week ending December 17, 1994, p. 8B.
7. *La Civilta*, Vol. iii, 1862, p. 11.
8. Peter de Rosa, *Vicars of Christ* (Crown Publishers, Inc., 1988), pp. 194-95.
9. Letter on file dated July 28, 1991.
10. Earl Paulk, *The Handwriting on the Wall* (booklet self-published by Paulk's Chapel Hill Harvester Church, Decatur, GA 30034); see pp. 17, 19-20.
11. Ibid.
12. David Chilton, *Days of Vengeance: An Exposition of the Book of Revelation* (Dominion Press, 1987), pp. 410, 443, 575.
13. *End-Times News Digest*, December 1987 (James McKeever Ministries Newsletter), p. 3.
14. Philip Mauro, *The Hope of Israel* (Grace Abounding Ministries, Inc., 1988), p. 17.
15. Mauro, op. cit., p. 261.
16. R.B. Yerby, *The Once and Future Israel* (Grace Abounding Ministries, Inc., 1988), pp. 96-97.
17. Ibid., p. 117.
18. *National & International Religion Report*, December 26, 1994, p. 2.

19. *The Jerusalem Post International Edition*, Week ending October 29, 1994, pp. 1, 10.
20. *News From Israel*, April 1995, p. 10.
21. J.H. Ignaz von Dollinger, op. cit., pp. 190-93.

Chapter 18—Antichrist and the Temple Rebuilt
 1. *Los Angeles Times*, December 26, 1989, p. A13.
 2. Lamb, op. cit., p. 226.
 3. *The Jerusalem Post International Edition*, Week ending April 1, 1995, p. 4.
 4. Ibid., p. 11.
 5. Ibid., pp. 2, 8, 11.
 6. Richard Kirby and Earl D.C. Brewer, "Temples of Tomorrow: Toward a United Religions Organization," in *The Futurist*, September-October 1994, pp. 26-28.
 7. *Chalcedon Report*, July 1988, p. 1.
 8. *Inside the Vatican*, October 1993, p. 18.
 9. Ibid., p. 4
10. *Inside the Vatican*, December 1994, p. 14.
11. Flannery, op. cit., Vol. 1, p. 740.
12. Moshay, op. cit., p. 25.
13. From an interview with Gershon Salomon, June 24, 1991, as reported in Thomas Ice & Randall Price, *Ready To Rebuild: The Imminent Plan to Rebuild the Last Days Temple* (Harvest House Publishers, 1992), p. 121.
14. *U.S. News & World Report*, December 19, 1994, p. 7C.
15. Marmaduke Pickthall, *The Meaning of The Glorious Koran: An explanatory translation* (Alfred A. Knopf, 1992), Introductory notes at beginning of Surah 17.
16. *Spokesman Review*, September 27, 1993, "National Digest" column.
17. *Inside the Vatican*, December 1994, p. 19.
18. Editorial, *Jewish Press*, September 2, 1994.
19. Art Kunkin, *Whole Life Times*, August 1979, "The Dalai Lama in Los Angeles: What Does Kalachakra Have To Do With World Peace?", p. 8.

Chapter 19—Where Are the Aliens?
 1. *GEO*, February 1982, "GeoConversation," an interview with Dr. Robert Jastrow, p. 14.
 2. John Gliedman, "Scientists in Search of God," in *Science Digest*, July 1982, p. 78.
 3. Sir John Eccles, with Daniel N. Robinson, *The Wonder of Being Human—Our Brain & Our Mind* (New Science Library, 1985), p. 54.
 4. Sir Arthur Eddington, *Science and the Unseen World* (Macmillan, 1937), pp. 53-54.
 5. Ken Wilbur, *Quantum Questions: The Mystical Writings of the World's Great Physicists* (Shambhala Publications, 1984), p. 170.
 6. *Research in Parapsychology 1972* (special dinner address by Arthur Koestler), p. 203.
 7. "An Interview with Hafez Assad," in *Time*, October 20, 1986, pp. 56-57.
 8. Copy of letter on file.
 9. Copy of memorandum on file.
10. Copy of memorandum on file.
11. From an interview by AP correspondent George W. Cornall, quoted from *Times-Advocate*, Escondido, California, December 10, 1982, pp. A10-11.
12. Sir Arthur Eddington, *The Nature of the Physical World* (Macmillan, 1953), p. 345.
13. Erwin Schroedinger, cited in Wilbur, *Quantum Questions*, pp. 81-83.
14. *Harpers*, February 1985, pp. 49-50.
15. Douglas Dewar and L.M. Davies, "Science and the BBC," in *The Nineteenth Century and After*, April 1943, p. 167.

Chapter 20—Double Cross and Armageddon!
 1. *U.S. News & World Report*, April 10, 1995, p. 14.
 2. *The Jerusalem Post International Edition*, Week ending January 14, 1995, p. 12.
 3. Associated Press, January 23, 1995, as reported in *The Bulletin*, January 23, 1995, front page.

4. Ibid.
5. *The Jerusalem Post International Edition*, Week ending January 14, 1995, p. 3.
6. *The Jerusalem Post International Edition*, Week ending April 1, 1995, p. 8.
7. Shlomo Gazit - Zeev Eytan, edited by Shlomo Gazit, *The Middle East Military Balance* (Tel Aviv University, 1994), p. 153.
8. Ibid., pp. 150-51.
9. *Inside the Vatican,* March 1995, pp. 8-10.
10. Ibid., p. 11.
11. *The Washington Post,* October 26, 1994, p. A26.
12. *News From Israel.* April 1995, pp. 6, 9.
13. *Time,* February 24, 1992, pp. 28-35.
14. *The Catholic World Report,* March 1994, p. 23.
15. Ibid.
16. *New York Times,* April 15, 1993.
17. *San Jose Mercury News,* April 17, 1993.
18. *San Jose Mercury News,* April 16, 1993.
19. Gerald Suster, *Hitler: The Occult Messiah* (New York, 1981), pp. 100, 107.
20. Jean-Michel Angebert, *The Occult and the Third Reich* (New York, 1974), p. 20.
21. *Time,* July 11, 1994, p. 41.
22. *Time,* November 21, 1994, pp. 82-83.
23. *The Jerusalem Post International Edition*, Week ending January 14, 1995, p. 9.
24. Ibid.
25. Ibid.

Chapter 21—"All Israel Shall Be Saved"

1. *Newsweek,* December 12, 1994, p. 54.
2. *The Jerusalem Post International Edition*, Week ending March 4, 1995, p. 6, Shmuel Katz, "Answers blowing in the ill wind."
3. *St. Petersburg Times,* February 13, 1995, p. 2A.
4. *The Jerusalem Post International Edition*, Week ending March 4, 1995, p. 24.
5. Alon Liel, "Killer today, official tomorrow," *The Jerusalem Post International Edition*, Week ending March 4, 1995, p. 7.
6. *The Catholic World Report,* April 1995, pp. 41-43.
7. *The Jerusalem Post International Edition*, Week ending September 3, 1994, p. 6, Uri Dan and Dennis Eisenberg, "Syria offered Carlos' head for the Golan."
8. *Our Sunday Visitor,* September 7, 1993, pp. 6-7.
9. *Parade Magazine,* April 9, 1955, p. 8.
10. *U.S. News & World Report,* December 19, 1994, pp. 62-71.
11. Ibid., p. 67.
12. Ibid., p. 62; *Bend Bulletin,* December 11, 1994, p. 2.
13. *Los Angeles Times,* April 20, 1993, p. A17.
14. Editorial, "Mainstreaming Madmen," in *Israel My Glory,* June/July 1994, p. 4.
15. *U.S. News & World Report,* December 19, 1994, pp. 62-71.
16. Ibid.
17. Ibid.

Chapter 22—The New Jerusalem

1. *U.S. News & World Report,* December 19, 1994, p. 64.
2. *Houston Chronicle,* February 24, 1995, as reported in *The Christian News,* April 17, 1995, p. 2.
3. *The Bulletin* (Bend, Oregon), April 25, 1995, p. A-2.
4. Ibid., April 28, 1995, p. A-2.
5. "Ofek-3 in orbit, 'Can read license plates in Baghdad,'" in *The Jerusalem Post International Edition*, Week ending April 15, 1995, p. 1.
6. *The Jerusalem Post International Edition*, Week ending April 15, 1995, p. 2.
7. Ibid., p. 3.

8. Editorial, "Nuclear terrorists," in *The Jerusalem Post International Edition*, Week ending August 27, 1994.
9. *Time*, August 28, 1994, p. 47.
10. *The Orange County Register*, September 5, 1992.
11. Ibid.
12. Editorial, "The peace of the naive," in *The Jerusalem Post International Edition*, Week ending September 3, 1994, p. 8.
13. Paul Horgan, *Rome Eternal* (New York, 1959).
14. *The Orange County Register*, September 30, 1993, p. NEWS 24.
15. From the "Statement on Jerusalem" adopted by the Central Committee of the World Council of Churches at its meeting August 14-22, 1980, paragraphs 1 and 2.
16. Ibid, sections 3-6.
17. Editorial, "The emerging police state," in *The Jerusalem Post International Edition*, Week ending September 3, 1994, p. 8.
18. "Gaza police chief: We won't shoot at Hamas," in *The Jerusalem Post International Edition*, Week ending August 27, 1994.
19. Ze'ev B. Begin, "A vital reassessment," in *The Jerusalem Post International Edition*, Week ending April 8, 1995, p. 6.
20. *Praise the Lord*, Trinity Broadcasting Network Newsletter, August 1994.
21. Ibid.
22. *The Good Olive Tree*, September/October 1994, p. 17.

Other Books by Dave Hunt

Beyond Seduction
Countdown to the Second Coming
Death of a Guru
Global Peace and the Rise of Antichrist
The God Makers
How Close Are We?
The New Spirituality
The Seduction of Christianity
Understanding the New Age Movement
A Woman Rides the Beast